EUROPEAN STUDIES ON CHRISTIAN ORIGINS

Editor
Michael Labahn

Editorial Board
Tom Holmén, Bert Jan Lietaert Peerbolte

Published under

JOURNAL FOR THE STUDY OF THE NEW TESTAMENT
SUPPLEMENT SERIES
243

Editor
Mark Goodacre

Christians as a Religious Minority in a Multicultural City

Modes of Interaction and Identity Formation in Early Imperial Rome

Studies on the Basis of a Seminar at the Second Conference of the
European Association for Biblical Studies (EABS) from July 8–12, 2001, in Rome

Edited by

Jürgen Zangenberg and Michael Labahn

T&T CLARK INTERNATIONAL
A Continuum imprint
LONDON • NEW YORK

Copyright © 2004 T&T Clark International
A Continuum imprint

Published by T&T Clark International
The Tower Building, 11 York Road, London SE1 7NX
15 East 26th Street, Suite 1703, New York, NY 10010

www.tandtclark.com

British Library Cataloguing-in-Publication Data
A catalogue record for this book is available from the British Library

Library of Congress Cataloging-in-Publication Data
A catalogue record for this book is available from the Library of Congress

Typeset by CA Typesetting, Sheffield
Printed on acid-free paper in Great Britain by CPI Bath

ISBN 0–8264–6670–2 (hardback)

CONTENTS

PREFACE

Early Imperial Rome truly was one of the most 'multicultural' cities in antiquity. Juvenal even dubbed it 'Greek Rome' and complained that 'the waters of the Syrian Orontes flow into the Tiber' (Sat. 3,61f). Syrians, Africans, Gauls, Egyptians, Jews and other groups flocked into the city and formed their communities – as well as Christians. How did these ethnic and religious minority groups maintain and develop their identity? How did the 'cultural majority' react towards these sometimes exotic groups? It turns out that early Imperial Rome did not simply function as a giant 'melting pot' that levelled off all individuality, the city rather provided a big stage on which these groups were able to interact with each other or disassociate from each other and, by that, express and develop their own identity. The early Christian group(s) in Rome are no exception here.

The articles, all but two first presented at a seminar during the Second Conference of the European Association for Biblical Studies (EABS) in conjunction with the International Meeting of the Society of Biblical Literature (SBL) from July 8– 12, 2001 in Rome, discuss exemplary aspects of the complex process of interaction and identity formation. The fact that they are written by internationally renowned experts in New Testament studies, Judaic studies, religious studies and archaeology, guarantees a broad perspective and different methodological approaches. The papers are arranged in three sections. The first section gives a general survey about living conditions in early Christian Rome and how minorities like Christians, Jews and Egyptians related to their urban context. The second part specifically focuses on the interaction between majorities and minorities in the early Christian community of Rome on the basis of selected New Testament texts and traditions. The question, how the city of Rome features in New Testament narrative contexts is also discussed. The third and final part follows the development of the post-New Testament Christian community into the second and third centuries. 1 Clem, the Pseudo-Clementine cycle and information about the Valentinians suggest that the variety of positions within the early Christian community to a large extent was also a result of interaction with and adaptation from their cultural context. The articles in their respective way convincingly demonstrate that identity formation always is a dialogue *within* a given community and with factors *outside* the own social and intellectual boundaries.

The editors are grateful to all who contributed to the seminar, the audience, the organizers of the conference and, above all, to all colleagues who presented their research and insights (among them also Eckart Plümacher who will include his paper into the forthcoming collection of essays). We are also grateful to all presenters who submitted their revised papers to us and made the present volume possible. Our thanks are also due to Philip R. Davies for his encouragement and support during various stages of preparing the seminar and this volume as well as to the editors of the series. Robert Bellin helped preparing the final version of the text.

The volume is respectfully dedicated to the blessed memory of the late Professor John C. O'Neill whose friendship and inspiration we treasure and deeply miss.

Jürgen Zangenberg
Michael Labahn

LIST OF ABBREVIATIONS

AB	Anchor Bible
AbhBAW	Abhandlungen der Bayerischen Akademie der Wissenschaften. Philosophisch-Historische Klasse
AE	L'Année épigraphique
AGAJ	Arbeiten zur Geschichte des antiken Judentums und des Urchristentums
AJA	*American Journal of Archaeology*
AJAH	American Journal of Ancient History
AKG	Arbeiten zur Kirchengeschichte
ANF	The Ante-Nicene Fathers
ANRW	Aufstieg und Niedergang der römischen Welt
Arch Korr	*Archäologisches Korrespondenzblat*
ARGU	Arbeiten zur Religion und Geschichte des Urchristentums
ASMA	Aarhus Studies in Mediterranean Antiquities
AW	*Antike Welt*
BAR	British Archaeology Reports
BARev	Biblical Archaeology Review
BBB	Bonner Biblische Beiträge
BCAR	*Bullettino della Commissione Archeologica Comunale Roma*
BECNT	Baker Exegetical Commentary on the New Testament
BETL	Bibliotheca Ephemeridum Theologicarum Lovaniensium
BGU	Ägyptische Urkunden aus den (Königlichen) Museen zu Berlin
BHTh	Beiträge zur historischen Theologie
Bib.	*Biblica*
BIS	Biblical Interpretation Series
BN	*Biblische Notizen*
BR	*Biblical Research*
BTB	*Biblical Theology Bulletin*
BZNW	Beihefte zur *ZNW*
CAH	Cambridge Ancient History
CBQ	*Catholic Biblical Quarterly*
CCh	Corpus Christianorum
CHJ	Cambridge History of Judaism
CIJ	*Corpus Inscriptionum Judaicaum*
CIL	*Corpus Inscriptionum Latinarum*
CRINT	Corpus Rerum Iudaicarum ad Novum Testamentum
EPRO	Etudes préliminaires aux religions orientales dans l'Empire romain
es.NF	Edition Suhrkamp. Neue Folge
FABT	Funde und Ausgrabungen im Bezirk Trier
FC	Fontes Christiani
FRLANT	Forschungen zur Religion und Literatur des Alten und Neuen Testaments
GLAJJ	Greek and Latin Authors on Jews and Judaism

GTB	Gütersloher Taschenbücher
HABES	Heidelberger Althistorische Beiträge und Epigraphische Studien
HDR	Harvard Dissertations in Religion
HNT	Handbuch zum Neuen Testament
HTKNT	Herders theologischer Kommentar zum Neuen Testament
HTR	*Harvard Theological Review*
ICUR	Inscriptiones christianae urbis Romae
IGCVO	Inscriptiones Graecae Christianae veteres Occidentis
IGUR	*Inscriptiones Graecae Urbis Romae*
ILS	*Inscriptiones Latinae Selectae*
JAC	*Jahrbuch für Antike und Christentum*
JAC.E	JAC Ergänzungsband
JBL	*Journal of Biblical Literature*
JECS	*Journal of Early Christian Studies*
JIGRE	Jewish Inscriptions of Graeco-Roman Egypt
JIWE	Jewish Inscriptions in Western Europe
JQR	*Jewish Quarterly Review*
JRA.Supp	Journal of Roman Archeology. Supplement Series
JRS	*Journal of Roman Studies*
JSNT	*Journal for the Study of the New Testament*
JSNT.Sup	Journal for the Study of the New Testament. Supplement Series
JSP.Sup	Journal for the Study of the Pseudepigrapha. Supplement Series
JSSt.Sup	Journal of Semitic Studies. Supplement Series
JRS	*Journal of Roman Studies*
JTS	*Journal of Theological Studies*
KAV	Kommentar zu den Apostolischen Vätern
KEK	Kritisch-exegetischer Kommentar
KVR	Kleine Vandenhoeck-Reihe
LCL	Loeb Classical Library
LD	Lectio Divina
LPGL	*G.W.H. Lampe, A Patristic Greek Lexicon (Oxford: Clarendon Press, 1961).*
MDAI.R	*Mitteilungen des Deutschen Archaeologischen Instituts, Römische Abteilung*
MPARA	*Memorie della Pontifica Accademia Romana di Archeologia*
NHMS	Nag Hammadi and Manichaean Studies
NICNT	New International Commentary on the New Testament
NRSV	New Revised Standard Version
NT	*Novum Testamentum*
NTOA	Novum Testamentum et Orbis Antiquus
NT.Sup	Novum Testamentum. Supplements
NTS	*New Testament Studies*
ÖTK	Ökumenischer Taschenkommentar
PBSR	*Papers of the British School at Rome*
PL	Patrologia Latina
PO	Patrologia Orientalis
RPARA	Rendiconti della Pontifica Accademia Romana di Archeologia
QD	Quaestiones Disputatae
RAC	*Reallexikon für Antike und Christentum*
RB	*Revue Biblique*
RHE	Revue d'Histoire Ecclesiastique
RöHM	*Römisch Historische Mitteilungen*
RHPhR	*Revue d'Histoire et de Philosophie Religieuse*

RivB	*Rivista Biblica*
RNT	Regensburger Neues Testament
RSR	*Religious Studies Review*
RVV	Religionsgeschichtliche Versuche und Vorarbeiten
SBL.DS	Society of Biblical Literature, Dissertation Series
SBL.SP	*Society of Biblical Literature, Seminar Papers*
SBS	Stuttgarter Bibelstudien
SC	Sources chrétiennes
SEG	*Supplementum Epigraphorum Graecum*
SJLA	Studies in Judaism in Late Antiquity
SMB	Série monographique de "Benedictina"
SNTS.MS	Society for New Testament Studies Monograph Series
SOC	Scritti delle origini cristiane
SPB	Studia Post-Biblica
STAC	Studien und Texte zum Antiken Christentum
StPatr	Studia Patristica
StUNT	Studien zur Umwelt des Neuen Testaments
SUC	Schriften des Urchristentums
SVF	*Stoicorum Veterorum Fragmenta*
TANZ	Texte und Arbeiten zum neutestamentlichen Zeitalter
TAPA	Transactions of the American Philological Association
ThHK	Theologischer Handkommentar zum Neuen Testament
ThLZ.F	Theologische Literaturzeitung. Forum
ThV	Theologia Viatorum
ThR	*Theologische Rundschau*
TKTG	Texte zur Kirchen- und Theologiegeschichte
TRE	*Theologische Realenzyklopädie*
TSAJ	Texte und Studien zum antiken Judentum
TU	Texte und Untersuchungen
TynB	*Tyndale Bulletin*
TZTh	*Tübinger Zeitschrift für Theologie*
UTB	Uni-Taschenbücher
VC	*Vigiliae Christianae*
VC.Sup	Vigiliae Christianae Supplementa
WBC	Word Biblical Commentary
WdF	Wege der Forschung
WUB	*Welt und Umwelt der Bibel*
WUNT	Wissenschaftliche Untersuchungen zum Neuen Testament
ZKG	*Zeitschrift für Kirchengeschichte*
ZNW	*Zeitschrift für die neutestamentliche Wissenschaft*
ZPE	*Zeitschrift für Papyrologie und Epigraphik*
ZRGG	*Zeitschrift für Religions- und Geistesgeschichte*
ZSRG.R	*Zeitschrift der Savigny Gesellschaft für Rechtsgeschichte. Romanistische Abteilung*

LIST OF CONTRIBUTORS

Ismo Dunderberg, Dr Theol., is Professor for New Testament at the Department of Biblical Studies, University of Helsinki, Finland.

Caroline Johnson Hodge, PhD, is Assistant Visiting Professor at the College of the Holy Cross, Worcester, MA, USA.

Christiane Kunst, Dr Phil., is Privatdozentin for Ancient History and Wissenschaftliche Mitarbeiterin at the Historische Institut of the University of Potsdam, Germany.

Michael Labahn, Dr Theol., is Wissenschaftlicher Assistent for New Testament at the Martin Luther University Halle-Wittenberg, Germany.

Peter Lampe, Dr Theol., is Professor for New Testament at the University of Heidelberg, Germany.

Martin Meiser, Dr Theol., is Privatdozent for New Testament and Wissenschaftlicher Mitarbeiter at the Seminar for Ecclesiastical History at the University of Mainz, Germany.

David Noy, PhD, is Lecturer at the Department of Classics at the University of Wales Lampeter, UK.

John C. O'Neill, PhD, † was Professor of New Testament Language, Literature and Theology at New College, University of Edinburgh, UK.

Antonio Pitta, Dr Theol., is Professor for New Testament at the Pontifical Faculty for South Italy, St. Thomas Aquinas, Naples, Italy.

Margaret H. Williams, PhD is Honorary Visiting Research Fellow at the Department of Classics at The Open University, Milton Keynes, UK.

Jürgen Wehnert, Dr Theol., is Privatdozent for New Testament at the University of Göttingen, Germany.

Jürgen Zangenberg, Dr Theol., is Privatdozent for New Testament at Barmen School of Theology and Wissenschaftlicher Assistent at the Bergische Universität Wuppertal, Germany.

Part I

Minorities Living in Early Imperial Rome

WOHNEN IN DER ANTIKEN GROSSTADT.
ZUR SOZIALEN TOPOGRAPHIE ROMS IN DER FRÜHEN KAISERZEIT

Christiane Kunst

Die Stadt Rom wurde in der frühen Kaiserzeit von ihren Bewohnern sehr unterschiedlich wahrgenommen. Sie berichten von einer engen Stadt[1] mit viel zu wenig erschwinglichem Wohnraum, sie preisen aber auch die Pracht ihrer Bauten (Strabo, *Geogr.* 5,3,8).[2] Einem scheinbar geordneten städtebaulichen Ausbau bei Vitruv (2,8,17)[3] steht eine ungeordnete, kosmopolite, lärmende Metropole[4] gegenüber, in der man sich kaum vorwärts bewegen konnte, weil wogende Menschenmengen und Gewerbe die Straßen verstopften.[5] Ungeheurer Luxus[6] stand neben bitterer Armut.[7] Das Rom des frühen Principats war eine Stadt im Wandel. Zwar hatten die *principes* seit Augustus Anstrengungen zur Infrastrukturverbesserung unternommen – etwa im Bereich der Wasserversorgung haben sie dafür gesorgt, dass mehr frisches Wasser die Metropole erreichte;[8] neue Marktanlagen und zahlreiche Erholungsbereiche wurden für die hauptstädtische Bevölkerung geschaffen. Gleichzeitig übte jedoch gerade der kaiserliche Bedarf an öffentlichem Raum ungeheuren Druck auf die Wohngebiete aus und trug zu einer eklatanten Verknappung des innerstädtischen

1. *Hanc frequentiam, cui vix urbis immensae tecta sufficiunt* (Seneca, *Consol. Helv.* 6,2. Die enge verwinkelte Stadt der späten Republik (Cicero, *Leg. Agr.* 96) begünstigte im Jahr 64 n. Chr. den verheerenden Brand (Tacitus, *Ann.* 15,38,3).

2. Andererseits sehnten sich auch diese Kritiker nach Rom, sobald sie es verließen, weil es voller Lebenskraft und Gesellichkeit steckte; vgl. Martial 12 praef. 7–14.

3. Aelius Aristides, *Orationes* 26,8 bewundert geradezu den vertikalen Stadtausbau 156 n. Chr.; cf. Plinius, *Nat. Hist.* 3,67 zur Größe Roms, wenn der horizontalen die vertikale Ausdehnung hinzugefügt wird.

4. H. Dahlmann, 'Über den Lärm', *Gymnasium* 85 (1978), pp. 206–27. Horatius, *Ep.* 2,2,65ff.; Seneca, *Ep.* 56; Juvenal, *Sat.* 3,234–8; Martial 12, 57.

5. Juvenal, *Sat.* 3,243ff.; Seneca, *Clem.* 1,6; Martial 7,61.

6. Einzelne Aristokraten bewohnen Häuser, die die Größe von Städten einnahmen oder besaßen mehrere Paläste in ausgesuchten Wohnlagen (Martial 7,73). Vedius Pollio: Cassius Dio 54,23; Sallust, *Cat.* 12; Seneca, *Ep.* 90,43 (*domos instar urbium*); 114,9; *Benef.* 7,10; Apuleius, *De deo Socratis* 22; Statius 1,2 bes. 141ff.; Plinius, *Nat. Hist.* 19,51; Vitruv 6,5; Martial 12,57,18–25: *domus* des Sparsus auf dem Ianiculum mit Landgut und Weinbergen verbunden.

7. Z. Yavetz, 'The Living Conditions of the Urban Plebs in Republican Rome', *Latomus* 18 (1958), pp. 500–17 (Nachdruck in *The Crisis of the Roman Republic*, [hg. v. R. Seager; Cambridge: Heffer, 1969], pp. 162–79); P. Brunt, 'The Roman Mob', *Past and Present* 35 (1966), pp. 3–27.

8. Agrippa verdoppelte die Wassermenge: H.B. Evans, 'Agrippa's Water Plan', *AJA* 86 (1982), pp. 401–11 (411).

Bodens bei. Die Stadt konnte aufgrund fehlender Transportinfrastruktur kaum in die Breite wachsen, wohl aber in die Höhe.[9] Die durch die Palastarchitektur vom Palatin abgedrängte Elite besetzte mit ihren luxuriösen Raum verzehrenden Einzelhäusern die klimatisch günstigen Höhenlagen und zwang die übrige Bevölkerung an die Hänge und in die fiebererzeugenden Senken. Periodisch wurde Rom von Naturkatastrophen und epidemischen Krankheiten heimgesucht, die keinen Unterschied machten zwischen arm und reich.[10] Augustus war in seiner frühen Regierungszeit mit einer Vielzahl von Überschwemmungen und Feuersbrünsten konfrontiert.[11]

Die Schaffung von Wohnraum war kein Anliegen des römischen Staates,[12] aber die Kaiser mühten sich, die Gefahren von Feuer und Brand beherrschbar zu machen, die Vernichtung von Wohnraum einzudämmen und zur Entwicklung von Wohngebieten beizutragen. Doch weder Brandschutzverordnungen, Materialstandardisierungen, Geschoßhöhenverordnungen noch Straßenerweiterungen erwiesen sich als geeignete Instrumentarien, die Probleme der Stadt im Bereich der Versorgung mit Wohnraum zu lösen.

Die beiden dominierenden Haustypen waren *insula* und *domus*[13] mehrgeschossige von Mietern bewohnte Bauten und von Einzelhaushalten genutzte Häuser, die ebenfalls häufig ganz oder teilweise vermietet waren. Denn als Nero Geld für den städtischen Wiederaufbau brauchte, verlangte er von den Mietern (*inquilinos*) *privatarum aedium atque insularum* eine Jahresmiete (*pensionem annuam*) an den Fiskus abzuführen (Suetonius, *Nero* 44,2). Diese Vermischung von *Insula*- und Privathausmietern deutet ebenso wie das Fehlen ausgesprochener Armenghettos oder Notstandssiedlungen in unseren Quellen auf eine starke vertikale Differenzierung der Stadt.[14] Und so scheint es lohnend zu untersuchen, inwieweit soziale

9. Weiterer Grund für die begrenzten Wachstumsmöglichkeiten waren die überschwemmungsgefährdeten suburbanen Areale entlang von Tiber und Anio, teilweise Sumpfgebiete.

10. B. Shaw, 'Seasons of Death. Aspects of Mortality in Imperial Rome', *JRS* 86 (1996), pp. 100–38; W. Speidel, 'Seasonal Mortality in the Roman Empire', in *idem* (ed.), *Measuring Sex, Age and Death in the Roman Empire. Explorations in Ancient Demography* (JRA.Supp 21; Ann Arbor, 1996), pp. 139–63.

11. Suetonius, *Aug.* 28,3; zu Hungerkatastrophen vgl. Plinius, *Nat. Hist.* 7,46; Suetonius, *Aug.* 16; 42.

12. Vgl. H. Braunert, 'Großstadt und Großstadtprobleme im Altertum' (1967), in idem, *Politik, Recht und Gesellschaft in der griechisch-römischen Antike. Gesammelte Aufsätze und Reden von H. Braunert* (hg. v. K. Telschow, M. Zahrnt; Kieler Historische Studien, 26; Stuttgart: Klett-Cotta, 1980), pp. 11–28 (24–25).

13. Das Feuer 64 n. Chr. verbrannte nach Suetonius (*Nero* 38,2) *immensum numerum insularum* und *domus priscorum ducum*, vgl. Suetonius, *Nero* 16,1. Zur *insula* als gängiger Haustyp vgl. Cicero, *Leg. Agr.* 2,96; Dionysius Halicarnassensis, *Ant. Rom.* 10,32,5; Vitruv 2,8,16ff.; Tacitus, *Ann.* 15,38.43; Gellius 15,1,2–3; Herodian 7,12,5–6; SHA, *Pius* 9. *Domus* ist das innerstädtische Haus im Gegensatz zur Vorstadtvilla (*villa urbana*) vgl. Martial 4,64,25.

14. Zur Mischbebauung Pompeiis vgl. G.F. La Torre, 'Gli impianti commerciali ed artigianali nel tessuto urbano di Pompei', in *Pompei. L'informatica al servizio di una città antica* (Rom: L'Erma di Bretschneider, 1988), pp. 75–102, A. Wallace-Hadrill, 'The Social Spread of Roman Luxury. Sampling Pompeii and Herculaneum', *PBSR* 58 (1990) pp. 145–90 (164; 190); zu Rom: E.S. Ramage, 'Urban Problems in Ancient Rome', in R.T. Marchese (ed.), *Aspects of Graeco-*

Zugehörigkeit weniger durch das Wohnen in bestimmten Gegenden als vielmehr auch durch das Bewohnen bestimmter Hausformen ausgedrückt wurde.

Zunächst ist stichprobenhaft zu prüfen, wieweit Wohngebiete sozial durchmischt waren.[15] Danach wird die soziale Durchmischung der Mieter zu untersuchen sein. Im dritten Teil soll dann die Differenzierung des Mietshauses selbst im Mittelpunkt stehen.

1. *Die Wohnquartiere*

Die Verteilung der Bevölkerung von etwa 1 Mio[16] festzustellen, ist aufgrund der Quellenlage für die Kaiserzeit ausgesprochen schwierig. Literarische wie archäologische Quellen lassen eine Gemengelage erkennen. Selbst dort, wo vermeintlich arme Bevölkerungskreise lebten, kommen vornehme Häuser vor. Wenden wir uns diesen wahrscheinlich schlechteren Wohnlagen zu, so kommen zunächst die in Frage, die in der Literatur übel beleumundet waren. Das traf vor allem dort zu, wo Kleingewerbe und Prostitution aufeinander trafen.[17] Dies galt für die Straßen rund um das Forum,[18] insbesondere für die Gegend der nach NO führenden Straßen vom Argiletum[19] und der Subura.[20] Am Argiletum boten die lederverarbeitenden Gewerbe wie Schuhmacher und Buchhändler ihre Waren an (Martial 2,17,3; 1,3,1; 1,117,9ff.).[21] Die beiden Cicero-Brüder besaßen hier Häuser,[22] Marcus eine oder mehrere *insulae*, Quintus ein Objekt im Wert von einer Million, was mehr auf

Roman Urbanism. Essays on the Classical City (BAR International Series, 188; Oxford: BAR, 1984), pp. 61–92.

15.   Zur sozialen, an Stadtviertel gebundenen Topographie vgl. P. Lampe, *Die stadtrömischen Christen in den ersten beiden Jahrhunderten. Untersuchung zur Sozialgeschichte* (WUNT, II/18; Tübingen: Mohr-Siebeck, 1987), pp. 10ff.

16.   Zur Bevölkerungszahl mit Diskussion vgl. F. Kolb, *Rom. Die Geschichte der Stadt in der Antike* (München: C.H. Beck, 1995), p. 414.

17.   Ein ausgesprochenes Rotlichtviertel gab es jedoch nicht. Die Arbeit von B.E. Stumpp, *Prostitution in der römischen Antike* (Antike in der Moderne; Berlin: Akademie Verlag, 1998), pp. 151ff. hat gezeigt, dass die Prostitution überall in der Stadt zu finden war, Schwerpunkte lediglich an den Ausfallstraßen, in der Nähe der Kasernen sowie an allen Orten, wo viele Menschen zusammenkamen, in Tempeln, Fora, Bädern, Parks und Theatern.

18.   Plautus, *Curculio* 462ff.; Plutarch, *C. Gracch.* 12,1; Zum Vicus Tuscus am südlichen Forum: Horatius, *Sat.* 2,3,228; Plautus, *Curculio* 462ff. Im *velabrum* der Senke zwischen Palatin und Kapitol fanden die Bäcker, Fleischer, aber auch die Wahrsager ein Auskommen (Plautus, *ibid.*). Vgl. U.E. Paoli, *Das Leben im alten Rom* (Bern: Francke, 1948), p. 42.

19.   J.C. Anderson, 'Domitian, the Argiletum and the Temple of Peace', *AJA* 86 (1982), pp. 101–03; E. Tortorici, *Argiletum. Commercio, speculazione edilizia e lotta politica dall'analisi topografica di un quartiere di Roma d èta republicana* (Bulletino della Commissione Archeologica Comunale di Roma Suppl., 1; Rom: L'Erma di Bretschneider, 1991).

20.   Juvenal, *Sat.* 3,5–9: *ego vel Prochytam praepono Suburae;/ nam quid tam miserum, tam solum vidimus, ut non/ deterius credas horrere incendia, lapsus/ tectorum adsiduos ac mille pericula saevae/ urbis.* Properz, 4,7,15.25; vgl. J.P. Poe, 'The Septizonium and the Subura', *TAPA* 108 (1978), pp. 147–54.

21.   Nicht weit entfernt am Vicus Sandilarius waren die Flickschuster Martial (1,117,10–1) ansässig.

22.   Marcus: Cicero, *Att.* 12,32,2. Quintus: Cicero, *Att.* 1,14,7.

einen *domus*-Bau weist. Prostitution war in der Subura, einem Viertel für nächtliche Ausschweifungen, sehr verbreitet.[23] Die häufigen Brände der Subura veranlassten Augustus beim Bau seines Forums eine riesige Brandmauer zum Schutz des Neubaus errichten zu lassen.[24] Als Ädil hatte Caesar in einem bescheidenen Haus des Viertels gewohnt (Suetonius, *Caes.* 46; Plinius, *Nat. Hist.* 19, 23).[25] L. Arruntius Stella, der Konsul 101 n. Chr. besaß eine stattliche *domus* in der Subura und etwas weiter zum Esquilin hin, am *clivus suburbanus*, hatte sich bis 15 v. Chr. der gewaltige Stadtpalast des steinreichen Vedius Pollio befunden. Nicht weit davon entfernt lag die *domus* des jüngeren Plinius.[26]

Transtiberim, das erst in der Republik allmählich besiedelt worden war, zählte ebenfalls zu den einfachen Vierteln. Schon aufgrund seiner Lage am anderen Flußufer benachteiligt, hatten sich hier Handwerker angesiedelt wie etwa Gerber und Walker, die wegen des Gestanks ihrer Betriebe keine bevorzugte Nachbarschaft darstellten.[27] Hier lebten Arbeiter des nahe gelegenen Hafens und Kleinproduzenten wie Tischler und Töpfer. Aber auch in Transtiberim gab es *domus*-Bestand. Martials Patron Gallus besaß ein luxuriöses Haus (1,108,2), ebenso der reiche Jurist Manius Aquilius Regulus (Plinius, *Ep.* 4,2,5; Martial 1,12,82).[28]

Die Gegenden in Flußnähe, die von den häufigen Tiberüberschwemmungen bedroht waren, müssen tendenziell einfache Wohnlagen aufgewiesen haben. Dazu sind das Forum Boarium und das Forum Holitorium zu rechnen, wo sich schon im 3. Jh. v. Chr. dreigeschossige Bauten fanden.[29] Nur bei besonders heftigen Überflutungen wie 69 n. Chr. erreichte das Wasser auch die höheren Lagen.[30] Nicht weit entfernt galt der Circus Maximus als verdächtige Gegend, in der sich abends lichtscheues Gesindel herumtrieb (Horatius, *Sat.* 1,6,110–128). Auch in dieser Region waren Brände an der Tagesordnung, hatten doch die Korbflechter hier ihre Werkstätten.[31] 64 n. Chr. hatte das verheerende Feuer von hier seinen

23. Prostitution in der Subura: Horatius, *Epod.* 5,57f; Martial 6,66,1–2; 9,37,1; 11,61,3.

24. Zur ideologischen Deutung vgl. P. Zanker, *Augustus und die Macht der Bilder* (2. Aufl.; München: C.H. Beck, 1990), p. 160.

25. Augustus wohnte als junger Mann ebenfalls in Forumsnähe: *iuxta Romanum Forum supra Scalas anularias* (Suetonius, *Aug.* 72).

26. C. Panella, 'L'organizzazione degli spazi sulle pendici settentrionale del colle oppio tra Augusto e i Severi', in *L'Urbs. Espace urbain et histoire. Actes du colloque international organisé par le centre national de la recherche scientifique et École française de Rome* (Collection de l' École française de Rome, 98; Rom: Boccard/L'Erma di Bretschneider 1987), pp. 610–51.

27. Martial 1,41,3ff.; 6,93,1; Juvenal, *Sat.* 14,202; zur Stadtrandlage Artemidorus, *Oneiro-criticus* 1,51.

28. Viele Lagen waren extrem fiebergefährdet wie der Vatikan (Tacitus, *Hist.* 2,93,2) und daher eher Wohngegenden unterprivilegierter Schichten (Ammianus Marcellinus 27,3,6). Auf dem Campus Vaticanus befanden sich jedoch auch die *horti* der Agrippina und der Domitia mit ihren vorstädtischen Villen.

29. Livius 21,62,3 vgl. Plutarch, *C. Gracchus* 12.

30. 20 Meilen (30 km) von Rom waren die Straßen durch eingestürzte Gebäude versperrt (Tacitus, *Hist.* 1,86; 2–3; Plutarch, *Otho* 4; Suetonius, *Otho* 8,3). *Ammianus Marcellinus* 29,6,18.

31. Fasti Ostiensis (Inscr. It. XIII 1, 189): *k(alendis) Nov(embribus) pars Circi inter vitores arsit, ad quod T[i(berius)] Caesar (sestertium miliens) public(e)/ [d(edit)].*

Ausgang genommen und sich in den Läden mit leicht entzündlichen Waren in Windeseile ausgebreitet (Tacitus, *Ann.* 15,38).

Viertel veränderten zudem beständig ihr Gesicht. Typische Mischbebauung zeigt der aus severischer Zeit stammende antike Marmorplan im Gebiet zwischen Fugatal und Cispius an der Porticus Liviae (Abb. 1). In dichter Nachbarschaft liegen ein unregelmäßig angelegtes Viertel mit engen Gassen, in dem bescheidene Wohnhäuser, *insulae* sowie zu *insulae* umgewandelte *domus* anzutreffen waren und planvollere Anlagen mit einem sternförmig verlaufendem Straßensystem. Nero hatte nach dem großen Brand 64 n. Chr. (Tacitus, *Ann.* 15,43) ein Stadt-erneuerungskonzept vorgelegt, das breite Straßen und gerade *vici* vorsah.[32] Doch die neronischen Planungen kamen nur ansatzweise zur Umsetzung.[33] Auf dem Caelius lässt sich das eindrucksvoll zeigen. Bei Ausgrabungen im Bereich der modernen Via Celimontana unter dem Tempel des Claudius wurden *insula*-Bauten freigelegt, die unmittelbar nach 64 n. Chr. entstanden und die neronischen Vorgaben zu verwirklichen suchten.[34] Um die Piazza Celimontana, im Gebiet des heutigen Militärhospitals, wurden frühkaiserzeitliche *domus* in neronisch-flavischer Zeit unter Beibehaltung des Straßensystems von *insula*-Bebauung abgelöst, die im 2. Jh. erneut in luxuriöse Wohnhäuser umgewandelt wurden.

Der neronische Wiederaufbau der Stadt nach dem großen Brand ging nur schleppend voran. Man mußte zu außergewöhnlichen Maßnahmen greifen. Nero versprach den reichen Freigelassenen Iuniani Latini das volle römische Bürger-recht, wenn sie eine *domus* für wenigstens 100.000 Sesterzen in der Stadt Rom bauten (*Gaius* 1,33).[35] Aber noch in flavischer Zeit waren die Baulücken in der Stadt gravierend. Vespasian (*CIL* VI 931 = *ILS* 245) sah sich 71 n. Chr. gezwungen; sie gegen den Willen der Besitzer von jedermann schließen zu lassen (Suetonius, *Vesp.* 8,5) und weitere Wohnraumvernichtung zu unterbinden (*Constitutiones* 8,10,2).[36]

Neben den Stadterneuerungs- bzw. Privatisierungskonzepten standen großan-gelegte Stadterweiterungsprojekte, die nur durch kaiserliche Intervention geschaffen worden sein können. Aus hadrianischer Zeit[37] stammen die soliden großen mehrge-

---

32. Es wurden regelmäßige Häuserzeilen (*vici*) und breite Straßen angelegt, die Höhe der Häuser beschränkt, freie Innenhöfe (*areae*) gelassen und Portiken angebaut, um die Front der Mietshäuser zu verdecken (s. Abb. 2).

33. Vgl. G. Carettoni *et al.*, *La pianta marmorea di Roma antica (Forma Urbis Romae)* (2 Bde.; Rom: Ripartizione del Comune di Roma, 1960), Bd. 2. Im östlichen Teil der *via sacra* zwischen dem Haus der Vestalinnen und dem Palatin zeigt die *forma urbis* große rechteckige Wohnblocks mit vorgelagerten Portiken und breite, gerade Straßen; Transtiberim im Bereich des Ianiculum zeigt, dass die *insula*-Bebauung bis an den Tiber vorgelagert war (Taf. 30, frgm. Nr.33–4). Ähnliches gilt für die Hafengegend am Aventin (Taf. 24 frgm. Nr. 23–4) und die Region um die Via Portuensis (Taf. 27).

34. C. Pavolini, 'Lo scavo di Piazza Celimontana. Un' idagine nel Caput Africae', in *L'Urbs. Espace urbain et histoire*, pp. 653–85.

35. Prämien zum zügigen Wiederaufbau von *domus* und *insulae* Tacitus, *Ann.* 15,43,3.

36. Vgl. E.J. Phillips, 'Roman Law on the Demolition of Buildings', *Latomus* 32 (1973), pp. 86–95.

37. Bereits in flavischer Zeit war durch eine Niveauanhebung eine Vorbereitung zur Urbanisierung des Campus Martius erfolgt vgl. Kolb, *Rom*, p. 410.

schossigen Bauten von 1000–2500 qm Grundfläche[38] östlich und westlich der Via Lata auf dem nördlichen Marsfeld.[39]

Umnutzungen fanden auch innerhalb der Häuser statt. *Domus* wurden in kleinere Wohneinheiten aufgeteilt[40] oder *insulae* zu prächtigen Privathäusern zusammengelegt. Das Fragment der *forma urbis* 543[41] zeigt, dass zwei von drei Atriumhäusern in kleinere Wohneinheiten aufgeteilt wurden. Ein mindestens vierstöckiger *insula*-Bau auf dem Caelius am Clivus Scauri unter SS. Giovanni e Paolo wurde dagegen im 4. Jh. in ein Privathaus durch Zusammenlegung von zwei *insulae* umgewandelt.[42] Mietwohnraum wurde in Gewerberaum verwandelt, parzelliert oder arondiert.[43] Während die Geschoßhöhen zur Straße immer wieder staatlichen Regulierungen unterlagen,[44] galten diese Verordnungen nicht, wo die Gebäude auf private Grundstücke und Straßen zuliefen,[45] so dass die Häuser im hinteren Bereich häufig in verschachtelte Gebäudeansammlungen übergingen, in die sich niemand ohne Ortskenntnis hineinwagte.[46] So konnte eine *domus* unmittelbar mit einer angrenzenden *insula* verbunden sein.[47] Enge Gassen und Durchgänge aber galten bereits als verrufen und gefährlich (*Catull* 58,4–5). Holzkonstruktionen ergänzten die Gebäude nach oben und zur Straßenseite etwa in Form von Vor- und Anbauten und rückten so Bauten dicht zusammen.[48] Temporäre Bretterbuden wurden neben oder auf öffentlichen Gebäuden, zwischen den Säulen der Portiken oder vor Läden errichtet.[49]

38. G. Gatti, 'Caratteristiche edilizie di un quartiere di Roma del II secolo d. C.', *Quaderni dell' Istituto die storia architectura* 31 (1961), pp. 49–66 zu den Bauten an der Piazza Colonna.

39. F. Rakob, 'Die Urbanisierung des nördlichen Marsfeldes. Neue Forschungen im Areal des Horologium Augusti', in *L'Urbs. Espace urbain et histoire*, pp. 687–712.

40. Digesta 7,1,13,8: *per cenacula dividere domum*; Digesta 32,91,4.

41. Vgl. G. Carettoni *et al.*, *La pianta marmorea di Roma antica (Forma Urbis Romae)* (2 Bde.; Rom: Ripartizione del Comune di Roma 1960), Bd. 2, Taf. 53.

42. M. Trinci Cecchelli, 'Osservazioni sul complesso della domus celimontana dei SS. Giovanni e Paolo', in *Atti del IX Congresso internazionale di archeologia cristiana*: Roma 21–27 Sett. 1975. 1: Imonumenti Cristiani praecostantiniani (Studi di antichità cristiana, 32,, Rom: Pontificio Istituto di Archeologia Cristiana 1978), pp. 551–62.

43. Vgl. C. Kunst, 'Ein Dach für Viele. Das römische Privathaus zwischen Ökonomie und Repräsentation', *ZRGG* 52 (2000), pp. 289–308.

44. Die Geschoßhöhen wurden unter Augustus auf 6–7 Stockwerke (= 70 Fuß, vgl. Strabo, *Geogr.* 5,3,7) festgelegt, was etwa 21 m entspricht, und von Trajan auf 5–6 (60 Fuß; vgl. Ps.-Aurelius Victor 13,13) reduziert, also etwa 18 m.

45. H. Vetters, 'Zu römerzeitlichen Bauvorschriften', in F. Krinzinger *et al.* (eds.), *Forschungen und Funde FS B. Neutsch* (Innsbrucker Beiträge zur Kulturwissenschaft, 21; Innsbruck: Verlag des Instituts für Sprachwissenschaft der Universität Insbruck 1980), pp. 477–85.

46. Herodian 7,12,5–6. Vgl. die Erklärung des Festus zu den *vici* (Fest. 508 L) innerhalb von Gebäudekomplexen.

47. Digesta 32,91,6: *Appellatione domus insulam quoque iniunctam domui videri, si uno pretio cum domu fuisset comparata et utriusque pensiones similiter accepto latas rationibus ostenderetur.* 39,2,15,4: *insula adiecem domui.*

48. Vgl. die Beschreibung, die Herodian (7,12,5–6) vom Straßenkampf im Jahre 238 n. Chr. gibt. Martial (1,86) konnte seinen Nachbarn Novius aus dem Fenster heraus berühren.

49. A. Scobie, 'Slums, Sanitation and Mortality in the Roman World', *Klio* 68 (1986), pp. 399–433 (402) mit Anm. 25. R. Pöhlmann, *Die Überbevölkerung der antiken Großstädte im*

Nur eine verschwindende Minderheit konnte sich den Luxus suburbaner Villen im Grüngürtel der Stadt leisten. Die innerstädtischen *domus* des severischen Plans weisen dagegen Grundflächen zwischen 364 und 1664 qm aus, was den *domus*-Typ zu einem Haus von sehr weit gefächerter sozialer Zuordnung macht. Wir wissen, dass auch die *domus* keineswegs einer einzigen Familie vorbehalten blieben. Dienerschaft[50] mußte ebenso untergebracht werden wie mehr oder weniger permanente Gäste,[51] Freigelassene und Klienten.[52] Die meisten *domus* verfügten über Gewerbeeinheiten, die ebenso wie Wohnungen im Obergeschoß[53] vermietet werden konnten.[54] Wenig Zweifel besteht daran, dass die Mehrheit der hauptstädtischen Bevölkerung darauf angewiesen war, in den mehrgeschossigen *insulae*[55] zusammenzuleben, die zum Teil schwindelerregende Höhen annahmen wie die *insula* Felicles in der *regio* IX (Circus Flaminius), die weit über Roms Grenzen hinaus einen Ruf als antiker Wolkenkratzer genoß (Tertullian, *Adv. Vat.* c.7: *meritorium factus est mundus, insulam Feliculae credas tanta tabulata coelorum – illic etiam Valentinianorum deus ad summas tegulas habitat*).[56]

Doch auch die Mehrgeschoßbauten nahmen Leute von unterschiedlicher sozialer Herkunft auf. Zum einen gab es die soliden, gut proportionierten *insulae* des Typs wie sie in Ostia erhalten sind, zum anderen verfügte die Stadt über zahllose weniger repräsentative *insula*-Bauten. Viele von ihnen waren schmale Häuser wie sie das Planfragment vom Esquilin zeigt, mit etwa 6–12 m breiten Fassaden und ähnlichen Grundflächen wie in Ostia zwischen, 200–400 qm (Abb. 1). Der Plan zeigt auch, dass kleine *domus* tendenziell in *insulae* umgewandelt wurden. *Insulae* sind wiederum nicht nur im Zentrum, sondern auch im *suburbium* zu finden. Die Digesten zeigen jedoch, dass es im Verlauf der Kaiserzeit zu einer immer stärkeren Verdichtung der Stadt durch die Schließung von *area* (Hofräumen) kam.[57]

Zusammenhang mit der Gesamtentwicklung städtischer Civilisation dargestellt (Preisschriften gekrönt und hg. von der Fürstlichen Jablonowski'schen Gesellschaft zu Leipzig, 24; Leipzig: Hirzel 1884 [Ndr. Leipzig 1967]), p. 96ff. zu angeblichen Kellerwohnungen. Dazu kritisch Scobie, *ibidem*, p. 403 Anm. 31.

50. M. George, 'Servus and *domus*: the Slave in the Roman House', in R. Laurence, A. Wallace-Hadrill (eds.), *Domestic Space in the Roman World. Pompeii and Beyond* (JRA.Supp 22; Portsmouth 1997), pp. 15–24.

51. Digesta 9,3,1,9; 9,3,5,1; 9,3,5,4; 19,2,11 Pr. 39,2,13,5; Marci. D. 20,2,5 Pr.

52. Digesta 9,3,5,1.

53. Livius 39,14,2–3.

54. Digesta 32,91,6. F. Pirson, 'Rented Accomodation at Pompeii: the Evidence of the Insula Arriana Polliana VI 6', in Laurence, Wallace-Hadrill (eds.), *Domestic Space in the Roman World*, pp. 165–81; F. Pirson, *Mietwohnungen in Pompeji und Herkulaneum. Untersuchungen zur Architektur, zum Wohnen und zur Sozial- und Wirtschaftsgeschichte der Vesuvstädte* (München: Pfeil 1999).

55. H.D. Bottke, *Römische Mietshäuser* (Diss. Duisburg 1999), pp. 51ff.; J.E. Packer, 'Housing and Population in Imperial Ostia and Rome', *JRS* 57 (1967), pp. 80–95; B.W. Frier, 'The Rental Market in Early Imperial Rome', *JRS* 67 (1977), pp. 27–37.

56. *Insulae* von der Höhe der städtischen Hügel vgl. Ammianus Marcellinus 29,6,18.

57. Digesta 8,2,14; 8,2,20,6; 8,2,27,1.

2. Gemieteter Wohnraum der Oberschicht [58]

Noch in der frühen Kaiserzeit lebten selbst Senatoren in gemietetem Wohnraum.[59] Auf relativ kurzfristiger Basis standen Häuser zur Verfügung, die den Repräsentationsbedürfnissen dieser Gruppe entsprachen.[60] Lebten hingegen mehrere Generationen senatorischer Familien unter einem Dach, galt dies als Zeichen materieller Bedürftigkeit.[61] Daher war es üblich, dass die Söhne sehr früh eine eigene Wohnung bzw. eine *domus* bezogen, die angemietet wurde.[62] Dabei gehe ich davon aus, dass hier das Erdgeschoß eines Mehrfamilienhauses gemeint ist[63] oder aber ein *cenaculum*[64] – eine abgeschlossene Wohnung, die aus mehreren Räumen (*cubicula, exedra, medianum*) im Obergeschoß bestand.

3. Soziale Differenzierung innerhalb der insula

Die vertikale Differenzierung einer *insula* läßt sich an den Überresten einer ca. um 100 n. Chr. errichteten *insula* am Nordwesthang des Capitols nachweisen, von der ein Flügel mit vier Geschossen erhalten geblieben ist (Abb. 2).[65] Im Erdgeschoß befanden sich ausschließlich Läden und Werkstätten mit darüber liegendem Zwischengeschoß als Wohnräumen. Vorgelagert waren Arkaden, wie sie in den Brandschutzverordnungen Neros gefordert wurden. Der zweite Stock wies zwei großzügig geschnittene *cenaculae* von etwa 200 qm auf. Fünf nebeneinander liegende Zimmer (zwei *exedrae* und drei dazwischen liegende *cubiculae*) wurden durch ein *medianum* auf der Vorderseite des Hauses verbunden. Auf der dritten Etage waren immer drei nebeneinander liegende Räume von jeweils 10 qm im rechten Winkel zur Fassade angeordnet. Der vierte Stock ist nur schlecht erhalten, weist aber auf eine ähnliche Raumaufteilung wie der dritte. Leichtere Wände lassen darauf schließen, dass hier billigere Wohnungen als im Stock darunter zu haben waren. Nach oben gab es möglicherweise zwei weitere Stockwerke aus Holzkonstruktionen.[66] Am Nordrand des Capitols gab es laut Tacitus (*Hist.* 3,71)

---

58. Zu Mietwohnraum für die oberen Schichten vgl. B.W. Frier, *Landlords and Tenants in Imperial Rome* (Princeton, 1980), pp. 39–47.

59. Cassius Dio 46,31,3; Velleius Paterculus, *Hist. Rom.* 2,10,1.

60. Vgl. Q. Cicero (Cicero, *Q. Fr.* 2,3,7) und L. Calpurnius Piso (Cicero, *Pis.* 61).

61. Valerius Maximus 4,4,8; Plutarch, *Aem. Paulus* 5.

62. Sulla (Plutarch, *Sulla* 1,2); M. Caelius (Cicero, *Cael.* 18); M. Cicero minor (Cicero, *Att.* 12,32,2); Q. Cicero minor (Cicero, *Att.* 12,38,1); Oktavian (Nic. Damas. 4 [FrGrH. 90]); Domitian wird die eigene Wohnung verweigert (Suetonius, *Dom.* 2,1); zu anderen Haussöhnen vgl. Digesta 44,7,5,5; 9,3,1,7; 39,2,21; Plinius, *Ep.* 4,13,5.

63. Bei Caelius ist dies sehr deutlich, denn er wohnt in der *insula* des Clodius (Cicero, *Cael.* 17), in einer *habitatio* (ibid), die an anderer Stelle mehrfach als *domus* bezeichnet wird. Vgl. bes. *conduxit in Palatio non magno domum* (*ibidem*, 18). Zu Sullas Quartier vgl. L.E. Reams, 'Sulla's Early Poverty and Roman Rent', *AJAH* 9 (1984), pp. 148–74 (163ff).

64. Varro l.l.5,162 hat dieses Raumensemble im Obergeschoß lokalisiert: *posteaquam in superiore parte cenitare coeperint, superioris domus universa cenacula dicta sunt.*

65. J.E. Packer, 'La casa di Via Giulio Romano', *BCAR* 81 (1968–69), pp. 127–48.

66. J.E. Packer, 'La casa di Via Giulio Romano', p. 131 fig. 2.

am Ende der julisch-claudischen Zeit *insula*-Bauten, die bis auf die Höhe des Capitols reichten.

Der archäologische Befund einer vertikalen Differenzierung wird vom literarischen Befund gestützt. Je weiter man im Haus hinaufstieg, desto schlechter wurden die Quartiere. Eine vertikale Gliederung findet sich auch in den Mietsquartieren des alten Neapel. Dort waren zu ebener Ebene die Bassi, die Quartiere der Armen. Der adlige Besitzer wohnte zumeist im 2. Stock, das mittlere Bürgertum im 1. und 3. Geschoß und die Handwerker und Kleinhändler in der 4. und 5. Etage.[67] In den kaiserzeitlichen *insulae* vom Typ Ostia, boten die *tabernae*, die das gesamte Erdgeschoß einnahmen, einer großen Zahl kleiner Handwerker und Gewerbetreibender und ihren Familien Arbeit und Obdach.[68] Die Ladenbesitzer wohnten mit ihren Familien in einem kleinen Raum über dem Laden in einem Zwischengeschoß (*pergula*).[69] *Natus in pergula* (in einer *pergula* geboren) war ein sprichwörtlicher Ausdruck für eine Herkunft aus ärmlichen Verhältnissen.[70]

Wer waren nun die Bewohner der *cenacula*? Der jüngere Seneca, ein Ritter, der in den Senat aufstieg, wohnte zeitweise in einem *cenaculum* im 1. Stock einer *insula* nahe der *meta sudans* in der Senke zwischen Caelius und Palatin (*Ep.* 56,1,4) unmittelbar über einem öffentlichen Bad (*balneum*). *Tabernae* befanden sich im gleichen Haus, von denen eine von einem Schmied betrieben wurde. In unmittelbarer Nachbarschaft übte ein Tischler sein Handwerk aus. Der Ritter Martial hatte auf der Westseite des Quirinal (1,108,3) *ad pirum* sein *cenaculum* drei Treppen hoch (1,117,6–7), was auf das zweite Geschoß über den *tabernae* schließen lässt. Hier beherbergte er auch Sklaven zu seiner Bedienung. Freunde und Freigelassene des Augustus wohnten in *cenacula*, u. a. sein Hofnarr Gabba.[71] Diese Räumlichkeiten waren so groß, dass Augustus hier – vermutlich mit einem kleinen Stab – übernachten konnte.[72] Der Jurist Aquilius Regulus brachte in einem seiner *insula*-Objekte den Redner Nicostratus in einem *cenaculum* unter (*dono et permitto tibi habitare*) als Ausgleich für dessen Verdienste.[73] Die Obergeschoßwohnung des Topographen Demetrius, in die 164–163 v. Chr. der exilierte König Ptolemaios mit 4 Bedienten Aufnahme fand, muß allein aufgrund der Größe ein *cenaculum* gewesen sein – möglicherweise im 2. oder 3. Stock.[74]

---

67. R. Legler, *Der Golf von Neapel* (4. Aufl.; Köln: Dumont 1995), pp. 378–79.

68. Asconius Pedianus, *Tog. Cand.* p. 32 (Clark): *dormientem in taberna*; Tacitus, *Hist.* 1,86,2 *tabernis et cubilibus*; Digesta 50,16,183 (Ulpian); in den Vermietungsanzeigen aus Pompeii werden jeweils *tabernae cum pergulis* angeboten *CIL* IV 1136 = *ILS* 5723; *CIL* IV 138 = *ILS* 6035.

69. Indikatoren für den Nachweis von Wohnraum sind: Küchen, Latrinen, Bettnischen und Schreine vgl. V. Gassner, *Die Kaufläden in Pompeii* (Dissertationen der Universität Wien, 178; Wien: VWGÖ 1986), pp. 36–43.

70. Petronius, *Sat.* 74,14. Ärmlichkeit: Horatius, *Carm.* 1,4,14–5: pauperum tabernas regumque turris; *Tabernae* als Sammelpunkt des Mobs vgl. Cicero, *Cat.* 4,17; *Dom.* 89.

71. Suetonius, *Aug.* 45,1 cf. Cassius Dio 57,11,4–5. Gabba: *cenaculum* (Quintilianus, *Institutio Oratoria* 6,3,64).

72. Suetonius, *Aug.* 78,2.

73. Digesta 39,5,27 pr.

74. Diodorus Siculus 31,18,2. Die Hetäre Manilia bewohnte eine Wohnung im Obergeschoß, die jedoch nicht näher typisiert wird (Gellius 4,14).

Tabernae und *cenacula* gehören zu den charakteristischen Wohnungstypen der *insula*. In den Vermietungsanzeigen Pompeiis, die zweigeschossige Häuser vermarkten, werden *tabernae* mit *pergulae* sowie *cenacula* angeboten. In der römischen *insula* Sertoriana am Forum Boarium gab es mehr als 6 *cenacula* und 11 *tabernae* sowie eine nicht spezifizierte Zahl von Unterkünften unter den Treppen (*CIL* VI 29791 = *ILS* 6034: *in his praedis insula Sertoriana bolo esse Aur. Cyriacetis filie meae cinacula* [sic] *n.VI, tabernas n. XI et repossone subiscalire*). Eine weitere *insula* (*CIL* VI 10248) verfügte über mindestens 24 *cenacula*.

Auch *cenacula* dürften von unterschiedlicher Qualität gewesen sein.[75] Die *cenacula* der pompeianischen *insula* Arriana Polliana werden ausdrücklich als *cenacula equestria* angepriesen.[76] Für Pompeii wie Herculaneum sind eine Reihe von wohl ausgestatteten, gut gelegenen *cenacula* nachweisbar, die über eine Ballustrade einen Blick in den Peristylgarten oder das Atrium hatten.[77] Der Umzug aus dem *cenaculum* in eine *domus* galt jedoch als Zeichen des sozialen Aufstiegs (Petronius, *Sat.* 38). Martial erwarb, nachdem er zu Ruhm gekommen war, eine *domus* auf dem Quirinal,[78] wechselte also nicht die Gegend, sondern die Wohnform.

Cenacula waren beliebig in Zimmer aufteilbar (Digesta 9,3,5 pr), aber der Plan der capitolinischen *insula* zeigt auch, dass die einfachen Wohnräume (*cellae*)[79] der literarischen Überlieferung ihre architektonische Entsprechung in den Einzelzimmern im 3. und 4. Geschoß fanden. In ihnen wohnen Leute mit einem mäßigen Einkommen, aber keineswegs die mittellosen, denn der Armutsbegriff der antiken Literatur war überaus weitgefasst.[80] Als Bewohner werden ein Schuster, ein Historiker und ein verarmter Hausbesitzer (Olus) genannt.[81] Martial beschwerte sich heftig, als ihm eine solche *cella* mit nur einem zugigen Fenster als Gästequartier angeboten wurde.[82] Eine *cella pauperis* richteten sich die Allerreichsten in ihren vornehmen Häusern ein, um gelegentlich das einfache Leben zu zelebrieren (Seneca, *Ep.* 18,7;100,6; *Dial.* 12,12,3; Martial 3,48).

Die miesesten Quartiere befanden sich, wenn man den antiken Quellen folgt; unter dem Dach (*sub tegulis*),[83] aber auch diese Mieter verfügten über ein beschei-

---

75. Schon im 2. Jh. bezeichnet es die Wohnung eines prestigereichen Mannes im Obergeschoß, vgl. Plautus, *Amphitruo* 861–63.

76. Digesta 9,3,1,8. (Ulp.). Hor. epist. 1,1,91: identifiziert das cenaculum mit dem weniger Begüterten.

77. I. Sutherland, *Colonnaded cenacula in Pompeian Domestic Architecture* (ungedruckte Diss.; Duke University 1989).

78. Martial 9,18,2; 97,8; 10,58,10 (vermutlich 94 n. Chr.).

79. Auch die Bezeichnung für die Kammern eines Bordells vgl. Martial 11,45,1.

80. C.R. Whittaker, 'Der Arme', in A. Giardina (ed.), *Der Mensch der römischen Antike* (Frankfurt: Campus 1991), pp. 305–36; M. Prell, *Sozialökonomische Untersuchungen zur Armut im antiken Rom. Von den Gracchen bis Kaiser Diocletian* (Beiträge zur Wirtschafts- und Sozialgeschichte, 77; Stuttgart: Steiner 1997), pp. 44ff.

81. *Cellae* bewohnen: Santra (Martial 7,20,21), Olus (*cella pauperis*: Martial 3,48,1–2), ein Schuster (Martial 9,73,4); der mittellose Historiker Telesinus (Juvenal, *Sat.* 7,27–9).

82. Martial 8,14,5–6.

83. Juvenal, *Sat.* 3,202; Tertullians Kritik am Gedankengebäude der Valentinianer, das er mit

denes Einkommen, wie zum Beispiel der Grammatiklehrer L. Orbilius Pupillus (Suetonius, *Gramm.* 9,3). Codrus, ein anderer Bewohner, besitzt eine winzige Bibliothek und eine Marmorstatuette (Iuvenal, *Sat.* 3, 205–6).

Wo wohnten nun die wirklich Armen? Die Quartiere unter den Treppen aus der *insula* Sertoriana werden von den Satirikern kaum erwähnt,[84] haben aber in den *domus* wohl als einfache Sklavenunterkünfte gedient.[85] Die Digesten kennen Pensionen (*meritorium, deversorium*)[86] als Dauerunterkünfte. Dazu gehören z.B. die Zimmer in *cauponae* und *stabula* (Digesta 47,5,1,6 für permanente Unterkünfte). Die Ärmsten freilich konnten nicht einmal eine solche dauerhafte Bleibe finanzieren. Sie hausten, wo es gerade einen Platz zum Schlafen gab,[87] unter Brücken,[88] im Freien, in den Thermen.[89] Kaum Beachtung finden die Quartiere der Sklaven. In den Digesten wird verlangt, dass jemand, der einen Sklaven nur zum Nießbrauch erhält, also nur ein befristetes Nutzungsrecht am Sklaven hat, das die Rechte des Eigentümers nicht verletzen darf, die Sklaven *sufficienter autem alere et vestire ... secundum ordinem et dignitatem* (Digesta 7,1,15,2) muß. Von einer akzeptablen Unterkunft ist jedoch nicht die Rede. Daran läßt sich gut zeigen, dass Obdach nicht als lebensnotwendiges Bedürfnis eingestuft wurde.[90] Die einfachen Sklaven verfügten daher im Hause des Herrn kaum über formalisierte Quartiere.[91]

4. Zugangsmöglichkeiten zu verschiedenen infrastrukturellen Kommoditäten

Um die vertikale Differenzierung der *insula* weiter zu überprüfen, sollen die Wohnungssegmente in Bezug auf Platz, Licht, Hygiene, Sicherheit und Preis betrachtet werden. Der Gegensatz zwischen urbanem und suburbanem (bzw. ländlichem) Wohnen wurde für die Menschen der Kaiserzeit vor allem durch zwei Dinge bestimmt. Auf dem Land gab es erstens genug Raum und damit Luft und Licht; zweitens war das *suburbanum* der Inbegriff der Ruhe. Der zermürbende Lärm der Stadt war eine Unbequemlichkeit, die alle Städter gleichermaßen ertragen mussten. Nur sehr Reiche, sagt Iuvenal (3,234f.), können in Rom schlafen.

a) Platz: In Hinblick auf Größe boten die *cenacula* schon wegen ihrer Vielräumigkeit mehr Platz als die einfachen *cellae*. Menschliche Bedürfnisse konnten in der Wohnung befriedigt werden (z.B. ungestörter Sex). Gäste konnten empfangen und bewirtet werden, was ein gewisses Maß an Repräsentation zuließ (Geschirr). Differenzierter Empfang war jedoch nur in einem sehr großen *cenaculum* bzw. in

---

der *insula* Felicles vergleicht, instrumentalisiert dieses Bild, wenn er spöttisch bemerkt, dass der Gott der Valentianer *ad summas tegulas habitat.*

84. Ein Hinweis könnte Martial 2,53,8 sein.

85. Zu *subscalaria* vgl. Scobie, 'Slums, Sanitation and Mortality', p. 403, Anm. 29.

86. Leben im *deversorium/taberna* vgl. Petronius, *Sat.* 76,6; 80,3, wo Encolpius sein Quartier einmal als *deversorium*, einmal als *taberna* bezeichnet. Frier, pp. 31–32.

87. Prell, *Sozialökonomische Untersuchungen*, p. 122, Anm. 50.

88. Martial 12,32.

89. Scobie, 'Slums, Sanitation and Mortality', p. 403.

90. Scobie, 'Slums, Sanitation and Mortality', p. 406 mit Anm. 57.

91. Horatius, *Sat.* 1,8,8: *angustis eiecta cadavera cellis*; George, 'Servus and *domus*', pp. 15–24.

der *domus* möglich. So besaß Martial, der Besuch empfing, beispiels–weise einen Herd, der einigen Aufwand zum Anheizen erforderte. Paulus, der zwei Jahre in einer gemieteten Unterkunft in Rom verbrachte, konnte hier ebenfalls Besuch empfangen und predigen. Ferner war hier Platz für seine Bewachung.[92] Die *cellae* boten dagegen nur als Schlafstelle und Aufbewahrungsort für Habseligkeiten Raum. Die Bewohner aßen in den Garküchen und lebten mehr oder weniger auf der Straße, weil ihre Wohnungen zu wenig Raum für andere Aktivitäten ließen. *Cenacula* und auch *cellae* konnten parzelliert werden und damit individuellen Raum verringern. In der Capitol-*insula* ermöglichten gewölbte Decken in erheblicher Höhe das Einziehen von Ziehböden. Wie wenig Raum vorhanden sein konnte, verdeutlicht das Beispiel Neapel im 19. Jh. Hier wurden 4–5 qm große Räume (halb so groß wie die *cellae* der Capitol-*insula*) durch horizontale Scheidewände getrennt und boten so ca. 20 Menschen Platz.[93] Aus dem ägyptischen Arsinoë liegt die Zensusdeklaration des Webers Herodes vor, der mit 20 Personen und 6 Untermietern im zehnten Teil eines Mietshauses im bithynischen Viertel wohnte.[94]

b) Licht: Ein wichtiges Kriterium zur Klassifizierung von Wohnraum war seine Belichtung. Eine ausreichende Versorgung mit Licht war ein Grundproblem der römischen Bauweise. Die *tabernae* im Erdgeschoß der Capitol-*insula* bekamen schon aufgrund der vorliegenden Arkaden fast kein Licht, ebenso die darüber liegenden *pergulae*, die ihr Licht durch Öffnungen über dem Eingang zur *taberna* erhielten. Die *cenacula* dagegen waren dem Licht zugewandt. Die *cellae* waren sukzessive vom Licht abgewandt. Allein die vorderen zur Straße ausgerichteten Räume erhielten hier überhaupt nennenswertes natürliches Licht. Die beiden nach innen liegenden Räume wurden durch einen schlecht belichteten Flur fast gar nicht erhellt. Eine der Wohnungen jedoch war von diesem Standpunkt aus eleganter, da sie über einen großen Eckraum verfügte, der von mehreren großen Fenstern direktes Licht erhielt. Eine dunkle Kammer (*fusca cella*) war das Synonym für eine bescheidene Unterkunft.[95]

Auf den städtischen Grundstücken gab es Baulasten, die verhindern sollten, dass man einem Nachbarn durch Erhöhung des eigenen Gebäudes oder durch Neubau Licht nahm. Diese Baulasten galten jedoch nur für fremde Grundstücke. Besaß ein Eigentümer eine Ansammlung von *insulae* bzw. einen Gebäudekomplex, konnte er das Grundstück nach Belieben verdichten und somit die Lichtverhältnisse in den einzelnen Etagen ohne Rücksicht verschlechtern. Denn Geschoßhöhenverordnungen

92. Apg 28,16–31. Zu leichterer Haft in eigener Wohnung vgl. Digesta 48,2,3; mit eigener Tätigkeit Dig. 4,6,10. Es spricht nichts dafür, dass er das Quartier wechselte. Zur Gleichsetzung von ξενία und μίσθωμα vgl. G. Stählin, ξενός, *ThWNT* 5 (Nachdr. 1990), p. 18 n. 137.

93. R. Pöhlmann, *Überbevölkerung*, p. 104, Anm. 4 auf der Grundlage eines Zeitungsberichts zum Ausbruch der Cholera im Dez. 1873. F. Snowden, *Naples in the Time of Cholera, 1884–1911* (Cambridge: University Press, 1995), p. 18f. erhebt für den Vico Fico, eine typische neapolitanische Gasse, Durchschnittsbelegungen von 7 Personen für einen 5 qm großen Raum, der auf diese Weise geteilt worden war. Dabei gab es auch Wohnquartiere, wo weniger als ein halber Quadratmeter pro Bewohner zur Verfügung stand.

94. BGU 1326 Nr. 115 (189 n. Chr.) = L. Mitteis, U. Wilcken, *Grundzüge und Chrestomathie der Papyruskunde*, 4 Bde. (Leipzig: Teubner, 1912 [Ndr. Hildesheim: Olms, 1963]), I,2 Nr. 203.

95. Martial 3,30,3; Juvenal, *Sat.* 3,225.

galten nicht, wo Gebäude aan private Grundstücke und Straßen grenzten,[96] so dass die Häuser im hinteren Bereich häufig in verschachtelte Gebäudeansammlungen übergingen.[97] Die kleinen *insulae* verfügten ohnehin über keinen lichtspendenden Innenhof. Licht bedeutete in den Digesten darüber hinaus nur „ein Stück vom Himmel sehen", was auf sehr düstere Verhältnisse deutet. Da es keine Scheiben gab oder nur in sehr kostspieligen Räumen, mußten bei schlechter Witterung die Fensterläden geschlossen werden, was zu weiterer Verdunkelung führte. Der Mangel an Licht für die Bevölkerungsmehrheit führte zu ernsthaften gesundheitlichen Problemen. So berichtet Soran (1,44,133), dass die Stadtrömer extrem unter Rachitis litten, auch wenn er die Krummbeinigkeit auf mangelnde Mutterliebe zurückführte.[98]

Die wachsende Dichte der städtischen Bebauung mit schmalen Straßen und geringem Abstand zum Nachbarhaus[99] (Kolb) spitzte das Lichtproblem extrem zu. Das macht verständlich, warum eine Aussicht ebenfalls durch eine Baulast gesichert wurde. Derartige *prospecti* waren ein spezielles Kennzeichen großer *villae urbanae*[100] und trugen in der Stadt nicht unwesentlich dazu bei, dem Wohnraum Exklusivität zu verleihen.[101] Martials *cenaculum* blickte auf die Porticus Vipsaniae (1,108,3–4); einige der *cenacula* von Freunden bzw. Freigelassenen des Augustus hatten Aussicht auf die Rennen im Circus (Suetonius, *Aug.* 45,1 cf. Dio Cassius, *Hist. Rom.* 57,11,4–5). Möglicherweise konnte Seneca von seiner Wohnung auf die *meta sudans* sehen.

c) Hygiene: Die hygienischen Verhältnisse war in der gesamten *insula* nicht zum besten gestellt, dennoch werden sie von den Satirikern kaum thematisiert und allgemein nicht als Problem wahrgenommen. Es gab in den oberen Stockwerken zumeist keine Wasserversorgung.[102] Im Idealfall existierte im Hofbereich ein Brunnen.[103] Immerhin erfahren wir von Frontin (*Aq.* 2,76), *curator aquarum* 97 n. Chr., dass das Wasser der Aquädukte „sogar in *cenacula*" abgeleitet worden waren. Die Capitol-*insula* jedoch verfügte weder über identifizierbare Wasserzuleitungen noch Latrinen. Üblicherweise standen entgeltlich öffentliche Latrinen zur Verfügung, die auch von höhergestellten Persönlichkeiten wie den Bewohnern der *cenacula* in Anspruch genommen wurden.[104] In Martials *cenaculum* gab es

---

96. Kolb, *Rom*, p. 446; Vetters, 'Bauvorschriften', pp. 477–85.

97. Herodian 7,12,5–6. Vgl. die Erklärung des Festus zu den *vici* (Fest. 508 L) innerhalb von Gebäudekomplexen.

98. Martial (10,12) verspottete die blassen Städter.

99. Novius (Martial 1,86). Der noch sichtbare *ambitus* zwischen den *horrea* und der *insula* unter San Clemente beträgt knapp 30 cm.

100. Martial 12,57; 4,64; Hor. *Epod.* 2,12; Plinius, *Nat. Hist.* 5,6,28; Tacitus, *Ann.* 15,42,1 (Kritik an Neros Domus Aurea).

101. Martial 7,73.

102. Seneca, *Ep.* 100,6.

103. Wir wissen nichts über die Verteilung der *lacus* in der Stadt. Pompeii verfügte über 40 öffentliche Wasserstellen, die gleichmäßig verteilt waren. Allein die Regio VI war spärlicher ausgestattet, ein älteres Wohnquartier, vgl. H. Eschebach, 'Die Gebrauchswasserversorgung des antiken Pompeji', *AW* 10 (1979), pp. 3–24. Für Rom spricht Frontin (78,3) von 591 Brunnen; die spätantiken Regionenverzeichnisse nennen 1352.

104. Suetonius, *Poet.* 31 über Lukan.

ebenfalls kein fließendes Wasser (8,67,7–8). Kaum Häuser waren in der Stadt Rom mit dem Straßenabwasser verbunden,[105] stattdessen gab es innerhäusliche Gruben und Latrinen. Es ist hinlänglich bekannt, dass letztere in Pompeii im Küchenbereich lagen, was nachhaltig gesundheitliche Beeinträchtigungen bedeutet haben muß. (In Ostia ist bisher eine *insula* identifiziert, wo ein Latrine im Obergeschoß mit einer Küchenlatrine im Erdgeschoß verbunden war.[106]) Vaccera, der mit Mutter, Schwester und Frau vermutlich in einer *cella* wohnte, benutzte einen Nachttopf (Martial 12,32,13). Die Entsorgung von Nachtgeschirren und anderem Müll auf die Straße war trotz drastischer Strafen ein weit verbreitetes Problem.

d) Sicherheit: Die Ordnung der antiken Stadt war überaus fragil.[107] Was die Sicherheit in den *insulae* betrifft, so waren sie wesentlich häufiger Ziel von Kleinkriminalität wie Diebstahl und Einbruch als die großen, gut geschützten Häuser. Die von einer Person bewohnten *cenacula* dürften leichter zu bewachen gewesen sein, als die von verschiedenen Leuten frequentierten Räume, auch wenn Sicherheitsriegel und anderes belegt sind. Die Bausicherheit wiederum betraf sämtliche Bewohner, allerdings war es leichter bei den häufigen Feuerkatastrophen im *cenaculum* mit dem Leben davon zu kommen, weil der Rettungsweg kürzer war.[108] Die obersten Stockwerke bestanden häufig ausschließlich aus leicht entflammbaren Holzkonstruktionen und waren eine Brandfalle. In keinem Stockwerk gab es Heizmöglichkeiten, so dass in allen Etagen mit feuergefährlichen Holzkohlebecken geheizt wurde. Die Baustandards ließen häufig zu wünschen übrig. Das lag einmal an einer möglichst kostensparenden Bauweise,[109] zum anderen auch daran, dass es keine vernünftigen Prüfmöglichkeiten für Materialen gab.[110] Das *cenaculum* von Augustus' Hofnarr Gabba war bei Regen feucht (Quintilian 6,3,64). Teile der Capitol-*insula* waren in den Berg gebaut. Dies dürfte ebenfalls für erhebliche Feuchtigkeit in den rückwärtigen Räumen gesorgt haben. Selbst *domus*-Besitzer fürchteten den Einsturz ihres Hauses (sowie Brand.)[111] Hier ist dann auch eher an die oben beschriebene regionale Differenzierung der Stadt zu denken. In den verdichteten Quartieren brach häufiger Feuer aus, in den Niederungen gelegene Häuser konnten bei Hochwasser eher unterspült werden. *Insula*-Einstürze waren jedoch ein generelles Problem. Allerdings konnte ein relativ hochgestellter

105. Scobie, 'Slums, Sanitation and Mortality', p. 409.

106. J.E. Packer, *The Insulae of Imperial Ostia* (Memoirs of the Am. Academy of Rome, 31, Rom: American Academy, 1971), regio III v. 1.

107. Unruhen in der augusteischen Stadt in Folge von Getreidepreiserhöhungen Suetonius, *Aug.* 25,2; nach der Niederlage in Germanien 23,1; Schlägereien Suetonius, *Aug.* 45,2. Vgl. T.W. Africa, 'Urban Violence in Imperial Rome', *Journal of Interdisciplinary History* 2 (1971), pp. 3–21; nächtliche Straßengewalt: Digesta 9,2,52,1.

108. Juvenal, *Sat.* 3,197–202. Bei manchen *insulae* macht die Höhe jeden Rettungsversuch unmöglich vgl. Seneca, *Contr.* 2,9.

109. Vitruv 2,8,20.

110. Vitruv 2,3,2 (Trocknungsgrade).

111. Seneca, *Ep.* 90,43.

Geschädigter offensichtlich erwarten, dass ihm bei der Wiederbeschaffung von Eigentum Unterstützung von seinesgleichen zukam. Diese Art der Solidarität war für die einfacheren Bewohner unerreichbar.[112]

e) Miete: Die Grabinschrift eines Freigelassenen sagt unmissverständlich, dass das Bezahlen der Miete zu den Alltagssorgen gehört, von denen der Tod ihn befreit hatte.[113] Allein die Tatsache, dass er sich einen Stein leisten konnte, deutet darauf hin, dass das Mietenproblem nicht allein die Mittellosen betraf. Ein Grund dafür war erstens Knappheit des Angebots und zweitens die indirekte Vermarktung von Wohnraum, mit einem Geflecht von Weiter- und Untervermietung. Übliche Praxis war es, ein ganzes Haus zu mieten, um die einzelnen Wohnungen weiterzuvermieten.[114] Ein *cenaculum* etwa konnte in Teilen oder als Ganzes untervermietet werden, wobei der Flur (*medianum*)[115] den Zugang zu den Räumen der Untermieter bot.[116] In der Regel wurden größere Objekte an einen Generalunternehmer vermietet, der sie seinerseits untervermietete.[117] Der Generalmieter zahlte im Voraus.[118] Die Laufzeiten der Verträge waren üblicherweise auf ein oder mehrere Jahre terminiert.[119] Frühestens am Ende eines Halbjahres war der Mietzins (*pensio*) für die vorangegangene Periode zu entrichten.[120] Die Armen mussten dagegen für ihre bescheidenen Unterkünfte täglich ihre Miete begleichen.

Ein Drittel Gewinn wird von Ulpian als übliche Rendite für denjenigen angenommen, der die Wohnungen selbst einzeln untervermietete.[121] Immerhin noch 20% Gewinn konnte man bei Vermietung an einen Gesamtuntermieter erzielen.[122] Darüber hinaus wurden gerade wegen der hohen Mieten auch Teile der Wohnungen erneut untervermietet,[123] so dass die kleinsten Räume proportional das meiste

---

112. Juvenal, *Sat.* 3, 209–22; Martial 3,52.

113. *CIL* VI 7193a.

114. Digesta 19,2, (59) 58; zu einem Mietvertrag vgl. BGU 1116, vgl. auch Frier, 'Rental Market', pp. 27–37.

115. G. Hermansen, 'The *medianum* and the Roman Apartment', *Phoenix* 24 (1970), pp. 342–47.

116. Digesta 9,3,5 pr. 1: *Si vero plures diviso inter se cenaculo habitent, actio in eum solum datur, qui inhabitabat eam partem, unde effusum est. ... nam et si quis cenaculariam exerceus ipse maximam partem cenaculi habeat, solus tenebitur: sed si quis cenaculariam exercens modicum sibi hospitum retinuerit, residuum locaverit pluribus, omnes tenebuntur quasi in hoc cenaculo habitantes, unde deiectum effusumve est.*

117. Digesta 13,7,11,5; 19,1,53pr.; 19,2,7–8. 30pr. 58pr. 60pr.

118. Digesta 19,2,7,30pr.

119. Vgl. Mietkontrakte *CIL* IV 1136; 138. Digesta 19,2,24,2; stillschweigende Verlängerung vgl. Digesta 19,2,13,11.

120. Digesta 43,32,1,4; Jahresabrechnung vgl. Suetonius, *Nero* 44,2; Digesta 36,2,12,5; mehrjährige Kontrakte: Digesta 19,2,24,2 (*domus*); 60pr.; 43,32,1,4; *CIL* IV 1136. Zu einer Liste publizierter Verträge vgl. Frier, 'Rental Market', Anm. 17. Vaccera war nach zwei Jahren ohne Mietzahlung geräumt worden (Martial 12,32).

121. Digesta 19,2,30pr.

122. Digesta 19,2,7.

123. Digesta 9,3,5 vgl. Anm. 116. Die Mieter wiederum können bei der Unsicherheit der Mietzahlungen wenig Druck ausüben.

kosteten[124] und Immobilienbesitz in der Hauptstadt trotz zahlreicher Risiken[125] ein lohnendes Geschäft darstellte.

Abb. 1

5. Zusammenfassung

Hauptverbreitungsgebiete der *insula*-Bauten waren die Senken im Bereich der Kernstadt und die der Stadt zugewandten Hänge von Quirinal, Viminal und Esquilin. In ihnen wohnten die Mittel- und Unterschichten, aber auch Angehörige der Elite, Söhne von Senatoren, Ritter. Auf den Hügelkuppen und im Suburbium besaßen die wenigen Reichen und sehr Vornehmen ihre Häuser. Kleinere, mittlere, aber auch ansehnliche *domus* waren auf die gesamte Stadt verteilt. Nur wenige Gegenden waren ausschließlich von einfachen Leuten geprägt wie die in den fluß-nahen Regionen. Soziale Differenzierung vollzog sich innerhalb der Wohnkomplexe

---

124. Juvenal, *Sat.* 3,223–5. Die Grenze der Zumutbarkeit war recht hoch: zu Licht vgl. Digesta 3,1,30; 8,2,10; zu Minderung 19,2,27pr.
125. Gellius 15,1; Herodian 7,12,6.

bzw. in unmittelbarer Nachbarschaft. Die wirklich Armen, diejenigen, die nur selten bis gar nicht über Einkommen verfügten, hatten überhaupt keinen festen Wohnsitz; bestenfalls hausten sie in einem provisorischen Bretterverschlag. Die Wohnverhältnisse der Bevölkerungsmehrheit waren insofern katastrophal, als das Gesundheitsgefährdung extrem hoch war. Brände, Hauseinstürze, unzureichende Abfallbeseitigung bzw. hygienisch ungenügende Wasserversorgung sowie Seuchen im Gefolge von Naturkatastrophen trafen alle Bevölkerungsschichten der Stadt.[126] Nervenzerrüttender Lärm und Gestank waren ebenfalls ein allgemeines Problem. Die Mittel- und Unterschichten waren jedoch in besonderem Maße gesundheitlich gefährdet, da sie auch in solide gebauten *insulae* nur bei entsprechendem Einkommen über genügend mit Licht, Luft und gegebenenfalls Wasser versorgten Wohnraum verfügen konnten. Je bescheidener die Einkommensverhältnisse um so dramatischer stellte sich diese Situation dar. Hinzu kam eine beständige Bedrohung durch mangelnde öffentliche Sicherheit. Die Bevölkerung der Hauptstadt war daher nicht zufällig ein hoch explosives Unruhepotential, das von den Autoritäten beständig bei Laune gehalten werden musste.

Abbildungsverzeichnis

1. Der Esquilin, aus: E. Rodríguez-Almeida, 'I confini interni della "regio V", Esquiliae, nella "Forma Urbis Marmorea"', in G. Pisani Sartorio (ed.), *L'archeologia in Roma capitale tra sterro e scavo* (Roma Capitale 1870–1911, 7; Venedig: Marsilio Editori, 1983) pp. 106–15, Taf. II p. 169.
2. a) Aufriß der Casa Giulio Romano, aus: J.E. Packer, 'La casa di Via Giulio Romano', *BCAR* 81 (1968–9) pp. 127–48, fig. 3, p. 132.

   b) Rekonstruktion der Casa Giulio Romano nach P. Connolly, *Die Antike Stadt* (Köln: Könemann 1998), p. 142.

ABSTRACT

While the provision of food supplies and water to urban centres were expected from public authorities or from private or imperial euegertism, the availability of housing was almost entirely left to the free market of supply and demand. The emperor only interfered in matters of housing as far as city planning was concerned. An overview of urban housing areas in Rome reveals that despite a tendency towards upper class occupation on top of the hills and poorer housing close to the River, generally a strong social mixture prevailed. The very poor, however, had mostly no proper housing available at all. The quality and accessibility of living space was directly related to the status of each individual and can therefore be regarded as a key to understand an individual's position within Roman society. Since the majority of the urban population lived in large apartment blocks, social diversification had to develop within the house itself. This vertical diversification of housing can be traced with the help of archaeological as well as literary sources and centres around the categories space, light, security and price. Despite all dif-

---

126. Vermutlich 22 v. Chr. brach in Rom die Pest aus vgl. Plinius, *Nat. Hist.* 7,46.

ferences within the various segments of a particular house, the overall quality of living in the City of Rome was rather dull due to the specific urban problems connected with sanitation standards, lack of security and devastating diseases.

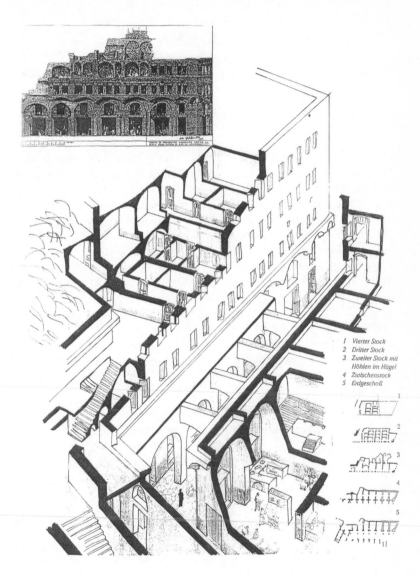

1   Vierter Stock
2   Dritter Stock
3   Zweiter Stock mit
    Höhlen im Hügel
4   Zwischenstock
5   Erdgeschoß

Abb. 2

EARLY CHRISTIANS IN THE CITY OF ROME. TOPOGRAPHICAL AND SOCIAL HISTORICAL ASPECTS OF THE FIRST THREE CENTURIES[1]

Peter Lampe

The waters of the Syrian river Orontes flow into the Tiber. They carry eastern rhythms, eastern music and eastern customs with them. The city of Rome is *Greek.* It was Iuvenal (*Sat.* 3.60ff.) who characterized the world's capital at the beginning of the second century CE in this way. The majority of the city's inhabitants were not born in Rome, as Seneca observed.[2] And what was true for the city population as a whole applied even more to the early Roman Christians. In Rome 'all detestable and appalling things from all over the world come together', Tacitus (*Ann.* 15.44.3) regretted, with particularly the Christians in mind. The Apostle Paul drastically illustrated this bad press under which the early Christian missionaries suffered: 'We have become like the rubbish of the world, the dirt of all things' (1 Cor. 4.13).

Bad press, immigrant status, being an unimportant ingredient in a melting-pot city of people from all over the empire, not being the centre of this centre of the world – this was early Christianity in the city of Rome. I propose to approach a look into the world of these early Christians by cutting several avenues through the historical material:

The Jewish congregations as the cradle of Roman Christianity;
Topographical aspects;
Social Strata;
Organizational aspects, especially fractionation;
Cultural aspects, especially pagan/Christian osmosis.

1. *Jewish Congregations as the Cradle of Christianity in the City of Rome*

Pompey, who conquered Judea in 63 BCE, deported large numbers of Jews to Rome as slaves. Soon, at the latest under Augustus, they were freed. At their manumission, most of them gained Roman citizenship and bequeathed it to their offspring.[3]

---

1. The paper will focus on the two first centuries predominantly, but tracks will be followed into the third century and beyond as well.
2. *Helv.* 6; cf. Pliny, *Nat. Hist.* 3.6.
3. Cf. Philo, *Leg. ad Caium* 155,157, and P. Lampe, *Die stadtrömischen Christen in den ersten beiden Jahrhunderten: Untersuchungen zur Sozialgeschichte* (WUNT 11/18; Tübingen: Mohr-

Other Roman citizens of Jewish faith in the city were freed persons of large Roman households such as the *Imperial house* or the houses of *Volumnius*, who once served as Augustus's legate to Syria, or of *Marcus Agrippa*; both were friends of King Herod.[4] Thus, when Tiberius expelled many Jews from the city in the year 19 CE, many Jewish freed persons and their offspring could not be forced to leave without individual trials because they enjoyed Roman citizenship. Tiberius used a trick to rid the city of a large number of Jews. He drafted 4,000 of Rome's Jewish freedmen into armed service to fight against Sardinia's bandits.[5] Jewish congregations, however, survived in the city of Rome. In the first century CE, we know of at least five synagogues existing in Rome, and at least three of them were founded by Jewish freed persons.[6] Altogether, the inscriptions mention around 14 Roman synagogues in imperial times.[7] All of these Jewish congregations in Rome were independent units and only loosely connected with one another. This factionalism was different from the situation in Alexandria, where the various synagogues constituted one political body. We will encounter the factionalism again in Roman Christianity.

Three areas can still be identified where Roman Jews resided in the first century CE.[8] Many lived in Trastevere, the crowded quarter west of the Tiber River across from Tiber Island. Others of poor economic means settled on the Appian Way outside the Capena Gate. A synagogue was also founded in the vicinity of the Viminal Gate. All three locations were outside the Republican Wall and the *pomerium* (for a similar situation in Philippi, see Acts 16.13). The Egyptian cults, with which Judaism was often associated by the Romans, were also banned from the *pomerium*.[9]

The Christian faith appears to have entered the city in the 40s of the first century through Jewish Christians who frequented one or several Jewish synagogues in town. Preaching about Christ, they stirred up turmoil within the synagogues and

---

Siebeck, 2nd edn, 1989), pp. 26, 66–67; English translation: P. Lampe, *From Paul to Valentinus: Christians at Rome in the First Two Centuries* (Minneapolis: Augsburg-Fortress, 2003).

4.   Synagogues of the *Augustesioi* (imperial freed persons), of the *Volumnenses*, and of the *Agrippesioi* are mentioned in inscriptions. See the epigraphical material in Lampe, *Die stadtrömischen Christen,* pp. 66, 367–68. 'Volumnius', a Roman *nomen gentile*, was the name of a Roman legate, a personal emissary of Augustus, who resided in Syria in 8 BCE. and whose friendship King Herod enjoyed (Josephus, *War.* 1.535, 538; *Ant.* 16. 277ff., 332, 354). This Volumnius most likely was the patron of the Jewish freed persons who founded the synagogue of the *Volumnenses*. The *Agrippesioi* were most probably freed persons (and their offspring) of the household of Marcus Agrippa, who in the east from the year 15 BCE. onward maintained a close friendship with Herod (Josephus, *Ant.* 16.44).

5.   Cf. Tacitus, *Ann.* 2.85.4; Suetonius, *Tib.* 36.1; Josephus, *Ant.* 18.81–85; see Lampe, *Die stadtrömischen Christen*, p. 67.

6.   Cf. n. 4 and the epigraphical material in Lampe, *Die stadtrömischen Christen*, pp. 66, 367–68.

7.   Lampe, *Die stadtrömischen Christen*, pp. 367–68; L.V. Rutgers, *The Jews in Late Ancient Rome: Evidence of Cultural Interaction in the Roman Diaspora* (Leiden: E.J. Brill, 1995); cf. L.V. Rutgers, *Subterranean Rome* (Leuven: Peeters, 2000).

8.   See the material in Lampe, *Die stadtrömischen Christen*, pp. 26–28.

9.   See Lampe, *Die stadtrömischen Christen*, p. 31.

thus attracted the attention of the Roman officials. The key persons in this *inner-*Jewish argument were apparently expelled by Claudius's administration in 49 CE.[10] Among those forced to leave were Prisca and Aquila (Acts 18.2). Following this disruption, the Christians appear to have assembled on their own. At the latest in the second half of the 50s CE, at the time of Paul's Letter to the Romans, the Christians in Rome met separately from the Jewish synagogues. The majority of Roman Christians now were Gentile, although many of these Gentiles may, before their baptisms, have been loosely connected with Jewish synagogues as sympathizers with Jewish monotheism. In 64 CE, even Nero could distinguish the Christians from the Jews in the city. In this year, a great fire had severely damaged 10 of the city's 14 regions. Nero unjustly accused the Christians[11] of arson, crucifying and burning many of them.

Despite separation from the worship of the synagogues, the Roman Christians maintained many Jewish traditions and influences in their thinking and teaching. *The First Epistle of Clement* and the *Book of Hermas* exemplify this well.[12] Social contacts between Christians and Jews in the city continued, as Callistus still demonstrated at the end of the second century,[13] and still in the second century, a group of Jewish Christians observed the Torah,[14] withdrawing fellowship from other Christians who did not, but probably maintaining contact with non-Christian Jewish synagogues.

2. *Topographical Aspects* [15]

Like the Jews, the early Christians lived at the periphery of Rome outside the sacred city limits, the *pomerium*: in Trastevere and in the valley of the Appian Way outside the Capena Gate. Both areas were permeated with immigrants from the provinces who swept into the city on the Appian Way and the Tiber River. People of the lower social strata populated these quarters. Martial (*Epigr.* 1.41) caricatures the typical Trastevere inhabitant: a buffoon who trades bits of glass for sulferized matches.

Other Christians dwelt between these two areas on the Aventine Hill, a very preferred residential area in imperial times, still others on the Campus Martius.

On a map, these areas infiltrated by Christians exhibit the shape of a sickle lying around the city centre. This was the typical situation of an immigrant eastern religious group. In the immediate neighborhood of the Christian cells, other eastern cults blossomed, such as the veneration of the god Sol of Palmyra, of the Syrian deities Hadad, Atargatis, Simios and Iuppiter Dolichenus or of Isis, Sarapis, Mithras and Cybele.[16]

---

10. See, e.g., Lampe, *Die stadtrömischen Christen*, pp. 4–9.
11. '...*quos...vulgus Chrestianos appellabat. auctor nominis eius Christus, Tiberio imperitante per procuratorem Pontium Pilatum...*' (Tacitus, *Ann.* 15.44).
12. See Lampe, *Die stadtrömischen Christen*, pp. 58–63, 174–82.
13. See Lampe, *Die stadtrömischen Christen*, pp. 282, 454, on Hippolytus, *Ref.* 9.12.
14. See Lampe, *Die stadtrömischen Christen*, pp. 455, on Justin, *Dial.* 47.
15. For the following, see Lampe, *Die stadtrömischen Christen*, pp. 10–52, plus maps.
16. Cf. Lampe, *Die stadtrömischen Christen*, pp. 41–43, 45, 48–49.

The sickle shape explains why Nero could so easily accuse the Christians of arson: Not only did they have the bad reputation of being misanthropes,[17] they also primarily lived outside the quarters that were affected by the disastrous fire in the year 64 CE.[18] Those in Trastevere could safely watch the fire from the other side of the Tiber River. They were the ideal scapegoats, facing the traditional punishment for arsonists of being burned alive. They were executed by being burned as torches in the Vatican gardens. It is probable that the Apostle Peter was among them. Already at the end of the first century CE, the *First Epistle of Clement*[19] claimed that both apostles, Peter and Paul, had suffered martyrdom in Rome.

What can be said about Peter's alleged burial place in the Vatican?[20] In the middle of the second century CE at the latest, that is three generations (at the most) after Peter's death, Christians identified a simple grave in the Vatican necropolis as the Apostle Peter's burial place. This is all that can be said in a scientifically responsible way about the history of this tomb prior to 160 CE. Around 160 CE, Roman Christians decorated this simple grave with a modest monument, an *aedicula*, before it gradually became the centre of more and more architectural activities.

3. Social Strata

Most of the Christians were of very modest means: *plerique pauperes,* as Minucius Felix (*Oct.* 36.3) described. The lower social strata predominated in the pre-Constantinian Roman house churches. However, as they also predominated in the city population as a whole,[21] there is nothing extraordinary in this finding.

Inspite of the *plerique pauperes* situation, Roman Christianity gradually infiltrated *all social levels*, even the senatorial. In the year 96 CE, for example, a relative of the Emperor Domitian, Flavia Domitilla, was banned to an island because of her Christian faith that did not allow her to acknowledge Domitian as a god.[22]

The higher we rise in the Roman social strata, the more Christian women and the fewer men we encounter.[23] This, of course, made it hard for aristocratic Christian women to find Christian spouses and created problems within the church.[24] It was primarily through the women that Roman Christianity entered the upper classes.

The farther we progress in time, the more people of socially advanced status we encounter. Thus, with time the average social position of all Roman Christians rose.

---

17. Tacitus, *Ann.* 15.44.
18. See, Lampe, *Die stadtrömischen Christen*, p. 35.
19. 5.4; see also Ignatius, *Rom.* 4.
20. Cf. Lampe, *Die stadtrömischen Christen*, pp. 82–94.
21. Cf. Lampe, *Die stadtrömischen Christen*, pp. 112–16, and Seneca, *Helv.* 12.1.
22. For the discussion, see Lampe, *Die stadtrömischen Christen*, pp. 166–72, especially p. 170.
23. See Lampe, *Die stadtrömischen Christen*, pp. 95–99, 297.
24. For the details, including early Christian birth control, see Lampe, *Die stadtrömischen Christen*, pp. 96–99.

In the first century CE, the group of socially elevated Christians was still small. Some Roman Christians even sold themselves into temporary slavery in order to raise money for the poor in the church.[25] Apparently there were no other profitable means available. It was not until the 90s of the first century that we hear about Christian *plousioi* ('wealthy people').[26] During the entire second century, however, the well-off Christians were able to raise respectable sums for charity. And at the turn of the second to the third century, not only the needy but also the church's office holders could be paid from these donations. In the last 20 years of the second century, under the Emperors Commodus and Septimius Severus, a *fair number* of generously giving imperial freed slaves, for instance, and *several* Christian senators and ladies of senatorial rank belonged to Roman churches.[27] A significant number of Christian senators is documented again around 258 CE.[28] In the prosopographical field, we are able to name almost 40 pre-Constantinian Christian members of the senatorial class, most of them living in the third century, with two-thirds of them being female.[29] The actual number presumably was higher than 40, with our prosopographical knowledge being more accidental than representative.

Parallel to this development within the church, the Roman Senate itself, since the times of Septimius Severus, consisted of many more members from the eastern provinces than before; the portion of eastern senators jumped to almost a third under Septimius Severus.[30] It is tempting to suppose that this increase of eastern senators also helped to push up the number of senators in the church. In the prosopographical field, we indeed know of a senator Astyrius from Syria-Palestine in the 60s of the third century and of members of the senatorial class from Phrygia and Lycaonia.[31]

Senators from the provinces had to invest at least a quarter of their capital into Italian real estate, and one of their residences had to be in Rome. Thus, Christian senators from the eastern provinces sat both in Roman church services *and* played roles in their provincial churches, which made them influential links between Roman Christianity and the churches of the east.

The correspondence between the increases of eastern personages in the senate on the one hand and of senators in the church on the other is not the only parallel between pagan and Christian social developments. The gradual rise of the average

25. See Lampe, *Die stadtrömischen Christen*, pp. 68–69.
26. One of the methodological problems that we face is that the sources often fail to give us enough clues for pinning down the specific social stratum of a person. The term 'rich' is almost useless. It is an entirely relative term, indicating a certain social stratification within Roman Christianity (poor/rich) without enabling us to attribute the 'rich' or the 'poor' to specific social strata. For more on the term '*pauper*', see below.
27. See the material in Lampe, *Die stadtrömischen Christen*, pp. 94–103, 296, and nn. 677–78.
28. See Lampe, *Die stadtrömischen Christen*, p. 95, n. 287.
29. Lampe, *Die stadtrömischen Christen*, p. 96, and n. 292; pp. 121–22. 40 persons out of about 15,000 senatorial individuals in the first three centuries equal the small amount of 0.27 per cent. Pagan traditionalists did not need to worry about the Roman Senate being undermined by Christianity.
30. Lampe, *Die stadtrömischen Christen*, p. 95, and n. 288.
31. Lampe, *Die stadtrömischen Christen*, p. 96 n. 289.

social status of the Roman Christians corresponds to a general development in the society of the Roman Empire as a whole: In the second century, the number of members of the higher social strata grew healthily, while the number of slaves decreased.[32] Thus, at least partially, the social history of Roman Christianity simply mirrors developments of the society as a whole. This was also true of the majority of *pauperes* (poor) both in the Roman church and in the city, as was demonstrated above.

What then differs from society in general? Does the social history of early Roman Christianity exhibit anything special that is not reflected in the pagan environment? I will mention at least one point. We already discussed those Christians who sold themselves into slavery in order to support the needy of their church. This kind of extreme solidarity among members of *lower* social strata is rare in Roman society. Only the upper classes of the pagan empire presented themselves as fairly consolidated groups, above all the senatorial *ordo* (class), while the lower strata lacked a collective consciousness and a supra-regional cohesion. The early Christian representatives of the lower social levels, however, exhibited exactly this: a supra-regional solidarity and a sense of belonging together in spite of ethnic and geographical distances. Christianity here contributed to the social integration of the Roman society as a whole.

The latter is also true in another respect. Within the realm of the church (although not exclusively there) members of *different* social strata became extremely close to one another, supporting each other. At least, this was the intention of Christian authors such as Hermas, for example. The *Book of Hermas,* written in Rome in the first half of the second century CE, painted the lovely image of a vine climbing up an elm tree, the vine being the poor and the elm the rich in the church.[33] The vine can only bear grapes, i.e. spiritual fruit, as long as the elm supports the vine. And the unfruitful elm can only bring forth fruit as long as the vine grows grapes among its branches. The different social levels need each other.

The donations and alms of the richer Christians *raised* the social position of those who, without Christian support, had scarcely scratched out a living. The church offered subsistence to the needy and in this way, again, contributed to the social integration of the Roman society as a whole.

A last remark in this passage needs to be made on *fragmentary statistics.*[34] In the middle of the third century, Bishop Cornelius counted 1,500 Christians who were receiving assistance from the church. However, this does not tell us how many Christian *pauperes* lived in Rome, because a *pauper,* a 'poor' person, usually *did* make a very modest living on his or her own. Thus, we are left in the dark when it comes to estimating the total number of Roman Christians.

Cornelius also counted 46 presbyters in the city; and during the first three decades of the third century around 800 Christians were buried in the subterranean S. Callisto cemetery, one of the first catacombs. However, we do not know by

32. Lampe, *Die stadtrömischen Christen*, p. 113.
33. Cf. Lampe, *Die stadtrömischen Christen*, p. 74.
34. See Lampe, *Die stadtrömischen Christen*, p. 116 and p. 22.

which factors these figures need to be multiplied. Already in the time of Nero, the Roman Christians formed an *ingens multitudo* (a large crowd), which constantly grew in the decades to come.[35] Irenaeus (*Haer.* 3.3.2) called Roman Christianity the biggest Christian unit in the world; no other city housed as many followers of the new faith. Modern guesses vary between 10,000–30,000 Roman Christians in the middle of the third century, while the total number of Roman Jews in early imperial times is estimated between 15,000–60,000 by different authors. We had better leave the murky waters of population statistics, coming clearly to the limits of our knowledge.

4. Organizational Aspects, especially Fractionation[36]

Early Christians in Rome formed various house churches. These groups met in private homes. There was no local centre for Roman Christianity. This factionalism, similar to that of the Jews in the city, facilitated a theological pluralism. Thus, second century Rome saw Christian groups following numerous theological directions: Marcionite, Valentinian, Carpocratian, Theodotian, Modalistic, Montanist and Quartodecimanian teachings. There were Cerdo's followers and house churches of (what was only later called) the 'orthodox' faith. There existed a Jewish-Christian circle that still observed the Torah (see above). Some groups exhibited a *logos* theology that was too complicated for lesser educated Christians. Some circles believed in the millennium and others did not. Roman Christianity was multicoloured and as such often also reflected the various geographical and educational provenances of Roman Christians.

These house churches, scattered over the city, were only loosely connected. Some sent portions of their eucharist to other Christian groups in the city to express fellowship and unity with them. Written material was also shared among the Christian groups in Rome.

On the whole, because of these loose connections, the various groups in the city tolerated each other during the first two centuries. With few exceptions, no Christian group labelled another as heretical before the last decade of the second century.[37] Consequently, communication with persons or congregations *outside* of Rome was often coordinated among the groups. As a result, outsiders could perceive the various Roman house churches as '*the* Roman church'.

A monarchical bishop, however, who oversaw at least the 'orthodox' house churches in the city, did *not* come into existence before the second half of the second century. Earlier, the various house churches were led solely by their own presbyters. The role of a monarchical bishop emerged in connection with the needs for a centralized coordination of the foreign contacts and affairs of the Roman Christians; the first pioneers and proponents of a monarchical episcopacy were in

---

35. Cf. Minucius Felix, *Oct.* 31.7.

36. For the detailed evidence, see Lampe, *Die stadtrömischen Christen,* pp. 301–45.

37. For the evidence, see Lampe, *Die stadtrömischen Christen*, pp. 323–34, for the exceptions, pp. 330ff.

fact those presbyters who acted as sorts of 'foreign ministers' of Roman Christianity. Also, the support of the poor called for more centralized structures in order to be effective. Christian theologians such as Irenaeus helped stabilize the monarchical episcopacy by introducing the Roman state's conceptions of order in the church. He was also the one who pushed the doctrine of apostolic succession in order to consolidate the authority of monarchical bishops in the cities of the empire.

One of the effects of the emerging monarchical episcopate was that the tool of excommunication began to be used more often. It was under Bishop Victor (about 189–199 CE) that Roman house churches, regarding themselves as 'orthodox', began to excommunicate other groups on a large scale. Victor, supported by Irenaeus, cut the ties to four Christian groups in the city.

5. *Cultural Aspects*

a) Languages:[38] In the immigrant culture of early Roman Christianity, Greek was used as the main language. It was not until the 240s CE that the preponderance shifted to Latin, indicating that the majority of Roman Christians now came from a Latin background.

In the second century, while Greek was the dominant language of the educated Christians in Rome, a rather uncultivated Latin was being used by some lower class Christian circles in town. In the first half of the third century, however, Latin and Greek were already equally represented on the catacomb inscriptions.

At the beginning of the third century, the Roman Christian lawyer Minucius Felix, a highly educated rhetorician probably of North African origin, composed a Latin dialogue of perfectly elegant style and Ciceronian form. The next important Latin author of the Christian faith in Rome, Novatianus, entered the stage in the middle of the third century. He was a man of profound rhetorical, philosophical and literary education, who skilfully used classical Latin writings; his knowledge of the stoic philosophy seems to be molded by Seneca. In the 250s CE, the Roman bishop's correspondence was exclusively composed in Latin, as Cyprian's letters reflect. But the more educated circles still were bilingual at that time. Both Latin *and* Greek could be used as liturgical languages until the fourth century. The funerary inscriptions of the Roman bishops of the third century also were still formulated in Greek. Bilingualism, however, slowly faded from the second half of the third century onwards.

One did not need to be a prophet to predict that this shift towards Latin would start to open a gap between the western and eastern church provinces in the Roman Empire.

38. For the following, see the material in Lampe, *Die stadtrömischen Christen*, pp. 117–19, 287–89, and A. Dihle, *Die griechische und lateinische Literatur der Kaiserzeit* (München: Beck, 1989), pp. 366–69, 396–98. Lampe, *Die stadtrömischen Christen*, p. 288 argues in favour of Minucius Felix' localization at Rome (*pace* Dihle, *Literatur*, p. 367). That Tertullian converted to Christianity at Rome (Dihle, *Literatur*, p. 359) is hardly supported by the evidence (Lampe, *Die stadtrömischen Christen*, p. 287). For the language situation of the Roman Jews, see H. Solin, 'Juden und Syrer im westlichen Teil der römischen Welt', *ANRW* 2.29/2 (1983), pp. 706–07.

b) Adopting elements of pagan education:[39] Within the *Greek*-speaking Christian circles of Rome, the ambitious assimilation of pagan education, of Greek literature and philosophy, already took place in the second century. The apologist philosopher Justin, for example, bridged Middle Platonism and Christian thought. The Roman Theodotians explained the Christian faith by means of post-Aristotelian logic. Others like Valentinus were rooted in Platonism. These intellectuals of the second century were the first Christians who extensively used and enjoyed the treasure chest of Greek culture and *paideia*.[40] They re-thought the Christian doctrine on the basis of pagan philosophical presuppositions. Already the *First Epistle of Clement*, at the end of the first century, exhibited Stoic elements, which probably had reached Roman Christianity via the Hellenistic synagogues.

c) Looking for a respectable place in the Greco-Roman Culture: Apologists such as Justin looked for as many points of congruence as possible between the Greco-Roman and Christian cultures. They tried to bring the Greek and Christian traditions into a harmonious relationship in order to find a respectable place for Christianity in the Roman political and societal systems. The Christians offered their loyal service to the pagan empire. Having insights into the allegedly definite truth – a truth that Moses and many Greek philosophers only partially had discovered – Christians such as Justin reasoned that they alone could properly assess the acting of governments and the legitimacy of institutions and laws. The question is whether or not the pagan environment was delighted with this offer of service.[41]

d) The reaction of the pagan environment to Christianity: For pagan Romans, the multitude of deities and cults undergirded the order of their multi-peopled empire. They therefore tolerated the religious and cultic diversity. A philosophically minded pagan, adhering to a non-exclusive philosophical monotheism, speculatively pondered the unity of the divine essence. At the same time, however, the same person, in every day religious praxis, participated in more than one of the many cults. Thus, for pagan Romans the *exclusive* monotheism of the Christians, which ruled out any other veneration of the divine besides their own, was impious and ungodly. The Christians therefore were met with suspicion. They were regarded as potentially dangerous for the Roman order. And every governor, upon denunciation, could examine Christians and punish or even sentence to death those who confessed their belief in Christ and refused to express cultic reverence for another deity or the *genius* of the emperor.

The apologists' writings did not change this legal position, but they probably altered the climate, at least slightly. Tacitus, Suetonius and Pliny had still labelled

---

39. For the following, see the material in Lampe, *Die stadtrömischen Christen*, pp. 172–300, 350–66.

40. For a fair number of other Roman examples, see Lampe, *Die stadtrömischen Christen*, pp. 172–300.

41. On the Christian side, this offer was sneered at by Justin's student Tatian. Although highly educated in Greek culture himself, he wrote a harsh polemic 'against the Hellenes', stating the incompability of the Christian faith with everything that Greek philosophy, rhetoric, science, art and religion had produced.

Christianity a 'superstition'.[42] From the second third of the second century on, however, Christian philosophers such as Justin worked on improving the Christians' image and claimed that Christianity was a respectable and loyal *philosophy*, worthy of being received into the Greco-Roman world of *paideia*.[43] Their words usually went unheard – but not always. The pagan authors Lucianus and Galenus indeed began to call Christianity a 'sophia' and a 'philosophy,' although they were not impressed by it. In their eyes this school lacked solid proof and was dogmatically incrusted.[44] However, more and more cultivated and distinguished pagans found their way to the baptismal font during the second half of the second century. Christianity was – albeit gradually and slowly – recognized as a *paideia*.

e) Educational processes within the church: The Christian tradition, its doctrines and moral teachings, sometimes fused with pagan cultural elements, was transmitted within the church as a culture of its own. This 'paideia in Christ', as the *First Epistle of Clement* (21.8) called it, was taught on three levels:[45]

– Independent teachers and philosophers such as Justin or Valentinus gathered circles of students around themselves and held lectures;
– Presbyters taught their house-church congregations. They also instructed the catechumens. *Traditio Apostolica,*[46] a Roman writing from about 215 CE, ruled which pagan candidates could be admitted to this education and which not;
– In the private homes children were taught by their parents. In the second century, husbands often also taught their wives. Only for the orphans and the widows in town did the Roman house churches appoint a special woman teacher.[47]

However, the Christian instruction of children did not replace the secular schools where one learned to read and write, to calculate and to analyse texts. The Christians consequently continued to send their offspring to the pagan elementary, grammar and rhetorical schools.[48] The exercise book of a fourth century Christian child in Egypt gives a touching illustration: the child writes down mythological names, pagan anecdotes of moral or sometimes risqué content, but at the beginning of every new page it draws a cross and a Christ monogram.[49] This little papyrological document says more about the clash of two cultures than any theoretical discourse.

f) Pagan/Christian osmosis on the level of common people:[50] The last example gives rise to the question of how much the Christian and pagan cultures amalga-

---

42. Tacitus, *Ann.* 15.44; Suetonius, *Claud.* 25.3, and *Nero* 16.2; Pliny, *Ep.* 10.96.8.

43. In the east, this apologetic thinking had been developed much earlier. It began with the author of Luke/Acts in the last third of the first century CE.

44. See Lampe, *Die stadtrömischen Christen,* pp. 300 and 235.

45. For the following, see the evidence in Lampe, *Die stadtrömischen Christen*, pp. 298–99.

46. 15ff., ed. Botte.

47. See Lampe, *Die stadtrömischen Christen*, pp. 121, 297–99, 338f.

48. Cf. Tertullian, *de idol.*

49. In Lampe, *Die stadtrömischen Christen*, p. 298.

50. For the following, see the evidence in Lampe, *Die stadtrömischen Christen*, pp. 298, 36ff., 91, 191ff., 280; cf. 18–20.

mated on the level not only of intellectuals (see above) but also of the ordinary Roman Christians who did not have the philosophical or rhetorical backgrounds of higher learning. This is an important facet for any study of Christian identity in Rome. Ordinary people often only come alive through the combination of various source genres. In the case of Roman Christianity, literary, archaeological and epigraphical sources reveal that many ordinary Roman Christians lived closely side by side with their pagan neighbours without any scruples or fear of contact. They often maintained pagan customs, particularly in the funerary domain. Still in the fourth century CE, Christians occasionally felt free to build tombs with openings for libations.[51] According to several graffiti, Christians of the second half of the fourth century practiced libation under S. Sebastiano and in the Catacomb of Priscilla. A Christian fresco and a drawing in the catacombs of Domitilla and of S. Ermete/ Bassilla depict the libation ritual as well.[52] This coincides with other epigraphical and literary evidence according to which Christians often celebrated meals for the dead at their tombs, still in the third and fourth centuries.[53] Augustine[54] writes that their meals for the dead did not differ from the superstitious pagan ones. They brought wine with them, and those who honored several tombs in one day ended up coming home tipsy from the cemetery. Paulinus of Nola,[55] a contemporary of Augustine, complained about the simple-mindedness of those Christians who poured wine over graves.

Around 200 CE, a cross and a Christian acrostichon ('Jesus Christ God's Son Saviour') were drawn into the wet plaster of an otherwise clearly pagan mausoleum under S. Sebastiano. In other words, Christians buried one or more of their family members close to pagan graves. The same is true for the S. Callisto cemetery: in the surface area above the two original nuclei of this catacomb, pagan and Christian graves lay peacefully side by side still in the fourth century. In the third century in the mausoleums of the Vatican necropolis, several Christians were buried in direct proximity to many pagan deceased; the Christians decorated one little mausoleum with a Christ/Helios mosaic, not far from pagan frescos and mosaics. In and above the two nuclei of the Pretestato Catacomb on the Appian Way, Christian and pagan tombs peacefully coexisted in the third century. Even Jews did not have scruples about burying their dead side by side with pagans, as the Jewish funerary inscriptions of Ostia show.[56]

In the year 217 CE, the freed persons of the Christian imperial freedman Marcus Aurelius Prosenes were responsible for an interesting mixture of pagan and Christian elements. Their patron died, and they ordered two inscriptions for a sarcophagus (*CIL* 6.8498). Their language shows mistakes, which appears to rank these freed persons among ordinary people. They juxtaposed the hint at Prosenes's

---

51. See Lampe, *Die stadtrömischen Christen*, p. 91; for the second century, see p. 90.

52. Lampe, *Die stadtrömischen Christen*, pp. 449–50.

53. Lampe, *Die stadtrömischen Christen*, pp. 90–91.

54. *Conf.* 6.2.

55. *Poem 27 St. Felix,* Carmen 9.

56. For the examples listed above, see Lampe, *Die stadtrömischen Christen*, pp. 18–20, 86–87.

Christianity, almost shyly hidden at the narrow side of the sarcophagus, with little cupids, with winged geniuses and with the usual pagan formula *divus Commodus*.[57] Another clearly Christian sarcophagus from the middle of the third century also shows winged geniuses.[58] On the Christian frescos and reliefs of the third century in Rome, the biblical figures – Daniel among the lions, the resting Jonah and others – are often placed in traditional idyllic landscapes known from pagan art. The pagan idyllic motifs even dominate the biblical ones, almost camouflaging the latter.[59]

Church officials like Cyprianus[60] were upset about the intense osmosis between Christianity and paganism in the cemeteries. However, the ordinary early Christians had more than one reason to absorb pagan elements. It was not only naiveté or lack of fear of coming into contact with other religious cultures that guided them. Tertullian[61] adds another aspect which helps to interpret these sarcophaguses, frescos and reliefs of the third century. According to Tertullian, Christian women defended their elegant attire and their ornaments by arguing that this is a sort of camouflage. If they did not wear it, everybody would know right away that they were Christians. Interestingly enough, the Christians' personal names usually were pagan until the middle of the third century. Specifically Christian or biblical names were avoided most of the time. This was also true of the Jews both in Rome and in the diaspora in general. One did not want to invite denunciations or molestations by constantly publicizing one's faith in daily life.

Sometimes ordinary people also speak through our literary sources. The *Book of Hermas* was composed in Rome by a Christian freedman in the first half of the second century. The author betrays an only mediocre education and naively mixes pagan elements into his Christian writing.[62] His Mother Church, an allegoric figure, exhibits features of the Sibyl of Cumae. Materials from pagan erotic novels and light reading are woven into the book. The pagan motif of the 'divine beloved' is happily used. Pagan bucolic literature inspires a great many pastoral motifs in the book. Popular Cynic-Stoic elements are picked up; the author, however, erroneously thinks that they are Pythagorean. His book 'christens' manifold popular pagan conceptions and motifs. And if it had not been for the more sophisticated theologians in the church, this book would have been included into the canon by the masses of ordinary Christians who loved it and gladly read it, generation after generation.

The *symbiosis of paganism and Christianity* can also be shown *within one and the same family*. Two examples – now we are in the socially elevated strata – are based on archaeological and literary evidence.[63]

---

57. See Lampe, *Die stadtrömischen Christen*, pp. 278–82.

58. See Lampe, *Die stadtrömischen Christen*, p. 454.

59. See Lampe, *Die stadtrömischen Christen*, p. 451.

60. *Ep.* 67.6.

61. *De cultu fem.* 2.11.

62. For the following details, see the evidence in Lampe, *Die stadtrömischen Christen*, pp. 191–98.

63. See Lampe, *Die stadtrömischen Christen*, pp. 122–23.

An anonymous catacomb on the Via Latina dates from the fourth century. This private hypogeum exhibits gorgeous frescos of both Christian and pagan contents side by side. In room 11, soldiers gamble for Jesus's tunica, and Jonah falls into the ocean, while in room 12, Hercules steals apples from the Hesperides. He kills a hydra and offers Athena his hand.

The second example is given by the noble family of the *Ceionii* from the end of the fourth and the first decades of the fifth centuries. Two brothers married two Christian ladies, but they themselves remained pagan. The daughters and grand-daughters of these two marriages grew up Christian and also married Christian spouses. But the *sons* of these two marriages again cultivated the old pagan roots of their family, although paganism had been officially suppressed. It was the women who gave the family the necessary Christian façade.

This example again illustrates Christianity being introduced into aristocratic circles primarily through the women (see above 3). However, it also shows how difficult it was to infect these circles with the Christian spirit. Even after Constantine, aristocratic families remained bastions of paganism. Almost all Roman nobles were still pagan at the beginning of the fifth century at the time of St. Augustine.[64] And before the second half of the fifth century, no Roman bishop originated from the leading circles of the empire. Even in the sixth century, pagan spirit and secular traditions of the city of Rome tenaciously survived in the Italian aristocracy under a thin Christian surface.

---

64. *Conf.* 8.2.3.

THE SHAPING OF THE IDENTITY OF THE JEWISH COMMUNITY IN ROME IN ANTIQUITY

Margaret H. Williams

Jewish identity in Graeco-Roman antiquity is generally talked about as if it were unchanging and homogeneous.[1] But common sense should tell us that different Diaspora communities are likely to have had different and changing identities, given the different circumstances in which they came into being[2] and the different influences to which they were subjected in the course of their histories. The main reason that scholars usually gloss over such variations and produce broad-brush sketches is the poor quality of the evidence. The majority of Jewish Diaspora communities are known to us through only a handful of inscriptions, usually not securely dateable, and quite a few are attested each by as little as a single epitaph.[3] So, in most instances, localised studies of Jewish identity are not possible. With the Roman Diaspora, however, that is not the case. Not only is the evidence, epigraphic, literary and artefactual, relatively plentiful[4] but its chronological distribution is such that it is feasible to try and work out, at least in general terms, how and why Jewish identity changed between 62 BCE, when the Roman Jewish community

1. For recent examples of this approach, see J.M.G. Barclay, *Jews in the Mediterranean Diaspora* (Edinburgh: T. & T. Clark, 1996), pp. 399–444 and M.H. Williams, 'Jews and Jewish Communities in the Roman Empire', in J. Huskinson (ed.), *Experiencing Rome: Culture, Identity and Power in the Roman Empire* (London: Routledge in association with The Open University, 2000), pp. 305–33 (especially 323–27).

2. For documented examples of communities arising from voluntary immigration, enforced settlement by a Hellenistic ruler and deportation into slavery, see M.H. Williams, *The Jews among the Greeks and Romans: A Diasporan Sourcebook* (London: Gerald Duckworth, 1998), Section I.2: 'Reasons for the diffusion of the Jews'.

3. For multiple examples, see W. Horbury and D. Noy (eds.), *Jewish Inscriptions of Graeco-Roman Egypt* (Cambridge: University Press, 1992); D. Noy (ed.), *Jewish Inscriptions of Western Europe* (2 vols., Cambridge: University Press, 1993–95), vol. I (= *JIWE* I).

4. For the epigraphic, see J.-B. Frey (ed.), *Corpus Inscriptionum Iudaicarum I* (Rome: Pontificio Istituto di Archeologia Cristiana, 1936, reprinted with a prolegomenon by B. Lifshitz, New York, 1975) = *CIJ* I and Noy, *Inscriptions* II (= *JIWE* II); for the literary, M. Stern (ed.), *Greek and Latin Authors on Jews and Judaism* (3 vols., Jerusalem: The Israel Academy of Sciences and Humanities, 1974–84) (= *GLAJJ*) and B. Bell, 'The Language of Classical Latin Poets as an Indication of Familiarity with Jewish Institutions', *Acta Classica* 35 (1992), pp. 61–71; for the artefactual (e.g. fragments of gold glasses), H.J. Leon, *The Jews of Ancient Rome* (revised by C.A. Osiek; Peabody, Massachusetts: Hendrickson Publishers, 1995 [1960]) and L.V. Rutgers, *The Jews in Late Ancient Rome: Evidence of Cultural Interaction in the Roman Diaspora* (Religions in the Graeco-Roman world, 126; Leiden: E.J. Brill, 1995).

was effectively founded, and the third and fourth centuries CE, the date usually assigned to the material from the Jewish catacombs there. The purpose of this study is to carry out such an investigation. In the process, we shall see that an identity, initially very 'nationalistic'and with a strong focus on the Temple cult and the Hasmonaean monarchy, lost those political aspects, largely as a result of political turmoil and revolt in Judaea, and became almost entirely oriented towards the local synagogue and (very Roman, this) the holding of office within it. But if there was change, there was continuity too – from first to last, the core of Jewish identity at Rome, namely, attachment to the ancestral customs enjoined by the Law of Moses, remained untouched.

1. The Formation of Jewish Identity at Rome (62 BCE–14 CE)

Although Jews are attested in Rome in the second century BCE,[5] there is no evidence for a settled community there before the second quarter of the first century BCE. The first substantial influx of Jews occurred in 62 BCE, when the defeated supporters of the Hasmonaean king, Aristoboulos II, were brought to Rome after the conquest of Judaea and the capture of the Temple by Pompey. The second was in 37 BCE, after Sosius' expulsion of the Parthians from Judaea and his replacement of their client ruler, Aristoboulos' son, Antigonos/Mattathiah, with Rome's nominee, the half-Jewish Herod.[6] The fate of the defeated supporters of Antigonos was the same as that meted out earlier to those who had fought for Aristoboulos – first, the humiliation of being displayed in a Roman triumph and then the ultimate degradation, sale into slavery. Inevitably experiences of that nature were to influence the identity of the community of which these deportees were, in effect, the Founding Fathers.

That a key element in that identity was a determination to continue to uphold the Temple cult should not surprise: Pompey's captives had, after all, fought tooth and nail in order to keep the Temple out of Roman hands, their defence so resolute that sacrifices were able to continue there unabated until the very moment of its capture (Josephus, *War* 1.148; *Ant.* 14.65–7). An early expression of the continuing adherence of those Jews to the Temple cult is to be seen in the foundation of associations (συναγωγαί), the first of them perhaps the Synagogue of the Hebrews,[7] a major function of which was to act as a collection point for the dues that every adult male Jew was obliged, under the Law of Moses, to pay annually towards the maintenance of the Temple itself and the sacrifices daily offered in it (Josephus, *Ant.* 14. 215, if accepted as genuine; Philo, *Leg. Gai.* 156–7, cited in full below).

---

5.   Valerius Maximus 1.3.3 = *GLAJJ* I # 147. For the various interpretations of this highly controversial passage, see Barclay, *Jews*, pp. 285–86 and E.S. Gruen, *Diaspora: Jews amidst Greeks and Romans* (Cambridge, MA, and London, England: Harvard University Press, 2002), pp. 15–19.

6.   For these and other likely influxes of Jewish captives in the Republican period, see E.M. Smallwood, *The Jews under Roman Rule from Pompey to Diocletian* (SJLA, 20; Leiden: E.J. Brill, 1976), p. 31.

7.   Leon, *Jews*, pp. 148–49.

Through Cicero's *Pro Flacco*, his speech in defence of L. Valerius Flaccus, one-time governor of the province of Asia, we get a clear glimpse of this facet of the identity of the early Roman Jewish community. Among Flaccus' alleged offences was the impounding of the gold collected by the Jews of his province for the Temple tax. Clearly it was of enormous importance to the Jews of Rome whether Flaccus' action was adjudged legal or not. If legal, then their own ability to collect the tax without interference from the Roman authorities might be at risk. Hence their keen interest in his trial in 59 BCE, for which, so Cicero informs us, they turned out in force (Cicero, *Pro Flacco* 28.669 = *GLAJJ* I # 68).

That a second conspicuous element in early Romano-Jewish identity was devotion to the Hasmonaean dynasty should also not surprise, given what we have seen above about the origins of the community. The enduring attachment of the Roman Jews to the ousted Hasmonaeans, with whom, initially, they shared their exile in Rome,[8] is beautifully illustrated by the so-called False Alexander episode. This was the attempt by a young Jewish man from Sidon to pass himself off as the youngest son of Herod the Great by his Hasmonaean wife, Mariamme, and so benefit from the confusion in Judaea after Herod's death (4 BCE). Although the real Alexander had actually been executed some three years earlier, so great was the Roman Jews' devotion to the Hasmonaean family and hope for its eventual political revival that they readily accepted the claims of this plausible young man and extended to him on his arrival in Rome a welcome appropriate for a king (Josephus, *War* 2.101–5; *Ant.* 17.324–38 (especially 330 and 335).

But it was not only in adherence to the Temple cult and loyalty to the Hasmonaean family that the Jews of Rome expressed their Jewish identity in the late Republic and early empire. Fundamental to it also was the faithful observance of ancestral customs (πάτρια νόμιμα / ἔθη), much older than the Temple itself. These consisted of practices, believed to have been ordained by God Himself, principally through Moses, which set Jews apart from others and marked them out as the 'Chosen People'. Among the traditional customs of the Jews at Rome, those that struck the Romans of the time most forcibly were (i) the worship of a single, imageless and, apparently, nameless sky god, (ii) complex dietary regulations, of which the most conspicuous and, in Roman eyes, the oddest was the ban on eating pork, their own favourite meat, (iii) circumcision and (iv) Sabbath observance – i.e. the setting aside of each seventh day as a day of rest and abstention from all work. Although the Romans, at a state level, had long acknowledged the Jews' right to follow their ancestral customs and in the period under discussion often publicly upheld that right both in the provinces and in Rome itself (Josephus, *Ant.* 14.213–5 and 223–7), as private individuals they tended to regard the distinctive practices of the Jews with amusement, as their literature from this period shows clearly.[9] That the Jews of Rome persisted with their ancient customs despite mockery from the host community and, in the case of Sabbath observance, considerable inconven-

---

8. Smallwood, *Jews*, p. 28.

9. Apart from Varro's admiring comment on the imageless worship of the Jews (*GLAJJ* I # 72a), all the other allusions to Jewish customs are derogatory in character. For full discussion, see Bell, 'Language'.

ience to themselves[10] is testimony to the fundamental role the Law of Moses played in the preservation of their identity as Jews.

Though of vital importance to the Jews of Rome, the customs noted in the previous paragraph were not peculiar to them but practised by Jews everywhere who kept the Mosaic Law. What does seem to have been a peculiarity of Roman Jewry is the widespread observance of the Sabbath not only as a day of rest but also as a day of fasting – a practice for which there was no legal prescription. Many Roman writers allude to this singular custom of the Jews. The earliest of them is the emperor Augustus, who, in an informal letter to his step-son, Tiberius, writes as follows: Not even a Jew, my dear Tiberius, fasts as diligently on his Sabbath as I have done today. It was not until after the first hour of night that I munched a couple of mouthfuls of bread in the bath prior to being oiled (Suetonius, *Divus Augustus* 76.2). Although none of these writers gives any reason for this unusual practice on the part of the Roman Jews, it is not difficult to suggest one. It had been on the Sabbath, so our sources make clear, that Jerusalem and its Temple fell to Pompey in 63 BCE and to Sosius in 37 BCE. That being so, that day will have had particularly sorrowful associations for the Jews of Rome, since it will have marked for them the loss of freedom and the beginning of their life in exile. Rather than celebrating it as a joyous occasion by refraining from work (something, which, as slaves, they would probably not have been permitted to do), they may have chosen instead to mark it by fasting. But, whatever the reason for it, the practice seems to have been a conspicuous ingredient of the identity of specifically Roman Jews, drawing comment from Latin writers from the time of Augustus down into the second century, when the literary sources for the Jews of ancient Rome come to an end.[11]

From the foregoing, it will be clear that the Jews who were uprooted and transported to Rome in the closing decades of the Republic did not dissolve in the capital's cultural melting pot, as happened to most ethnic groups conquered by the Romans. While there may well have been Jews for whom the pressures of slavery resulted in total assimilation, enough of them managed to retain and develop a sufficiently strong sense of their ethnic, religious and political identity for a clearly identifiable Jewish community to become established at Rome.[12] Suetonius attests to its high public profile in the 40s BCE (Suetonius, *Divus Iulius* 84.5). By Augustus' reign (31 BCE–14 CE), the prayer-houses (προσευχαί) where associations, such as the Synagogue of the Augustesians,[13] met to study the Law

10. This can be deduced from the comments of Philo (*Leg. Gai.* 158) about the administration of the corn dole at Rome: in praising Augustus for enabling needy Roman Jews to collect on the day after the Sabbath their share of the free corn distributions made on that day, he clearly implies that until that concession was made by the authorities they had had to go without.

11. Though most scholars reject the evidence for Sabbath-fasting at Rome, its reliability has recently been defended. For a full discussion, see M.H. Williams, 'Being a Jew in Rome: Sabbath Fasting as an Expression of Romano-Jewish Identity' in J.M.G. Barclay (ed.), *Negotiating Diaspora: Jewish Strategies in the Roman Empire* (Library of Second Temple Studies, 45; London, New York: T & T Clark International, 2004), pp. 8–18.

12. Both Cicero (*Pro Flacco* 28.66) and Horace (*Sermones* 1.4.142–3) comment on the cohesiveness of the Jews.

13. Attested epigraphically only in the third and fourth century CE (*CIJ* I 284, 301, 338, 368,

of Moses each Sabbath and to pay their annual dues for the Temple in Jerusalem had become a marked and accepted feature of the urban landscape, as the following passage from Philo makes clear: Augustus knew that they had prayer-houses (in Transtiberinum = modern Trastevere) and met in them, especially on the holy seventh day, when publicly they undergo instruction in their ancestral philosophy. He also knew that they collected sacred monies from the first-fruits and sent them to Jerusalem by means of envoys who would offer sacrifices (on their behalf). Nonetheless, he neither expelled them from Rome nor deprived them of their Roman rights because they were mindful of their Jewish ones. Nor did he introduce any changes into their prayer-houses or prevent them from assembling for the exposition of the Law or obstruct their offering of the first-fruits (Philo, *Leg. Gai.*156–7). Given such long-standing official acceptance, few in the Roman Jewish community in 14 CE can have expected the complete reversal that was to happen to Romano-Jewish fortunes in the Julio-Claudian period and the challenges, external and internal, that would be made in the course of it to their very identity as Jews.

2. Jewish Identity at Rome in the Julio-Claudian Period (14–68 CE)

a. External attacks

The first attack came only five years into the Julio-Claudian period. In 19 CE, the emperor Tiberius (14–37 CE), for reasons which are still disputed but which I believe are connected with his concern over law and order,[14] turned on the Jewish community of Rome and expelled it from the city. A special punishment was reserved for Jewish males of military age – in a clear break with the past, an order went out that they were to be conscripted into the Roman army (Tacitus, *Ann.*

416 and 496), this association is generally believed to have been founded in the time of Augustus (Leon, *Jews*, p. 142), probably by Jewish slaves and freedmen in the imperial household (see E. Schürer, *The History of the Jewish People in the Age of Jesus Christ* [rev. and ed. G. Vermes, F. Millar, M. Black and M. Goodman; 3 vols., Edinburgh: T. & T. Clark, 1973–87], vol. III, p. 96). The Synagogue of the Volumnesians (*CIJ* I 343, 402, 417 and 523) could also be of Augustan date. W. Horbury, 'Herod's Temple and Herod's Days', in W. Horbury (ed.), *Templum Amicitiae: Essays on the Second Temple presented to Ernst Bammel* (JSNT.Sup, 48; Sheffield: Sheffield Academic Press, 1991), pp. 103–49 (here p. 142) defends the idea that this association was comprised of Jewish slaves in the household of Volumnius, procurator of Syria at the time of Augustus. For the Synagogue of the Agrippesians, probably also of Augustan date, see n. 18 below.

14. M.H. Williams, 'The Expulsion of the Jews from Rome in AD 19', *Latomus* 48 (1989), pp. 765–84. For a similar view, see L.V. Rutgers, 'Roman Policy towards the Jews: Expulsions from the City of Rome during the First Century CE', *Classical Antiquity* 13 (1994), pp. 56–74 (= L.V. Rutgers, *The Hidden Heritage of Diaspora Judaism* [Contributions to Biblical Exegesis and Theology, 20; Leuven: Peeters, 1998], pp. 171–97 and = Rutgers in K.P. Donfried and P. Richardson [eds.], *Judaism and Christianity in First-Century Rome* [Grand Rapids, Michigan and Cambridge, UK: Eerdmans, 1998], pp. 93–116). For re-statements of the view that the expulsion was caused by Jewish proselytizing, see Barclay, *Jews*, pp. 298–300 and J. Carleton Paget, 'Jewish Proselytism at the Time of Christian Origins: Chimera or Reality?', *JSNT* 62 (1996), pp. 65–103 (especially 88–90 – arguments against Williams).

2.85.5; Suetonius, *Tiberius* 36; Josephus, *Ant.* 18.83–4). Hitherto exemption from military service had regularly been granted Jews on religious grounds – it was accepted that their ancestral customs of resting on the Sabbath and requiring special foodstuffs were incompatible with life in the Roman army (Josephus, *Ant.* 14.225–7). Tiberius' volte face was, in effect, if not in primary intent, an attack upon Jewish identity. It should hardly come as a surprise, therefore, that large numbers of these conscripts declined to serve, preferring to undergo the severest of punishments from the Roman authorities, rather than to break the Law of Moses (Josephus, *Ant.* 18.84).

Expulsion, as a method of social control, was notoriously inefficient – in general, the expelled seem to have experienced little difficulty in returning to the city and the Jews proved to be no exception. By 30 CE, if we are to believe Philo (*Leg. Gai.* 159–61), they were back in the capital again. But although they had managed to regain a footing in the city, their situation continued to be fraught with danger and their identity as Jews to be at risk: Sejanus, Tiberius' mighty minister, was ill-disposed towards them and the emperor Gaius (37–41 CE), an unstable megalomaniac, felt nothing but antipathy for their ways. Had the former not fallen suddenly from power in 31 CE, they might well have suffered another expulsion or worse;[15] and had the latter not been assassinated in 41 CE, they could well have seen a key element of their identity as Jews fatally undermined. For Gaius made no secret of his hostility to the Temple cult in Jerusalem and of his determination to have a cult statue of himself installed in the Holy of Holies.[16]

When Claudius unexpectedly came to power and, equally unexpectedly, revived the Judaean monarchy in the person of his friend, Agrippa (Josephus, *War* 2.215; *Ant.* 19. 274), the Roman Jews surely must have believed that any threat of attack, whether to their persons or to their identity, had now been removed: Agrippa, a descendant of the Hasmonaean kings, had recently (41 CE) shown himself to be not only a most effective champion of the Temple cult[17] but an influential friend of Claudius too (Josephus, *Ant.* 19.236–8 and 265); and Claudius himself had revealed very early in his reign that he intended to model his rule upon that of Augustus, a good friend, as we saw above, of the Roman Jews. But those beliefs, if they were held, though not unreasonable, turned out to be overly optimistic. Agrippa's elevation brought to the Jews of Rome no tangible benefit.[18] As for the rule of Claudius (41–54 CE), it proved to be even more detrimental to their interests than that of Tiberius had been. The new reign had scarcely got underway before Jewish asso-

15.   Philo, *Leg. Gai. 159–61*, our only source for this threatened attack, does not specify what Sejanus had in mind. For recent discussions of this passage, see Barclay, *Jews*, p. 301 n. 49 and Gruen, *Diaspora*, pp. 32 and 35–36.

16.   For full accounts of the crisis this produced, see Philo, *Leg. Gai.* 184–334 and Josephus, *Ant.* 18.261–309. Although Gaius abandoned the idea as a consequence of the skilful advocacy of the Jewish prince, Agrippa, the fear remained that the idea might be revived. See Tacitus, *Ann.* 12.54.

17.   See n. 16 above.

18.   Unless the Synagogue of the Agrippesians, attested in third and fourth century CE inscriptions, is taken as a sign of his patronage. For this view, see Leon, *Jews*, p. 141. Most scholars, however, believe that this association takes its name from Marcus Agrippa, Augustus' right-hand man.

ciations became subject to an imperial banning order (Dio, *Hist. Rom.* 60.6.6). Although the synagogues were not alone in being closed down (in attempting to reduce lawlessness in the city, Claudius acted against clubs and taverns too), that will hardly have been a consolation to the Jews. Sabbath assembly, as was shown above, was fundamental to the maintenance of Jewish identity and this unprecedented act on Claudius' part represented a serious undermining of it.[19] In 44 CE, it was dealt another blow: on Agrippa's sudden death, Claudius, again in the interests of sound government, suppressed the monarchy in Judaea, Agrippa's teenage son, also called Agrippa, not being considered 'up to the job' of ruling such a difficult area (Josephus, *Ant.* 19.362). Nor was it just Jewish identity that was adversely affected by Claudius' concern with good government. In 49 CE (?),[20] the Jews found themselves once again subject to expulsion from the city, the emperor having grown tired of the turmoil in which, allegedly, they were constantly involved (Suetonius, *Divus Claudius* 25.4).

Unpleasant as Claudius' measures must have been for the Roman Jewish community at the time of their enactment, outwardly, at least, their long-term impact was minimal. Within a few years of the expulsion, Jews are found back in the capital once more and, if the comments of Seneca and Persius are taken as reflections on contemporary Jewish life, openly carrying on a traditionally Jewish lifestyle.[21] But, if little appears to have changed on the outside, inwardly that cannot have been the case. The vicissitudes experienced by Rome's Jews during the previous thirty years must have left them feeling deeply insecure about not only their personal well-being but the very survival of their Jewish identity. No wonder, then, that they reacted so strongly when that identity came under threat from within the synagogue itself.

b. *Internal Challenge*

Precisely when the Christian 'message' was brought to the Jewish community in Rome is unknown but it may have been as early as the reign of Gaius (37–41 CE).[22]

---

19. On the important role played by Sabbath assembly in the re-affirmation of Jewish communal identity at Rome, see J.M.G. Barclay, ' "Do We Undermine the Law?": A Study of Romans 14.1–15.6', in J.D.G. Dunn (ed.), *Paul and the Mosaic Law* (Grand Rapids, Michigan and Cambridge, UK: Eerdmans, 2001), pp. 287–308 (esp. p. 296).

20. The evidence for Claudius' dealings with the Jews of Rome is controversial and much debated. See now Barclay, *Jews*, pp. 303–06 and Gruen, *Diaspora*, pp. 36–41. For arguments supporting the chronology adopted here, see Smallwood, *Jews*, pp. 210–16; H.D. Slingerland, 'Suetonius, *Claudius* 25.4 and the Account in Cassius Dio', *JQR* 79 (1989), pp. 305–22 and (in more detail) *idem*, *Claudian Policymaking and the Early Imperial Repression of Judaism at Rome* (South Florida Studies in the History of Judaism, 160; Atlanta, Georgia: Scholars Press, 1997).

21. At *Epistulae Morales* 95.47 Seneca refers to the lighting of the Sabbath lamps and in *De Superstitione*, as cited by Augustine at *De Civitate Dei* 6.11, to the custom of resting on the Sabbath. Persius, meanwhile, at *Saturae* 5.176–84 gives a graphic account of Jewish practice in Rome on the so-called Day of Herod (=? the Sabbath).

22. W.H.C. Frend, *Martyrdom and Persecution in the Early Church* (Oxford: Basil Blackwell, 1965), p. 160 suggests that 'the Church was founded' either by the proselytes from Rome, mentioned in the account of the first Pentecost (Acts 2.10), 'or by a similar group of pilgrims.' Certainly there was a Christian presence in Rome in the first part of Claudius' reign – among the

No narrative account survives of early Christian activity in the capital but its impact can be deduced from the Epistle to the Romans, believed to have been written in the early years of Nero's reign (c. 56–57 CE). From Paul's impassioned rhetoric there on the subject of circumcision (Rom. 2.25–9) and his pleas for harmony over food and 'keeping the (Sabbath) day' (Rom. 14.1–6 and 13–23) it may readily be inferred that the Roman Jewish community was being torn apart by disputes over practices fundamental to Jewish identity.[23] It is easy to see why that state of affairs had arisen. The Roman Jewish community, like many other Jewish communities within the Roman empire, had long had a Gentile component – interested members of the host community who attended the synagogue and adopted some Jewish practices, most commonly Sabbath-observance, but usually stopped well short of conversion to Judaism and full subscription to the Law of Moses.[24] As in those communities, so at Rome, these people had proved far more amenable to the Christian message than the Jews – a fact that is hardly surprising, given the nature of that message. In his zeal to win converts to the Christian cause, Paul, seeing himself as God's chief apostle to the Gentiles, had deliberately downgraded the Mosaic Law, claiming that it had been fulfilled with the coming of Jesus the Messiah, and, in consequence, superseded. And so, while there was no harm in continuing to observe the Law of Moses, there was no necessity to do so. Faith was all that mattered now. Those strong in faith should try and show compassion for those weak souls who still needed the Mosaic Law to prop up their lives. As for the Temple, that was as irrelevant as the Law of Moses – believers in Christ should think of themselves as 'the temple of God'.[25]

For Jews whose whole sense of identity was grounded in the Temple and the Mosaic Law (and, as we have seen, at Rome there were many such), Paul's radicalism was a challenge which had to be faced head-on and defeated, if necessary by severing ties with those characterized by him as 'the strong' – i.e. those less dedicated to the Law.[26] Mutual forbearance was no answer to the problems facing the community, for it now contained people whose identities were not only differ-

Jews expelled by him were the Christian converts, Aquila and Priscilla (Acts 18.2). Whether Suetonius, *Divus Claudius* 25.4 ('Iudaeos impulsore Chresto assidue tumultuantes Roma expulit') is to be taken as a reference to Christian activity in the capital under Claudius continues to be debated (see Slingerland, 'Suetonius, Claudius 25.4' and *idem, Claudian Policymaking*; Barclay, *Jews*, p. 304 n. 52; I. Levinskaya, *The Book of Acts in its Diaspora Setting* [The Book of Acts in its First Century Setting, 5; Grand Rapids, Michigan: Eerdmans; Carlisle: Paternoster Press, 1996], pp. 178–82).

23. For powerful arguments that the epistle deals with live issues in the Roman churches and is not generalized paraenesis, see J.M.G. Barclay, ' "Do we undermine the Law?": A Study of Romans 14.1–15.6' in J.D.G. Dunn (ed.), *Paul and the Mosaic Law* (Grand Rapids, Michigan and Cambridge, UK: Eerdmans, 2001), pp. 287–308 (here esp. pp. 288–93).

24. The earliest allusion to such people at Rome is to be found in Horace, *Sermones* 1.9.60–72. The earliest attested proselyte at Rome is Fulvia, wife of Gaius Sentius Saturninus, a friend of the emperor Tiberius. See Josephus, *Ant.* 18.81–4.

25. Barclay, *Jews*, pp. 384–87.

26. That expulsion from the Jewish community could be the consequence of not following the requirements of the Law had penetrated the consciousness even of Roman writers of the period. See Petronius, *Frag. No. 37 = GLAJJ* I #195.

ent but irreconcilable. The end result we know. Before Nero's reign was out (68 CE), the gulf between observant Jews and converts to Christianity (the latter consisting of Jews as well as Gentiles) had become so wide that even the Roman authorities had no difficulty distinguishing between the two groups. Their targeting of the Christian sect in the aftermath of the Great Fire of 64 CE (Tacitus, *Ann.* 15.44.2) is a clear indication that by then significant numbers of Jews and Christians must have had distinct identities.[27]

3. *Jewish Identity at Rome in the Flavian Period (70–96 CE) – the Destruction of the Temple and its Consequences*

Within only a few years of traditionally observant Jews in Rome seeing off the local Christian challenge to their identity, they found themselves having to cope with a fresh, and far more serious, assault upon it. In 70 CE, with Titus' capture and destruction of the Temple, the revolt of the Judaean Jews against Rome effectively collapsed. The Temple now being a heap of ruins, and condemned by Rome to remain so, the Temple cult automatically fell into abeyance. Since cultic activity had now come to a halt, Jews everywhere, Rome included, must have expected that the tax that had sustained that activity would stop as well. But they were in for a nasty surprise. Far from being suspended, the tax was actually extended by the new emperor, Vespasian (70–79 CE): whereas only adult male Jews had paid the old Temple dues, all those who 'continued to embrace the ancestral customs' (Cassius Dio, *Hist. Rom.* 66.7.2) were liable for the new Jewish Tax of two drachmas per annum – i.e. women as well as men, and children as well as adults. Nor was that all – the revenue so raised was to have a new destination: no longer was Jewish money to go to the Jewish God at Jerusalem to maintain his cult; it was to be paid instead to Jupiter at Rome, whose temple on the Capitol had been recently burned down and needed re-building.[28]

Previous assaults by Roman emperors on Jewish identity had been, as we saw above, largely the indirect result of measures taken in the interests of law and order, whether in Rome or in Judaea. But Vespasian's attack was different. As someone with recent, personal experience of Judaea, having been Nero's commander against the Jewish rebels between 66 and 68 CE, he was aware of the fundamental importance of the Temple and its cult to the maintenance of Jewish identity. As the central institution of the Jewish people (ἔθνος), it commanded the loyalty of Jews everywhere. Every year, as he will have known and may even have seen for himself,[29] pilgrims in their thousands flocked to it, not just from Judaea,

---

27. J.C. Walters, 'Romans, Jews, and Christians: The Impact of the Romans on Jewish/ Christian Relations in First-Century Rome', in Donfried and Richardson (eds.), *Judaism and Christianity in First-Century Rome*, pp. 179–80.

28. For the key texts relating to the Jewish tax, see Williams, *The Jews among the Greeks and Romans*, Section IV.8 (c).

29. For the presence of pilgrims in Jerusalem even at the height of the Jewish revolt, see M. Goodman, *The Ruling Class of Judaea* (Cambridge: Cambridge University Press, 1987), p. 179, citing Josephus, *War* 6.421.

but from all over the inhabited world, including the city of Rome (Acts 2.10). For good as it was to re-affirm one's Jewishness through payment of the Temple tax in one's local community, an even better way of demonstrating one's fidelity to the Law of Moses was to visit the Temple in person, especially at the time of the great festivals (e.g. Tabernacles). By leaving the Temple in ruins and thus terminating the Temple cult, what Vespasian had in mind was nothing less than the complete re-shaping of Jewish identity. While ancestral practices of a socio-religious nature were to be permitted, at a price, anything that smacked of the political was to be suppressed. Thus, for the younger Agrippa, who from 49 CE down to the revolt of 66 CE had been the curator of the Temple, there was to be no further role in Judaea. Nor was the temple of Yahweh at Leontopolis in Egypt, the only other place where the Jews offered sacrifice to their national god, to be allowed to function any more. Around 73 CE, orders went out for its closure – Vespasian had no intention of allowing that pale shadow of the Jerusalem Temple to become a substitute for it in the consciousness of the Jewish people (Josephus, *War* 7.420–35).

What the Jews of Rome made of this assault upon Jewish identity is impossible to say. Although Latin writers of the period make frequent reference to them, mocking their strange 'Mosaic' customs (Juvenal, *Sat.* 14.96–106) and relishing their abject and impoverished state (Martial, *Ep.* 7.55.7–8 and 12.57.13; Juvenal, *Sat.* 3.14–16 and 6.542–7), on the subject of Jewish feelings and attitudes, they are, unsurprisingly, silent. That the Roman Jews will have felt deeply humiliated by Flavian triumphalism in Rome may be safely inferred.[30] Not only will they have seen their compatriots led in triumph and the sacred treasures from the Temple (e.g. the seven-branched, golden candelabrum) put on permanent public display in the Temple of Peace but they will also have had to endure the mortification of observing Jupiter's temple rising in splendour from the ashes thanks to their money! And that, not once but twice! For the temple built by Vespasian between 70 and 75 CE lasted only five years before succumbing to the same fate as its predecessor and so had to be rebuilt by Vespasian's son, the emperor, Domitian.[31] But whether the demise of the Temple induced them, at this stage, to think about re-shaping or re-focusing their identity is unknown.[32] In Judaea, in the period after the First Revolt, we know that the leading rabbis tried to compensate for the disappearance of the Temple and the whole social order that it represented by placing much greater emphasis on the oral law. But whether the leaders of the Jewish community in Rome attempted anything similar is disputed. Although there is some late Talmudic evidence for an analogous development at Rome, its historicity has recently been strongly challenged.[33] More likely than not, the Roman Jews, their numbers

30. M. Goodman, 'Josephus as a Roman Citizen', in F. Parente and J. Sievers (eds.), *Josephus and the History of the Graeco-Roman Period: Essays in Memory of Morton Smith* (SPB, 41; Leiden: E.J. Brill, 1994), pp. 329–38 (here esp. 331–32).

31. D. Dudley, *Urbs Roma: A Sourcebook of Classical Texts on the City and its Monuments* (Great Britain: Phaedon/Aberdeen University Press, 1967), pp. 55–58.

32. For a rather speculative treatment of Josephus' identity problems at this period, see Goodman, 'Josephus as a Roman Citizen', pp. 333–38.

33. Rutgers, *Jews*, pp. 203–04.

now inflated by the latest batch of captives from Judaea, will have felt too demoralized to think about the future. Even if they did, it surely will have been with the hope that the Temple would rise again. After all, the Second Temple had risen from the ashes of the First within a couple of generations. A major aim of the Bar Kochba Revolt (132–135 CE), as the coins struck by the rebels show,[34] was the restitution of the Temple and its cult.

4. *The Modification of Jewish Identity at Rome after the Bar Kochba Revolt*

But if such hopes remained after the Flavian destruction of the Temple, they surely must have all but evaporated after the failure of the Bar Kochba Revolt. Precisely when Hadrian took the decision to erect on the derelict Temple site a temple to Jupiter Capitolinus and turn Jerusalem into a pagan city, to be named Aelia Capitolina after himself[35] and Jove, is uncertain and does not matter here.[36] The crucial fact is that once the revolt had failed, there was nothing to impede the implementation of that project. As with Vespasian's decision about the Temple in 70 CE, so with this, Rome's last and most violent assault on Jewish identity,[37] its immediate impact on the Jews of Rome goes unrecorded. With regard to its long-term effects, however, we are better informed. Thanks to the abundant, first-hand evidence for Roman Jewry in the third and fourth centuries CE, most of it supplied by three Jewish catacombs in Rome, we can see how, during the silent decades of the latter half of the second century, Jewish identity in Rome had undergone modification.

The first noticeable change is that the Temple barely figures any more as an element in Jewish identity. Some scholars have attempted to see a reference to it in the colonnaded, pedimented structure depicted on a fragment of gold glass (*CIJ* I 515 = *JIWE* II 588).[38] Others think that the object depicted at the base of the epitaph of Tychikos from the Monteverde catacomb (*CIJ* I 412 = *JIWE* II 107) is an incense shovel and hence is an allusion to Temple ritual.[39] Both interpretations have been challenged. But, even if they are accepted, as they have been most recently by David Noy in *JIWE* II, the two items in question amount to no more than a tiny fraction of the available iconographic evidence.[40] Further, there is no

---

34. Smallwood, *Jews*, pp. 444–45; F. Millar, *The Roman Near East (31 BC–AD 337)* (Cambridge, Massachusetts and London, England: Harvard University Press, 1993), p. 372.

35. Hadrian's family name was Aelius and his full name Publius Aelius Hadrianus.

36. Millar, *Roman Near East*, pp. 106–07 and 372 sees no reason to disbelieve Dio's statement (*Hist. Rom.* 69.12.1–2) that the decision was taken before the revolt and hence was a contributory factor to it. For a detailed discussion of the evidence, see Schürer, *History* [revised], I, pp. 536–41.

37. This involved supressing the name Judaea with its ethnic reference and replacing it with the un-Jewish Syria Palaestina, see Millar, *Roman Near East*, p. 108 for documentation of the process.

38. Leon, *Jews*, pp. 222–23; Rutgers, *Jews*, pp. 82–83.

39. Leon, *Jews*, p. 203, following Goodenough.

40. Unless the ubiquitous menorah be taken as referring to the great golden candelabrum that stood in the Temple until 70 CE. On this vexed question, see now the excellent, nuanced discussion in L.I. Levine, *The Ancient Synagogue: The First Thousand Years* (New Haven and London: Yale

sign of the practice, to be seen in Jewish epitaphs elsewhere from this period, of using the Destruction of the Temple as a means of dating.[41]

But while the Temple has receded almost to the point of invisibility, as have Hasmonaean names too,[42] the synagogue, which in earlier times had been secondary and in some ways ancillary to the Temple (Philo, *Leg. Gai.* 156–7), now comes to the fore. Objects used in the synagogue and in synagogal worship dominate the pictorial record left by the Jews of Rome.

In addition to the menorah (n. 40), numerous depictions occur of the Ark of the Law, by now an established item of synagogal furniture,[43] the shofar, blown in the synagogue at Rosh ha-Shanah (John Chysostom, *Adversus Iudaeos* 1.1), and the palm branches and citrons (*lulavim* and *ethrogim*) carried around the prayer-house during the Festival of Tabernacles. These symbols are to be found not only on the marble plaques that marked the burial places of the dead but also on several of the gold glass fragments and, in one spectacular instance, as the principal subject of an elaborate tomb fresco.[44]

But, it is not only in the pictorial record that the centrality of the synagogue to Jewish life is to be seen. The inscriptions from the Jewish catacombs of Rome abound in references both to the city's many synagogues, no fewer than eleven of which are specifically named[45] and to the plethora of offices that were held in them (*JIWE* II, Index Vb). The reason that the latter are mentioned so often is that tenure of synagogal office is now used by the prosperous members of the Roman Jewish community (of whom, by this stage, there were very many) as their principal marker of status and identity.[46] It is not just the office-bearers themselves who use this mode of self-definition but also non-office bearing members of the community who had, or claimed to have, some relationship with them. One example must suffice – *CIJ* I 319 = *JIWE* II 560, which, translated, runs:

University Press, 2000). While not ruling out that there may be an allusion to the Temple (p. 333), he thinks it more likely that the reference is to synagogal menorot (pp. 215–17). For some three-dimensional examples of these, see Levine, *Synagogue*, p. 334 and S. Fine (ed.), *Sacred Realm: the Emergence of the Synagogue in the Ancient World* (New York and Oxford: Oxford University Press and Yeshiva University Museum, 1996), pp. 37 (Fig. 2.12) and 43 (Plate X).

41. For a recent example from Zo'ar, Arabia, see H.M. Cotton, J.J. Price, 'A Bilingual Tombstone from Zo'ar (Arabia) (Hecht Museum, Haifa, Inv. No. H-3029, Naveh's list no. 18)', *ZPE* 134 (2001), pp. 277–83; for earlier examples, see M.H. Williams, 'The contribution of Jewish inscriptions to the study of Judaism' in W. Horbury, W.D. Davies and J. Sturdy (eds.), *The Cambridge History of Judaism* III (Cambridge: Cambridge University Press, 1999), pp. 75–93 (here p. 88). For a Jewish example from Rome of the use of Roman consular dating, see *CIJ* I 482 (probably, contra *JIWE* II 564, from the Monteverde catacomb).

42. Frey in *CIJ* I lists three possible examples: an Agrippinus, a [Bere]nice (the name of Agrippa II's notorious sister) and an Agrippa (*CIJ* I 322; 461 and 500). Noy, however, has recently rejected the restoration, Berenice, in *CIJ* I 461, preferring instead to leave the text as [...]nice, and has cast doubt on the Jewishness of Agrippa in *CIJ* I 500. See *JIWE* II 181 and 627 (i).

43. Levine, *Synagogue*, pp. 327–28.

44. Leon, *Jews*, pp. 195–210, 220–22 and fig. 43.

45. Leon, *Jews*, pp. 140–59; *JIWE* II, Index Vc.

46. Williams, 'Contribution of Jewish Inscriptions', p. 78; D. Noy, *Foreigners at Rome: Citizens and Strangers* (London: Gerald Duckworth with the Classical Press of Wales, 2000), p. 265.

> Here lies Eirena, maiden wife of Klodios (= Clodius), brother of Kountos Klaudios
> Synesios (= Quintus Claudius Synesius), Father of the Community (συναγωγή)
> of the Campesians at Rome. Peace (*shalom*)!

In this epitaph, the deceased woman is commemorated principally for having been the wife of a man whose brother was a Father of the Synagogue!

In using office in this way, the Jews of Rome reveal not only how the synagogue has usurped the role of the Temple in Jewish identity but also how Romanized that identity has now become.[47] Using office as a marker of status and identity is a quintessentially Roman practice. To the Romans' way of thinking, public office was not a burden but an honour for self and family. Hence their term for public offices – *honores* (honours). Hence also their custom of inscribing on the honorific statues that cluttered the public spaces of their city and on the tombstones that lined the roads leading out of it the titles of the offices once held by the honorand and the deceased. That the Jews of Rome should have fallen under the influence of this ideology, most clearly expressed in the formula *honoribus omnibus functus* (= having held all the public offices) in the epitaph of the *archon* and *archisynagogus*, Stafylus,[48] is only to be expected: by the time the catacomb inscriptions came to be carved, most Jews had probably been in the city for some time[49] and some Jewish families had been settled there for generations. The *gentilicia* of the Roman Jews (i.e. the Latin family names they would have acquired from their Roman citizen owners at the time of their liberation and enfranchisement) are very instructive here: while those named Flavius and Aelius are probably the descendants of slaves brought to Rome after the First and Second Jewish Revolts by Vespasian and Hadrian and subsequently manumitted by them,[50] those called Pompeius (*CIJ* I 259 = *JIWE* II 366) may well go back to Jews brought to Rome and in due course liberated by Pompey himself.

But if much has changed, much has also remained constant since 135 CE. Just as in the earlier phases of the community's history, so in this, the attachment to the Law of Moses remains strong, as the unusually large number of allusions to it in the material from the catacombs shows. Iconographically, this is demonstrated not just by the Ark of the Law (mentioned above) but by the depiction of the circumcision knife on some loculus closures[51] and the engraving of individual Torah scrolls on others.[52] Onomastically, it finds reflection in the popularity of Sabbath-type names, such as Eusabbatius, Sabbatius and Sabbatis (*JIWE* II Index II). And verbally it is to be seen in the epithets chosen to characterize the deceased –

---

47. Williams, *Jews*, Section VI.4 (a).

48. Full text to be found at *CIJ* I 265 = *JIWE* II 322. On the commonness of the formula in Roman civic epigraphy, see Frey's note (*CIJ* ad loc.).

49. Noy, *Foreigners at Rome*, p. 282 n. 445. Although Jewish immigration to Rome was still going on in the third and fourth centuries CE, the evidence for it is very limited, see *JIWE* II, Index IV.

50. See, for instance, *CIJ* I 208 (= *JIWE* II 285) – Aelia Alexandria and Aelia Septima (mother and daughter) and *CIJ* I 457 (= *JIWE* II 179) – Aelius Primitivus and Flavia Maria (husband and wife).

51. As, for instance, in *CIJ* I 200 = Leon, *Jews*, fig. 35.

52. Leon, *Jews*, pp. 200–01.

φιλόνομος (lover of the Law), φιλέντολος (lover of the commandments), ὅσιος (devout – i.e. *hasid*)[53] – and the esteem meted out to the dead for their φιλόνομος and *observantia legis* (*CIJ* I 482 and 476, line 10).

5. *Summing Up*

In this study we have surveyed the history of the Jewish community at Rome from 62 BCE down to the third and fourth century CE, with attention to the question of Jewish identity. After pinpointing the chief elements of that identity – namely, Temple, monarchy, synagogue and Mosaic Law, we showed how each of those elements came under attack in the Julio-Claudian period – the Temple cult being threatened by Gaius, synagogal life at Rome and the monarchy in Judaea being suppressed by Claudius, and the Law itself coming under intense pressure through the teaching of Paul and the activities of local Christian converts. But devastating as all this will have been for many Jews at the time, the overall effect upon Jewish identity appears to have been slight. Yet, in due course, Jewish identity did change – as we saw in the final part of our study, the ways in which the Jews of third and fourth century Rome chose to express their Jewishness were different from those used by their ancestors. Not only was the synagogue more important to them than the Temple but the way in which they used the synagogue was different too. Whereas in the early days synagogues were purely collective organisations[54] for group activities (Philo, *Leg. Gai.* 156–7), now they have also become arenas for individuals to display their wealth and status within the Jewish community. In the main, the shift had been brought about by the events described above in Section 3– the destruction of the Temple in 70 CE and the measures deliberately taken by Vespasian in the aftermath of the First Revolt to re-shape Jewish identity. But another powerful factor in shaping the identity of the Roman Jews was the influence of the Roman environment itself.

But, if most of the elements that went into the making of Jewish identity at Rome in the late Republican period had vanished or changed by the third and fourth century CE, one certainly had not – namely, devotion to the Mosaic Law.[55] As the evidence shows, at least among those Jews who chose to be buried in a Jewish cemetery, an important way of underlining their Jewishness was to emphasize their love and respect for the Law of Moses.

---

53. For these epithets, see *JIWE* II Index III f and P.W. van der Horst, *Ancient Jewish Epitaphs* (Contributions to Biblical Exegesis and Theology; 2; Kampen: Kok Pharos, 1991), pp. 65–68.

54. This is shown by their titles, Synagogue of the Augustesians, Volumnesians and so on. See n. 13 above. Contrast these with the private synagogues, named after their owners, such as that of Asabinos at Antioch. See Williams, *Jews*, V.29 with V.9.

55. What happened to Sabbath-fasting, we do not know. The kind of evidence that mentions this practice (i.e. literary texts) fails after the mid-second century CE. See discussion relating to n. 11 above.

BEING AN EGYPTIAN IN ROME.
STRATEGIES OF IDENTITY FORMATION

David Noy

The modern label 'Egyptian' covers several different identifiers used in inscriptions at Rome. Most people seem to have defined themselves, or more precisely to have been defined by their commemorators, either as Egyptians or as Alexandrians, not as both. Only one inscription (I.Porto 23) appears to use both terms, and that depends on a rather debatable restoration. People who enlisted in the armed forces, usually to serve in the Roman fleet, could be described as *natione Alexandrinus* or *natione Aegypt(i)us*, but not both. The difference appears to have survived into late antiquity: two Christian epitaphs commemorate Alexandrians (*ICUR* 6415, 12856) and in another (*ICUR* 4032 = *IGUR* 939) the people involved style themselves 'Egyptians'.

Alexandrians would no doubt normally have wished to identify themselves as 'Greeks' rather than 'Egyptians', and the label 'Alexandrian' implies 'non-Egyptian'. However, this distinction apparently meant little to most of the population of Rome, and there is no evidence that they recognized a separate category of 'Alexandrian'. The stereotyped Roman image of Egyptians concentrated on the aspects of their behaviour perceived as most outlandish, particularly the worship of animal-gods,[1] and largely ignored the Greek component of their culture, even though that may have been better represented at Rome in real life. There seems to be something of a contradiction between image and reality which may be due at least in part to anti-Cleopatra propaganda and its legacy.

The first Egyptians to come to Rome in the Republic fall into three categories: members of the Ptolemaic royal family, priests of Egyptian cults, and slaves. Egyptian slaves are mentioned as early as the time of Plautus. At first they would only have reached Rome through the regular slave trade, but large numbers were probably brought back as prisoners of war for Octavian's triumph in 29 BCE, and more after the revolt of 25 BCE.[2] By the first century CE, Egyptian slaves and ex-slaves had allegedly achieved great influence at Rome. Philo complains about Caligula's domestic servants, 'The majority of these were Egyptians (*Aigyptioi*), a seed bed of evil in whose souls both the venom and the temper of the native crocodiles and asps were reproduced.'[3] They included the chamberlain Helicon,

1. C. Ricci, 'Egiziani a Roma', *Aegyptus* 73 (1993), pp. 71–91 (71–73).
2. Ricci, 'Egiziani a Roma', p. 76.
3. Philo, *Leg. Gai.* 166–78.

who is said to have used his influence on behalf of the Alexandrian Greek delega-
tion against the Jews. He may have been an Alexandrian rather than an Egyptian,
since Philo would naturally use the most pejorative (in his view) term available.[4]
The lack of epigraphic evidence for imperial slaves with distinctively Egyptian
names may also indicate that the 'Egyptians' around the emperor were more likely
to be of Greek extraction, or at least to wish to appear so. The association between
Egyptians and slavery found in literature of the late first and early second centuries
CE suggests that Egyptian slaves were still present at Rome in significant numbers
then,[5] although none of the Egyptians recorded in inscriptions are specifically said
to be slaves. Egyptian slaves are mentioned in literature as entertainers, such as the
dancer Bathyllus (a freedman of Maecenas),[6] one of the actors named Paris,[7] and
Lucius Verus' actor freedman Apolaustus.[8] Egypt was also a source of gladiators,[9]
and there is an epitaph for a *citharoedus*.[10]

Ptolemy VI, Ptolemy XII and Cleopatra VII all lived at Rome temporarily due
to combinations of political and personal circumstances, but the permanent migration of members of the Egyptian elite to Rome was very unusual. Egypt did not
produce any senators until the second century CE. Crispinus, a pickled-fish seller
from Canopus mentioned frequently by Martial and Juvenal, allegedly reached at
least equestrian rank at Rome under Domitian, and a few other Alexandrians held
equestrian governmental posts, but they were exceptional.[11] The pancratiast
M. Aurelius Asclepiades Hermodorus came from an office-holding Alexandrian
family, but was presumably at Rome in pursuit of an athletic career and not for
political reasons.[12] Normally the Alexandrian elite were more likely to visit Rome
as members of delegations, like the rival Greek and Jewish embassies to Caligula
and Claudius, and others mentioned in the *Acts of the Alexandrian Martyrs*. Alexandrians were active at Rome in the world of letters as writers, teachers and philosophers, from the time of Augustus at least until Claudian came to Rome in
394.[13] The grain trade also brought Alexandrian merchants to Rome,[14] where their
business activities extended to other commodities, too. According to Suetonius,
Augustus was honoured while sailing through the Bay of Puteoli by the passengers
and crew of an Alexandrian ship, who thanked him for making the seas safe, and
he responded by giving his staff money to spend on Alexandrian goods.[15] Two

---

4.   Cf. S. Pearce, 'Belonging and not belonging: Local perspectives in Philo of Alexandria', in
Jewish Local Patriotism and Self-Identification in the Graeco-Roman period (ed. by S. Jones and
S. Pearce; JSP.Sup, 31; Sheffield: Sheffield Academic Press 1998), pp. 79–105.

5.   Ricci, 'Egiziani a Roma', p. 76.

6.   Ricci, 'Egiziani a Roma', p. 76.

7.   Martial 11.13.

8.   SHA *Verus* 8.10–11; *CIL* 6.10117.

9.   *CIL* 6.10194, 10197; *IGUR* 939 = *ICUR* 4032; AE 1988: 24.

10.   *IGUR* 1034.

11.   Ricci, 'Egiziani a Roma', p. 78.

12.   *IGUR* 240.

13.   Ricci, 'Egiziani a Roma', pp. 74–75.

14.   I.Porto 2–3; *IGUR* 393.

15.   Suetonius, *Aug.* 98.

peregrini with Egyptian-sounding names are recorded as members of the ship-wrights' guild (*corpus fabrum navalium*) of Ostia.[16] Someone known from a papyrus may have been at Rome dealing in cotton.[17] Other products of Egypt, notably papyrus, linen and stone, must also have brought traders to Rome, although there is no direct evidence for Egyptians dealing in them. Strabo (17.1.44) mentions people coming from Dendera to Rome with the crocodiles which were sent from there.

There are references to Egyptian doctors,[18] most of whom were probably Alexandrians or at least trained at Alexandria. The Elder Pliny, a notorious hater of doctors, comments on their coming from Egypt to make a profit by treating a new skin disease called *mentagra* which had spread from Asia,[19] and mentions a doctor from Egypt called to treat Nero's friend Cossinus.[20] The Younger Pliny was treated for a serious medical condition, presumably at Rome, by an Egyptian *iatralipta* (translated by Lewis & Short as 'ointment-doctor' and OLD as 'masseur') named Arpocras, for whom he successfully asked Trajan for Roman citizenship.[21] This man was the freedman of a *peregrina* named Thermuthis wife of Theon, evidently an Egyptian herself without Roman citizenship. Plotinus was treated until his death in 270 by an Alexandrian doctor, Eustochius.[22]

Another group among whom Egyptians seem to have been well represented was astrologers.[23] These were perhaps more likely to be native Egyptians. An Egyptian named Serapion, presumably an astrologer, is mentioned by Dio Cassius (*Hist. Rom.* 79[78].4.4–5) as predicting the death of Caracalla and succession of Macrinus.

The various designations used in inscriptions for people from Egypt are shown in the following table.

Egyptian	13[24]
Alexandrian	21
Other cities	3
Villages	4

Table 1. *Designation of people from Egypt in inscriptions*

Most of the people identified in inscriptions as 'Egyptians' are sailors from the Roman fleet, recorded with very Latin-sounding names such as T. Flavius Maximus and C. Iulius Priscus which they almost certainly acquired on enlistment. Most 'Alexandrians' are civilians, and they tend to have Greek names, but there are a few Egyptian ones such as Aurelia Boubastous (*IGUR* 395), and the very

16. *CIL* 14.256; C. Ricci, 'Egiziani a Roma', p. 90.
17. P.Mich. 8.500–1.
18. Ricci, 'Egiziani a Roma' lists the known doctors from Egypt.
19. Pliny, *Nat. Hist.* 26.3.
20. Pliny, *Nat. Hist.* 29.93.
21. Pliny, *Ep.* 10.5–6.
22. Porphyry, *Vit. Plot.* 7.
23. Ricci, 'Egiziani a Roma', p. 75.
24. 12 of these use *Aegypt(i)us*, one mentions both Egypt and Alexandria.

Latin-sounding family of Julia Pia and her son Julius Hilarus (*IGUR* 610). The other cities mentioned are Memphis, Hermopolis, and Babylon; the 'city of the Nile' in *IGUR* 1321 might, as suggested by Moretti, be Alexandria rather than Nilopolis. Villages are mentioned only in Christian inscriptions: one reference to *kōmēs Megalēs Pottheōs* and three, probably from the fifth century, to Koprithis; there was evidently a small community from the village at Rome then.[25] The predominance of Alexandrians in the evidence is clear, and there is a distinct lack of references to any other Egyptian cities. This suggests either a genuine shortage of non-Alexandrian Egyptians at Rome or, perhaps more plausibly, a reluctance to identify themselves as such in view of the strong hostility to Egyptians. The label 'Alexandrian' may sometimes indicate not a native of Alexandria but someone who moved there from somewhere in the Egyptian *chora* and then moved on to Rome, a pattern of migration which is certainly to be expected on the basis of modern evidence; Ricci suggests that the designation *Alexandrinus* for two gladiators may indicate that they came from the Alexandrian gladiatorial school, rather than being Alexandrian citizens.[26]

The languages used in the inscriptions are exclusively Greek (mainly for the civilians) and Latin (mainly for the military personnel). There is no sign of the Egyptian language being inscribed in epitaphs or other personal inscriptions, and no use of hieroglyphics except for decorative purposes in Isis temples (in contrast to the apparently symbolic use of the Hebrew alphabet in some Jewish inscriptions). Perhaps there was a lack of any competent stonecutters, but since amateurish attempts were made to inscribe languages such as Palmyrene, this may not be a sufficient explanation.

Two other Egyptian practices which did make their way to Rome may have had some connection with Egyptian immigrants: the worship of Isis and other Egyptian gods, and the mummification of the dead. However, on closer investigation these appear not to have been the vehicles for maintaining Egyptian identity which might be imagined.

The cult of Isis at Rome was probably established by the early first century BCE, but was repressed repeatedly from the 50s BCE, although the triumvirs set up a temple of Isis and Serapis in 43 BCE.[27] Despite some further setbacks up to and including the reign of Tiberius, the cult achieved such prominence that one of the regions of Rome came to be known as *Isis et Serapis*. The cult was not exclusive to, or even dominated by, Egyptians, but there is some evidence that Egyptians often held the priesthoods.[28] Embes, described as *prophetes* and *pater* of the college

25.   Reference to a native village is commoner at Rome among Thracians, Galatians and Syrians; D. Noy, *Foreigners at Rome: Citizens and Strangers* (London: Duckworth/Classical Press of Wales, 2000), pp. 219, 232, 237.

26.   Ricci, 'Egiziani a Roma', p. 89.

27.   G. La Piana, 'Foreign Groups in Rome during the First Centuries of the Empire', *HThR* 20 (1927), pp. 183–403; R. Turcan, *The Cults of the Roman Empire* (Oxford *et al.*: Basil Blackwell, 1996), pp. 85–87.

28.   M. Beard, J. North and S. Price, *Religions of Rome*. Vol. 1. *A History* (Cambridge: Cambridge University Press), p. 294.

of Paeanistai of Serapis in 146 CE, was almost certainly an Egyptian.[29] The *neokoros* of the temple of Serapis at Portus in c. 200 was an Alexandrian,[30] and later in the third century, Plotinus met an Egyptian priest who had come to Rome and conjured up a spirit in the temple of Isis.[31]

The Greek language seems to have been obligatory for dedications to Isis and Serapis. The Egyptian calendar (to be discussed later) was occasionally used too. The epitaph of a girl named Isias commemorated by her parents Antinous and Panthia suggests the influence of Egyptian worship on naming practice, but does not necessarily indicate that the people were themselves Egyptians.[32] The cult was very attractive to some upper-class Romans, and the role of Egyptians seems to have been fairly limited beyond supplying the priests. When it was temporarily suppressed by Tiberius after a scandal, the priests were crucified, which indicates that they must have been slaves or *peregrini*.[33] However, the lack of any associated expulsion of Egyptians then or in any of the previous suppressions may indicate that it was not thought to be limited to one national group. At Ostia, where Isis' popularity was no doubt increased by her patronage of sailing and by the regular arrival of the grain fleet from Alexandria, the same man was priest of both 'Ostian Isis and Mater Deorum of Trastevere',[34] showing that the cult did not require exclusive adherence.

Visual links with Egypt and traditional Egyptian religion were part of the attraction of Isis-worship, as exemplified in the Domitianic temple at Rome.[35] Objects such as obelisks of Aswan granite were imported to add to the Egyptian atmosphere. However, it does not appear that this was for the benefit of real Egyptians, but rather for cultural tourists who wanted to be reminded of a visit to Egypt or compensated for a visit which they would never make.[36] In the Flavian period, the association of Alexandria with the dynasty's rise to power may have been an additional attraction. Egyptian workmen probably came to Rome to work on the temples, but they were not the people for whom the temples were built.

The epigraphic evidence does not indicate the involvement of many immigrants in the cult, or any close connection between Egyptian gods and Egyptian identity. This is demonstrated by the inscriptions for Serapis. The *prophetes* Embes who appears to have been Egyptian, with a group of *paianistai* who probably were not,

29. *IGUR* 77; Ricci, 'Egiziani a Roma', no. A12; L. Vidman, 'Ägypter ausserhalb von Ägypten in der Kaiserzeit', in M. Ta'eva and D. Bojad'iev (eds.), *Studia in honorem Borisi Gerov* (Sofia: Sofia Press, 1980), pp. 259–66 (263).

30. Vidman, 'Ägypter', p. 262.

31. Porphyry, *Vit. Plot.* 10.

32. *CIL* 6.19716; contra Ricci, 'Egiziani a Roma', no. A16.

33. Noy, *Foreigners*, pp. 43–44.

34. M. Floriani Squarciapino, *I culti orientali ad Ostia* (*EPRO*, 3; Leiden: E.J. Brill, 1962), pp. 15, 30; *CIL* 14.429.

35. F.E. Brenk, 'The Isis Campensis of Katja Lembke', in *Imago Antiquitatis. Religions et iconographie du monde romain* (Mélanges offerts à R. Turcan; ed. by N. Blanc and A. Buisson; De l'archéologie à l'histoire; Paris: De Boccard, 1999), pp. 133–43 (133).

36. See Brenk ('Isis Campensis') for discussion and bibliography.

associated the god with the imperial cult.[37] At Portus, he was honoured by a father and son from Alexandria.[38] On the other hand, the priest Vibius made a dedication to him, 'on the god's orders'.[39] The Arellii Severus and Fuscus (very Latin names) and the 'holy order of *paianistai* in Rome' also honoured him in Greek.[40] The *hierodoulos* C. Avidius Trophimianus made a vow to him for the safety of the emperor (probably Caracalla).[41] He was identified with Zeus Helios in a thanksgiving inscription.[42] The cosmopolitan nature of the cult means that it cannot have functioned as a communal focus for Egyptians at Rome.

Egyptian gods other than Isis and Serapis were also worshipped, and in these cases there are some clearer connections with people who came from Egypt. An Alexandrian councillor honoured 'the ancestral gods' at Portus.[43] 'Antinous the companion of the gods in Egypt' was honoured with a dedication from the *prophetes* M. Ulpius Apollonius, who gives no further information about himself but, as the title and divinities are unusual at Rome, seems very likely to have come from Egypt.[44]

Chioffi has thirty likely examples of mummification or embalming from Rome, including fifteen from S. Sebastiano. Suggested dates range from the Augustan period to the second and third centuries; those from S. Sebastiano may in some cases be fourth or fifth century. Mummification in the strict sense (involving drying out the body with natron and removing the internal organs) was a highly specialized art, and there do not seem to be any definite examples of its use at Rome; the bodies described as 'mummies' appear in fact to have been preserved inside a layer of resinous mixture which kept them from the air.[45] There is therefore no reason to connect any of these burials with Egyptians. Embalming in honey was practised by various people at Rome: there is a possible reference in an epitaph for a Laodicean.[46] Lucretius mentions embalming in honey as a possibility in his time, and Statius says that Priscilla, the wife of Domitian's secretary Abascantus, was embalmed; they do not suggest that the practice had any particular ethnic connotations.[47] The pyramid of C. Cestius shows the attraction of Egyptian burial practices for some Italians. The so-called 'Tomb of the Egyptians' (tomb Z in the Vatican necropolis) takes its name from the depictions of Egyptian gods in national

37. *IGUR* 77; Ricci, 'Egiziani a Roma', no. A12; Vidman 'Ägypter', p. 263.
38. I.Porto 16.
39. *IGUR* 100.
40. *IGUR* 188, 77.
41. *IGUR* 190.
42. *IGUR* 193; *IGUR* 187, 189, 191, 192, 194 are also Serapis inscriptions.
43. I.Porto 21.
44. *IGUR* 98.
45. L. Chioffi, *Mummificazione e imbalsamazione a Roma ed in altri luoghi del mondo romano* (Opuscula epigraphica dell'Università degli Studi di Roma La Sapienza, Dipartimento di Scienze Storiche, Archeologiche, Antropologiche dell'Antichità, 8, Roma: Quasar, 1998), pp. 21, 24, 48, 53.
46. *IGUR* 1288, according to Sacco's interpretation cited by Moretti ad loc.
47. Lucretius 3.890–3; Statius, *Silv.* 5.1; J.M.C Toynbee, *Death and Burial in the Roman World* (Aspects of Greek and Roman Life; London: Thames & Hudson, 1971), p. 41.

costume. Since this tomb, which was only for inhumations, in a period when cremation was still dominant, had an Egyptian-style interior but apparently no external Egyptian features, it seems likely that it was originally used by Egyptian migrants rather than by people wanting to make a show of their egyptianizing tastes.[48] However, it is very much the exception. There do not appear to have been any exclusively or even predominantly Egyptian burial areas (unlike the Jewish catacombs).

Few distinctively Egyptian names are recorded in inscriptions at Rome. The commonest seems to be Horus, but that only occurs five times, all in Latin inscriptions.[49]

Slave	2
Freedman	2
Duo/tria nomina	1

Table 2. *Status of people called* Horus

The same association with servile status applies for this as for many other local names.[50] The one bearer of the name with a recorded child (a freedman of Galba) had a daughter named Basilia, which is consistent with the usual reluctance of the bearers of local names to pass them on to their children.[51]

One other epigraphic way of showing Egyptian identity was by using the Egyptian calendar, the only non-Roman calendar which was regularly inscribed at Rome. This is something for which there is substantial evidence. It was only used in inscriptions written largely or entirely in Greek, and it seems to have been commonest in the fifth century. Three Christian epitaphs use it for people who are stated to be immigrants: Paulus of Alexandria died on Phaophi 24;[52] a man from Koprithis died on Payni 22;[53] Ammon from Alexandria died on Mecheir 21.[54] There is also a Christian epitaph in which the details of the deceased are almost entirely lost but a date in Phaophi is given;[55] another very fragmentary one which seems to use both Greek and Latin has a date in Pharmouthi;[56] and both give the year by consular dating (471 and 458 or 474). Someone whose name is largely lost died on Hathyr 7,[57] and there is another fragmentary date in Pharmouthi.[58] An

48. Noy, *Foreigners*, pp. 189–90.
49. Vidman, 'Ägypter', p. 261.
50. Noy, *Foreigners*, pp. 182–83.
51. *CIL* 6.26959.
52. *ICUR* 12856.
53. *ICUR* 4957; the year is given by consular dating.
54. *ICUR* 6415.
55. A. Ferrua, 'Antichi iscrizioni inedite di Roma', *Epigraphica* 1 (1939), pp. 142–50 (148 no. 11); *SEG* 30.1215; cf. A. Avraméa, 'Mort loin de la patrie. L'apport des inscriptions paléochrétiennes', in *Epigrafia medievale Greca e Latina. Ideologia e funzione. Atti del seminario di Erice (12–18 sett. 1991)* (ed. by G. Cavallo and C. Mango; Biblioteca del 'Centro per il Collegamento degli Studi Medievali e Umanistici in Umbria'; 11; Spoleto: Centro Italiano di Studi sull'Alto Medioevo, 1995), pp. 1–65.
56. *IGCVO* 1066.
57. *ICUR* 12864.
58. *ICUR* 19855c.

epitaph which may be Jewish records the death of [Theo]dosia on Tybi 20.[59] An inscription dated to 589 which seems to record a benefaction has a date in Pharmouthi.[60]

Egyptian dates were not restricted to a Christian context, although that is where most occur. In two inscriptions concerning the cult of Serapis, the date is carefully given according to both systems: 'one day before the Nones of May, which is according to the Alexandrians Pachon 11',[61] and 'six days before the Kalends of April, Pharmouthi 1';[62] both give the year by the normal consular dating. The mainly (but not exclusively) Egyptian practice of writing L for 'year(s)', either in a date or in someone's age, is also found in several Greek inscriptions at Rome.[63]

On the other hand, Aurelius Apion of Hermopolis died on the Kalends of December.[64] The important difference is that Apion's epitaph is in Latin, whereas all those which use Egyptian dates are in Greek. It was evidently felt that a Latin epitaph required a date according to the Roman system, but that the Egyptian dating system and the Greek language went together naturally. It is not clear if the people commemorated with Egyptian dates were all immigrants from Egypt themselves, although some clearly were. While non-Egyptians might adopt the Egyptian calendar for religious reasons, the fact that the large majority of the examples given above are Christian shows that this was not usual. More probably, the inscribing of dates from their own calendar was a small statement of Egyptian identity made by Egyptians themselves and perhaps also (although this is not provable) by people of Egyptian ancestry.[65]

The inevitable conclusion is that Egyptians at Rome lacked any form of communal organization. Isis and Serapis worship could have united Alexandrians with other Egyptians, but only along with people from a variety of other backgrounds. There is no evidence of any other institution which provided a focus for Alexandrians or other Egyptians, and only the people from fifth-century Koprithis seem to have been anxious to preserve a form of local identity. As far as we can tell from the surviving evidence (remembering that there may have been a whole level of oral culture among immigrants which has left no trace) people who came to Rome from Egypt were likely to experience fairly rapid assimilation rather than maintaining their own distinctive institutions in the way that the Jews did.[66]

59. *JIGRE* 141.

60. *ICUR* 3974.

61. *IGUR* 77.

62. *IGUR* 191 = L. Vidman, *Sylloge inscriptionum religionis Isiacae et Sarapiacae* (*RVV*, 28; Berlin: W. de Gruyter, 1969), p. 398 [SIRIS], dated 299.

63. *IGUR* 333, 452, 644, 884.

64. *ICUR* 1170.

65. P. Lombardi, 'Le iscrizioni greche cristiane nei Musei Vaticani', in I. di Stefano Manzella (ed.), *Le iscrizioni dei Cristiani in Vaticano. Materiali e contributi scientifici per una Mostra Epigrafica* (Inscriptiones Sanctae Sedis, 2; Rome: Quasar, 1997), pp. 45–51, considers that the people who used Egyptian dates and gave no place of origin are more likely to be from Cyrenaica than from Egypt, but I can see no reason for thinking that Cyrenaica is *more* likely, in view of the small number of known immigrants from there.

66. Noy, *Foreigners*, p. 287.

Part II

ROME, ROMAN CHRISTIANS AND THEIR RELATIONSHIP
IN EARLY CHRISTIAN WRITINGS AND ARCHAEOLOGY

Part IIa
New Testament Reflections on the Early Christian Community of Rome

'BOLDLY AND WITHOUT HINDRANCE HE PREACHED THE KINGDOM OF
GOD AND TAUGHT ABOUT THE LORD JESUS CHRIST' (*ACTS* 28.31).
PAUL'S PUBLIC PROCLAMATION IN ROME AS THE *FINALE* OF A SHIPWRECK

Michael Labahn

The city of Rome is rarely explicitly mentioned in the New Testament.[1] The ancient metropolis is generally recognized as a centre of political power with which New Testament authors were in conflict. Often and in an enigmatic manner, Rome is identified with the well-known Old Testament opponent of Israel: Babylon (1 Pet. 5.13; Rev. 14.8; 16.19; 17.5; 18.2, 10, 21). This equation opened up a vivid exegetical discussion on its meaning, its range, and historical consequences, e.g. for the dates of 1 Peter and Revelation.[2]

Indisputably, Rome plays a distinct role within the literary depiction and the historical concept of Acts. As it was recently emphasized by Carsten Burfeind, the city of Rome is the final goal of the Lukan plot in Acts.[3] Often, Rome was presented as the destination at which all efforts to proclaim the Kingdom of God (κηρύσσων τὴν βασιλείαν τοῦ θεοῦ, Acts 28.31) would finally arrive; this assumption is challenged by an interpretation that links the programmatic hint in Acts 1.8 (…and you will be my witnesses in Jerusalem, in all Judea and Samaria, and to the ends of the earth; *NRSV*) with Rom. 15.23ff. and takes it as an indication of Paul's mission in Spain[4] whose realization is nowhere reported or alluded to in the New Testament.

---

1. There are only eight references for 'Ῥώμη' in the New Testament, five of them belong to Acts: 18.2; 19.21; 23.11; 28.14, 16.

2. Cf., e.g., D.E. Aune, *Revelation 6–16* (WBC, 52B; Nashville, TN: Thomas Nelson, 1998), pp. 829–31. – On a new, less offensive interpretation of Babylon as symbol for Rome in 1 Peter 5.13 cf. now L. Thurén, 'Jeremiah 27 and Civil Obedience in 1 Peter', in M. Labahn and J. Zangenberg (ed.), *Zwischen den Reichen. Neues Testament und Römische Herrschaft* (TANZ, 36; Tübingen, Basel: Francke, 2002), pp. 215–28.

3. In his important article 'Paulus muß nach Rom. Zur politischen Dimension der Apostelgeschichte', *NTS* 46 (2000), pp. 75–91, C. Burfeind stresses an orientation of Acts towards Paul's proclamation in Rome. Burfeind proposes a critical attitude of the author of Acts against Rome based on theological prejudices (for a different and more neutral approach to the critical attitude towards Roman power within the Lukan work cf. now M. Meiser, 'Lukas und die römische Staatsmacht', in M. Labahn and J. Zangenberg [eds.], *Zwischen den Reichen*, pp. 175–93). I argue for a more universal interpretation of the proclamation in Rome which stands for a final, universal target.

4. E.g. Earle E. Ellis who even suggests an exact location and proposes the region of Gades

The readers of Acts finally arrive at Rome in Acts 28. Paul, who is declared innocent by Roman and Jewish authorities (26.31; further statements of Paul's innocence are to be found in 18.14–5; 20.26; 23.3, 9, 29; 24.12–3; 25.18, 25; according to Daniel Marguerat this aspect is a 'Leitmotiv' within these chapters[5]), still insists on his right to appeal to Caesar in Rome and be heard by the Roman *princeps*. A new horizon opens up in Acts 28.30–1 which points to the final fulfilment of Acts 1.8 by mentioning the bold and free preaching of Paul (see below ch. 4): the term 'the ends of the world' is to be taken geographically and points to the preservation of the Gospel by God until it is universally heard, which is exemplarily shown in the protection of the Apostle Paul during his shipwreck. So the final focus of Acts is the world-wide dissemination of the Gospel as far as Rome *and even beyond*. That means Rome is not the target of the proclamation envisaged in Acts 1.8[6] but rather the gate through which universal proclamation has to go through.

Some scholars describe Acts 27–28 as the *centre*[7] of the entire narrative of Acts.[8] Because both chapters present the final words of the narrative, it seems more

west of Gibraltar as the background of Acts 1.8: ' "The End of the Earth" (Acts 1.8)', in E.E. Ellis, *History and Interpretation in New Testament Perspective* (BIS, 54; Leiden: Brill 2001), pp. 53–63; *idem*, ' "Das Ende der Erde" (Apg 1,8)', in C. Bussmann and W. Radl (eds.), *Der Treue Gottes trauen. Beiträge zum Werk des Lukas. Für G. Schneider* (Freiburg *et al.*: Herder, 1991), pp. 277–87.

5. D. Marguerat, 'The End of Acts (28.16–31) and the Rhetoric of Silence', in S.E. Porter and T.H. Olbricht (eds.), *Rhetoric and the New Testament. Essays from the 1992 Heidelberg Conference* (JSNT.Sup 90; Sheffield: Sheffield Academic Press, 1993), pp. 74–89 (83).

6. A view often taken into account and equally often severely criticized; cf. now H. Omerzu, 'Das Schweigen des Lukas. Überlegungen zum offenen Ende der Apostelgeschichte,' in F.W. Horn (ed.), *Das Ende des Paulus. Historische, theologische und literaturgeschichtliche Aspekte* (BZNW, 106; Berlin, New York: W. de Gruyter, 2001), pp. 127–56 (131–33).

7. G.B. Miles and G. Trompf, 'Luke and Antiphon: The Theology of Acts 27–28 in the Light of Pagan Beliefs about Divine Retribution, Pollution, and Shipwreck', *HTR* 69 (1976), pp. 260–67 (260).

8. The use of 'narrative' and of 'narrative plot' in this article presupposes a broad meaning of 'narrative' (cf., e.g., R. Barthes, 'Einführung in die strukturale Analyse von Erzählungen', in *idem*, *Das semiologische Abenteuer* [es.NF 441, Frankfurt am Main: Suhrkamp, 1988], pp. 102–43 [102]) which focuses on a text as generator of meaning out of past events (cf. also J. Straub, 'Über das Bilden von Vergangenheit. Erzähltheoretische Überlegungen und eine exemplarische Analyse eines Gruppengesprächs über die "NS-Zeit"', in J. Rüsen [ed.], *Geschichtsbewußtsein. Psychologische Grundlagen, Entwicklungskonzepte, empirische Befunde* [Beiträge zur Geschichtskultur, 21; Köln *et al.*: Böhlau, 2001], pp. 45–113) which is not restricted to a literary genre. (For the meaning of 'historical narration' in modern discussion on the theory of history cf., e.g., J. Rüsen, *Historische Orientierung. Über die Arbeit des Geschichtsbewußtseins, sich in der Zeit zurechtzufinden* [Köln *et al.*: Böhlau, 1994], especially pp. 37–39).

Modern theorists of history claim that the basic approach to history is a narrative one: cf. E. Reinmuth, *Neutestamentliche Historik. Probleme und Perspektiven* (ThLZ.F, 8; Leipzig: EVA, 2003), pp. 41–45 (p. 41: 'Die Grundform der Vergegenwärtigung von Vergangenem ist das Erzählen eigener und überlieferter Erfahrungen.'); J. Rüsen, *Historische Vernunft. Grundzüge einer Historik I: Die Grundzüge der Geschichtswissenschaft* (KVR, 1489; Göttingen: Vandenhoeck & Ruprecht, 1983), pp. 52–57.

appropriate to speak of a *climax* rather than a centre.[9] As demonstrated below, Acts 27–28 present the significant final target of the Lukan writing activity, taking up key words from the beginning of Acts with the proclamation of the earliest Christian community in Rome and even from the start of Jesus' own proclamation according to Luke's gospel.

Acts 27–28 are part of the final section of the characterization of Paul in Acts which also contains the Lukan depiction of Paul's trial: 21.15–28.31. Hence, Paul is brought to Rome in Acts 27.1–28.18,[10] in Rome he stays under arrest in *custodia militaris*[11] and, finally, he preaches boldly and without hindrance the kingdom of God in that city (Acts 28.31). The connection of the whole narrative to the final section of Acts' trial sequence seems loose and in some aspects unsatisfactory,[12] so that its open questions 'constantly call for re-examination'.[13] The appeal to Caesar appears twice in the last two chapters in Acts – in Paul's apology in front of the Jews, Acts 28.19 and in Acts 27.24. Both texts underscore that the sea voyage will finally end safely: The voyage cannot fail because Paul has to go to Rome in order to appear before Caesar. That aspect seems to be the main target of the last section of Acts, for according to these remarks Paul is not primarily brought there in order to preach in Rome. These two alternative interpretations of Paul's trip to Rome outline two main issues for the interpretation of Acts 27–28. First, the narrative gap between the guided expectation of the reader (Paul's defense before Caesar) and the events actually reported in the narrative (Paul's bold and free preaching) have to be noted. Second, although there is an aporia or a gap between the reader's expectation and the already narrated final act of Paul in Rome, the events *in Rome* and the events on the trip *to Rome* seem to be closely connected.[14]

For the purpose of this article I do not have to define the literary genre of Acts. Despite its specific literary genre, Acts is structured around narrative strategies and even has a narrative plot.

9.   According to P. Pokorný, 'Die Romfahrt des Paulus und der antike Roman', *ZNW* 64 (1973), pp. 233–44 [233], Acts reaches its zenith in Paul's journey to Rome.

10.   Cf. now P. Seul, *Rettung für alle. Die Romreise des Paulus nach Apg 27,1–28,16* (BBB, 146; Berlin, Wien: Philo, 2003).

11.   On various kinds of military custody of a prisoner, cf. B. Rapske, *The Book of Acts and Paul in Roman Custody* (The Book of Acts in its First Century Setting, 3; Grand Rapids: Eerdmans; Carlisle: Paternoster Press, 1994), pp. 28–29. References on custody in *one's own house* cf. Tacitus, *Ann.* 14.60.2 as well as Josephus, *Ant.* 18.235, 237 (assumed to facilitate the captivity of Agrippa I). For an impressive examination especially of the juridical conflicts in Acts 16–25, cf. now H. Omerzu, *Der Prozeß des Paulus. Eine exegetische und rechtshistorische Untersuchung der Apostelgeschichte* (BZNW, 115; Berlin, New York: W. de Gruyter, 2002); on Acts 27.1–28.31 cf. *ibidem*, pp. 498–501.

12.   Cf. the classical remarks of A. Harnack, *Neue Untersuchungen zur Apostelgeschichte und zur Abfassungszeit der synoptischen Evangelien* (Beiträge zur Einleitung in das Neue Testament, 4; Leipzig: J.C. Hinrichs, 1911), pp. 66–67, who finds here an 'intolerable aporia' ('unerträglichen Aporie').

13.   C.K. Barrett, 'The End of Acts', in H. Lichtenberger (ed.), *Geschichte–Tradition–Reflexion. FS M. Hengel. Vol. III: Frühes Christentum* (Tübingen: Mohr-Siebeck, 1996), pp. 545–55. A critical survey of explanations about the open end of Acts is given by H. Omerzu, 'Das Schweigen des Lukas', pp. 128–44.

14.   A recent interpretation of the end of Acts is given by H. Omerzu, 'Das Schweigen des Lukas', pp. 151–56. She points to a lack of information of the author of Acts who does not invent

The apostle brought to Rome on his appeal to Caesar proclaims the gospel there and is only partially hindered by his house arrest: κηρύσσων τὴν βασιλείαν τοῦ θεοῦ καὶ διδάσκων τὰ περὶ τοῦ κυρίου Ἰησοῦ Χριστοῦ μετὰ πάσης παρρησίας ἀκωλύτως (Acts 28.31). The fact that Paul is taken in before Caesar – in the same way as, for example, Apollonius of Tyana in Philostrate's vita – is not mentioned, neither is the outcome of the process referred to by the narrator, so that the question arises, how the narrator handles this climax: it forms another literary gap[15] that leads the reader's focus away from the fate of the proclaimer and turns it to the proclamation itself: 'boldly and without hindrance'.

In this article, I deal with the second aspect and look at a detail of the subject just raised. In continuation with my previous article 'Paulus – ein *homo honestus et iustus*',[16] I will try to explain the sea rescue story in Acts 27.1ff. as *an intended narrative requirement of Paul's free proclamation in Rome*. As a literary hinge, the sea rescue story connects Paul's appeal to Caesar (and, therewith, the trial scenes in Acts 22ff.) with his preaching in Rome. The purpose of the sea voyage is not simply to bring the main character from Palestine to Rome but rather *to develop a crisis in the narrative flow which enables the readers to understand the strong protection of God for the gospel's proclaimer and even more his proclamation.*[17] The *krisis* could either cause the demise of both, the proclaimer and its proclamation, or the proclaimer overcomes the danger. Such lucky outcome from a life-threatening shipwreck is not only a subject of ancient novels entertaining the public with the demonstration that the hero is loved by Gods and/or Tyche. The lucky outcome is also frequently expressed in public as praise of gods and goddesses

---

episodes against the traditions available to him: 'Da ihm jedoch für den Romaufenthalt selbst keine Informationen mehr vorlagen, verzichtete er auf eine selbständige Darstellung etwa einer Verhandlung vor dem Kaiser' (p. 153). Acts presents Paul's fate in the light of the passion of Jesus and he blames the Jewish people to be responsible for his death (pp. 154–55).

15. That Luke knew about the death of Paul according to Acts 20.17–35 is a firm assumption (cf. Acts 20.38; 21.11 [remembering the death of Jesus; cf., e.g., D. Marguerat, 'End of Acts', p. 75]): cf., e.g., H. Conzelmann, *Die Apostelgeschichte* (HNT, 7; Tübingen: Mohr-Siebeck, 2nd edn, 1972), p. 127; E. Haenchen, *The Acts of the Apostles. A Commentary* (Philadelphia: Westminster, 1971), pp. 596–97 (cf. the revised German edition: *idem, Die Apostelgeschichte* [MeyerK, 3; Göttingen: Vandenhoeck & Ruprecht, 7th edn, 1977], pp. 570–72); G. Schneider, *Die Apostelgeschichte II. Teil. Kommentar zu Kap. 9,1–28,31* (HTKNT, V/2; Freiburg *et al.*: Herder, 1982), p. 411. Differently, A. Harnack, *Untersuchungen*, pp. 66–69: Acts is written before the death of Paul.

16. M. Labahn, 'Paulus – ein *homo honestus et iustus*. Das lukanische Paulusportrait von Apg 27–28 im Lichte ausgewählter antiker Parallelen', in F.W. Horn (ed.), *Das Ende des Paulus*, pp. 75–106.

17. Therefore, the last voyage of Paul's falls into the second category of narrative functions of travel accounts mentioned by L. Alexander, '"In Journeyings Often": Voyaging in the Acts of the Apostles and in Greek Romance', in C.M. Tuckett (ed.), *Luke's Literary Achievement. Collected Essays* (JSNT.Sup, 116; Sheffield: Sheffield Academic Press, 1995), pp. 17–49 (19): 'The travelling itself may simply serve as a linking device which transports the characters from one scene to another, so that the exotic location (and the adventures which take place there) are more important in narrative terms than the route by which it is reached; or the travel may itself become the focus of attention.'

responsible for help. This narrative strategy provides evidence that the path the Gospel takes to Rome aiming at free proclamation harmonises with God's will and indicates the future success of world-wide preaching that started in Rome.[18]

In a first step I will locate the shipwreck account and its entire structure within its actual literary context by pointing out that it forms an important part of the whole text. In a second step, I shortly introduce and analyse different ancient texts to discover how the survival of a shipwreck is presented in different literary genres. It will be shown that the event was connected with gods and their favour, that it is made public, sometimes proclaiming the nature of gods, and that it triggers hope for future safety or prosperity guaranteed by the gods' favour. In the third step, I will investigate the narrative role of Paul's bold proclamation. The final chapter ties the bands together and reads the end of Acts as an intentional conclusion that opens the readers' eyes for the future realization of Acts 1.8 prefigured in Paul's bold and unhindered preaching: enabled by the rescue from the shipwreck which shows God's engagement in the Gospel, Paul's proclamation in Rome is a symbol for God's continuing care.

1. *The Rescue of Paul from Shipwreck as Part of the Final Composition of Acts*

In his *Poetics*, *Aristotle* establishes a basic scheme for 'tragedy' which is relevant for any literary work (*Poet* V 11, 3–7 1450b7). That strategy is even present and further developed in modern narrative theories, for example it is connected with the theorem of the 'plot' of a story:[19]

> A whole is what has a beginning and middle and end. A beginning is that which is not a necessary consequent of anything else but after which something else exists or happens as a natural result. An end on the contrary is that which is inevitably or, as a rule, the natural result of something else but from which nothing else follows; a middle follows something else and something follows from it. Well constructed plots must not therefore begin and end at random, but must embody the formulae we have stated.[20]

In contrast to some imbalances of the Lukan story, which may disturb modern readers and which may force exegetes to use their literary-critical scalpel, the aim of Luke is to establish a well organized story line. That point should not be denied at all – therefore the question of how the end of Acts should be assessed in terms of

---

18. L. Alexander, 'Journeyings Often,' pp. 22–23, marks a clear difference of Acts compared to ancient novels in that Acts 'does not share the outward-and-return structure'.

19. Cf. P. Ricoeur, *Zeit und Erzählung. Band 1: Zeit und historische Erzählung* (Übergänge, 18,1; München: Wilhelm Fink, 1988), pp. 54–104 (referring to book VII of Aristotles's *Poetics* by using the catchword 'Fabel' which should be read in accordance with the English term 'plot'); see also J. Straub, 'Temporale Orientierung und narrative Kompetenz. Zeit- und erzähltheoretische Grundlagen einer Psychologie biographischer und historischer Sinnbildung', in J. Rüsen (ed.), *Geschichtsbewußtsein*, pp. 15–44 (25–30).

20. Translation: W.H. Fyfe, *Aristotle in 23 Volumes, Vol. 23* (Cambridge, MA: Harvard University Press; London: Heinemann, 1932), p. 31.

its literary function needs to be raised seriously. For what reason does the author narrate the last two chapters of Acts after having declared Paul's innocence, and how does he motivate his narrative of the arrested Paul? According to Luke, it is Paul himself who forces his way to Rome by appealing to Caesar although both, Roman and Jewish authorities have already stated Paul's innocence, and nothing but Paul's own appeal prevents his release from Roman custody. Also, Luke in his description of Paul's transfer to Rome clearly and several times portrays the apostle as an innocent and free man; Paul is still able to visit his friends and fellow Christians in Sidon and is supplied by them with goods for his journey to Rome (Acts 27.3) and he is – among others activities – even involved in discussions with the authorities on board about the winter quarters of the ship.[21]

Delays are frequent features in ancient narratives on naval travel,[22] so it is no surprise at all that the narrator of Acts uses such a well known element from ancient travel experiences to shape his story. Furthermore, the frequent use of shipwreck-narratives in the ancient Greek and Latin literature, e.g. in the Homeric Hymns or in the poetry of Homer up to late-antique novels, may well be explained from common experience of people who more or less lived close the Mediterranean Sea, whose occasional heavy storms and high waves often caused danger to any traveller.[23] A further ancient example, taken from the New Testament itself, is Paul's own statement in the list of hardships in 2 Cor. 11.25: *three times I was shipwrecked* (τρὶς ἐναυάγησα); *for a night and a day I was adrift at sea* (*NRSV*). On the one hand, Paul's lament illustrates that ancient travellers always faced the potential danger of shipwreck and, on the other hand, that shipwreck may even pose a life-threatening danger, although it does not necessarily lead to death. Paul does not give any details of these perilous events, nor does Luke tell anything about them which must have taken place before Paul's last voyage to Rome.[24]

21. Cf. M. Labahn, 'Paulus', pp. 82–86. P. Seul shows that Paul's behaviour is in accordance with ancient sea law (cf. Seul, *Rettung*, p. 60). However, Paul the prisoner acts as a free passenger on board with great authority.

22. Cicero, *Familiares* 14.5.1: 'On the 14th of October I arrived at Athens, after experiencing unfavourable winds and a slow and unpleasant voyage (*cum sane adversis ventis usi essemus tardeque et incommode navigassemus*).' Translation: E. Shuckburgh (http://perseus.mpiwg-berlin.mpg.de/cgi-bin/ptext?doc=Perseus%3Atext%3A1999.02.0022&layout=&loc=F+14.5). Similar reports on delays can be found, e.g., in Pliny, *Epistulae* X 15, 17a2.

23. Cf., e.g., T. Hägg, *The Novel in Antiquity* (Oxford: Basil Blackwell, 1983), p. 103: 'Shipwreck and capture by pirates were…realities in the Mediterranean of Hellenistic times, even if the frequency is, for obvious reasons, unrealistically high in the novels'; L. Alexander, 'Journeyings Often,' pp. 31–37 (p. 33: 'The popularity of this kind of voyage narrative among the Greeks…must reflect the importance of the sea, and especially of the coastal voyage, in the Greek perception of the world.'); cf. the following remarks on ship voyages in different types of ancient literature from various times: Lucretius 2.1–5; Lukian, *Toxaris vel Amicitia* 20; Martialis 4.63; Ailianos, *Epistulae* 18 and many others. On the basic role of travel for the narrative plot in ancient novels cf. L. Alexander, 'Journeyings Often,' pp. 17–49.

24. E. Haenchen, 'Acta 27,' in E. Dinkler (ed.), in co-operation with H. Thyen, *Zeit und Geschichte. Dankesgabe an Rudolf Bultmann zum 80. Geburtstag* (Tübingen: Mohr-Siebeck, 1964), pp. 235–54 (238) builds up only the following alternative: 'Entweder Lukas wußte von

However, rescue from shipwreck and maritime disasters belong to the reality of Paul's apostolic existence and to the life of other Mediterranean people.[25]

The report of Paul's sea journey in Acts 27.1–28.14 can be structured according to the stop-overs on the route. After a summary "headline" mentioning the journey to Italy together with other prisoners in custody of the *centurio* Julius, a first stage describes the trip on a ship from Adramyttium in Palestine via Sidon and then, passing around Cyprus, through the Cilician and Pamphylian Seas to Myra in Lycia: Acts 27.2–5. In a more detailed passage Acts 27.6–44 describes the next phase, including a storm and the shipwreck, to an island with the Greek name Μελίτη on an Alexandrian ship.[26] On the island, the travellers spend the winter, running into new exciting adventures.

The extended passage Acts 27.6–44 can again be subdivided. Acts 27.6–8 report the first phase of the journey aboard the Alexandrian ship. The ship is sailing off Cnidus when a gale prevents the continuation of the journey. Finally, on lee side of Crete the ship arrives at *Kaloi Limenes*. Here, a conversation about possible hibernation and the subsequent departure to Phoenix takes place, pointing to the future catastrophe: vv. 9–13. Actually, the ship is caught in a storm named Eurakylon[27] which finally causes a shipwreck: vv. 14–44. Here, divergent stages can be distinguished, too: the crew's maneuvers to save the ship in the storm (vv. 14–20),

alledem nichts. Dann war er über die Paulusreisen nur sehr mangelhaft unterrichtet. Oder aber er schwieg von den früheren Schiffbrüchen, um nicht die Spannung bei der Geschichte von der Romreise zu mindern. Damit tut sich das Entweder/Oder auf: Unzureichende Überlieferung oder bewußt unhistorische Darstellung.' Blaming Luke does not help to understand his narrative and/or his theological achievement. If Luke knew anything about Paul's earlier shipwrecks, he kept his information for the final event which not only intends to entertain his readers like in ancient novels, but rather illustrates God's providential protection of the Gospel and those who preach it to bring it to Rome.

25. On the apostolic self-understanding of Paul cf. now, e.g., U. Schnelle, *Paulus. Leben und Denken* (W. de Gruyter Lehrbuch; Berlin, New York: W. de Gruyter, 2003), pp. 262–69.

26. Myra belongs to the route which Egyptian grain ships took on their way to Italy. The city of Rome imported 1/3 of its grain from Egypt (cf. Josephus, *War* II 386) through individual merchants (cf. Sueton, *Claud.* 18–19). Thus, the portrait of the scenery corresponds to contemporary economic customs; that can be illustrated by a passage from Lionel Casson: 'Probably the most ambitious maritime enterprise of the ancient world was the transport of the grain that Rome imported from Egypt, 150,000 tons which travelled annually from Alexandria to Rome during the first three centuries CE and required the services of a fleet of the biggest and fastest freighters available'. Grain is brought to Rome in spring when shipping resumes after the winter break. There are two possible divergent routes: a *southern lane* follows the North African shore and a *northern route* 'by way of Cyprus, Myra, Rhodes or Cnidos, south of Crete, Malta, Messina'. The latter is relevant for the Lukan report in Acts. The ships reach Italy in the beginning of May and then return for a second delivery of grain to Rome which ends just before the next winter break (L. Casson, *Ships and Seamanship in the Ancient World* [Baltimore, London: The Johns Hopkins University Press, 1995], pp. 297–98; quotations: 297). For the organization of Rome's food supply during the Early Empire cf. F. Kolb, *Rom. Die Geschichte der Stadt in der Antike* (Beck's Historische Bibliothek; München: Beck, 1995), pp. 514–39.

27. On the name of the storm cf. now M. Reiser, 'Von Caesarea nach Malta. Literarischer Charakter und historische Glaubwürdigkeit,' in F.W. Horn (ed.), *Das Ende des Paulus*, pp. 49–73 (62–67).

Paul's speech announcing eventual rescue (vv. 21–26),[28] and the actual rescue by running the ship aground (vv. 27–44). This literary structure corresponds to ancient analogies.[29] Distress and rescue including a description of the storm and its dangers, search for rescue in a protected mountain zone, throwing equipment overboard, divine appearances (e.g. an angel proclaiming salvation), the stranding, and finally the loss of the ship.

During the last episode the pace of the narrative slows down.[30] A comparatively short timespan is covered in a long and extended episode: the arrival on land, the plan of the seamen to flee, thwarted by Paul (27.27–32), Paul's call on the seamen to eat (27.33–8), and finally the stranding of the ship and Paul's rescue by the Roman officer (27.39–44). It is obvious that the headword 'salvation/rescue' is used twice: 27.43 (ὁ δὲ ἑκατοντάρχης βουλόμενος διασῶσαι τὸν Παῦλον): the officer tries to save Paul, and 27.44 (καὶ οὕτως ἐγένετο πάντας διασωθῆναι ἐπὶ τὴν γῆν): everybody is saved at this stage of the narrative – the passive verb may indicate a *passivum divinum*. The last rescue refers back to Paul's speech in 27.22ff., especially to the frame 27.22 and 27.26 announcing the stranding and the loss of the ship on the one hand and the survival of everyone on the other.[31] The angelophany does not eliminate the rescue of all seamen; however, it puts Paul into the centre of the scope, because he is ought to appear before Caesar. Hence, Paul's rescue fulfills the angels' proclamation. Simultaneously, saving Paul leads to the rescue of all: καὶ ἰδοὺ κεχάρισταί σοι ὁ θεὸς πάντας τοὺς πλέοντας μετὰ σοῦ (*and indeed, God has granted safety to all those who are sailing with you* [NRSV]; 27.24). The

28. On the rhetorical structure of Paul's speech cf. K. Löning, 'Das Gottesbild der Apostelgeschichte im Spannungsfeld von Frühjudentum und Fremdreligionen', in H.-J. Klauck (ed.), *Monotheismus und Christologie. Zur Gottesfrage im hellenistischen Judentum und im Urchristentum* (QD, 138; Freiburg *et al.*: Herder, 1992), pp. 88–117 (117).

29. The opinion of M. Reiser, 'Caesarea', p. 51, that there is 'keine wirkliche Parallele zu Act 27' demonstrates the necessity to clarify the term 'Parallele' but does not really give justice to the narrative motifs and structures of the parallels mentioned below (cf. n. 59). Furthermore, texts like the Homeric epics are well known in the Hellenistic world and belong to the *intellectual realm* of most ancient readers or hearers (to the term and its relevance cf. M. Labahn, '"Heiland der Welt". Der gesandte Gottessohn und der römische Kaiser – ein Thema johanneischer Christologie?', in *Zwischen den Reichen*, pp. 147–73 [147–48. *lit.*]), so that these texts belong to the material which should be taken into account if one attempts to understand the impact of a text on its reader – other texts, like the material referred to in this article, show how the ancients constructed meaning out of their fate by *narrating* these incidents sometimes in very abriged from and in different genres. An exegete should also take the impact of such texts into account in order to interpret the function of an ancient narrative plot. Therefore, Reiser's hints at '*literarische* Schilderungen wirklicher Seereisen' (Reiser, 'Caesarea', pp. 53–61 [italics are mine]) are helpful and provide a welcome supplement to the corpus of texts relevant to the interpretation of Acts 27.

30. On the narratologic function of variation of the 'narrated time' cf., e.g., G. Genette, *Die Erzählung* (2. Aufl., München: Fink, 1998), pp. 61–80; M. Martinez/M. Scheffel, *Einführung in die Erzähltheorie* (C.H. Beck Studium; München: C.H. Beck, 1999), pp. 39–44; J.H. Petersen, *Erzählsysteme. Eine Poetik epischer Texte* (Stuttgart, Weimar: Metzler, 1993), pp. 44–45.

31. On the element of saving prediction and subsequent salvation cf., e.g., R. Söder, *Die apokryphen Apostelgeschichten und die romanhafte Literatur der Antike* (Würzburger Studien zur Altertumswissenschaft, 3; Stuttgart: W. Kohlhammer, 1932), p. 166.

conformity of Paul's speech to the report of the angelophany, as well as the stranding of the ship and the rescue of Paul and all his companions demonstrate in an exemplary way that the tension is deliberately built up by Luke. This impression becomes even stronger if one notes that, at the same time, the announcement of the coming misfortune is analeptically picked up by Paul (27.10), thus making Acts 27.21–6 the hinge of the narrative.

According to Acts 28.11, another Alexandrian ship takes Paul and his companions to Italy. The travel route runs to Puteoli via Syracuse and Rhegium. Mentioning the arrival in Rome like a frame, Acts 28.14–6 describes the end of the voyage and at the same time opens the view at events happening now in Rome. On the way to Rome, an encouraging contact between Paul and local Christian brethren takes place (28.15), since the narrator remarks that Paul thanks God and regains courage (ἔλαβε θάρσος). Undoubtedly, Luke refers to the courage that only God can give and which Paul needs for his testimony – a testimony, that Paul will pass to the synagogue (28.17–22) and also through his bold, unhindered proclamation before all the people: Acts 28.30–1.

Acts 28.17–28 subdivides in three passages: first, an apology before the leaders of the Jews (οἱ ὄντες τῶν Ἰουδαίων πρῶτοι) in Rome: Acts 28.17–22, which covers Paul's speech (vv.18–20) and the reply of the leaders, that prepares the next scene (vv. 21–22). The next scene consists of a short report of Paul's missionary proclamation (28.23: *testifying to the kingdom of God and trying to convince them about Jesus both from the law of Moses and from the prophets* [*NRSV*]), which precedes a note on Paul's partial success[32] and thereafter a reflection on the relationship between gentiles and Jews in Paul's speech. Paul quotes Isa. 6.9–10; however, it may be disputed whether the quotation might refer to permanent obduracy and therefore indicates a fundamental shift from the Jews to the gentiles,[33] or if it allows a general openness (Acts 28.23–8).

Thus, in the pericope concerning the events in Rome, Luke still follows the principle expressed in Acts 13.46, namely that Paul first of all proclaims the Gospel in the Jewish synagogues.[34] Admittedly, Paul does not preach in Acts 28.17–22, but rather gives an apology for his appeal to Caesar. Preaching, indirectly mentioned in 28.23, happens only in a second step. That topic is worth to be taken seriously in view of Paul's deeds in Acts 28.17ff., a passage that does not present him as a 'Judenmissionar' to fulfill his job, as it was proposed by Jacob Jervell.[35] The quotation from Isaiah refutes Jervell's proposal, because Isa. 6 disassociates him from the Jewish community and prepares for the universal openness of the bold proclamation of the Gospel by Paul in 28.30–1.[36]

---

32. Shifts among the people are also reported in Acts 14.4; 17.32.

33. E.g., G. Schneider, *Apostelgeschichte*, pp. 408–409, 418–20.

34. Cf. already E. Zeller, *Die Apostelgeschichte nach ihrem Inhalt und Ursprung kritisch untersucht* (Stuttgart: C. Mäcken, 1854), p. 292; now, e.g., J. Jeska, *Die Geschichte Israels in der Sicht des Lukas. Apg 7,2b–53 und 13,17–25 im Kontext antik-jüdischer Summarien der Geschichte Israels* (FRLANT, 195; Göttingen: Vandenhoeck & Ruprecht, 2001), p. 246.

35. J. Jervell, *Die Apostelgeschichte* (MeyerK, 3, Göttingen: Vandenhoeck & Ruprecht, 1998), p. 623.

36. M. Rese, 'The Jews in Luke–Acts. Some Second Thoughts', in J. Verheyden (ed.), *The*

2. *Rescue from Peril at Sea as a Publicly Visible Deed of a Deity*

Travel in the ancient world[37] always was a dangerous business, but voyaging on sea presented an exceptional amount of danger.[38] Therefore, it comes by no surprise that the hardships of maritime travel are reflected in various texts from divergent literary genres. Apart from a potential threat to life, the risk of losing cargo and property was not far, aspects which are also mentioned quite often.[39] Already these remarks demonstrate that not every shipwreck does ultimately lead to death.

What is the function of the report of Paul's rescue in the last two chapters of Acts? John Clayton Lentz made an interesting proposal when he claims that 'the last eight chapters of Acts are encomiastic in nature'. This encomiastic function is especially present in Paul's depiction as a 'model Christian' and an 'example for his readers to respect and imitate'.[40] Undoubtedly, the portrait of Paul is thoroughly and crucially reshaped in this passage;[41] but Paul's rescue itself, as well as its narrative function within the literary context also have to be taken into account for the interpretation of the passage so that the apostle is not so much a Christian model, instead the whole passage reveals something about divine protection.

To interpret the passage, I would like to single out three examples of ancient shipwreck stories by different authors, underscoring the aspect of *divine saving* and divine grace connected with the rescue motif. Because the reports come from different literary genres, the various usages of the motif suggest its widespread circulation. All stories introduced here share the same character as a *public act of expressing gratitude to* the deity, which everyone who enjoyed such an act of divine favour had to perform. The public act of paying tribute to the deity resulted in different personal and religious consequences.[42]

Unity of Luke–Acts (BETL, 142; Leuven: Peeters, 1999) pp. 185–201 (201), pleads that there is 'not the slightest tract of an interest in the fate of the unbelieving Jews'. Differently, J. Jeska, *Geschichte*, p. 270: 'So kann geschlußfolgert werden, dass die Erstadressatenschaft des jüdischen Volkes auch über die Abkehr von den Juden in Rom (Apg 28,26–28) und das offene Ende der Apostelgeschichte hinaus gilt.'

37. Cf. in general, e.g., L. Casson, *Reisen in der Alten Welt* (München: Prestel, 1976; English edition: *Travel in the Ancient World* [London: Allen, 1974; London: Book Club Associates, 2nd edn, 1979); M. Giebel, *Reisen in der Antike* (Düsseldorf *et al.*: Artemis, 1999).

38. Cf. the Anacharsis' laconic remarks in Diogenes Laertius, *Vitae Philosophorum* I 104: 'To the question what vessels were the saftest his reply was, "Those which have been hauled ashore"', and in the same paragraph: 'When someone inquired which were more in number, the living or the dead, he rejoined, "In which category, then, do you place those who are on the seas?"' (Translation: R.H. Hicks, *Diogenes Laertius, Lives of Eminent Philosophers with an English Translation. vol. 1* [reprint; LCL; Cambridge, MA: Harvard University/London: Heinemann, 1991], p. 109). A minimum degree of security for one's life can only be attained by being on land; whoever is going aboard enters a situation between life and death.

39. E.g. Ailianos, *Epistulae* 18.

40. J.C. Lentz, Jr, *Luke's Portrait of Paul* (SNTS.MS, 77; Cambridge: Cambridge University Press, 1993), p. 63.

41. Cf. M. Labahn, 'Paulus', *passim* (with critical remarks on J.C. Lentz: *ibidem*, 78 n. 7).

42. Cf. R. Merkelbach, *Isis regina – Zeus Sarapis. Die griechisch-ägyptische Religion nach den*

Lucian, De Mercede Conductis Potentium Familiaribus 1:

So it was not without interest and attention that I listened to them while they spun yarns about their shipwreck and unlooked-for deliverance, just like the men with shaven heads who gather in crowds at the temples and tell of third waves, tempests, headlands, strandings, masts carried away, rudders broken, and to cap it all, how the Twin Brethren[43] appeared (they are peculiar to this sort of rhodo-montade), or how some other deus ex machina sat on the masthead or stood at the helm and steered the ship to a soft beach where she might break up gradually and slowly and they themselves get ashore safely by the grace and favour of the god (αὐτοὶ δὲ ἀσφαλῶς ἀποβήσεσθαι χάριτι καὶ εὐμενείᾳ τοῦ θεοῦ).

Those men, to be sure, invent the greater part of their tragical histories to meet their temporary need, in order that they may receive alms from a greater number of people by seeming not only unfortunate but dear to the gods (καὶ θεοφιλεῖς τινες εἶναι δοκοῦντες);...[44]

This text is written in scathing sarcasm – the address to the reader recalls well-known temple scenes which mention numerous people who claim to be favourites of the gods and thereby seek to gain the favour of their fellow humans in form of alms. Regardless of the exaggerations, one should not doubt that this is a typical scene. The structure of the rescue stories described by the beggars seems to be traditional, too: the sea voyage – storm and bad weather with catastrophic outcome – divine intervention (particularly of the Dioskouroi responsible for such events[45]) – the landing and destruction of the ship – and the rescue of all humans. This structure corresponds well with the report in Acts 27.1–44. However, it does not mean that I claim any literary dependence.

The lamenting beggars in Lucian located in temples of unspecified deities (πρὸς τοῖς ἱεροῖς) hope to get bigger alms by telling their stories. Most of all, the reasons given are interesting: the narrators earn particular alms because they are favoured by the gods: εὐμενείᾳ τοῦ θεοῦ. Having experienced deliverance from peril at sea honours the individual person for his or her rescue because it is due to a special proximity of the individual to the deity. Thus, the miraculous rescues were made public in sanctuaries, an act which aims at the individual's own advantage, according to the judgement of Lucian.

(2) The second type of texts – examples expressing personal gratitude due to a vow taken in actual distress –, which I want to consider in this chapter, also presents a public reaction to a deliverance from peril. Aelius Aristides, who still has not

---

Quellen dargestellt (Stuttgart, Leipzig: Teubner, 1995), p. 342: 'Wen Götter von Krankheit geheilt hatten, wer aus Seenot gerettet worden war und wer mit Hilfe der Götter im Prozeß gesiegt hatte, der war verpflichtet, öffentlich Dank abzustatten. Das geschah im Vorhof oder in den Räumen eines Tempels. Dort gab es immer ein Publikum, das durch erstaunliche Berichte unterhalten werden wollte.' The following quotation from Luc Merc 1 illustrates the scene Merkelbach mentioned.

43. Sc. the Dioskouroi.

44. Translation: A.M. Harmon, *Lucian with an English Translation in Eight Volumes III* (repr.; LCL, Cambridge, MA: Harvard University; London: Heinemann, 1947), pp. 413–15.

45. Cf., e.g., Euripides, *Electra* 1348–1355; Epictetus, *Dissertationes* II 19.28; Aelius Aristides, *Orationes* 43.25; Lucian, *Navigium* 9; cf. on this point briefly M. Labahn, *Offenbarung in Zeichen und Wort. Untersuchungen zur Vorgeschichte von Joh. 6,1–25a und seiner Rezeption in der Brotrede* (WUNT, II/117; Tübingen: Mohr-Siebeck, 2000), pp. 202–03 with n. 30.

received due attention for the understanding of contemporary Hellenistic religiosity,[46] links the origin of two hymns to a deliverance at sea.

First, I want to quote the relevant passages from his *Hymn to Zeus* (Aelius Aristides, *Orationes* 43.2–3):

> [2] … But I seem now to understand quite well that I was in great danger and lost my self-control because of the sea, when I made such a vow, which is not easy to fulfil, and attempting which perhaps inspires no confidence in my moderation, since I promised that I would deliver a hymn to Zeus, and at that in prose. [3] Indeed, then the sea was great and it made me do and say everything. Still – for no vow must be neglected, as they say, but any kind of payment is better than absolute neglect – let us try in some way or other to fulfil our religious obligation to the god.[47]

It is interesting to see, that the experience of rescue, which is explicitly ascribed to Zeus, is not combined with a portrayal of the saving act itself. He only briefly mentions his dispair and rescue at sea as reasons for the hymn. The poet publicly gives thanks to the god by celebrating him as creator and preserver of the world.[48] Regarding the content as well as the structure, this aspect sets Aelius Aristides' hymn apart from the rescue stories of the beggars reported by Lucian, as well as from Acts 27 and from various other ancient novels, which are mentioned as parallels for the portrait of Paul's deliverance in Acts.

In the Zeus hymn, Aristides praises the god for being an eminently effective protector of the world. The prose hymn somehow 'preaches' Zeus as creator (43.7–18) and preserver (43.19–28) of mankind. A similar assumption can also be made concerning the *Sarapis-Hymn*. After fundamental remarks about why he chose a prose hymn, Aelius Aristides turns to the nature and the acts of the Sarapis; yet at the end of the hymn, he specifies his reason for writing it (Aelius Aristides, *Orationes* 45.33):

> O universal light for all mankind, you who were recently manifested to us when, at the time that the vast sea rose from all sides and rushed in upon us and nothing was visible except the destruction which was approaching and had well-nigh arrived, you stretched out your hand, revealed the hidden heavens, and granted us to behold the earth and to make port, so much beyond our expectation that we were unconvinced even when we set foot on shore.[49]

In the reference to the reason for the hymn we find more information about the rescue from danger at sea than in the previously mentioned hymn to Zeus. The

---

46. Cf., e.g., S.C. Muir, 'Touched by a God: Aelius Aristides, Religious Healing, and Asclepius Cults', in *SBL.SP* 34 (1995), pp. 362–79 (362ff.).

47. Translation: P. Aelius Aristides, *The Complete Works. Vol. II. Orations XVII–LIII* (trans. into English by C.A. Behr; Leiden: E.J. Brill, 1981), p. 251.

48. Cf. J. Amann, *Die Zeusrede des Ailios Aristeides* (Tübinger Beiträge zur Altertumswissenschaft, 12; Stuttgart: W. Kohlhammer, 1931), pp. 28–46.

49. Translation: P. Aelius Aristides, *Complete Works II*, p. 268; for the interpretation cf., e.g., A. Höfler, *Der Sarapishymnus des Ailios Aristeides* (Tübinger Beiträge zur Altertumswissenschaft, 27; Stuttgart-Berlin: W. Kohlhammer, 1935).

occasion for the hymn is also not more than the structuring topic of the hymn. This contains a more comprehensive reflection about the activity of the god Sarapis and about the way, how his actions benefit mankind.

(3) The last exemplary text, which ought to be introduced here, represents a third literary genre, the genre of inscriptions and epigrams, in which public gratitude is expressed for rescue from distress at sea.[50] First, I come to the inscription of a certain Theodotus from the temple of Pan in El-Kanais near Edfu (*CIJ* II 1537; second or first century BCE):

> Praise for god. Theodotus, son of Dorion, a Jew, he was saved from open sea.[51,52]

Like in the texts previously mentioned, the rescue from distress at sea is made public by giving thanks to the god for the preservation of one's life.[53] If the god is to be identified either with Pan or with Yahweh is still a matter of debate.[54] An explicit portrayal of the act of deliverance is absent.

50.   Inscriptions and epigrams as well as the erection of votive tablets share a custom of giving thanks to gods for sea-rescue to which a scholiast to Juvenal, *Sat.* 12.28 provides information: '*Antiquitus enim solebant qui naufragio liberati essent pro voto pingere tabellas et in templo Isidis ponere*'; text and German translation by R. Merkelbach, *Isis regina*, p. 67.

51.   Similar expressions are also to be found in non-public texts like the letter of Apion to his father Epimachos: 'I thank the lord Serapis that when I was in danger at sea he straightaway saved me' (ὅτι μου κινδυνεύσαντος εἰς θάλασσαν ἔσωσε εὐθέως; *BGU* II 423,6–8; translation: A.S. Hunt and C.C. Edgar, *Select Papyri I. Non-Literary Papyri Private Affairs* [repr.; LCL; London: Heinemann/Cambridge, MA: Harvard University Press, 1952], p. 305; cf. H.-J. Klauck, *Die antike Briefliteratur und das Neue Testament. Ein Lehr- und Arbeitsbuch* [UTB, 2022; Paderborn et al.: Schöningh, 1998] pp. 29–33). According to this parallel, I prefer a translation of the inscription from the Pan temple which presupposes a situation of explicit distress at sea instead of assuming just a fortunate ending of travel on sea (considered by W. Horbury, and D. Noy, *Jewish Inscriptions*, p. 121: 'saved from the sea'). Admittedly, the safe arrival at a harbour, e.g. at the time of the winter break of seafaring, may be regarded as saving from sea: cf. Theophylaktos Simokattes Ep. 61.

52.   θεοῦ εὐλογία· | Θεύ[ο]δοτος Δωρίωνος | Ἰουδαῖος σωθεὶς ἐκ με|λ<άγ>ους (W. Horbury, and D. Noy, *Jewish Inscriptions of Graeco-Roman Egypt* [Cambridge: Cambridge University Press, 1992], nº 121). On the inscription cf., e.g., W. Horbury, and D. Noy, *Jewish Inscriptions*, pp. 208–09, M.H. Williams, 'The Meaning and Function of Ioudaios in Graeco-Roman Inscriptions', *ZPE* 111 (1997), pp. 249–62 (255); M. Labahn, *Offenbarung*, pp. 203–04.

53.   Prof. Dr. Bernd Janowski, Tübingen, kindly drew my attention to the interesting article by W. Röllig, 'Altorientalische Schiffsmetaphorik', in V. Drehsen, D. Henke, R. Schmidt-Rost, W. Steck (eds.), *Der „ganze Mensch'. Perspektiven lebensgeschichtlicher Individualität* FS D. Rössler (Arbeiten zur praktischen Theologie, 10; Berlin, New York: W. de Gruyter, 1997), pp. 13–18, who analyses an ensemble of inscriptions and graffiti from a chamber grave in Ḥirbet Bēt Layy (seventh century BCE). Next to pictures of ships, we find pleas to Yahweh for rescue of a mother in cases of giving birth to a child. If one considers the location of the graffiti found close to maritime imagery, one may understand them as articulating dangers of giving birth compared to dangers at sea, an interpretation which can be established on grounds of metaphorical comparisons with ancient parallels.

54.   The find context of the inscription suggests to take it as a dedicatory inscription to Pan. M. Hengel, *Juden, Griechen und Barbaren. Aspekte der Hellenisierung des Judentums in vorchristlicher Zeit* (*SBS*, 76; Stuttgart: KBW, 1976), p. 142, argues for an identification of Pan

An epigram of Philippos from Thessalonike (first half of the first century BC) goes a step further. Sacrificial offerings given to the deity as a sign of gratitude for rescue on sea are connected with a further request (*Anthologia Graeca* 6.231):

A   O Ruler over the black earth of Egypt,[55] Goddess within the linen dress,/ exercise your very holy priesthood! /

B   because for you there lays as offer on a tablet an unpretentious cake / and a pair of grey gooses living on the water / and dried nard with grainy dried figs all around, / and raisins and sweet breathing incense.[56] /

C   Save Damis, like (once) from distress on sea, also from poverty (εἰ δ' ὡς ἐκ πελάγους ἐρρύσαο Δᾶμιν, ἄνασσά, κἠκ πενίης), /

D   o Queen – than he will offer you a male fawn with golden horns.[57]

Arranged in four parts: (A) address, (B) description of the offerings demonstrating Philippos' gratitude, (C) request and (D) vow to give another offering if the deity acts favourably, the epigram made the rescue public. At the same time, having gained the previous favour triggers a new, quite general request for prosperity (εἰ ὡς). The motivation to ask a new favour obviously results from the fact that Philippus acknowledged the divine intervention as act of special appreciation by the deity. Thus, the epigram shares that aspect with the self-definition of the beggars in the Lucian scene discussed above. The request is again connected with the promise of a more luxurious offer corresponding to the more substantial divine saving act.

If one asks for the *pragmatics*[58] of Acts 27 in the context of the conclusion of the narrative and if one looks for meaning in other ancient parallels, the interest should not merely be restricted to the well known narrative parallels from ancient novels.[59]

However, these remarks do not intend to argue against the value of the ancient narrative parallels for the depiction of Paul's shipwreck in Acts. On the contrary,

---

with Yahweh by its Jewish dedicator which seems to be highly plausible. Another proposal comes from William Horbury and David Noy (*Jewish Inscriptions*, p. 208) who stress the frame and the location of the inscription and argue against an identification with Pan.

55. Isis.

56. On the connection of rescue from distress at sea and offerings cf. also *Achilles Tatios* 1.1.

57. For the interpretation of the epigram cf. R. Merkelbach, *Isis regina*, p. 98 n. 12.

58. On the methodological approach cf., e.g., W. Egger, *Methodenlehre zum Neuen Testament. Einführung in linguistische und historisch-kritische Methoden* (Freiburg *et al.*: Herder, 3rd edn, 1993), §10.

59. For a comprehensive list cf. E. Plümacher, *Lukas als hellenistischer Schriftsteller. Studien zur Apostelgeschichte* (StUNT, 9; Göttingen: Vandenhoeck & Ruprecht, 1972), pp. 14–15 n. 43: Lucian, *Toxaris vel Amicitia* 19–20; *Verae Historiae* I 6; *Navigium* 7–9; *Achilles Tatios* 3.1–5; *Chariton* 3.3.10; Heliodorus, *Aethiopia* 5.27 und Historia Apollonii regis Tyri 11–2; P. Dublin C 3 (cf. now: R. Küssl, *Papyrusfragmente griechischer Romane. Ausgewählte Untersuchungen* [Classica Monacensia, 2; Tübingen: Narr, 1991], pp. 103–40). Cf. already E. Norden, *Agnostos Theos. Untersuchungen zur Formengeschichte religiöser Rede* (repr.; Darmstadt: WBG, 1956), p. 313. Other ancient texts frequently considered parallels to Acts 27 are the Homeric ship voyaging narratives; e.g., D.R. MacDonald, 'The Shipwrecks of Odysseus and Paul', *NTS* 45 (1999), pp. 88–107, who regards these texts as model followed by Luke in Acts 27.

they illustrate that the positive outcome of his shipwreck was due to divine will, respectively to the plan of Tyche. Therefore, the ancient parallels are close to Acts 27 in a central point. If one follows Reinhold Merkelbach[60] and assumes that such novels serve a religious aim for a community – which is in the form proposed by Merkelbach far from universally accepted –,[61] then there is an even more remarkable proximity, because in both cases the narrative serves the self-assurance of a community. The connection of rescue and proclamation, just as in Acts 27–28, is amply illustrated through the pragmatics of the texts discussed here.

(1) In terms of function, the texts introduced in this chapter show that stories about rescue at sea *generally aim at the public*. Deliverance from maritime dangers require public acts of gratitude performed by the rescued person for the helpful deity. The catchword 'gratitude' is, by the way, neither explicitly mentioned in Hellenistic texts nor in Acts 28.30–1 (nor in the entire context Acts 27–28); the religious function of the gratitude, however, is expressed by the location of the acts of gratitude (a sanctuary), by a vow, or by a sacrificial offering. Thus, the term 'gratitude' is derived from texts describing the behaviour of a person after having been rescued from peril (i.e. setting up a votive tablet, etc.).[62]

(2) The public expression of gratitude does not necessarily need to contain a description of the rescue itself nor its circumstances. The point made publicly, rather, is to be seen in the activity of the deity – although the divine activity is not limited to the rescuing acts alone – like Aristides' hymns show. The public response to the deity's activity proclaims *the nature and the character of the deity in general* – and may it only materialize in bigger alms from people visting sanctuaries.

(3) The presentation of the rescue creates *confidence in continuing help from the deity for the rescued person*.

A similar function can be found in Acts 27–28. The rescue of Paul and his companions *aims at public recognition*. The purpose of the last two chapters of Acts is to present Paul's proclamation of the kingdom of God to the inhabitants of Rome. Rome is the final destination where public and unhindered proclamation by Paul can take place because of his survival at sea. The rescue from shipwreck may perhaps also underscore the motif of Paul's innocence, but it certainly means more: Paul's rescue demonstrates that God himself is acting. In connection with the reader-guiding, programmatic statement in Acts 27.24, the danger and rescue at sea emphasize that Paul's public proclamation of the Gospel is authorized by God – although the public response undisputedly shifts from self-defense before Caesar (which is given as motivation for the trip to Rome) to final proclamation before all who want to listen. Even if the orientation towards the public in rescue stories is motivated differently in ancient texts (display of gratitude or hope for alms) than in Acts 27–28 – the closest parallels come from Aristides who uses the rescue as

60. R. Merkelbach, *Roman und Mysterium in der Antike* (München: C.H. Beck, 1962), who forcefully claimed that the extant ancient novels are 'Mysterientexte'.

61. In his critique of Merkelbach's thesis, T. Hägg, *Novel*, pp. 101–04 accepts that there is a 'religious component': 'Even on the surface religion plays a remarkably important role. Gods, oracles, cults of different kinds are organically integrated into the course of events'.

62. See above page 68 n. 50.

motivation for his encomium of the deity –, the pragmatics of Acts 27.24 can still be placed within ancient literary narrative customs.

3. *The Bold Proclamation of the Kingdom of God*

As mentioned previously, the problems of the final chapters of Acts exist due to the logic of the text itself, insofar as the narrator insists on Paul's appeal to Caesar in the last two chapters, but neither mentions a trial nor Paul's end, which still seems to be known to the author.[63] Various theories attempt to solve the problem by either assuming that the author intended to write a more extensive, but never finished book, or that some information was deleted for unknown reasons.[64] A possible explanation for the problems in Acts 27–28 seems not to lie in historical or literary historical options or operations. The entire text under consideration is the object of our interpretation; the author raises an expectation which he does not fulfil in the way expected by the reader. In the beginning we have referred to the literary technique of *narrative gaps (Erzähl-Leerstellen)*, which, according to Wolfgang Iser, work by provoking a reader's judgement and establishing his or her own estimation.[65] That means for the end of Acts that Paul's free proclamation as well as God's will and the guidance of the Sprit need to be seen as parts of one and the same plot. Daniel Marguerat made an important proposal which should be taken into account in all further investigations of the aporia in Acts 27–28 when pointed to the concept of 'Rhetoric of Silence', a narrative clue by which the reader supplements the end of the book from information provided in the rest of the entire narrative.[66]

The end of Paul's activity and thereby the end of his life are referred to in Acts 28.30 by the aorist ἐνέμεινεν indicating a limited remaining timespan (διετίαν ὅλην).[67] In light of the narrative stream of the entire text[68] it is unlikely that the text suggests Paul's release.[69] The final sentence of Acts is of special importance here:

κηρύσσων τὴν βασιλείαν τοῦ θεοῦ
καὶ διδάσκων τὰ περὶ τοῦ κυρίου Ἰησοῦ Χριστοῦ
μετὰ πάσης παρρησίας ἀκωλύτως (v.31).

---

63. The problem is convincingly stated by D. Marguerat, 'End of Acts', pp. 74–75.

64. Cf. the interpretation of G. Schneider, *Apostelgeschichte*, p. 411.

65. W. Iser, 'Indeterminacy and the Reader's Response in Prose Fiction', in J.H. Miller (ed.), *Aspects of Narrative. Selected Papers from the English Institute* (New York, London: Columbia University Press, 1971), pp. 1–45; U. Eco, *Lector in fabula. Die Mitarbeit der Interpretation in erzählenden Texten* (3. Aufl., München, Deutscher Taschenbuch Verlag, 1998), pp. 63–64.

66. Cf. basically D. Marguerat, 'End of Acts', pp. 75–82; *ad* Acts 27–28: *ibidem*, pp. 82ff.

67. Cf. D. Marguerat, 'End of Acts', pp. 87–88.

68. Cf. above p. 59 n. 15.

69. According to B. Rapske, *The Book of Acts*, p. 2, all juridical conflicts in the Lukan depiction primarily intend 'to defend or justify the prisoner missionary Paul to the reader'. However, Rapske presupposes that the Lukan story primarily seeks to present Paul's final release which Acts does not contain anymore (cf. *ibidem*, p. 191).

> proclaiming the kingdom of God
> and teaching about the Lord Jesus Christ
> with all boldness and without hindrance (v.31; NRSV).

Paul's activity is described with two parallel expressions: κηρύσσων (proclaiming) and διδάσκων (teaching). By proclaiming the kingdom of God, Paul participates in Jesus' own activity[70] which is now reactivated in Rome and which is open to be accepted by 'all, who entered' (Acts 28.30). The term πάντες takes up Acts 1.8, literally, 'all who are willing to enter' are those who enter Paul's apartment. However, πᾶς is an open term. It includes the expectation that the Christian message will reach the 'world's end'. The proclamation of the kingdom of God corresponds to the duty with which the earthen Jesus is characterized in his initial preaching in Nazareth after his temptation (Lk. 4.18–9) and in his first healings in Lk. 4.43–4 (cf. Lk. 8.1).[71] At the end of the Miletus speech, Paul mentions his approaching death and characterizes his own work in Asia Minor as ἐν οἷς διῆλθον κηρύσσων τὴν βασιλείαν (Acts 20.25).

According to Acts 18.1, Paul's activity in Corinth could be described as διδάσκων ἐν αὐτοῖς τὸν λόγον τοῦ θεοῦ (see also 15.35). The teaching of the Lord Jesus Christ corresponds to the word of God and contrasts the false accusations of the rebellious Jews from Asia Minor accusing Paul to disturb the (Jewish) people by teaching against the law and its temple (21.28). Furthermore, Paul's message corresponds to the activity of Jesus himself: cf. Lk. 4.31; 5.17; 13.10, 22 etc. Paul conveys the Christian message of salvation in a powerful as well as fundamental way and brings it especially to all those who are willing to listen to it (Acts 28.30).

It is underscored that Paul's speech happens μετὰ πάσης παρρησίας (v. 31). The frankness, which recalls the Greek democratic ideal of free speech,[72] is linked by Luke especially to the apostolic proclamation.[73] The connection between Luke's

---

70. Cf., e.g., J.D.G. Dunn, *The Acts of the Apostles* (Narrative Commentaries; Valley Forge, PA: Trinity Press International, 1996), p. 356.

71. The combination of the proclamation of God's kingdom with the title 'kyrios' leads C. Burfeind, 'Paulus', pp. 89–91, to his crucial political interpretation, assuming a critical attitude against Rome and Caesar within the last verses of Acts.

72. On the term παρρησία in general cf. e.g., A. Momigliano, 'Freedom of Speech in Antiquity', in P.P. Wiener (ed.), *Dictionary of the History of Ideas. Studies of Selected Pivotal Ideas II* (New York: Charles Scribner's Sons, 1973), pp. 252–63; see also M. Foucault, *Diskurs und Wahrheit. Die Problematisierung der Parrhesia* (ed. by J. Pearson; Internationaler Merve-Diskurs, 197; Berlin: Merve, 1996); M. Labahn, 'Die παρρησία des Gottessohnes im Johannesevangelium. Theologische Hermeneutik und philosophisches Selbstverständnis', in J. Frey, and U. Schnelle (eds.), *Kontexte des Johannesevangeliums. Das vierte Evangelium in religions- und traditionsgeschichtlicher Perspektive* (WUNT; Tübingen: Mohr-Siebeck, 2004) (in print) – on the term in Acts: S.C. Winter, 'Παρρησία in Acts', in J.T. Fitzgerald (ed.), *Friendship, Frankness and Flattery of Speech. Studies on Friendship in the New Testament World* (NT.Sup, 82; Leiden: E.J. Brill, 1996), pp. 185–202.

73. In his pentecostal preaching, Peter talks about David μετὰ παρρησίας, articulating that when David died he already expressed hope in God to fulfil his promise (2 Sam. 7), which materialized in the resurrection of Christ. Against the threat of the 'high priests' and the elders the Jerusalem community asks for the proclamation of the divine word μετὰ παρρησίας (Acts 4.29). Their plea is immediately fulfilled by the gift of the spirit, that comes, penetrates the community, and leads to proclamation μετὰ παρρησίας (28.31).

final statement and his depiction of the early Christian community in Jerusalem can hardly be ignored and enables us to understand the final statement of Acts as intentional strategy and, according to Aristotle's sense, as successful conclusion of Acts or even of the entire Lukan two-volume work.[74] Paul's preaching and teaching proclaims the Jesus-based message of the earliest congregation. It is a teaching full of the Spirit and in freedom, which maintains continuity with the early congregation and Jesus and which brings the Spirit-guided proclamation of Acts closer to its aim (cf. Acts 1.8).

After all, the way of the proclamation is a way to the gentiles. Paul's apology and proclamation before the leaders of the Jewish community in Rome are presupposed and have created division among the Jews (28.24–5), but did not cause any acceptance of Paul's message (28.26–7 quoting Isa. 6.9–10). The program 'first to the Jewish people' seems to come to its end. Although the separation among the Jews may still contain a silent expectation that at least some Jews might accept Paul's bold and unhindered proclamation, his message is now universally open and addressed to all people (cf. 28.30: and welcomed all [πάντας] who came to him [*NRSV*]). Insofar the reaction in Acts 28.28 is connected with a formulation alluding to Isa. 40.5(LXX), the narrator closely links the end of his second book to the beginning of his first: Lk. 3.6.[75] The powerful proclamation is directed to all gentiles and Jews without any privilege; this sort of proclamation stands in accordance and in continuation with God's will, which resumes the activity of Jesus himself.

The last word of Acts is a *hapax legomenon* in the New Testament. Pauls proclamation happens 'unhindered' (ἀκωλύτως). Sometimes, exegetes have referred to the juridical meaning of the term – it can be found in Papyri of the second century CE[76]–, and assumed the passage implies Luke's assurance that the Roman authorities declared the Christian message innocuous.[77] Nevertheless, the objective of the final statement is not so much the Roman authority than the Christian community; the proclamation will go its way – it can neither be restricted nor hindered. That means that Luke's text is a closely composed whole, but as a hermenutically open text it provokes further reflection, it is in fact open to address future generations as well. This means that not Paul the proclaimer is important, rather the proclamation he brought.[78] At the end of Luke's second book, the perspective of the narrator shifts from the Paul's individual fate to the decisive matter itself. The proclamation is driven forward by the Spirit and has finally reached its destination through Paul's appeal to Caesar. Thus, Paul's presupposed death does not object against

---

74. Cf. G. Schille, *Die Apostelgeschichte des Lukas* (ThHK, 5; Berlin: EVA, 3rd edn, 1989), p. 480.

75. Cf. H.-J. Klauck, *Magie und Heidentum in der Apostelgeschichte des Lukas* (SBS, 167; Stuttgart: KBW, 1996), p. 134, hinting also to the hymn of praise by Simon, Lk. 2.30–2.

76. P.Oxy. III 502.31; VIII 1127.16.

77. Vgl. H.W. Tajra, *The Trial of St. Paul. A Juridical Exegesis of the Second Half of the Acts of the Apostles* (WUNT, II/35; Tübingen: Mohr-Siebeck, 1989), p. 193.

78. Cf. P. Pokorný, 'Romfahrt', p. 233: Paul 'steht im Schatten seiner Verkündigung des Reiches Gottes und des Herrn Jesus Christus'; see also *idem, Theologie der lukanischen Schriften* (FRLANT, 174; Göttingen: Vandenhoeck & Ruprecht, 1998), p. 27; cf. my remarks in *Bib.* 80 (1999), pp. 433–38 (435).

the assumption of a Spirit-led and God-favoured proclaiming church, because the proclamation finally reaches its intended destination supported by God's protection. The death of the proclaimer is integrated in the overall purpose of the Lukan narrative, which finally reaches its destination.[79]

4. *Conclusions*

Acts 27–28 provide a deliberately crafted conclusion of the narrative of Acts. This observation will have to be taken into account as an interpretative key to the narrative aporias of this passage in general. The above mentioned ancient parallels are analogies permitting a more precise understanding of the final composition that Luke created at the end of his writing. However, I do not intend to consider them as indicating any direct literary relationship.

Paul, not only innocent, but recognized as innocent, makes his way to Italy and Rome; he himself appeals to Caesar in order to promote the spread of the Gospel, a development which results from the guidance of the Spirit. Acts 27–28 tell the story of Paul's transfer to Rome as a narrative about shipwreck and rescue – a story which leads into a *crisis* and its solution produces a hero (the proclaimer) and a subject (the proclamation) that come out of the managed crisis stronger than before. Both follow the *favour of God* and demonstrate that the gospel, *God's story with Jesus* will finally *spread out into the general public*.

The story contains a deep religious dimension, like it has already been shown in different contributions to Acts 27. Admittedly, the point of the story, first of all, is not to prove Paul's justice or innocence as Gary B. Miles and Garry Trompf assume to justify the relatively open end of Acts.[80] Paul is already vindicated as innocent before he makes his way to Rome. In contrast to the ancient texts mentioned by Miles/Trompf and later by David Ladouceur,[81] Paul suffers a shipwreck which might have indicated his guilt rather than his innocence. Only if Acts 27 is read as part of the overall composition including the survival of a poisonous snake bite (Acts 28.3–6), the shipwreck episode as well as Paul's lucky rescue emphasize Paul's innocence, a conclusion already given before.[82]

Another proposal was raised by F. Scott Spencer, who sees Paul's shipwreck and the capture already told before as a dynamic process of loss and regain of status.[83] However, Luke's portrait of Paul as '*homo honestus et iustus*' seems to contradict the notion that captivity and shipwreck can be taken as indicators for loss and restoration of status.[84] However, it has to be admitted that there is a dynamic

---

79. Luke incorporates historical traditions in his narrative strategy, so that the fact that the narrator uses the appeal to Caesar and the accounts in Jerusalem to reach the goal of his narrative plot may be due to historical memory.

80. G.B. Miles, and G. Trompf, 'Luke and Antiphon', p. 266.

81. D. Ladouceur, 'Hellenistic Preconceptions of Shipwreck and Pollution as a Context for Acts 27–28', *HTR* 73 (1980), pp. 435–49.

82. Cf. M. Labahn, 'Paulus', pp. 89–90.

83. F.C. Spencer, 'Paul's Odyssey in Acts: Status Struggles and Island Adventures', *BTB* 28 (1998), pp. 150–59 (156).

84. Cf. M. Labahn, 'Paulus', pp. 78–79.

element in the narration itself. Paul's shipwreck poses a serious danger for the final conclusion of Acts. Here, everything which has been of any importance so far is put into question. Simultaneously, the prospect of the final rescue of Paul and his companions is secured through the divine plan to bring Paul to Rome – God's perservance is therefore acknowledged through the crisis itself (27.23–4).

A story of shipwreck and rescue, located in a temple by Lucian and considered typical, has its particular place in the entire context of Acts.[85] Aelius Aristeides dedicates his encomion/hymn to Zeus and to Sarapis because he saw them responsible for his rescue from shipwreck. Inscriptions found in sanctuaries like the graffiti in the Pan Temple near Edfu (*CIJ* II 1537) show public expressions of gratitude to a deity for deliverance from shipwreck.

Thus, rescue is granted by gods and the *fact of being rescued was made public* as an act of gratitude *for the promotion of the benevolent deity. The bold proclamation of the kingdom of God is also directed towards the general public, including the transfer of Paul to Rome*: shipwreck and rescue attain their goal by Paul's survival as the one who is obliged to bring the message of his rescue and deliverance by God to the public in Rome, a message not concerned with God's help in shipwreck, but about God who wants to be the saviour of all mankind, the saviour of those who are ready to accept the proclamation (27.24).[86] However, it should not be overlooked that the readers have the story of shipwreck and rescue in mind when they hear the Lukan passage of proclamation – they knew that both themes are connected by the author.

The element that 'ein *göttlicher, übernatürlicher Schutz* ... waltet und immer gerade im *Augenblick der höchsten Not* eingreift und aus jeglicher Gefahr ... rettet', plays an important role in the narrative.[87] Hence, that aspect includes a special message: the hero will not only be saved himself, he even guarantees rescue for all (27.24). Paul and his presence, however, will only provide rescue insofar as Paul manages to bring the message of God's kingdom to the public (cf. Acts 28.6); for that purpose, he is protected by God.

In this context, biographical questions concerning the fate of Paul in Rome become less important; reporting the negative outcome of Paul's adventures and eventually his death[88] – already indicated in Acts 20.17–35 (see also 20.38; 21.11) – would be counterproductive for the narrative strategy. The 'biographical' passage

---

85. The Lukian reference can also be read as indicating a special feature of a rescued individual, because the writer mentions, not without irony, that telling those stories offers a high amount of alms because the stories report a particular divine merit.

86. Cf. J.C. O'Neill, *The Theology of Acts in Its Historical Setting* (London: SPCK, 1961), pp. 156–57.

87. R. Söder, *Apostelgeschichten*, p. 162; on this narrative motif cf. the whole §9 (pp. 162–71). V.K. Robbins, 'By Land and By Sea: The We-Passages and Ancient Sea Voyages,' in C.H. Talbert (ed.), *Perspectives on Luke–Acts* (Perspectives in Religious Studies. Special Studies Series, 5; Danville, VA: Association of Baptist Professors of Religion, 1978), pp. 215–42 (233) identifies god's saving activity in the light of an ancient seafaring stories as the clue of the seastorm narrative: 'Divine destiny holds the controlling hand when storm and shipwreck dash ships and mortals back and forth upon the sea'.

88. Cf., e.g., U. Schnelle, *Paulus*, pp. 425–31.

of Paul's rescue promulgates God's activity and his saving act. God's activity and Paul's rescue refer to Rome. The 'gap' between Paul's appeal to Caesar and his free proclamation is due to the deliberate intention to present the bold proclamation in Rome, the most significant city of the Roman *princeps* and the centre of the entire ancient world as the final destination and climax of the literary strategy of Acts. God himself guarantees the freedom of proclamation in Rome by his own activity – mentioned only indirectly by the divine δεῖ (Acts 27.24),[89] but already obvious in ancient sea rescue stories mentioning divine favour.

Luke presents his entire narrative in Luke-Acts by a circle linking the sea rescue episode with the beginning of Jesus' ministry (Lk. 4.18–9, 43–4). The entire Lukan document reaches its final destination in Rome, the climax, where the bold proclamation guaranteed by God's will takes place. If – as it is very likely – Luke knew of Paul's death, than he expected a continuation of the Gospel proclamation in the light of Paul's rescue[90] and its triumphal progression from Rome[91] – a triumphal progression which later produced numerous martyrs and also caused sometimes fatal results which the Lukan narrator probably did not at all expect. The rescue stands for Luke's expectation that God will continue to protect the proclamation. Even in a disaster – like during a shipwreck – rescue will come in order to bring the gospel to its final destination; therefore, not even a catastrophe like Paul's death in Rome to which Luke only alludes to can restrict the expectation of a continuous proclamation which Paul once has started in Rome. The rescue from peril at sea rather symbolizes the progress of the proclamation which can by no means be interrupted.[92] In that way the proclaimer has to stay behind the proclamation, and the dynamics of Acts are concentrated on the divine δεῖ (Acts 27.24) which will bring the proclamation 'to the ends of the earth' (Acts 1.8 [NRSV]).[93]

89.   C.H. Cosgrave, 'The Divine Δεῖ in Luke–Acts. Investigations into the Lukan Understanding of God's Providence', *NT* 26 (1984), pp. 168–90 (173, 178–79: refering to Acts 27.24, etc.), stresses the correlation of human and divine will. According to the Lukan portrait, Paul can easily be integrated into the scenario of divine will because he plays an outstanding role in it, as can be shown from the careful social and religious shaping of his portrait by the narrator.

90.   Therefore, the city of Rome is more than the final destination in the Lukan portrait in Acts, envisaged in Acts 1.8, so that the narrative is not just a model for later 'imperial' constructions of time linked with a kind of symbolic value of Rome (cf. to this A. Assmann, *Zeit und Tradition. Kulturelle Strategien der Dauer* [Beiträge zur Geschichtskultur, 15; Köln *et al.*: Böhlau, 1999], pp. 25–27; to the term: pp. 24–31).

91.   Cf. A. Hummel, 'Factum und fictum. Literarische und theologische Erwägungen zur Romreise des Paulus in der Apostelgeschichte (Apg 27,1–28,16)', *BN* 105 (2000), pp. 39–53 (53).

92.   Cf. P. Seul, *Rettung*, p. 524.

93.   I am grateful to Jürgen Zangenberg for a revision of the English of my article.

OLIVE TREES AND ETHNICITIES.
JUDEANS AND GENTILES IN ROM. 11.17–24[1]

Caroline Johnson Hodge

Christianity is widely understood, by both scholars and laypeople, to be separate from and immune to differences related to kinship and ethnicity. People perceive Christianity as a 'universal' religion, one that transcends ethnic and familial particularities. Denise Kimber Buell calls attention to such scholarly portrayals of early Christianity: 'Most historical reconstructions published in the last 20 years depict earliest Christianity as an inclusive movement that rejected ethnic or racial specificity as a condition of religious identity.'[2]

Those who claim such a de-ethnicized Christianity fail to recognize that certain aspects of Judean culture are normative for Christians and that historically, Christians rank Judean culture over pagan or polytheistic culture. Christians have accepted the Judean master narrative, the story of this particular ethnic people, the God of their homeland, their myths about creation and the ordering of the cosmos, and the morals inscribed in their sacred scripture. Yet Christians – with the support of Pauline scholarship – have translated these particular markers of identity into an ethnically neutral, all-inclusive tradition which is somehow beyond the normal human characteristics of culture, its discourses and practices.

---

1.   This article was first presented as a paper at the Society of Biblical Literature International Meeting, July 10, 2001 (Rome). This research stems from a larger project on kinship and ethnicity in Paul which began as a dissertation (C. Johnson Hodge, ' "If Sons, Then Heirs": A Study of Kinship and Ethnicity in Paul's Letters' [PhD dissertation, Brown University, 2002], and is now forthcoming with Oxford University Press). Page numbers in this article refer to the dissertation version.

2.   D.K. Buell, 'Rethinking the Relevance of Race for Early Christian Self-Definition', *HTR* 94 (2001), pp. 449–76 (453). Buell quotes Frank Snowden who claims, 'Christianity swept racial distinctions aside' (*Before Color Prejudice: The Ancient View of Blacks* [Cambridge, MA: Harvard University Press, 1983], p. 99) and Rosemary Radford Reuther who remarks, 'class, ethnicity, and gender are…specifically singled out as the divisions overcome by redemption in Christ' ('Sexism and God-Language,' in J. Plaskow and C.P. Christ (eds.), *Weaving the Visions: New Patterns in Feminist Spirituality* [San Francisco: Harper and Row, 1989], pp. 151–62 [156]). Buell's article is based on the research from her forthcoming book: *'Why This New Race?': Ethnic Reasoning in Early Christianity* (New York: Columbia University Press, forthcoming). I am grateful to Buell for making the manuscript for the book available to me before publication; I have benefited greatly from our many conversations about our common topic and I am particularly grateful for her comments on a draft of this article.

In traditional Pauline scholarship, this portrait of Christianity as a universal, transcendent religion that escapes the particularities of history and culture has been located in and justified by the letters of Paul. Interpreters claim that Paul – by allegedly rejecting his own Judean identity and forming non-ethnic communities of 'Christians' – eliminates ethnicity or at least separates it from what is important about Christianity.[3]

I seek to challenge this perception of an ethnically-neutral 'Christianity' in Paul. In the following two-part analysis of Romans, I draw upon recent work in anthropology, Classics, and early Christianity which highlights the importance of ethnicity to religious identity and social formation.[4] My approach affords a new way to read Paul's olive tree metaphor of Rom. 11.17–24 and demonstrates that Paul did not imagine a new group of Judeans and gentiles united as 'Christians'. Rather, he envisioned a more complex scenario in which the gentiles-in-Christ are affiliated with Judeans as an associate people who share the same ancestor, Abraham.[5]

Two related points support this contention. First, the olive tree image should be understood in terms of kinship and ethnicity. Paul takes advantage of a popular motif in ancient literature in which agricultural images serve as metaphors for familial and ethnic relationships. Second, Paul uses this arboreal image both to link and to rank Judeans and gentiles as distinct peoples of the Judean God. This picture of a 'family tree' allows Paul to articulate a hierarchy in which the Judeans – as 'natural' branches or descendants – enjoy a more secure status than gentiles, the grafted branches or adopted descendants. While many scholars have recognized this ranking, most have not acknowledged the importance of kinship and ethnic categories in this configuration of peoples.

This analysis of the olive tree passage in turn helps us to develop a portrait of Paul's encoded audience. These are not necessarily the historical readers of the

---

3.   I think it is anachronistic to talk about 'Christianity' or 'Christians' in Paul. There is no evidence that Paul imagined a group that could be called 'Christians', and followers of Christ did not refer to themselves as 'Christians' until well after Paul. I prefer to use phrases such as 'gentiles-in-Christ' or 'followers of Christ' to describe those who have been baptized into Christ in Paul.

4.   Some examples that have been helpful to me are the following: S.K. Stowers, *A Rereading of Romans: Justice, Jews and Gentiles* (New Haven: Yale University Press, 1994); D. Konstan, 'Defining Ancient Greek Ethnicity', *Diaspora* 6 (1997), pp. 97–110; *idem*, '*To Hellenikon ethnos*: Ethnicity and the Construction of Ancient Greek Identity', in I. Malkin (ed.), *Ancient Perceptions of Greek Identity* (Cambridge, MA: Harvard University Press, 2001), pp. 29–50; J.M. Hall, *Ethnic Identity in Greek Antiquity* (Cambridge: Cambridge University Press, 1997); Buell, 'Rethinking the Relevance of Race'; *ead.*, 'Ethnicity and Religion in Mediterranean Antiquity and Beyond', *RSR* 26 (2000), pp. 243–49; *ead.*, 'Race and Universalism in Early Christianity', *JECS* 10 (2002), pp. 429–68; G. Baumann, *The Multicultural Riddle: Rethinking National, Ethnic, and Religious Identities* (New York: Routledge, 1999); J.A. Nagata, 'What is a Malay? Situational Selection of Ethnic Identity in a Plural Society', *American Ethnologist* 1 (1974), pp. 331–50; C.F. Keyes, 'Towards a New Formulation of the Concept of Ethnic Group', *Ethnicity* 3 (1976), pp. 202–13; S.J.D. Cohen, *The Beginnings of Jewishness* (Berkeley and Los Angeles: University of California Press, 1999).

5.   For a similar argument, see D.K. Buell and C. Johnson Hodge, 'The Politics of Interpretation: The Rhetoric of Race and Ethnicity in Paul' (paper presented at the Annual Meeting of the Society of Biblical Literature, Toronto, November 25, 2002), *JBL* 123.2 (2004), pp. 235–51.

letter, about whom we know little, but the ideal readers Paul constructs as he writes. Rom. 11.17–24 corroborates other clues in the letter that these readers are gentiles associated with Judeans, loyal to the Judean God, and followers of the Judean Christ. The olive tree metaphor represents Paul's effort to explain to his gentile audience how they fit into the larger narrative of the history and future salvation of Israel.

1. *Note on Translation*

One of my chief aims is to call attention to Paul's ethnic language in order to counter the tendency in traditional Pauline scholarship to translate this language into abstract concepts, spiritual categories or theological metaphors. With this goal in mind, I render the Greek term *Ioudaioi* as 'Judeans' instead of the more common 'Jews.' I prefer *Ioudaioi* for two linked reasons. First, I want to avoid the term 'Jew,' which in the modern world can evoke a concept of a religious identity separate from an ethnic one. In ancient Mediterranean cultures, religious identity and ethnic identity were interrelated and mutually constituting. The term 'Jew', because of its modern associations, can mask this relationship.

Second, I use 'Judean' in order to maintain the parallels inherent in the Greek with other ethnic designations such as 'Greek', 'Egyptian', 'Roman', and so on. The interrelatedness of ethnic and religious identities is clear in the various ways these terms are defined by ancient authors. Each term could encompass geographic homelands, claims of descent from particular ancestors, loyalty to certain gods, religious practices, adherence to laws, moral standing, or any combination of these. Furthermore, all of the major ethnic peoples of Paul's era had substantial diaspora populations that continued the use of designations that referred to the homeland or a supposed homeland. If we allow the term 'Greek', for example, to translate *Hellen* and to include the various possible components of 'Greekness', then we should do the same for Judean and *Ioudaios*. I see no reason to use an additional term, 'Jew', especially when it is potentially misleading as I mentioned above.[6]

---

6. Cohen discusses exactly these issues in *The Beginnings of Jewishness* (Berkeley and Los Angeles: University of California Press, 1999), chs. 3–5. He makes a clear distinction between a mutable 'Jewish' identity (which he claims is based on religious and cultural factors such as belief in God and following ancestral ways) and an immutable 'Judean' identity (which he describes as ethnic – in that it is based on ancestry – and geographic). He argues that starting during the Maccabean period (second century BCE), the concept of a 'Jewish' identity emerged alongside the traditional 'Judean' identity. For the first time, Cohen argues, gentiles could become 'Jews' by changing their beliefs and practices.

I am convinced by Cohen's case for an added dimension to Judean ethnic identity, one based on achievement rather than ascription, during the Maccabean period, and that these Judeans were following a Greek model. I do not agree, however, with Cohen's distinction between a 'Jew' and a 'Judean', the former based on achievement and therefore mutable and the latter based on ancestry and geography and therefore immutable. I see no part of ethnic identity that is immutable and not subject to manipulation and negotiation, not even kinship. Further, as Cohen himself points out, the achievement-oriented characteristics that define 'Jew' (religious affiliation and ancestral customs) are similar to those used to describe 'Greek' in some cases, or they might be used negatively to

Using 'Judean' encourages us to consider anew Paul's ethnic language, partly because it is a more accurate, literal rendering and partly because it is simply unfamiliar to modern ears.

2. *Olive Tree as 'Family Tree': Rom. 11.17–24*

In Rom. 9–11 in general, and in 11.17–24 in particular, Paul cultivates a tension between Judeans and gentiles which propels his version of salvation history. In Rom. 11.17 Paul tells the gentiles that they are a 'wild olive shoot' (ἀγριέλαιος) which has been grafted onto (ἐνεκεντρίσθης) a cultivated olive tree to benefit from the richness of the tree (11.17). Paul warns them not to boast about this arrangement:

> If you boast, remember that you do not support the root but the root supports you. (v. 19) Therefore you will say, 'The branches have been broken off so that I might be grafted on.' (v. 20) True. They have been broken off by unfaithfulness (τῇ ἀπιστίᾳ), but you have stood by means of faithfulness (τῇ πίστει). Do not consider high things, but be afraid. (v. 21) For if God did not spare the natural branches (τῶν κατὰ φύσιν κλάδων), he will in no way spare you. (v. 22) See the kindness and severity of God: severity upon those who have fallen, but the kindness of God upon you. Unless you remain in his kindness, you will be cut off. (v. 23) Also those people, if they do not remain in unfaithfulness, they will be grafted on. For God is able to graft them on again (πάλιν ἐγκεντρίσαι). For if you are cut off from an olive tree which is wild by nature, and, beyond the bounds of nature, you are grafted onto a cultivated tree, how much more will these natural branches be grafted onto their own olive tree (Rom. 11.18–24).

Various explanations have been offered for what the roots and branches, and the tree itself, represent in this passage. Yet many have missed what I would argue is the interpretive key to this passage: this agricultural metaphor refers to kinship, ethnicity and lineages. This is an ancient 'family tree', which delineates the relationship between the Judean God and his peoples.

Although a few interpreters note the connections between Paul's olive tree and his arguments about kinship and ethnicity, they nevertheless have not recognized the implications of this reading. Several scholars, for example, label the roots of the olive tree as the patriarchs and the branches as descendants, which seems to assume an implicit connection between lineage and Paul's olive tree. Joseph Fitzmyer even argues that the olive tree passage needs to be interpreted in the context of Rom. 4 and Gal. 3.29 (both of which address the new status of gentiles as

---

define 'Egyptians' (for example, 'Egyptians' are those who worship the wrong gods). Indeed, it was a common strategy in ethnic definition to forefront a collection of specific cultural and religious attributes (see Buell, 'Rethinking the Relevance' and *Why This New Race*; Johnson Hodge, 'If Sons, Then Heirs'). This is still very different from a modern notion of religion as a choice or option. Therefore, I prefer to maintain the parallels between terms like *Ioudaios, Hellen,* and *Aigyptos* by translating *Ioudaios* 'Judean'.

Cohen is right to have recognized two strands to Judean ethnic identity, one that is heritable and one that is achieved. They just cannot be as neatly separated as he suggests. The essentializing and constructed components of identity interact in complex ways, and they often reinforce each other.

descendants of Abraham).[7] But he never explains why. John Lodge connects the grafting of the gentiles to their new status as descendants of Abraham, but he refers to this connection as a 'mixing of metaphors.'[8] It is striking that scholars can link the olive tree passage and the kinship arguments yet neglect to explain why this might make sense to Paul and to his audience.[9]

I think this oversight is due in part to a modern use of agricultural metaphors for kinship: the phrase 'family tree' is the perfect example. Our own familiarity with the metaphor makes it seem like we do not need to explicate it in Paul. I would argue that a proper interpretation of this passage depends upon an awareness of the close associations between agricultural imagery and kinship and ethnic relations and an understanding of how they work in the ancient world. Paul's olive tree passage does not presuppose just any sort of membership in a group; it specifically speaks about those relationships created through lineages and ancestors. Once we recognize that the olive tree is an analogy for related lineages, then Paul's strategy becomes more apparent. He uses the tree to construct a relationship between Judeans and gentiles as distinct peoples of the Judean God.

That an ancient audience would have implicitly understood that Paul's argument builds on ideas about kinship and lineages is not difficult to demonstrate. Agricultural imagery was a favourite trope for ancient authors in many cultures discussing ethnic and familial relationships. Procreation itself was often imagined as sowing seeds in the earth, a metaphor which captures the gendered roles of the active male sower and the passive female recipient.[10] For example, Plutarch writes that menstruation, as a cleansing process which prepares the womb to receive the seed, renders 'the womb, in season, like fertile ground for plowing and sowing.'[11] In

---

7. J.A. Fitzmyer, *Romans* (*AB* 33; New York: Doubleday, 1993), p. 610.

8. J. Lodge, *Romans 9–11: A Reader-Response Analysis* (Atlanta, GA: Scholars Press, 1996), p. 181.

9. Many commentators who agree that the tree is some representation of Israel think that the roots must be Abraham or the patriarchs and the branches the descendants. These also do not make explicit connections between agricultural imagery and the relationships between ethnic groups; see J.D.G. Dunn, *Romans 9–16* (WBC 38B; Dallas, TX: Word Books, 1988), p. 659; R.H. Bell, *Provoked to Jealousy: The Origin and Purpose of the Jealousy Motif in Romans 9–11* (WUNT II/63; Tübingen: Mohr-Siebeck, 1994), p. 121. Others draw a distinction between the 'historical' or 'ethnic' Israel and the 'eschatological' Israel and claim that the branches of the olive tree, with gentile Christians incorporated, represent the latter; see Dunn, *Romans 9–16*, p. 672. I argue against this sort of split in 'If Sons, Then Heirs', pp. 113–17. Some scholars argue that the roots and the tree are not Israel but Christ and the attached and broken branches represent believers and unbelievers respectively. For example, see M.M. Bourke, *A Study of the Metaphor of the Olive Tree in Romans 11* (Washington, DC: Catholic University of America, 1947), pp. 79ff., 111. Bell also discusses this reading in *Provoked to Jealousy,* p. 122. I find it more convincing that Paul's larger category (represented by the olive tree) is Israel, not Christ. As I argue below, both Judeans and gentiles-in-Christ belong to Israel and Christ is the specific point where the gentiles are grafted on. The Judeans are already 'natural' outgrowths of the tree.

10. See P. duBois, *Sowing the Body* (Chicago: Chicago University Press, 1988), pp. 39–85; D.K. Buell, *Making Christians: Clement of Alexandria and the Rhetoric of Legitimacy* (Princeton, NJ: Princeton University Press, 1999), pp. 32–49.

11. Plutarch, *On Affection for Offspring* 495 E. Translation amended from Loeb: *Plutarch's*

Book VI of the *Iliad*, Glaukos is asked if he is human or god. He responds by comparing the mortality of humans to the perpetual regeneration of a tree: 'Why ask of my generation (γενεήν)? As is the generation (γενεή) of leaves, so is that of humanity. The wind scatters the leaves on the ground, but the live timber burgeons with leaves again in the season of spring returning. So one generation (γενεή) of men will grow while another dies.'[12]

As Paul would have known, biblical authors often compare God's peoples to plantings. The Psalmist writes: 'They that are planted in the house of the Lord shall flourish in the courts of our God' (Ps. 91.13 LXX).[13] Hosea, who describes Israel's return to its God as the new growth of plants, specifically uses the fruit-bearing olive tree as an image of the thriving Israel: '[Israel] shall bloom as the lily and cast forth its roots as Lebanon. Its branches shall spread, and it shall be as a fruitful olive (ἐλαία κατάκαρπος)' (Hos. 14.6–7 LXX).[14]

Jeremiah also compares Israel to an olive tree and – key for our purposes – uses it to describe God's response when Israel strays: 'The Lord called your name a fair olive tree (ἐλαίαν), of a goodly shade in appearance. At the noise of its being lopped, fire was kindled against it; great is the affliction coming upon you. Her branches have become good for nothing. And the Lord that planted you has pronounced evils against you because of the iniquities of the house of Israel and the house of Judah' (Jer. 11.16–7 LXX).[15] Here we have an image of violent separation in which the Judean God threatens to destroy the olive tree which is Israel.

Similarly, Isaiah addresses how God will root out corruption in the tribes of Israel, leaving only a remnant to survive: 'Look, the Sovereign, the Lord of hosts, will lop the boughs with terrifying power; the tallest trees will be cut down, and the lofty will be brought low. He will hack down the thickets of the forest with an ax, and Lebanon with its majestic trees will fall. A shoot shall come out from the stump of Jesse, and a branch shall grow out of his roots' (Isa. 10.33–11.1).[16] Paul uses these same motifs – the peoples of God as trees or branches and God's punishing act as cutting them down – in the olive tree pericope in Rom. 11. Notice that the hope amidst the destruction takes the form of the new growth that will issue from the 'stump of Jesse.' Thus the lineage of Jesse, the remnant which survives, is represented as a new shoot emerging from a stump.

Moralia, vol. VI (translated by W.C. Helmbold; LCL; Cambridge, MA: Harvard University Press, 1939), p. 345.

12. Homer, *Iliad*, 6.145–9. Translated by R. Lattimore, *The Iliad of Homer* (Chicago: University of Chicago, 1951), p. 157. Greek from Loeb edition: *Homer. Iliad. Books 1–12* (translated by A.T. Murray and revised by W.F. Wyatt; LCL; Cambridge, MA: Harvard University Press, 1999), p. 285.

13. Translation amended from *The Septuagint With Apocrypha: Greek and English* (translated by L.C.L. Brenton; Peabody, MA: Hendrickson Publishers, 1986; originally published in London: Samuel Bagster & Sons, 1851), p. 754.

14. Translation amended from Brenton, p. 1080.

15. Translation from Brenton, p. 917.

16. This passage is from the Hebrew version of Isaiah. Translation is from the *NRSV*. In Romans 15, Paul cites a similar Isaiah passage (Isa. 11.10 LXX), and connects the root of Jesse to Christ: 'There will come the root of Jesse, the one who rises to rule the gentiles (ἐθνῶν); in him the gentiles shall hope' (Rom. 15.12).

Later Judean authors also used arboreal imagery to trace lineages between generations. Philo compares Shem to a root, '…and from that root sprung up wise Abraham, a tree yielding sweet nutriment, and his fruit was Isaac…,' and Jacob in turn was Isaac's seed.[17] This image of a tree as a lineage works so well because kinship, like plant growth, is considered organic and contiguous. Each descendant (or new plant) is literally an elaboration of the 'stuff' of its ancestor.[18] Thus horticultural imagery, like the language of kinship and ethnicity, assumes an organic connection between forebears and offspring.

Adoption, which is an excellent example of producing kinship, can also be imagined in horticultural terms: as new branches grafted on to an existing tree. In a passage which bears a striking resemblance to Paul's olive tree metaphor, Philo likens grafting to adoption. He explains that a gardener can improve plants which yield poor crops '… by inserting grafts into the stem near the roots and joining them with it so that they grow together as one (συμφυεστάτη ἑνώσει).'[19] The same thing happens, Philo continues, when adopted sons, who, although aliens by birth, nevertheless fit right in to their adopted families.[20] Thus agricultural language provided a rich harvest of metaphors for reproduction, the creation and maintenance of lineages, and the power structures these familial relationships imply.[21]

Many of these images appear in Paul's olive tree metaphor in Rom. 11. Paul imagines the peoples of God as the branches of an olive tree. In this aggregation of related peoples, some are 'natural' and some are 'grafted.' As adopted sons, the gentiles are the grafted branches, and Paul reminds them of their dependence on the root which sustains them. This natural/unnatural divide is destabilized, however, by the power of the Judean God, the horticulturist who is able to graft on new branches or lop off existing ones as he sees fit. Although the gentiles currently 'stand by means of faithfulness,' they should nevertheless be wary, for God can easily cut them off and graft others on again.

Paul establishes a hierarchy by associating gentiles with the wild olive tree and Judeans with the cultivated one. While a cultivated tree would have been tall and would have borne fruit and oil, the wild olive would have been more like a shrub, with a few hard fruits on it.[22] Paul sharpens this point by distinguishing between natural and unnatural branches: 'For if you are cut off from an olive tree which is wild by nature, and, beyond the bounds of nature, you are grafted onto a cultivated tree, how much more will these natural branches be grafted onto their own olive tree' (Rom. 11.24). Paul contrasts Judeans and non-Judeans: the Judeans are the

17. Philo, *Sobr.* 65.

18. Thanks to S.K. Stowers for this observation. C. Delaney addresses similar themes in *Seed and Soil: Gender and Cosmology in Turkish Village Society* (Berkeley and Los Angeles: University of California Press, 1991).

19. Philo, *Agr.* 6.

20. Philo, *Agr.* 6.

21. Buell, *Making Christians*, pp. 50–68, 71–76, 79–86.

22. A.G. Baxter, J.A. Ziesler, 'Paul and Arboriculture in Romans 11.17–24', *JSNT* 24 (1985), pp. 25–32 (27).

'natural' branches and the gentiles are the grafted ones. The gentiles, as shoots from a different tree altogether, are in a particularly precarious situation.

Following the logic of Paul's metaphor, Christ would serve as the point at which the gentiles are grafted onto the olive tree. This idea echoes Paul's earlier agricultural image to describe uniting with Christ in baptism: to be planted together (σύμφυτος in Rom. 6.5). As I mention above, Philo employs similar imagery in his comparison of adoption to grafting in *De Agricultura*. Philo even uses the same word as Paul, the adjective form of *symphytos*, to describe the joining of the graft into the stem, and thus the adopted child into the family.

The olive tree metaphor allows for both similarity and difference between Judeans and gentiles. On the one hand, as branches of the same tree, they share the same roots and they are both vulnerable to being cut off if the tree is pruned. Thus Judeans and gentiles are descendants of a common founding ancestor and both are subject to God's judgment and mercy. On the other hand, they are distinct as separate branches and thus different lineages in a common genealogy. As the 'natural' branches of the cultivated, fruit-bearing tree, the Judeans rank higher in the hierarchy. The gentiles, originally from the wild, fruitless olive, are attached only through grafting and their status is less certain. Thus Judeans and gentiles are distinct peoples and remain so; the Judeans claim their link to Abraham by birth and the gentiles by adoption.

Scholars have missed the meaning of Rom. 11.17–24 not solely because of modern familiarity with agricultural metaphors for kinship and ethnicity. A larger issue limits our understanding of this passage: modern assumptions about kinship and ethnicity as 'natural.' A fundamental assumption of my work is that kinship and ethnicity are social constructions. While both of these, as categories of identity, claim a primordial or natural base, they are nevertheless human creations. Kinship, for example, may be formulated in terms of biological relationship, but it is often established by other criteria (such as common practices, language, religion, geographical region). How and whether a relationship is defined as one of kinship is contingent on the specific context and interests involved. Similarly, ethnic identity is often constructed upon a naturalized understanding of kinship (for example, appeals to common ancestry) but it, too, is a mutable construct that can be shaped by various criteria and contexts. The paradoxical nature of these concepts – 'natural' yet malleable – renders them effective tools in organizing people and power, shaping self-understanding and defining membership. Rom. 11.17–24 is a good example of the construction of kinship and ethnicity at work.

I have emphasized that Paul actively brings Judeans and gentiles into a shared lineage using the image of grafting. This strategy of creating ethnic ties is widespread in antiquity – what Jonathan Hall calls 'aggregative' ethnic self-definition.[23]

---

23. Hall, *Ethnic Identity*, pp. 47–51. Hall, who has written on the strategic use of ethnic language in genealogies from Archaic Greece, distinguishes between two modes of ethnicity construction: aggregative and oppositional. In the oppositional mode, a group defines itself by a series of contrasts with another group. For example, the concept of the 'Greek' developed over and against the concept of the 'barbarian', which encompassed everything a Greek was not. The same construction is evident in Paul's pairing the terms 'Judean' and 'gentile', or 'Judean' and 'Greek'. For

In the aggregative mode, ethnic identity is constructed not by contrast with others but by affiliation with others, usually to gain some advantage, such as a higher pedigree.[24] One expression of this affiliation is what Hall terms 'ethnic genealogies,' whereby various ethnic groups link themselves together as descendants of a common ancestor.[25] Hall reconstructs the earliest example of such a genealogy, which links Dorians, Ionians and Achaeans as descendents of *Hellen*.[26] Each of these names corresponds to ethnic groups which claim these men as their ancestors.

The function of this genealogy is to place these in relation to each other: they all claim *Hellen* as their founding ancestor, yet each group retains its own eponymous ancestor, signaling a certain degree of independence within the larger group.[27] Thus some ethnic groups can relate to each other as cousins, some as brothers, others as fathers and sons. Just as in ancient households not all relations are equal, so, too, with linked genealogies: the more direct line to *Hellen*, the higher the status of the ethnic group. Thus an aggregative linking does not erase previous ethnic distinctions. In fact, it often serves to establish hierarchies among them, as Hall notes, '...the Hellenic genealogy employs the metaphor of kinship to construct a system of *ranked* relationships between the groups that are represented by their eponyms.'[28] Hall's concept of aggregative ethnicity construction helps us to understand Paul's rhetoric in Rom. 11.17–24. In this olive tree passage, Paul uses agricultural imagery to arrange Judeans and gentiles as related but distinct peoples of the Judean God.

Reading the olive tree passage in terms of kinship and ethnicity coheres with Paul's larger argument for gentile salvation, which he frames in terms of aggregative kinship. Through baptism into Christ and the reception of the spirit, gentiles become adopted sons of the Judean God, descendants of the ancestor Abraham, co-heirs with Christ.[29] Through this adoption, the gentiles are added onto a larger family genealogy.

Like the Hellenic groups in Jonathan Hall's model of aggregative ethnic construction, Judeans and gentiles in Romans are separate, but hierarchically related peoples. The horticultural metaphors of trees, grafting and pruning allow Paul not

---

more on Paul's use of both the aggregative and oppositional modes, see Johnson Hodge, 'If Sons, Then Heirs', chapters 3 and 4. My thanks go to D.K. Buell, who first linked Hall's observations to Paul in her article, 'Ethnicity and Religion in Mediterranean Antiquity and Beyond', *RSR* 26 (2000), pp. 243–49 (248). Buell develops these ideas with respect to second- and third-century constructions of Christian identity in 'Race and Universalism', pp. 12–15, 48–50, and in her forthcoming book, 'Why This New Race?'

24. Hall, *Ethnic Identity*, p. 51.

25. Hall, *Ethnic Identity*, p. 41.

26. Hall reconstructs this 'Hellenic genealogy' from Pseudo-Hesiod's *Catalogue of Women* and recent papyrus discoveries: 'war-loving king Hellen' is the father of Doros, Xouthos and Aiolos; Doros is the father of Aigimios who is the father of Dymas and Pamphylos; Xouthos begets Ion and Akhaios (Hall, *Ethnic Identity*, pp. 42–43; see diagram on p. 43).

27. Hall, *Ethnic Identity*, p. 43.

28. Hall, *Ethnic Identity*, p. 43.

29. For a detailed study of these themes in Paul, see Johnson Hodge, 'If Sons, Then Heirs'.

only to articulate this relationship but also to illustrate how the Judean God manages the peoples who belong to him.

3. *Paul's Audience*

What can this reading of Rom. 11.17–24 tell us about Paul's audience and about first-century Christ-followers in Rome? I think it is important to exercise caution when attempting to answer this question. Especially in recent decades, scholars who have addressed ethnicity and Paul have been tempted to use Romans as a tool for reconstructing the 'early church' in Rome. The general thesis of much of this work, which has centred on Romans, is that Paul is attempting to solve problems that have arisen between 'Jewish Christians' and 'gentile Christians' in Rome. According to this view, Paul specifically addresses tensions between these two social groups in Rom. 14, where he speaks of the 'weak' (understood as 'Jewish Christians' who were expelled from Rome and are now returning) and the 'strong' (understood as 'gentile Christians' whose numbers have grown). This argument relies upon a historical reconstruction of the composition of the 'early church' in Rome to explain Judean/gentile relations as a pertinent issue. Romans is then interpreted in terms of this reconstruction.[30]

I find this approach to be methodologically flawed for two reasons. First, we have little if any knowledge of the first-century 'church' in Rome outside of Paul's letters. The reconstruction of the 'church' in Rome often relies upon a particular reading of Romans itself, resulting in a circular argument: this is what the first-century Roman 'church' was like (based on Paul's letter); therefore this is what Paul's letter to the Romans means.

Second, this argument results in part from a lack of critical awareness of issues related to audience.[31] It is important to distinguish between two groups: the empirical reader (anyone who may have read these texts) and the encoded reader (the audience which the author constructs).[32] In the case of Paul, we have little or no information about the empirical reader, but we can use the text to determine its

---

30. Some examples are J.D.G. Dunn, *Romans 1–8* (WBC 38B; Dallas, TX: Word Books, 1988), especially pp. xliv–liv; J.C. Walters, *Ethnic Issues in Paul's Letter to the Romans: Changing Self-Definitions in Earliest Roman Christianity* (Valley Forge, Pa.: Trinity Press International, 1983); and C.D. Stanley, ' "Neither Jew Nor Greek": Ethnic Conflict in Graeco-Roman Society', *JSNT* 64 (1996), pp. 101–24; J.A. Fitzmyer, *Romans*; J. Marcus, 'The Circumcision and Uncircumcision in Rome', *NTS* 35 (1989), pp. 67–81. This approach is not entirely new. In the nineteenth century, F.C. Baur suggested that Paul was writing to respond to the tensions among Judeans and gentiles in Rome: *Paul* (2 vols.; London: Williams and Norgate, 1873, 1875).

31. Stowers argues this point in *Rereading of Romans*, pp. 21–29.

32. The encoded reader is the audience found in the text itself, e.g. when Paul writes 'I am writing to you, gentiles'. The encoded reader can also be less obvious, however, and can be discerned by examining the assumptions Paul makes about his audience. For example, when he writes about the law or about eating sacrificed meat, he writes as though his audience is familiar with these practices and cultural codes. The encoded reader is thus a characteristic of the text itself. The empirical reader, on the other hand, is anyone who reads the texts, whether in the first century or today. This reader does not inform us about the audience as Paul constructed it in the text. Again, see Stowers, *Rereading of Romans*, pp. 21–29.

encoded reader. The historical-reconstruction approach collapses these two discrete categories. It claims that since there were both Judeans and gentiles in Rome when Paul wrote, he must have been writing to both groups.[33] This way of reading correlates empirical readers (Greeks and gentiles and Judeans who might have been in Rome at the time) with the ethnic labels in the text. Scholars then read Judeans into Paul's audience, a move which is not supported by Paul's letters.[34] When we blur these two groups – empirical readers (or in this case speculations about these readers) and the readers indicated in the text – then we lose sight of Paul's own ethnic constructions and strategies.

Of course, when Paul wrote Romans, more than likely he was trying to construct plausible arguments for his Roman audience, so that the encoded and empirical readers are not entirely unrelated to each other. Because Paul and the historical recipients of his letter shared common cultural codes, it is reasonable to assume that there is some connection between Paul's attempts to persuade and the frameworks of meaning the audience would bring to the text. Conceptually, it is possible to appreciate this common ground while still recognizing the distinction between the encoded and empirical readers.

That said, I think it is more reliable, and ultimately more fruitful, to focus on Paul's encoded audience, the constructed, ideal readers of the text. We seek not for evidence about historical communities, but for the ways Paul portrays his audience – how he creates their identity. Clues from the letter itself allow us to reconstruct these readers. First, they are gentiles. Paul is clear that he is the apostle to the gentiles and that he is writing *to* gentiles, even if he also writes *about* Judeans.[35] Regardless of who might have been in Rome at the time or read Paul's letter, it addresses gentiles described as living in Rome.

Although they are gentiles, Paul assumes they are familiar with Judean practices and scripture. In addition to repeatedly citing biblical passages to support his arguments, Paul also states: 'I am speaking to those who know the law…' (Rom. 7.1).[36] Furthermore, these gentiles are able to understand themselves in terms of Judean identity. This is clear from two terms Paul uses for his audience: 'gentiles' and 'uncircumcised.' These are not terms of self-description, but labels used by Judeans to describe ethnic and religious 'others.'[37] *Akrobustia*, which literally means 'foreskin' and is usually translated 'uncircumcised', specifically defines

---

33. The (flawed) logic goes something like this: Bob in New York writes to someone in Boston. He calls this person Sally in the letters and addresses her as 'you'. In a few letters, Bob asks after their mutual friends, Ruth and Fred. Then a later reader (a scholar, for example) studies the letters and reasons: 'Bob must also have been writing to Ruth and Fred because according to the letter they are friends of Sally's who also live in Boston and besides there are people named Fred in the phone book.'.

34. See Stowers, *Rereading of Romans*, pp. 29–33.

35. For examples of Paul explicitly identifying his encoded readers, see Rom. 1.5–6, 13; 11.13; 15.6.

36. See Stowers, *Rereading of Romans*, pp. 258–84, for a persuasive argument that Paul adopts a gentile persona in Rom. 7.7ff.

37. Paul also uses 'Greeks' to describe non-Judeans. Unlike 'gentiles' and 'uncircumcised', 'Greeks' can be a term of self-description for those who claim a Greek identity.

Paul's encoded audience as a people that does not practice circumcision.[38] These terms only make sense in a Judean context. Thus I concur with other scholars who have suggested that Paul addresses so-called 'godfearers'.[39] I think it is likely that they are culturally Greek gentiles who are somehow affiliated with Judean communities and who are followers of the Judean Christ.

Paul does not expect these gentiles-in-Christ to practice the law in the way that faithful Judeans do, but he does expect that the 'just requirement of the law' will be fulfilled in them (Rom. 8.4). This is made possible by life in the spirit, which Paul describes in Rom. 8. In chs. 12–15, he outlines some of the specifics of this new moral standard, offering guidelines for moral behaviour for these gentile followers of Christ.

Through this encoded reader, Paul forges a new identity for gentiles-in-Christ. He expects that they will have left behind their indigenous gods and religious practices to be loyal to the Judean God. Although the Judean God becomes their only God and Judean scripture becomes their scripture, and although Abraham becomes their founding ancestor and they are baptized into the Judean Christ, Paul does not expect them to become Judeans. Paul does not require them to practise the law like Judeans, especially not circumcision. Thus they are not Judeans but they are not quite gentiles either, at least not as they used to be. Through Christ these gentiles become an affiliated people of the Judeans, sharing ancestry, scripture and God.

Paul's task in his letter to the Romans is to lay out for these gentiles how they fit into the larger story of Israel. He does not expect them to become Judeans, nor does he expect them to replace Judeans. Paul uses the olive tree metaphor to explain that they have been grafted onto the tree, like adopted sons are 'grafted' into a family. This agricultural image expresses Paul's version of the master narrative: how Judeans and gentiles can relate to each other now that Christ has made possible a place for the gentiles in the genealogy of Israel.

4. *Conclusion*

My analysis of the olive tree passage and Paul's audience demonstrates that Paul's thinking is shaped by the story of a specific people and their God. He speaks not as a Christian theologian, but as a first-century Judean teacher of gentiles.[40] He writes not to all humans, or all Christians, but to those particular peoples in a particular time who remain alienated from the Judean God. I do not deny that Paul had universal aspirations: he devoted his life to reaching as many non-Judeans as possible. But these aspirations come from the point of view of a first-century Judean who

38. J. Marcus argues that 'foreskin' is an 'ethnic slur' used by Judeans about gentiles (Marcus, 'Circumcision', p. 78).

39. Stowers, *Rereading of Romans*, pp. 21–22, 30–33, 71–72, 277–78. See S. McKnight, *A Light Among the Gentiles: Jewish Missionary Activity in the Second Temple Period* (Minneapolis: Fortress Press, 1991), chs. 6 and 7.

40. L. Gaston makes this point in *Paul and the Torah* (Vancouver: University of British Columbia Press, 1987), p. 6.

understands Israel as a 'light to the nations.' Ethnicity is not removed from this universal goal; it lies at the core of his mission.

Recognizing the close relationship between ethnicity and Paul's gospel enables us to perceive a more complex picture of constructions of identities of early Christ-followers. In his letter to the Romans, Paul crafts ideal readers who are not 'Christians' following a religion free of ethnic ties, but gentiles who become ethnically linked with Judeans through baptism into Christ. The olive tree metaphor depicts a development in the story of Israel; God has added a branch to the family tree so that both Judeans and gentiles-in-Christ might be saved.

This analysis calls into question those interpretations which attribute to Paul an erasure of ethnic and other social identities.[41] Rom. 11.17–24 imagines Christ followers not as free of ethnic affiliations, but as part of a larger 'family tree'. This horticultural image presents a complex arrangement in which distinct branches share common roots and yet are also ranked in relation to each other. According to Paul, the Judean God plays the all important role of the gardener who prunes and grafts according to his mercy and judgment. Instead of erasing boundaries, Paul conceives of God's salvific actions in terms of the redrawing of ethnicity and kinship boundaries: through Christ God has made a place for gentiles in the ethnic genealogy of Israel.

---

41. Many scholars cite Gal. 3.28 to support such an interpretation. With a growing number of scholars, I agree that while Gal. 3.28 speaks of solidarity 'in Christ', it does not imply a modern notion of equality or sameness among Christ-followers. See S.K. Stowers, 'Paul and Slavery: A Response', *Semeia* 83–84 (1998), pp. 295–311, and Johnson Hodge, 'If Sons, Then Heirs', pp. 178–222.

THE STRONG, THE WEAK AND THE MOSAIC LAW IN THE CHRISTIAN COMMUNITIES OF ROME (ROM. 14.1–15.13)

Antonio Pitta

One of the most debated questions on the letter to the Romans concerns the function and the content of Rom. 14.1–15.13. It is well known that, in this section, Paul exhorts the 'strong' to welcome the 'weak' on the background of some dietary problematics.[1] Besides the vague distinction between the strong and the weak, is it possible to establish their identity and convictions with more accuracy? Who are they? Do they belong to the Christian communities in Rome, or does Paul simply raise again the conflict between the strong and the weak witnessed in the community in Corinth (cf. 1 Cor. 8.1–10.33)? If the contrast really reflects the situation of the adressees, what is their relationship to the Jewish communities of the capital? And what is the significance of the controversy for the letter itself? Is it only a secondary topic, merely mentioned in passing towards the conclusion, or does it shed light in a different way on some topics dealt with before in the course of Romans?

The silence of the major part of the exegesis, preceding the contemporary debate on Romans, has left ample space for numerous questions, probably the great part of

---

1. Apart from the commentaries on Romans for the most meaningful issues on Rom. 14.1–15.13, cf. J.M.G. Barclay, ' "Do We Undermine the Law?". A Study of Romans 14.1–16.6', in J.D.G. Dunn (ed.), *Paul and the Mosaic Law,* (WUNT, 2/89; Tübingen: Mohr-Siebeck, 1996), pp. 287–308; R.A. Gagnon, 'The Meaning of ΥΜΩΝ ΤΟ ΑΓΑΘΟΝ in Rom. 14.16', *JBL* 117 (1998), pp. 675–89; C. Heil, *Die Ablehnung der Speisegebote durch Paulus* (BBB, 96; Weinheim, Berlin: Beltz Athenaum, 1994); R. Karris, 'Romans 14.1–15.13 and the Occasion of Romans', in K.P. Donfried (ed.), *The Romans Debate. Revised and Expanded Edition* (Edinburgh: T. & T. Clark, 1991), pp. 65–84; W.A. Meeks, 'Judgment and the Brother: Romans 14.1–15.13', in G.F. Hawthorne and O. Betz (eds.), *Tradition and Interpretation in the New Testament, Festschrift E.E. Ellis* (Grand Rapids: Eerdmans and Tübingen: Mohr, 1987), pp. 290–300; M. Reasoner, *The Strong and the Weak. Romans 14.1–15.13 in Context* (SNTS.MS, 103; Cambridge: University Press, 1999); J.P. Sampley, 'The Weak and the Strong: Paul's Careful and Crafty Rhetorical Strategy in Romans 14.1–15.13', in L.M. White and O.L. Yarbrough (eds.), *The Social World of the First Christians, Festschrift W.A. Meeks* (Minneapolis: Fortress Press, 1995), pp. 40–52; N. Schneider, *Die 'Schwachen' in der christlichen Gemeinde Roms: Eine historisch-exegetische Untersuchung zu Röm. 14,1–15,13* (Diss. Theol., Kirchliche Hochschule; Wuppertal: 1989); M.B Thompson, *Clothed with Christ: The Example and Teaching of Jesus in Romans 12.1–15.13* (JSNT.Sup, 59; Sheffield: JSOT Press, 1991), pp. 161–236; P.J. Tompson, *Paul and the Jewish Law: Halakha in the Letters of the Apostle to the Gentiles* (CRINT, 3.1; Minneapolis: Fortress Press, 1990); F. Watson, 'The Two Roman Congregations: Romans 14.1–15.13', in Donfried, *Romans Debate,* pp. 203–15.

them destined to remain unresolved because of the picture that reflects on the matter in the same letter. We will try to focus our attention on the strong and the weak first by dealing with the 'literary-rhetorical' function of Rom. 14.1–15.13, in order to reach the historic context and, finally, return to its relevance for Romans.

1. *The Same Bricks but Different Buildings*

The fact that dietary questions have been treated at different levels and contexts in the New Testament means that they must have created many difficulties in the early Christian communities: they are already debated at the synoptic level, using the language of 'pure' and 'impure';[2] then they are taken up again in different contexts within the Pauline letters and in Acts.[3] Prior to Rom. 14.1–15.13, Paul has already addressed issues of diet in 1 Cor. 8.1–10.33 with reference to the idols, and in Gal. 2.11–4 he has recalled the Antiochean incident with Peter about common meals between Christians from Jewish origin and those from Gentile origin. Also the deutero- and post-Pauline tradition will deal with such a problematic, in Col. 2.16–23 and in Tit. 1.15, reflecting on the dietary purities and on their insignificance in respect to salvation.

Staying in the context of Paul's letters, the event most similar to ours is that of 1 Cor. 8.1–10.33, since the two sections are joined by a Pauline exhortation to bear with the conviction of the 'weak', while such a background does not become evident at Antioch. At first sight, we cannot deny the following semantic and argumentative connections between the two sections.[4]

a) In 1 Cor. 8–10 and in Rom. 14–15 Paul is first of all worried about community building, founded upon the rule of mutual love: ἡ γνῶσις φυσιοῖ, ἡ δὲ ἀγάπη οἰκοδομεῖ (1 Cor. 8.1); Ἄρα οὖν τὰ τῆς εἰρήνης διώκωμεν καὶ τὰ τῆς οἰκοδομῆς τῆς εἰς ἀλλήλους (Rom. 14.19).[5]

b) In both cases the food issue is posed, which is shown by the use of the nouns βρῶμα (see 1 Cor. 8.8, 13; 10, 3; Rom. 14.15, 15, 20) and βρῶσις (see 1 Cor. 8.4; Rom. 14.17) and of the verb ἐσθίειν (see 1 Cor. 8.8; 9.4; 10.31; Rom. 14.2, 3, 6, 20, 21, 23).

c) The scandal and the stumbling block for the 'brother' provide a further element of coherence between the two sections: διόπερ εἰ βρῶμα σκανδαλίζει

---

2. See Mk 7.14–23; Mt. 15.10–20. Even if at first sight the polemic on pure and impure transmitted in these two synoptic traditions seems to belong to the Jesuan level of synoptic material, it is more probable that it reflects a crisis risen in the later Christian communities. So also V. Fusco, *Le prime comunità cristiane. Tradizioni e tendenze nel cristianesimo delle origini* (Bologna: EDB, 1995), pp. 197–98.

3. See Acts 10.1–33; 11.1–18; 15.22–9.

4. On the relationship between 1 Cor. 8–10 and Rom. 14–15 see Karris, 'Occasion', pp. 73–75, even if some parallels are forced, as for instance that between Rom. 15.3 and 1 Cor. 11.1 dealing with the example of Christ and Paul, or the one between Rom. 14.17 and 1 Cor. 8.8 on the nature of the Kingdom of God.

5. On ἀγάπη in the two sections see 1 Cor. 8.1; Rom. 14.15; for the use of the verb οἰκοδομεῖν see 1 Cor. 8.1, 10; 10.23; see also the noun οἰκοδομή in Rom. 14.19; 15.2.

τὸν ἀδελφόν μου, οὐ μὴ φάγω κρέα εἰς τὸν αἰῶνα ἵνα μὴ τὸν ἀδελφὸν μου σκανδαλίσω (1 Cor. 8.13); Μηκέτι οὖν ἀλλήλους κρίνωμεν ἀλλὰ τοῦτο κρίνατε μάλλον τὸ μὴ τιθέναι πρόσκομμα τῷ ἀδελφῷ ἢ σκάνδαλον (Rom. 14.13).[6]

d) The brother (see 2 Cor. 8.11, 12, 13; Rom. 14.10, 13, 15, 21) who must not be harmed by scandal is in both cases defined as 'weak' (see ὁ ἀσθενῶν in 1 Cor. 8.11, 12; Rom. 14.1, 2).

e) With respect to the 'weak' of the two communities, in a particular way, the relationship with Christ who died for them receives stronger emphasis: ἀπόλλυται γὰρ ὁ ἀσθενῶν ἐν τῇ σῇ γνώσει ὁ ἀδελφὸς δι᾽ ὃν Χριστὸς ἀπέθανεν (1 Cor. 8.11); μὴ τῷ βρώματί σου ἐκεῖνον ἀπόλλυε ὑπὲρ οὗ Χριστὸς ἀπέθανεν (Rom. 14.15).[7]

f) For that, all believers are invited to restore their relationship with the Lord: καὶ εἷς κύριος Ἰησοῦς Χριστὸς δι᾽ οὗ τὰ πάντα καὶ ἡμεῖς δι᾽ οὗ δι᾽ αὐτου (1 Cor. 8.6); ὁ φρονῶν τὴν ἡμέραν κυρίῳ φρονεῖ καὶ ὁ ἐσθίων κυρίῳ ἐσθίει (Rom. 14.6).[8]

g) Even the reason for 'pleasing the neighbour' and not oneself joins the two sections together: μηδεὶς τὸ ἑαυτοῦ ζητείτω ἀλλὰ τὸ τοῦ ἑτέρου (1 Cor. 10.24); ἕκαστος ἡμῶν τῷ πλησίον ἀρεσκέτω εἰς τὸ ἀγαθὸν πρὸς οἰκοδομήν (Rom. 15.2).

The connections between 1 Cor. 8–10 and Rom. 14–15 cannot be ignored. Therefore, some scholars do not hesitate to consider the exhortation of Romans as a simple resumption of what was already expressed in 1 Corinthians and, consequently, deny its relevance to the situation of the communities in Rome.[9] Alongside these elements of coherence, it is necessary to underline the following data of discontinuity between the two sections:

a) Only in Romans two groups are mentioned: the weak *and* the strong while, as we have pointed out, 1 Cor. 8–10 only deals with the weak in terms of γνῶσις (see 1 Cor. 8.1) and the freedom of the others (see 1 Cor. 8.9; 10.29).[10]

b) In Rom. 14.3 Paul also mentions the criticism of the weak against the strong while the reactions of the weak are not described in 1 Cor. 8–10: ὁ δὲ μὴ ἐσθίων τὸν ἐσθίοντα μὴ κρινέτω (Rom. 14.3).

c) While in 1 Cor. 8–10 Paul adresses the issue of idol sacrifices (εἰδωλόθύτον in 1 Cor. 8.1, 4, 7, 10; 10.19), in Rom. 14–15 he pays attention to those who eat only vegetables (see λάχανον in Rom. 14.2).

---

6.   In connection with the 'scandal', see also the use of πρόσκομμα in 1 Cor. 8.9; Rom. 14.13, 20 and προσκόπτειν in Rom. 14.21.

7.   See also the use of ἀποθνῄσκειν in Rom. 14.7, 8, 9.

8.   See also the references to the κύριος in 1 Cor. 8.5; 9.1, 2, 5, 14; 10.21, 22, 26; Rom. 14.4, 8, 11, 14; 15.6, 11.

9.   As Karris, 'Occasion', pp. 81, 84.

10.   See also M.B. Thompson, 'Strong and Weak', in G.F. Hawthorne, R.P. Martin and D.G. Reid (eds.), *Dictionary of Paul and his Letters* (Downers Grove and Leicester: Inter Varsity Press, 1993), p. 917.

d) In 1 Cor. 8–10 the controversy about 'pure' and 'impure' is not debated, while it is found in the centre of the quarrel in Rom. 14, as is evident by the use of καθαρός and κοινός in Rom. 14.14, 20.

e) While Paul pays attention to the conscience of the weak in 1 Cor. 8–10 (see συνείδησις in 1 Cor. 8.7, 10, 12; 10.29), which is threatened by the freedom of the others, in Rom. 14 the emphasis shifts to the firm belief of the strong and the weak (see πίστις Rom. 14.1, 22, 23).[11]

f) While in 1 Cor. 8–10 Paul presents himself as a model of solidarity with the weak as evident in the extensive self-praise of 1 Cor. 9.1–27, in Rom. 14.1–15.13 this model function is fulfilled only by Christ (see Rom. 15.1–13). Such a change is mainly due to the fact that in Romans Paul is talking to a community not founded by him: the motive of the periautology, just mentioned in Rom. 11.1, would create the opposite effect in a letter like Rom., while it is repetitively used in letters sent to 'his' communities like 1 Corinthians.

g) The exhortation to accept the weak is mentioned only in Romans (see Rom. 14.1, 3; 15.1, 7), allowing us to assume, at least from this point of view, the existence of a much deeper crisis than it appears to be evident in 1 Cor. 8–10.

The differences between the two sections are more consistent than the coherences, which proves that Paul does not simply repeat a general exhortation in Rom. 14.1–15.13, brought up with rhetorical skill from 1 Corinthians but without any contextual relevance,[12] but that Paul addresses real difficulties among the communities in Rome.[13] At the same time we have to recognize that Paul indeed takes up some motives from the exhortation in 1 Cor. 8–10, but he alters and adapts them with respect to the recipients in Rome. Something similar can already be observed by the use of material from Gal. 4.4–7 in Rom. 8.14–7 about the relationship between the believers and the Spirit, and in the case of motives first evident in 1 Cor. 12.1–13 and reappearing in Rom. 12.3–21 which refer to ministries and mutual ἀγάπη in the community. In our case we can equally assert that the 'bricks' are the same but the 'buildings' are quite different, confirming the basic originality of Rom. 14.1–15.13 in comparison to 1 Cor. 8–10.

2. *Ethical Rather than Ethnical Identity*

The actual and situational character of Rom. 14.1–15.13 imposes great attention on the context of the whole letter to prevent us from falling into what someone described as the 'Lutheran trap'; in other words, we do not find ourselves confronted

---

11. The fact that in the previous section Paul uses the noun συνείδησις (Rom. 13.5), but leaves it out in Rom. 14–15, confirms that the case is quite different from the one he faced in Corinth.

12. Cf. Karris, 'Occasion', p. 71.

13. Similar also Barclay, 'Undermine the Law?', p. 288; G. Barbaglio, *La teologia di Paolo. Abbozzi in forma epistolare* (Bologna: EDB, 1999), p. 705; C. Bryan, *A Preface to Romans. Notes on the Epistle in Its Literary and Cultural Setting* (Oxford: Oxford University Press, 2000), pp. 216–27; Reasoner, *Strong*, p. 41; Sampley, 'The Weak', pp. 40–52; Schneider, *Die 'Schwachen'*, pp. 69–70; D. Zeller, *La Lettera ai Romani* (Brescia: Morcelliana, 1998), p. 352.

with a *doctrinae christianae compendium* (Melanchton) of Pauline thought, supposedly unrelated to all actual historical conditions. The trend to contextualize Paul's statement first of all is evident in M. Reasoner's essay who intends to place the letter in its socio-economical framework within the Romano-Christian communities.[14]

The point put forward by Reasoner and others who place Romans in its socio-historical context must certainly be welcomed, but we have to acknowledge that the results of the analysis are unpersuasive as are its aims. It is difficult, if not impossible, to establish that the strong indeed correspond to the *potentes*, and the weak to the *inferiores* in Roman social stratification and to try to corroborate this hypothesis by pointing to Pauls' reference to 'those of the household of Aristo-bulus and Narcissus' (see Rom. 16.10–1).[15] How can one assert that the weak of the Christian communities in Rome belong to the *collegia tenuiorum* of the capital, while the strong come from an elevated social level?[16] Similarly, the historical con-text of Romans cannot be clarified by the simple assumption on the basis of Rom. 13.8–14 that some cases of sexual immoralities might have taken place in the addressed communities.[17]

With all frankness, we have to note that in order to avoid the 'Lutheran trap' more than only a few scholars instead fall into an even more dangerous pit, namely the 'mirror reading' trap: not all the sender's statements correspond to real actions or events on the part of the recipients and vice versa! Such a claim is erroneous especially for the Pauline letters where, by using the picture of the trap, Paul himself falls into the 'theological' pit without forgetting the socio-historical background of his remarks. If, in other words, it is undeniable that Rom. 14.1–15.13 really reflects the controversy among the recipients of the letter, it cannot be denied that Paul himself tries to understand and then to settle the strife from a kerygmatical point of view in relationship to the death and resurrection of Christ. There are many situations in his letters which, even in regard to questions of less importance, e.g. the behaviour of women at the assembly (see 1 Cor. 11.1–16), are addressed by Paul with reference to faith and not simply in a fortuitous way. Therefore, if it is advisable to re-read Pauline argumentations without a confes-sional 'pince-nez', it is equally important, if not necessary, not to fall into arbi-trary claims about background and situations which cannot be verified, thereby risking to minimize the depth of Paul's argumentations.

If it is impossible in Rom. 14.1–15.13 to identify the strong with the *potentes* and the weak with the *inferiores*, the well known identification between the strong with Gentile-Christians and the weak with Jewish-Christians can not be maintained either.[18] From this point of view, it is significant that, corresponding to the devel-

14. As Reasoner writes: 'Romans is an occasional Letter, then we need to read the whole Letter as such' (*Strong*, p. 87).

15. Contrary to Reasoner, *Strong*, p. 203.

16. Different Reasoner, *Strong*, p. 51.

17. Contrary to Reasoner, *Strong*, p. 67.

18. This is the traditional interpretation of the two fronts in Rom. 14–15 already recognizable in the commentary of Origen, *Commento alla Lettera ai Romani* (F. Cocchini, trans.; Genova: Marietti, 1986), vol. II, p. 136 that explains them like this: 'And surely, that can seem to be said to

opment of the demonstration in Rom. 14.1–15.6, the pairs 'Jews-Gentiles' or 'Jewish-Greek' are completely missing and only the 'weak' and the 'strong' are mentioned. The ethnical polarity reappears in what we can define as the rhetorical 'peroration' of the section[19] in Rom. 15.7–13 in which Paul seems to invoke the universality of salvation, as demonstrated in Rom. 1.16–11.36, to exhort the strong and the weak to accept each other.[20] In fact, bearing witness to the radicality of the problems and typical of his manner of argumentation, Paul in Rom. 15.7–13 intends to refer to the polemic of the strong and the weak not to equate them to Gentile-Christians or Judaeo-Christians but in order to emphasize that, if the universal justification is well-grounded for everybody – Jews *and* Gentiles alike (see Rom. 1.16–7) – then how much more are the strong themselves called or better bound to bear with the illness of the weak.[21] In this sense, we can talk of an *a fortiori* argumentation, founded on Christ accepting both, Jews *and* Gentiles.

For this reason, we are not confronted with two ethnic groups or two separate congregations exhorted to accept each other on the basis of the Pauline gospel,[22] but with two morally or ethically defined segments of the congregation that cannot be properly understood with the distinction of 'Judaeo-Christianity' versus 'Gentile-Christianity'. Rather, these two parties belong to a form of 'Common Judaism' which in Christ finds its centre of adhesion and polarization.[23] In the Christian

those who have believed coming from gentiles hence were courageous in the freedom of faith…contrary to those who have believed coming from circumcision and still do observe the distinction of food according to the tradition of the Law'. As also Teodoreto di Ciro, *Commento alla lettera ai Romani* (L. Scarampi and F. Cocchini, trans.; Rome: Borla, 1998), p. 194; Thomas Aquinas, *Commento alla lettera ai Romani* (L. De Santis and M. Rossi, cur.; Rome: Città Nuova, 1994), vol. II, p. 167. Among contemporary scholars see M. Bockmuehl, *Jewish Law in Gentile Churches. Halakhah and the Beginning of Christian Public Ethics* (Edinburgh: T. & T. Clark, 2000), p. 73; J.D.G. Dunn, *Romans 9–16* (WBC, 38B; Dallas: Word Books, 1988), 799–802; T. Engberg-Pedersen, *Paul and the Stoics* (Edinburgh: T. & T. Clark, 2000), pp. 278–80; J.A. Fitzmyer, *Romans* (AB 33; New York: Doubleday, 1993), p. 687; D.J. Moo, *The Epistle to the Romans* (NICNT; Grand Rapids: Eerdmans, 1996) p. 835; C.M. Pate, *The Reverse of the Curse: Paul, Wisdom, and the Law* (WUNT 2.114; Tübingen: Mohr Siebeck, 2000), pp. 273–74; T.R. Schreiner, *Romans* (BECNT, 6; Grand Rapids: Baker Book House, 1998), p. 712; G.S. Schogren, 'Is the Kingdom of God about Eating and Drinking or isn't?' (Romans 14.17), *NT* 42 (2000), pp. 238–55; Watson, 'Two Roman Congregations', pp. 206–07.

19. On the function of the rethorical *peroration* see Aristotle, *Rhetorica* 3.19.1419b–1420a; Cicero, *Partitiones Oratoriae* 15.52; *De Inventione* 1.52.98; Cornificius, *Rhetorica ad Herennium* 2.30.47–2.31.50; Quintilian, *Institutio Oratoria* 6.1.1.

20. Even if in Rom. 15.7–13 the noun Ἰουδαῖος is lacking, the noun περιτομή is used (v. 8), so are quotations from Deut. 32.43 in Rom. 15.10 and Isa. 11.10 in Rom. 15.12 concerning the Jews. On ἔθνος for Gentiles see Rom. 15.10–1.

21. On the *peroratio* of Rom. 15.7–13 we refer to our detailed analysis in A. Pitta, *Lettera ai Romani* (Cinisello Balsamo: EP, 2nd edn, 2001), pp. 485–92; for the ethical meaning of the epithet 'strong and weak' see also S.K. Stowers, *A Rereading of Romans. Justice, Jews, and Gentiles* (New Haven and London: Yale University Press, 1994), p. 321.

22. Contrary to F. Watson, *Paul, Judaism and the Gentiles. A Sociological Approach* (*SNTS.MS*, 56; Cambridge: University Press, 1986), pp. 94–102; *idem*, 'Two Roman Congregations', pp. 203–15.

23. Because of the use of Ἰουδαϊσμός in its singular form in Gal. 1.13 we prefer to speak of

communities of Rome former adherents of paganism are also united to Christ not by ignoring the Mosaic Law, but through it (Rom. 7.1 refers to all the addressees). Such historical-social reconstruction corresponds well to what Ambrosiaster has written in his commentary on Romans:

> Since, amongst the Jews there were those that had introduced the Romans to faith in Christ, having united them to the Law, as I have restated at the beginning of the letter. Therefore, some believed not to have to eat the forbidden meat. To others that followed Christ without regarding the Law, the contrary seemed appropriate, namely that it was right to eat and, exactly for this, there were discussions amongst them.[24]

To confirm this conclusion, it is important to note the use of the noun ἀδελφός in Rom. 14.10, 13, 15, 21 and the reciprocal pronoun ἀλλήλους in Rom. 14.13, 19; 15.5, 7: beyond the ethnic description of Jews or Gentiles or that of being strong and weak, we can observe the mutual sharing of the same faith that permits the members of the community to recognize themselves as 'brothers'. With respect to the relevance of the many *domus ecclesiae* scattered in Rome, we do not see how M.D. Nanos could identify the weak only with the Jews and the strong with those who had accepted the Gospel.[25] The strong and the weak share the same faith in Christ and, at the same time, belong to a form of Judaism that develops and lives alongside other religious groups in Claudian and Neronian Rome.

Rather, the distinctive nature of personal names and the existence of different domestic communities attested in Rom. 16.1–16 show that both the strong and the weak belong to the social class of *humiliores* just like the Jewish communities spread out in the poor quarters of Rome.[26] With some exceptions, the Jewish communities of Rome came from the lowest stratum of society: most of them were slaves or freedmen and not merchants or craftsmen like the members of Jewish communities located in Puteoli and Ostia.

This picture is supported by burial inscriptions from Rome: they confirm the inclusion of Christians into Romano-Judaism and the lack of a synagogue or a

---

'common Judaism' instead of 'Judaisms' prevalent in the first century CE. So also M. Hengel and R. Deines, 'E.P. Sanders' "Common Judaism", Jesus, and the Pharisees', *JTS* 46 (1995), pp. 1–70 (39–40); while on the term 'Judaisms' see G. Boccaccini, *Il medio Giudaismo. Per una storia del pensiero giudaico tra il terzo secolo a.e.v. e il secondo e.v.* (Genova: Marietti, 1993).

24. See Ambrosiaster, *Commento alla lettera ai Romani* (A. Pollastri, trans.; Rome: Città Nuova, 1984), p. 285.

25. See M.D. Nanos, *The Mystery of Romans. The Jewish Context of Paul's Letter* (Minneapolis: Fortress Press, 1996), pp. 127, 159–63; *idem*, 'The Jewish Context of the Gentile Audience in Paul's Letter to the Romans', *CBQ* 6 (1999), pp. 293–304. For a critique of Nanos' hypothesis see R.A.J. Gagnon, 'Why the "Weak" at Rome Cannot Be Non-Christian Jews', *CBQ* 62 (2000), pp. 64–82; Pate, *Curse*, pp. 274–75; M. Theobald, *Der Römerbrief* (Darmstadt: Wissenschaftliche Buchgesellschaft, 2000), p. 32.

26. Regarding to this see the excellent contribution of P. Lampe, *Die stadtrömischen Christen in den ersten beiden Jahrhunderten. Untersuchungen zur Sozialgeschichte* (WUNT, 2/18; Tübingen: Mohr-Siebeck, 1989); *idem*, 'The Roman Christians of Romans 16', in Donfried, *Romans Debate*, pp. 216–30; E.W. Stegemann and W. Stegemann, *Storia sociale del cristianesimo primitivo. Gli inizi nel giudaismo e le comunità cristiane nel mondo mediterraneo* (Bologna: EDB, 1998), pp. 493–98.

central church instead of various *domus ecclesiae* scattered in the Roman Empire.[27] Despite the important testimony of Suetonius about the edict to ban the Jews from Rome under the emperor Claudius (49 CE),[28] it is still difficult to establish the quantitative proportions of the strong and the weak and assume that the weak might be the minority of former Jews from the capital while the strong might be the dominant part consisting of former Gentiles.[29] Even if the edict struck Jews like Prisca and Aquila (cf. Acts 18.2), it is practically impossible to define the impact of Jews on the society in Rome whose number increased from 20,000 to a maximum of 40,000 inhabitants around those years.

Insofar, one needs to be careful to maintain the distinction between the 'strong' and the 'weak' without falling into the trap of ethnic assimilation of a different kind which, at first sight, seems to be fascinating, but which risks to simplify a situation which actually was more complex and to impose a frame too narrow or too wide on the recipients of Romans.

3. *The Apple of Discord*

Unlike in 1 Cor. 8–10, the reason for the controversy between the Romano-Christian communities refers to dietary Laws: οἶδα καὶ πέπεισμαι ἐν κυρίῳ Ἰησοῦ ὅτι οὐδὲν κοινὸν δι᾽ ἑαυτοῦ, εἰ μὴ τῷ λογιζομένῳ τι κοινὸν εἶναι, ἐκείνῳ κοινόν (Rom. 14.14). On the one hand, we find those who do not consider any kind of food impure and for this reason regard themselves as 'strong', while on the other we find those who observe dietary Laws and for that reason are considered 'weak'. Paul does not hesitate, in terms of principles, to take side by the 'strong' and not by the 'weak': ὀφείλομεν δὲ ἡμεῖς οἱ δυνατοὶ τὰ ἀσθενήματα τῶν ἀδυνάτων βαστάζειν καὶ μὴ ἑαυτοῖς ἀρέσκειν (Rom. 15.1).

In addition to this 'apple of discord', some scholars also refer to questions of calendar observance and of intoxicating drinks like wine. On the basis of the development of Pauline argumentation, it can be noted that the observance of the calendar indeed finds great attention in Rom. 14.5–6a (ὃς μὲν κρίνει ἡμέραν παρ᾽ ἡμέραν, ὃς δὲ κρίνει πᾶσαν ἡμέραν· ἕκαστος ἐν τῷ ἰδίῳ νοί πληροφορείσθω. ὁ φρονῶν τὴν ἡμέραν κυρίῳ φρονεῖ),[30] while the issue of permitted is alluded to in Rom. 14.17, 21 (οὐ γάρ ἐστιν ἡ βασιλεία τοῦ θεοῦ βρῶσις καὶ πόσις | καλὸν τὸ μὴ φαγεῖν κρέα μηδὲ πιεῖν οἶνον), perhaps more for the sake of rhetoric polarity with the food than because of any real correspondence to the situation in the Romano-Christian communities.[31] How-

---

27. Cf. R. Penna, 'The Jews in Rome at the Time of the Apostle Paul', in *idem, Paul the Apostle. Jew and Greek Alike*, (Collegeville, MN: Liturgical Press, 1996), I, pp. 19–47; P. Richardson, 'Augustan-Era Synagogues in Rome', in K.P. Donfried and P. Richardson (eds.), *Judaism and Christianity in First-Century Rome* (Grand Rapids: Eerdmans, 1998), pp. 17–29.

28. See Suetonius, *Claudius* 25,4: 'Iudaeos impulsore Chresto assidue tumultuantes Roma expulit'.

29. Different Dunn, *Romans 9–16*, p. 798.

30. See H. Weiss, 'Paul and the Judging of Days', *ZNW* 86 (1995) pp. 137–53.

31. Also in 1 Cor. 10.31 there are some hints to 'drinking' because of a simple rhetoric polarity with 'eating' although only the idols are directly mentioned.

ever, these issues find real equivalents in extra-Pauline texts of Second Temple Judaism[32] and Greco-Roman sources.[33] In these cases, the observance of the Sabbath and the prohibition of alcoholic drinks (motivated by the avoidance of pagan libations rather than by food Laws), should be taken into consideration.[34] Among the quoted sources, Flavius Josephus' autobiography demands special attention:

> Between the twenty-sixth and twenty-seventh year it happened me to leave for Rome, for the reason that now I'm going to tell you. When Felix was procurator of Judaea, he had sent to Rome some priests, who according to me were extremely good people and had been arrested for scornful accusation, in order that they could justify themselves before the emperor. I, then, thinking on how to save them, and most of all, because I came to know that even in such disgrace they did not forget piety toward God and they were feeding themselves on fig-fruits and walnut-fruits, I left for Rome, running great risks along the way (*Life* 3, 13–4).

The event reported by Josephus is contemporary to Romans: Marcus Antonius Felix was a procurator in Judea from 52 to 60 CE, between Claudius and Nero, while the same Flavius Josephus was selected for the trip under Porcius Festus' procuratorship (61–62 CE) and arrived in Rome under that of Lucius Albinus (62–64 CE).

The extra-Pauline parallels and the use of terms like καθαρός and κοινος[35] in Rom. 14, 14.20 demonstrate that the argument encountered by Paul does not concern practices of philosophical asceticism, such as those practised among the neo-Pythagoreans, nor dietary traditions of Jewish sectarian groups, e.g. the Ebionites, nor Gnostic tendencies,[36] but some *halakhot* or oral norms of Torah inter-

---

32. See Dan. 1.8–16; Est. 14.17; *Jdt.* 12.1–2; *Tob.* 1, 10–2; *T. Iss.* 4.5–6; 2 Macc. 5.27; *4 Macc.* 1, 34; *Jos. Asen.* 7.1; 8.5; *1QS* 5, 16–8. See also Philo, *Leg. Gai.* 361; *Vit. Cont.* 4.37; Josephus, *Ant.* 11.346; *Apion* 2.282.

33. See Juvenal, *Satirae*, 14, 9b.10b; Horace, *Satirae* 1.9.67–72; Ovid, *Ars Amatoria* 1.16.415–6; *Remedia Amoris* 219–20; Tacitus, *Hist.* 5.4.2–4. It can be noted that, as often in such witnesses, Jewish food traditions are combined with those of the calendar and the Sabbath. On the diffusion of Jewish traditions in Rome and the context of the Diaspora see Barclay, *Undermine the Law?*, pp. 293–95; L.H. Feldman, *Jew and Gentile in the Ancient World: Attitudes and Interactions from Alexander to Justinian* (Princeton, NJ: Princeton University Press, 1992), pp. 127–76; M. Stern, *Greek and Latin Authors on Jews and Judaism* (Jerusalem: Israel Academy of Science and Humanities, 1974–84), vol. I-III.

34. Like Reasoner, *Strong*, pp. 140–58. About Jewish prohibitions of wine because of pagan libations see Dan. 1.13–6; 10.3; *T. Rub.* 1.10; *T. Jud.* 15.4.

35. Apart from Acts 2.44; 4.32; Tit. 1.4 and Jude 3 where κοινός means 'common', in the other instances in the NT the term refers to impurity, above all of a dietary type (see Mk 7.2, 5; 10.14, 28; 11.8; Heb. 10.29). See also the cognate verb κοινοῦν in Mk 7.15, 18, 20, 23; Mt. 15.11, 18, 20; Acts 10.15; 11.9; 21.28; Heb. 9.13. For the LXX see Sir. 18.1; 1 Macc. 1.47, 62; *3 Macc.* 2.33. For the use of καθαρίζειν in the context of dietary purity see Mk 7.19; Mt. 23.25; Lk. 11.39; Acts 10.15; 11.9. On Jewish-Hellenistic parallels on κοινός to Rom. 14.14 see also Fitzmyer, *Romans*, p. 688; Reasoner, *Strong,* p. 73; Schneider, *Die Schwachen*, pp. 69–70.

36. See the references to these forms of asceticism in Philo, *Vit. Cont.* 37.73; Philostratus, *Vita Apollonii* 1.8; Irenaeus, *Adversus Haereses* 1.24.2; Eusebius, *Hist. Eccl.* 4.29. See also Seneca, *Epistulae Morales* 108.22.

pretation.[37] Perhaps it is good to emphasize that it concerns the Torah and its oral tradition in the context of Diaspora Judaism, because in fact no Jewish tradition prohibits the consumption of meat.

Therefore, the Pauline strategy of mutual acceptance of the strong and the weak is marked by the respect towards different convictions of the recipients who, through the adhesion to a *form of Judaism* and the written Torah together with the oral traditions, encountered and eventually joined the Christian current of Roman Judaism. If they had practised pagan asceticism, perhaps the Pauline argumentation would have been less respectful, as is shown in the case of Galatians where Paul does not hesitate to blame the addressees for following the Jewish calendar: 'You pay special attention to certain days, months, seasons, and years. I am worried about you that all my work for you has been for nothing' (Gal. 4.10–1M).

At first sight, Paul's attitude seems to be contradictory: on the one hand, he reproaches the Galatians for the observance of the Jewish calendar while, on the other hand, he proves respectful to observance of the calendar shown by the 'weak' among the Christian communities in Rome. Actually, we have two different cases: the first relates to Gentile-Christians who, after accepting the Pauline gospel, want to be circumcised and still submit themselves to Jewish norms;[38] the second case refers to the weak and the strong regardless of their ethnic origin who moved from the knowledge of the Torah and the practices of its *halakot* to the union in Christ.

4. *The Strong, the Weak and the Mosaic Law*

If, as we have tried to demonstrate, the controversy between the strong and the weak is a result of the historic situation of the recipients of Romans, it is important to deal with possible echoes of what Paul has dictated in Rom. 1.1–13.13. At first sight, the absence of the binominal terms of 'strong' and 'weak' in the preceding sentences[39] and of any reference to dietary matters, seems to confirm the idea of those who consider the parenesis or, much better, the paraclesis of Rom. 14.1–15.13 as out of context and generic. Such a tendency seems to be confirmed by the lack of any allusions to conflicts within the Christian communities in Rome. Instead, in Rom. 1.8–15 Paul profusely applauds the faith of all the recipients: 'Your faith is proclaimed all over the world' (v. 8b).

A deeper analysis allows us to understand that the dispute in Romans reflects exactly on one of the more important topics addressed by Paul in his letter: the Torah, even if in Rom. 14.1–15.13 the noun νόμος is lacking.[40] We have already

37. With Tompson, *Paul*, pp. 237–45, even if the author translates ἀσθενοῦντα with 'delicate' and not with 'weak' (p. 243). What is in question in Rom. 14.1–15.13 is the weakness or the strength of the faith and not simply dietary delicacy.

38. For the social-historic context of Galatians see A. Pitta, *Lettera ai Galati* (SOC, 9; Bologna: EDB, 2nd edn, 2000), pp. 27–30.

39. The verb ἀσθενεῖν is found in Rom. 4.19; 8.3 while the adjective δυνατός appears in Rom. 4.21; 9.22; 11.23; 12.18; 15.1. Only in Rom. 4.19–21 it refers to weakness and strength, but the first term is attributed to Abraham, the second to God.

40. With Barclay, *Undermine the Law?,* pp. 287–308.

shown that 'pure' and 'impure' diet refers to Jewish Torah practice in a Diaspora context. Besides, it is not the case that Paul alludes to the binominal terminology of 'strength' versus 'weakness' with reference to the Mosaic Law only in Rom. 8.3 τὸ γὰρ ἀδύνατον τοῦ νόμου ἐν ᾧ ἠσθένει διὰ τῆς σαρκός. In Rom. 14.1–15.13 the weak are also in such a state, not because of their immoral behaviour or because of a certain lack of faith, but because of their dietary practices that come from their observance of the Torah, even though they consider themselves, like the strong, dead to the Law (see Rom. 7.4) in order to serve the Lord in the newness of the Spirit (see Rom. 7.6).

With such a background, the novelty concerning the Law in Romans becomes clear in comparison to that expressed above all in Galatians.[41] In Galatians, Paul could never have said that 'the Law is holy, and that the commandment is holy, right and good' (see Rom. 7.12), and neither that the same Law is 'spiritual' (see Rom. 7.14) nor that it is 'of God' (see Rom. 7.25). Rather, in Galatians, Paul tried to show that the Law has been promulgated 430 years after the promise given to Abraham (Gal. 3.17) that there is a terrible effect of the Law from which only Christ has set us free (see Gal. 3.13–4) and that those who are led by the Spirit are not subject to the Law (see Gal. 5.18). Paul would never have said that the circumcision is a 'sign of justice deriving from faith' (see Rom. 4.11), nor that 'Christ became the servant of the circumcision for being faithful to God's truth' (see Rom. 15.8), but he has strongly emphasized the opposition between Christ and circumcision: ἴδε ἐγὼ Παῦλος λέγω ὑμῖν ὅτι ἐὰν περιτέμνησθε, Χριστὸς ὑμᾶς οὐδὲν ὠφελήσει (Gal. 5.2).

Of course, even in Romans Paul does not miss some negative sentences on the Law and its actions: through the Law there is only the full knowledge of sin (see

41. As is well known, the issue of the Law in Paul inspired a wide field not only of contemporary exegetic debate and therefore an extensive bibliography. To limit ourselves to the more important and recent contributions on Galatians and Romans, see J.-N. Aletti, 'Fede e Legge in Romani', in *idem*, *La Lettera ai Romani e la giustizia di Dio* (Rome: Borla, 1997), pp. 71–144; *idem*, 'La Loi mosaique en Romains', in *idem*, *Israel et la Loi dans la Lettre aux Romains* (LD, 173; Paris: Cerf, 1998), pp. 267–94; R. Bergmeier, 'Das Gesetz im Römerbrief', in *idem*, *Das Gesetz im Römerbrief und andere Studien zum Neuen Testament* (WUNT, 121; Tübingen: Mohr-Siebeck, 2000), pp. 31–102; B. Byrne, 'The Problem of νόμος and the Relationship with Judaism in Romans', *CBQ* 62 (2000), pp. 294–309; K. Kuula, *The Law, the Covenant and God's Plan, I, Paul's Polemical Treatment of the Law in Galatians* (Publications of the Finnish Exegetical Society, 72; Helsinki: Vandenhoeck & Ruprecht, 1999); R. Penna, 'Come interpretare la "giustizia della Legge" in Rom. 8,4', in L.Padovese (ed.), *Atti del VI Simposio di Tarso su s.Paolo Apostolo* (Rome 2000: Antonianum), pp. 25–46; A. Pitta, 'Un conflitto in atto: la Legge nella Lettera ai Romani', *RivB* 49 (2001), pp. 257–82; H. Räisänen, *Paul and the Law* (WUNT, 29; Tübingen: Mohr-Siebeck, 1987); W. Reinbold, 'Gal. 3,6–14 und das Problem der Erfüllbarkeit des Gesetzes bei Paulus', *ZNW* 91 (2000), pp. 91–106; E.P. Sanders, *Paul, the Law and the Jewish People* (Philadelphia: Fortress Press, 1983); M.A. Seifrid, 'Natural Revelation and the Purpose of the Law in Romans', *TynB* 49 (1998), pp. 115–29; V.M. Smiles, *The Gospel and the Law in Galatia. Paul's Response to Jewish-Christian Separatism and the Threat of Galatian Apostasy* (Collegeville: Liturgical Press, 1998); F. Thielman, *From Plight to Solution: A Jewish Framework for Understanding Paul's View of the Law in Galatians and Romans* (NTSup, 61; Leiden: E.J. Brill, 1989); F.E. Udoh, 'Paul's View on the Law: Questions About Origin (Gal. 1.6–2.21; Phil. 3.2–11)', in *NT* 42 (2000), pp. 214–37.

Rom. 3.20), and it was introduced to increase the fall (see Rom. 5.20). For this, believers are no longer under the Law but under God's grace (see Rom. 6.14). The conflict between the positive and the negative statements on the Law reaches its climax in Rom. 7.7–25 in which its impotence concerning the power of sin is added to that of the 'ego'.[42] Therefore, we maintain that the novelty of the positive propositions on the Law in Romans, in comparison to those prevailing negatively in Galatians, is in fact due to the different historical-social contexts of the two letters. Because the Galatians need to be subjected to the Law and to circumcision after their union to Christ, it is necessary to underline above all the negative view of the same Law in relationship to justification by faith. Because of the transfer from the Law to Christ that has involved all the believers of Rome, Paul's point of view is different in the letter to the Romans. It is not the case that in Rom. 14.1–15.13 Paul never asks the weak to become strong and not to pay attention to the Jewish dietary practices, but he requires the strong to renounce their convictions for the positive reception of the weak: καλὸν τὸ μὴ φαγεῖν κρέα μηδὲ πιεῖν οἶνον μηδὲ ἐν ᾧ ὁ ἀδελφός σου προσκόπτει. σὺ πίστιν [ἣν] ἔχεις κατὰ σεαυτὸν ἔχε ἐνώπιον τοῦ θεοῦ. μακάριος ὁ μὴ κρίνων ἑαυτὸν ἐν ᾧ δοκιμάζει (Rom. 14.21–2).

At this point the question arises on why Paul takes up such a controversy so close to the conclusion of the letter, namely in the paracletic section (cf. Rom. 12.1–15.13) and not properly in the kerygmatic one. We think the main reason should be seen in the continuous discussion of the Law in Galatians and in Romans, in spite of differences we did not hesitate to point out. We refer to the axiom of justification by faith and not by works of the Law, expressed for the first time in Gal. 2.16 and emphasized again in Rom. 3.20. Also, the Christian believers in Rome agree on the axiom of righteousness by faith in Christ which represents a fundamental datum of convergence with the Pauline gospel. Nevertheless, the weak continue to follow some Jewish norms without considering them as soteriological prerequisits.

The ecclesial rather than kerygmatic nature of the debate has caused Paul to deal with the topic of Rom. 14.1–15.13 in the paracletic section of the letter, even if the conflict itself allows us to clarify the original treatment of the Law in Romans and leads us to understand that the kerygmatic and ethic or paracletic passages are less distant and less separate from each other than one might have thought.[43] The deep relationship between the Pauline exhortation to the weak and the strong and the treatment of the Mosaic Law that we have pointed out requires greater attention to the concluding paracletic sections of his letters, putting away with all forms of prejudice, e.g. of those who consider these passages generic and less relevant for the epistolary background of the sender and the recipients.

---

42. For a detailed analysis see Pitta, 'Conflitto', pp. 270–75.

43. On the relationship between kerygmatic and paracletic sections in the Pauline letters see A. Pitta, 'Esortazione morale e kerygma paolino', in A. Vanhoye (ed.), *La foi agissant par l'amour (Gal. 4,12–6,16)* (SMB, 13, Rome: Abbaye de S.Paul, 1996), pp. 219–40.

5. *Conclusion*

The exhortation directed to the strong in the Christian communities in Rome to welcome their weak fellows represents fundamental evidence about the pragmatic relevance of the Mosaic Law: the Law, without changing anything in regard to the justification by faith, can continue to be observed by those who joined Christ properly through it. In that sense, Paul corroborates the lapidary answer of Rom. 3.31: 'Do we abrogate the Law by means of faith? No, not at all; instead we uphold the Law'. The soteriologic inefficacy of the Law and its permanence are not in contradiction to Pauline assertions but they show how, from Christ onwards, the same Law is indifferent.

Some have likened Paul's exhortation towards the strong and the weak in Romans to the Trojan horse to which the axiom *timeo Danaos et dona ferentes* could be applied.[44] In reality, one could think of that trap if Paul had sustained the abrogation of the Law and if the weak in Rome would have considered the Law as a condition for justification. Instead, such conclusions are absent in Romans and in all Pauline letters in which, as far as the Law is described in a negative way like in Galatians, it is never retained as abrogated. The conflict in the Christian communities in Rome induces Paul to work out a more complex position about the Mosaic Law as can be seen in the tension between his positive and negative statements.

Paying attention to the identity of the strong and the weak has not led us to ignore their ethical identity determined by their relationship to the Law and their Jewish oral traditions. One cannot apply the distinction of 'Judaeo-Christians' and 'Gentile-Christians' to the recipients, nor the social distinction between *potentes* and *inferiores*, nor, even much less, between two separate groups invited to unify through the Pauline gospel. Of the one or of the other group they can make part both the Jewish-Christians or ethnic-Christians, because all of them share the only faith in Christ. We do not even know the numerical proportion of the two sides, to determine if the strong or the weak constituted the majority or the minority in the Christian communities in Rome. These questions are destined to remain unsolved, even if we have attained important results concerning the Roman background of the Pauline exhortation and on the relevance of the Law in order to distinguish the strong from the weak. Taking into account the important self-praise statement of 1 Cor. 9.1–27, Paul 'has become one under the Law so that I might win those who are under the Law ... to those who are without the Law so that might win those who are without the Law' (1 Cor. 9.20–1) and because of this instance, not as a trap or to a strategic concession towards the weak,[45] 'He became weak for the weak, in order to save someone at any cost' (1 Cor. 9.22).

---

44. As instead Barclay, *Undermine the Law?*, p. 308.

45. Against Pate, *Curse*, p. 271 who considers Rom. 14.1–15.13 'as a concession for the sake of the unity of the church rather than as a manifestation of his (Paul's) convictions'.

Part IIb
Persons and Positions in the Early Christian Community of Rome

WHO BURIED PETER AND PAUL?

John C. O'Neill[†]

There are traditionally three streets in Rome associated with the martyrdoms of Peter and Paul. A hymn attributed to Ambrose runs:

> *Trinis celebratur viis*
> *Festum sanctorum martyrum.*[1]

The three sites are the Via Aurelia on the Vatican for Peter, the Via Ostiensis for Paul, and the Via Appia at the Catacombs for both Peter and Paul. Louis Duchesne and Hans Lietzmann have proposed that Peter was first buried near the place of his crucifixion on the Vatican, that Paul was first buried near the place of his decapitation on the Ostian Way, that both bodies were moved to a common burial place in a cave cemetery called the Catacombs during the persecution of Christians by the Emperor Valerian in 258 CE, only to be restored to their original resting places in the fourth century (336 CE).[2]

This theory is too complicated and runs beyond the evidence. Since the Emperor Valerian had barred Christian cemeteries to all visitors, an exhumation from two sites and an inhumation in the Catacombs in 258 CE is unlikely. Strangely enough, there is no report of a fourth century exhumation from the Catacombs and two inhumations at the Vatican and on the Ostian Way. The only dated account of such a move is in the fifth century *Acts of Sebastian* and the date given is in the pontificate of Cornelius, 251–253 CE.[3]

Henry Chadwick has argued that a private cult of Peter and Paul arose in the third century in the Catacombs. This was embarrassing for the official cults at the Vatican and the Ostian Way. Pope Damasus, 382 CE, was glad to use this cult to buttress his claim for the supremacy of Rome over the East. The single commemoration on 29 June associated with the Catacombs was taken over and superseded the two separate feast days associated with the other two shrines. Pope Damasus laid to rest the cult at the Catacombs with a graceful inscription and arranged that the other shrines, the

---

1. Hymns 71 (*PL* 17.1254).
2. H. Lietzmann, *Petrus und Paulus in Rom: Liturgische und Archäologische Studien* (Bonn: A. Marcus und E. Weber, 1915; Berlin und Leipzig: W. de Gruyter, 2nd rev. edn, 1927). H. Chadwick, 'St. Peter and St. Paul in Rome: The Problem of the Memoria Apostolorum ad Catacumbas', *JTS* 8 (1957), pp. 31–52, notes on p. 41 that the learned Cambridge scholar John Pearson (1613–1686), later Bishop of Chester, already proposed this theory.
3. Lietzmann, *Petrus und Paulus in Rom*, p. 131; 2nd edn, p. 180.

places of martyrdom, alone receive papal visits on 29 June. This theory gives up any attempt to be certain about the true sites of the apostolic graves.

The cult at the third milestone of the Appian Way, in the Catacombs, is both so persistent and so embarrassing that it is possible to argue that when Peter and Paul were executed their bodies were indeed laid there rather than at the site of their deaths. Neither the reported words of Gaius (Eusebius, *Hist. Eccl.* 2.25.7) nor the evidence gathered from the excavations of the Catacombs rules out this possibility. Once we ask who were likely to have buried Peter and Paul, a connection with the caves used for burial by the Jews in Rome begins to appear possible.

First, we should question the argument that the dialogue of Gaius cited by Eusebius rules out the existence of a cemetery called 'Peter and Paul' about the year 200 CE.

Before we examine Gaius's statement, notice that Eusebius in *Hist. Eccl.* 3.31.1 summarizes the events of the execution of Paul and Peter in words that imply, perhaps erroneously, an earlier account by which the two apostles were buried together in one place on their death. 'We have already shown the time and the manner of the end of Paul and Peter and, besides, the place of the deposition of their corpses after their departure from life.' The earlier account is probably that one given in *Hist. Eccl.* 2.25.5. Since that earlier account was confirmed by an extract from a writing of Gaius that refers to two separate 'trophies' of the apostles, on the Vatican and in the Ostian Way, and as Eusebius himself says that the sacred σκηνώματα of the apostles were there, using a word which could (but need not) refer to their bodies (2 Pet. 1.13), this earlier account seems to point to two separate cemeteries. If, as will be argued below, Gaius meant by 'trophies' shrines rather than tombs, is is advisable to amend Eusebius to allow him to give an account in *Hist. Eccl.* 2.25.5 that matches his summary in 3.31.1. 'It is related that, under Nero, Paul was beheaded in Rome itself and Peter was likewise crucified, and the still prevailing designation of the immediate cemetery (τοῦ αὐτόθι κοιμητηρίου) as "Peter and Paul" confirms the story…'. In favour of this conjectural emendation, it would be passing strange if two separate graves had the single designation 'Peter and Paul'.

Gaius's controversy with Proclus the Montanist cited by Eusebius in *Hist. Eccl.* 2.25.7 refers to τὰ τρόπαια of the apostles. He is answering his interlocutor's claim to have at Hieropolis in Asia (and at Ephesus) the tombs of the four daughters of Philip who were prophetesses, and the tomb of their father (*Hist. Eccl.* 3.31.4). Carcopino has produced some late fourth-century texts where τρόπαια refer to the bodies of martyrs, and he rejects both the translation 'cenotaphs' and 'tombs'.[4] The use of τρόπαια in reply to Proclus's 'tombs' is likely to be a trumping argument: 'You Montanists have tombs; we have trophies, for Peter and Paul were martyred by cross and axe, mystic signs of a divine significance, hidden from the executors but visible to the eyes of faith' (cf. Justin, 1. *Apol.* 1.55).

4.   J. Carcopino, *De Pythagore aux Apôtres: Études sur la conversion du Monde Romain* (Paris: Flammarion, 1956), pp. 253–54. The translation 'tombs' is espoused by E. Kirschbaum, *The Tombs of St Peter and St Paul* (Translated from German, 1957; London: Secker & Warburg, 1959), p. 79.

Carcopino relies further on Eusebius's introduction to the citation from Gaius, particularly on his use of the word σκηνώματα. Although it is possible to take the word in the metaphorical sense as 'bodies' (2 Pet. 1.14), it more naturally refers to temples or shrines. 'Gaius ... speaks as follows concerning the places where the sacred shrines of the named apostles are set up (as a memorial).'[5] If my reconstruction of Eusebius's earlier remarks, bringing them into line with the later summary in *Hist. Eccl.* 3.31.4, is right, Eusebius assumes that Gaius, in drawing attention to the two separate trophies at the Vatican and on the Ostian Way, is not contradicting the tradition that there was one common tomb of both apostles elsewhere, known as 'Peter and Paul'.

The archaeological evidence for the 'Memoria Apostolorum ad Catacumbas' indicates that the Memoria was constructed between 238 and 260 CE. The inscription on the tomb preceding the Memoria refers to members of the imperial household who took as *cognomina* the names of their imperial masters Pupienus and Balbinus. One of the graffiti in the *tricula* dates back to 9 August 260. The walls of the *tricula* and courtyard are marked with graffiti asking the prayers of Peter and Paul and attesting the holding of meals in honour of the dead apostles.[6]

It is likely that the Catacombs originally formed a Jewish cemetery. Carcopino deciphers one inscription on a tomb preceding the building of the Memoria in which two Jewish women invoke, according to pagan custom, the soul of their dead mother for their own good. Perhaps Jews could do this (*CIJ* 193 from the Catacomb of the Vigna Randanini, close by Catacumbas).[7] Jeremiah was said to be praying for the people and the holy city, and in vision he gave Onias the high priest a sword (2 Macc. 15.12–6; cf. Philo, *Praem. Poen.* 165; Dan. 3.86 LXX; Mk 15.35).[8] The imperial servants buried there who belonged to the fraternity of the Innocentii may well have been Jews: '*Lavabo inter innocentes manus meas et circumdabo altare tuum, Domine*' (Ps. 25.6 Vg.).[9]

The area is surrounded by Jewish catacombs, notably Randanini, a little to the north (dating at least from the end of the first century), and Cimarra, a little to the south.

Let us turn to the key questions: Who are likely to have buried Peter and Paul?, and: Where are they likely to have buried them? Christians were cruelly persecuted by Nero. Paul was certainly executed on his orders and Peter most likely also. The small congregations of Christians, almost certainly Jews and godfearers, would have been inhibited by fear from claiming the apostles' bodies. Jews who had not accepted that the Messiah had come and been crucified by the Romans would yet feel it a sacred duty to give burial to their fellow Jews, Peter and Paul. If so, they would have placed their bodies in simple graves in their own catacombs. They would not have wanted to bury the bodies in the pagan cemeteries, full of cremated

---

5. See the acute remarks of Chadwick, 'St. Peter and St. Paul in Rome', pp. 43–44. He notes *1 Clem.* 5.4, 'Peter...having given his testimony went to the due place of glory', his Golgotha.

6. See Chadwick, 'St. Peter and St. Paul in Rome', pp. 32–34, especially p. 33 n. 1.

7. Carcopino, *De Pythagore aux Apôtres*, pp. 344–46.

8. W. Horbury, 'The Cult of Christ and the Cult of the Saints', *NTS* 44 (1998), pp. 444–69 (455).

9. Carcopino, *De Pythagore aux Apôtres*, pp. 346–49.

bodies, near the two places of execution. They already had their own catacombs, and to those they would most likely have taken them.

The later traditions that ascribe names to those who buried Peter and Paul do not contradict my assumption that the men involved were devout Jews. The Syriac *Doctrine of Simon Cephas in the City of Rome* says, 'And Isus the Guide arose and took up their bodies by night and buried them with great honour, and a house of assembly for many was made there.'[10] In the *Actus Petri cum Simone* containing the Μαρτύριον τοῦ ἁγίου ἀποστόλου Πέτρου a certain Marcellus put Peter's body in his own tomb. Peter then appeared to him and converted him (it seems).[11]

I could rest my case here, but it is hard not to draw a little support from the strange traditions that pious men from the east took the bodies and buried them at the Catacombs. The *Martyrium Petri et Pauli* 66[12] states that certain devout men from the east (in the Greek version) wanted to snatch the remains of the holy apostles. An earthquake hindered them and they fled. The Romans put the bodies in a place at the third milestone on the Appian Way. In the Greek version, the bodies lay there for one year and seven months, 'until they (the Romans) made a place in which they were about to bestow them. And after that, while all were assembled with praise and hymns, they laid them in the place they had constructed for them.' The Latin version says that the bodies were kept in the Catacombs on the Appian Way for one year and seven months until the two resting places were constructed, one on the Vatican and the other at the second milestone on the Ostian Way. The shorter Greek version is to be preferred. The devout men from the east are foiled; the bodies are laid, presumably in the Catacombs at the third milestone, for 19 months until one common resting place has been built, where they were laid to rest with festal song. I assume that the constructed resting place would have been elsewhere in the same Catacombs. The Latin version embroiders the shorter Greek account with the addition of festive processions to two resting places, at the Vatican and on the Ostian Way. It is unlikely that such a double procession through the streets of Rome would have been possible less than two years after the execution of the two apostles. The exhumation of the two bodies and their inhumation on the separate sites of their execution would probably require more settled times than the era of the first Jewish Revolt (66–70 CE).

A similar account is appended to the Syriac *Acts of Sharbil*, set at the time of Pope Fabian (235–250).[13] There are two layers to this tradition. The earlier layer tells of a popular Roman movement to expel strangers from Rome. The strangers ask and are given permission to remove the bones of their dead, particularly the bones of Peter and Paul. Permission is granted, but as they were removing the

---

10. W. Cureton (ed.), *Ancient Syriac Documents relative to the Earliest Establishment of Christianity in Edessa and the Neighbouring Countries* (London: Williams & Norgate, 1864), pp. 35–41 (40). Cureton supposes that Isus the Guide is the same as Ansus (i.e. Linus), whose appointment by Peter as his successor had just been mentioned in the same document.

11. R.A. Lipsius (ed.), *Acta Apostolorum Apocrypha 1: Acta Petri. Acta Pauli. Acta Petri et Pauli. Acta Pauli et Theclae. Acta Thaddaei* (Leipzig: Mendelssohn, 1891), pp. 45–103 at pp. 98–100.

12. Lipsius, *Acta Apostolorum Apocrypha*, I, pp. 174–77.

13. Cureton, *Ancient Syriac Documents*, pp. 41–62 (61–62).

bones an earthquake occurred which led the Romans to relent in their desire to expel the strangers. They intreated the strangers to return the bones to their former places of burial. The strangers are clearly Jews, who did not cremate their dead. That story is overlaid by another describing the mass conversion of Jews and Pagans at the time of Fabian, who is Pope of a flourishing Christian church, but no attempt is made to explain how that double conversion relates to the earlier account where the strangers own the bodies of Peter and Paul.

Gregory the Great in an epistle to the Empress Constantina in June 594 CE (4.30; *PL* 77.703; *CCh* 140.249–50) reported the common view that, at the time of the sufferings of the two apostles, faithful men from the east claimed their bodies as being those of their fellow citizens. They took them as far as the second milestone and placed them in the cemetery called *Catacumbas*. But when the entire multitude of them gathered to move them from there, they were terrified by thunder and lightning and dispersed. In due course worthy Romans came out and exhumed their bodies and placed them where they are now buried (on the Vatican and in the Ostian Way).

Two stories seem to have been run together. The first is of *fideles* from the east, believers, but possibly simply good Jews, who put the bodies in the catacombs at the time of martyrdom. That story is enlarged by a second story about an entire multitude of men from the east who wanted to move the bodies on. This seems to reflect the ideological tussle under Pope Damasus about the doctrinal authority of Rome against the Eastern Church; Peter and Paul may have come from the east but they were martyred at Rome and at Rome their relics were treasured.

It seems that the tradition that Peter and Paul were buried by devout men at the third milestone on the Appian Way may represent an ancient event, the burial by devout Jews of their misguided compatriots who had fallen foul of Nero.

GEBEINE DES APOSTELFÜRSTEN?
ZU DEN ANGEBLICH FRÜHCHRISTLICHEN GRÄBERN
UNTER DER PETERSKIRCHE IN ROM

Jürgen Zangenberg

Es geht uns darum, die heute oft in Vergessenheit geratene Doppelung der historischen Quellen in Erinnerung zu bringen. Weder Profan- noch Kirchengeschichte können auf die Einbeziehung der monumentalen Zeugnisse der Vergangenheit neben den literarischen verzichten.[1]

Eine besondere Rolle für das Selbstverständnis der antiken stadtrömischen Christengemeinde und bis heute für die Römisch-Katholische Kirche spielt die Tradition vom Märtyrertod und Begräbnis der Apostel Petrus und Paulus in Rom.[2] Während klare Hinweise auf diese Ereignisse im Neuen Testament fehlen,[3] berichtet der nach Meinung der Forschungsmehrheit um 95 n.Chr. entstandene *1 Clem*[4] bereits vom Märtyrertod vieler Christen in der Stadt, darunter auch der beiden Erzapostel (5.1–6.2). Gegenstand dieser Untersuchung soll aber nicht die literarische Überlieferung sein, die bereits mehrfach aufgearbeitet worden ist,[5] sondern archäologische Befunde, die von 1939/40 bis 1949 und 1953 bis 1957 unter der Apsis der Peterskirche auf dem Vatikan ergraben wurden.[6]

1. E. Dinkler, 'Petrus und Paulus in Rom', *Gymnasium* 87 (1980), pp. 1–37 (3).
2. Dazu siehe z.B. den Beitrag von John C. O'Neill in diesem Band.
3. Dinkler, 'Petrus', pp. 3–6.
4. Vgl. Anm. 1 des Beitrags von Martin Meiser in diesem Band.
5. H. Lietzmann, *Petrus und Paulus in Rom. Liturgische und archäologische Studien* (2. Aufl., AKG, 1; Berlin, Leipzig: Marcus und Weber); H.G.Thümmel, *Die Memorien für Petrus und Paulus in Rom. Die archäologischen Denkmäler und die literarische Tradition* (AKG, 76; Berlin, New York: W. de Gruyter, 1999), pp. 3–14; Dinkler, 'Petrus', dort jeweils weiterführende Literatur.
6. Im gegebenen Zusammenhang beschränke ich mich daher auf die archäologische Problematik, Fragen der Biographie des Petrus, der römischen Christengemeinde und der oft diskutierten „Zuverlässigkeit der römischen Petrustradition" können nur indirekt oder am Rande behandelt werden. Die erste, von Papst Pius XII. angeregte Grabungsphase dauerte von 1939–1949 und wurde 1951 in B.M. Apollonii Ghetti, A. Ferrua, E. Josi, E. Kirschbaum, L. Kaas, *Esplorazioni sotto la confessione di S.Pietro in Vaticano eseguite negli anni 1940–1949* (Città del Vaticano: Tipografia Poliglotta Vaticana, 1951) veröffentlicht. Die Arbeiten von J.M.C. Toynbee, 'The Shrine of St. Peter and its Setting', *JRS* 43 (1953), pp. 1–26; *idem*, J.B. Ward Perkins, *The Shrine of St. Peter and the Vatican Excavations* (New York: Longmans and Green, 1956); J. Ruysschaert, 'Réflexions sur les fouilles vaticanes. Le rapport officiel et la critique', *RHE* 48 (1953), pp. 573–631 basieren auf Autopsie des damals freigelegten Befundes und bestätigen sie im

Wesentlichen. Weitere Grabungen veranstalteten zwischen 1953 und 1958 Adrianio Prandi und Domenico Mustilli, sie liegen vor in A. Prandi, *La zona archeologica della confessione vaticana. I monumenti del II° secolo* (Città del Vaticano: Tipografia Poliglotta Vaticana, 1957) und *idem*, ‚La tomba di San Pietro nei pellegrinaggi dell'età medievale', in: *Pellegrinaggi e culto dei santi in Europa fino alla Iª crociata, 8.-11.10.1961* (Convegni del Centro di studi sulla spritualità medievale 4; Todi: Presso l'Accademia Tudertina, 1963), pp. 283–447 mit Fig. 1-159. Margherita Guarduccis Forschungen zu Gräbern des 1. Jh. in der Vatikangegend aus dem Jahre 1956 liegen vor in M. Guarducci, 'Documenti del primo secolo nella necropoli vaticane', *RPARA* 29 (1956–57), pp. 111–37. Sie müssen nun ergänzt werden durch E.M. Steinby, 'La necropoli della Via Triumphalis. Pianificazione generale e tipologia dei monumenti funerari', in H. v. Hesberg, P. Zanker (eds.), *Römische Gräberstraßen. Selbstdarstellung, Status, Standart. Colloquium in München 28.-30.10.1985* (AbhBAW, 96; München: Verlag der Bayerischen Akademie der Wissenschaften, 1987), pp. 85–110. Guarducci publizierte ihre seit 1953 betriebenen und heftig umstrittenen epigraphischen Forschungen im Jahre 1958 in M. Guarducci, *I graffiti sotto la confessione di San Pietro in Vaticano I-III* (Città del Vaticano: Tipografia Poliglotta Vaticana, 1958) sowie die Untersuchungen zu den wiederaufgefundenen menschlichen Knochen im Jahre 1965 (ich verwende die deutsche Ausgabe von 1967: *idem, Hier ist Petrus – ΠΕΤΡΟΣ ΕΝΙ. Die Gebeine des Apostelfürsten in der Confessio von St. Peter. Mit dem vollständigen Untersuchungsbericht von Professor Venerando Correnti und den anderen grundlegenden Gutachten der Professoren Luigi Cardini, Carlo Lauro und Gian Carlo Negretti, Maria Luisa Stein und Paolo Malatesta* [Regensburg: Josef Habbel, 1967]. Als abschließende Zusammenfassung ihrer Arbeit aus dem Jahr 1963 kann gelten *idem*, ‚Die Ausgrabungen unter St. Peter', in R. Klein (ed.), *Das frühe Christentum im römischen Staat* (2. Aufl., WdF, 267; Darmstadt: Wissenschaftliche Buchgesellschaft, 1982), pp. 364–414 und den letzten Stand wiedergebend v.a. *idem, Petrus. Sein Tod, sein Grab. Chronik einer Entdeckung* (Regensburg: Friedrich Pustet, 1975). Den Verlauf der Grabungen an der eigentlichen Petrusmemoria 1941 stellt Thümmel, *Memorien*, pp. 21–26 zusammen. Die Literatur zum Petrusgrab ist inzwischen nahezu unübersehbar. Eine hilfreiche Zusammenstellung der bis 1964 erschienenen Studien bietet die Bibliographie von A.A. De Marco, *The Tomb of St. Peter. A Representative and Annotated Bibliography of the Excavations* (NT.Sup 8; Leiden: E.J. Brill, 1964), zur Archäologie bes. pp. 144–256. Bis 1961 ist u.a. E. Dinkler, 'Die Petrus-Rom-Frage. Ein Forschungsbericht', *ThR* 25 (1959), pp. 189–230 und 289–335; 27 (1961), pp. 33–64 heranzuziehen. An englischsprachigen Titeln sind besonders Toynbee und Ward Perkins, Excavations sowie J.E. Walsh, *The Bones of St. Peter* (New York: Doubleday & Co., 1982) zu nennen. Für den deutschsprachigen Raum sind insbesondere wichtig E. Kirschbaum, *Die Gräber der Apostelfürsten. St. Peter und St. Paul in Rom, mit einem Nachtragskapitel von Ernst Dassmann* (3. Aufl., Frankfurt: Societäts-Verlag, 1974). Kirschbaum stellt die gesamten Ergebnisse in Auseinandersetzung mit Kritikern aus der Sicht des Ausgräberteams, dem er selbst angehört hatte, nochmals ausführlich zusammen und erweitert die Diskussion der Befunde von St. Peter mit denen von Alt-St.Paul; wichtig ist jedoch der kritische Nachtrag von E. Dassmann, 'Ist Petrus wirklich darin?' in der 3.Auflage von Kirschbaum, *Gräber*, pp. 223–48) und die Arbeiten von J. Fink, 'Das Petrusgrab. Glaube und Grabung', *VC* 32 (1978), pp. 255–75 und *idem*, 'Die Ausgrabungen unter St. Peter in Rom. und die Frühgeschichte des Petrusgrabes', *RöHM* 26 (1984), pp. 57–89 sowie *idem*, H.M. Schmiedinger, *Das Petrusgrab in Rom.* (Innsbruck: Tyrolia, 1988). W. Jordan, *Das Apostelgrab, der sakrale Grundstein der Vatikanischen Basilika* (Schriftenreihe des Rheinischen Landesmuseums Trier 4; Trier: Selbstverlag des Rheinischen Landesmuseums, 1990) bietet eine zuweilen sehr polemische Verteidigung der Ergebnisse der „offiziellen" Sicht, vermag aber manches interessante Detail zur Fundgeschichte mitzuteilen. Wichtig ist ferner P. Lampe, *Die stadtrömischen Christen in den ersten beiden Jahrhunderten. Untersuchungen zur Sozialgeschichte* (2. Aufl.; WUNT II/18; Tübingen: Mohr-Siebeck, 1989), pp. 82–94. Alle diese Forschungen wurden in Thümmel, *Memorien* umfassend geprüft und auf eine neue kritische Basis gestellt. Angesichts aller mit der Grabung verbundenen Schwierigkeiten und der oft geäußerten Kritik an den Unzulänglichkeiten der Dokumentation und Publikation sei auf die Worte Margherita

1. *Geschichte und Ergebnisse der Grabungen unter St. Peter*[7]

Nachdem man 1939 bei Bauarbeiten in den Grotten von St. Peter auf antike Baureste gestoßen war, begannen im Jahre 1940 intensivere Nachforschungen, in deren Verlauf man unter dem Fußboden der heutigen Peterskirche (hier Phase III) und den Resten ihres konstantinischen Vorgängerbaus (Phase II) (Abb. 1) einen beträchtlichen Abschnitt einer mittelkaiserzeitlichen Nekropole mit zum Teil hervorragend erhaltenen, in zwei Reihen der Via Cornelia folgenden Mausoleen (Phase I) freilegte (Abb. 2).[8] Insgesamt über zwanzig Grabanlagen wurden angeschnitten oder zum Teil ganz ausgegraben.[9] Direkt unterhalb der Apsis der konstantinischen Kirche, am Südende des erhaltenen Teils dieser Nekropole stieß man auf ein freies, nicht überdachtes Grundstück („Grabhof P"), der im Süden durch Mausoleum S, im Osten zum Teil durch Mausoleum O und im Westen durch eine rot getünchte Mauer (MR für *muro rosso*) mit einer Nische (N[1]) und einer *aedicula* begrenzt war. Daran angesetzt war eine kurze Mauer g mit unbekannter Funktion (Abb. 3). Das stratigraphische Verhältnis der einzelnen Bauelemente ist umstritten. Während die Ausgräber von der Gleichzeitigkeit von MR, Nische und Aedicula ausgehen, bringt Hans Georg Thümmel gute Argumente dafür vor, dass MR mit einer einfachen Nische *vor* die Anfügung von Mäuerchen g zu datieren ist und in einem dritten Schritt die Aedicula hinzukam, die ihrerseits im

Guarduccis verwiesen: „Man kann sicher nicht sagen, dass die beauftragten Personen ihrer Aufgabe nicht mit Hingabe gedient hätten. Das haben sie getan, ohne Zeit zu sparen und Kräfte zu schonen, lange, anstrengende und auch gefährliche Mühen auf sich nehmend. Es ist aber ebenfalls sicher, dass schon von Anfang an nicht immer alles so lief, wie es hätte laufen müssen. […] So wurde zum Beispiel niemals ein Ausgrabungstagebuch geführt, und trotz des guten Willens der Ausgräber ist ihnen das eine oder andere entgangen oder ging unwiderbringlich verloren" (*Petrus*, p. 49; vgl. Thümmel, *Memorien*, pp. 18–20). Viele Fragen werden sich daher nicht mehr mit der wünschenswerten Genauigkeit klären lassen.

7.   Zur archäologischen Forschungsgeschichte vgl. jetzt Thümmel, *Memorien*, pp. 15–26.

8.   Vorher hatte allein H. Grisar am Ende des 19. Jh. eigene Untersuchungen unter der Palliennische in St.Peter unternommen, vgl. H. Grisar, 'Le tombe apostoliche al Vaticano ed alla Via Ostiense', in *idem, Analecta Romana I* (Rom: Libreria Cattolica Internazionale, 1899); Thümmel, *Memorien*, p. 15.

9.   Die wissenschaftliche Publikation der Gräberstraße ist noch im Gang. Bisher liegt die Bearbeitung der Mausoleen A-D (H. Mielsch, H. v.Hesberg, K. Gaertner, *Die Heidnische Nekropole unter St.Peter in Rom. Die Mausoleen A-D* [Memorie della Pontificia Accademia Romana di Archeologia, XVI/1; Rom: L'Erma di Bretschneider, 1986]) sowie E-I und Z-Psi (H.Mielsch, H.v.Hesberg, *Die heidnische Nekropole unter St.Peter in Rom. Die Mausoleen E-I und Z-Psi* [Memorie della Pontificia Accademia Romana di Archeologia, XVI/2; Rom: L'Erma di Bretschneider, 1995) vor. Leider ist der Band über den für unsere Fragestellung besonders wichtigen Teil um den Grabhof P noch nicht erschienen. Vgl. bisher Prandi, *Zona*; Guarducci, *Petrus*, pp. 54–57 und H. v. Hesberg, 'Planung und Ausgestaltung der Nekropolen Roms im 2. Jh. n. Chr.' in v. Hesberg und Zanker, *Gräberstraßen*, pp. 43–60 und zu den Inschriften W. Eck, 'Inschriften und Grabbauten in der Nekropole unter St. Peter' in G. Alföldy (ed.), *Vom frühen Griechentum bis zur römischen Kaiserzeit. Gedenk- und Jubiläumsvorträge am Heidelberger Seminar für Alte Geschichte* (HABES, 6; Stuttgart: Steiner, 1989), pp. 55–90; *idem*, 'Römische Grabinschriften. Aussageabsicht und Aussagefähigkeit im funerären Kontext' in v. Hesberg und Zanker, *Gräberstraßen*, pp. 61–83.

Laufe der Zeit wieder verändert wurde (Abb. 4).[10] Nach Thümmel ist MR mit Nische als Teil von Grabhof P im Zuge der Errichtung der Gräberstraße entstanden,[11] die Aedicula entgegen der älteren Forschung aber erst später.[12] Die etwa 1,70 m hoch erhaltene Aedicula (bzw. besser mit Thümmel deren Vorgängerin: MR mit Nische) identifizierte man mit dem vom römischen Presbyter Gaius um 200 n.Chr. erwähnten τροπαῖον des Petrus auf dem Vatikan (s. Eusebius, H.E. 2.25.7).[13] Diese Identifikation ist bisher wohl zu Recht nicht bestritten worden.[14]

Einige Stempel auf Ziegeln, die in einer unter der Gräberstraße verlaufenden Wasserleitung verwendet wurden, datieren den Bau des Grabhofes P und seines benachbarten Ensembles in die Zeit um 160–165 n.Chr. Damit würde die Chronologie der archäologischen Befunde der Identifikation der Nische mit dem τροπαῖον zumindest nicht widersprechen. Das gesamte bis dahin entstandene Ensemble wurde nicht vor 319 n.Chr.[15] von Konstantin mit Marmor eingekleidet und in die neu errichtete Petersbasilika einbezogen. Massive Aufschüttungen begruben alle übrigen Reste der ehemaligen Gräberstraße bis zu 7 m tief unter sich. Damit ist auch der *terminus ante quem* sowohl für die Entstehung der angeschnittenen Teile der Gräberstraße entlang der Via Claudia mitsamt τροπαῖον als auch für alle daran vorgenommenen Veränderungen gegeben.

Besondere Brisanz erhielten die Grabungen vor allem dadurch, dass man sowohl in Grabhof P als auch in dessen Umgebung eine Anzahl recht einfacher Erdgräber fand, die zumindest zum Teil älter waren als die mittelkaiserzeitliche Gräberstraße inklusive seiner um den Grabhof P gruppierten Teile (Abb. 5). Dabei schien das um 160–165 n. Chr. erbaute τροπαῖον auf eines dieser Gräber in gewisser Weise Rücksicht zu nehmen (dazu s.u.). Also, folgerten die Ausgräber, muss diesem Grab eine besondere Bedeutung zugekommen sein, die durch die *Ausrichtung des τροπαῖον* ihren Ausdruck finde. Da das τροπαῖον aber seit frühester Zeit mit Petrus in Verbindung gebracht wird, lag der Schluss nahe, dass eben dieses durch das τροπαῖον hervorgehobene Grab das des Petrus sei, zumal wenn weitere Beobachtungen angeführt werden, die belegen sollen, dass sich das τροπαῖον des 2. Jh. in der Tat auf ein einzelnes, klar identifizierbares Grab bezieht. Zu diesen Beobachtungen gehört zum einen die Auswertung der vorkonstantinischen *Graffiti* auf der Nordseite von Mauer g, die u.a. auch den Namen des Petrus erwähnen und von Margherita Guarducci als frühe Zeugnisse christlicher Pilgerfrömmigkeit

---

10. Zur Diskussion der komplexen Fragen s. Thümmel, *Memorien*, pp. 26–62.

11. Vgl. die Argumentation bei Thümmel, *Memorien*, pp. 32–45.

12. Thümmel, *Memorien*, pp. 50–52.

13. Der Text lautet: ἐγὼ δὲ τὰ τρόπαια τῶν ἀποστόλων ἔχω δεῖξαι. ἐὰν γὰρ θελήσῃς ἀπελθεῖν ἐπὶ τὸν Βατικανὸν ἢ ἐπὶ τὴν ὁδὸν τὴν Ὠστίαν, εὑρήσεις τὰ τρόπαια τῶν ταύτην ἱδρυσαμένων τὴν ἐκκλησίαν. Zu Gaius, dem Presbyter und gebildeten Mitglied des stadtrömischen Klerus zur Zeit des Zephyrinus (198–217) vgl. Lampe, *Christen*, p. 295.

14. So auch jüngst Thümmel, *Memoria*, pp. 6–7. Aufgrund seiner Untersuchungen des Befundes kommt Thümmel freilich zu einer von der „offiziellen" Sicht abweichenden Rekonstruktion der Aedicula, vgl. *ibidem*, pp. 50–52.

15. Dies beweist eine Münze, die sich in der Urne mit der Asche einer Frau namens Trebellena Flacilla befand, dazu Guarducci, *Petrus*, p. 56.

interpretiert wurden, zum anderen auch die Behauptung, unter den aus dem Grab stammenden *Knochen* seien die des Petrus gewesen.[16]

Wie dem auch sei – aufgrund des τροπαῖον, der Anrufungen Petri auf der Graffitimauer und der baulichen Verbindung zur konstantinischen Basilika stand für die Ausgräber zweifelsfrei fest, dass man hier die ältesten Relikte der frühchristlichen Petrus*verehrung* vor sich hatte. Die kirchenpolitische Bedeutung der „Entdeckungen" mitten in den Bedrohungen des Zweiten Weltkrieges ist überdeutlich: nicht nur glaubte man die literarische Tradition des 2. Jh. auf Ereignisse des 1. Jh. zurückführen zu können, vielmehr schien sich auch zu bestätigen, dass sich die *bis heute* verankerte Berufung des römischen Bischofs auf Petrus auch auf archäologisch aufzeigbare „Tatsachen" stützt.[17] Die „Objektivität" der Archäologie diente als willkommenes Mittel gegen all diejenigen, die an der Zuverlässigkeit der Tradition zweifelten. Es verwundert daher nicht, dass die von den Ausgräbern entwickelte Theorie offizielle Bestätigung von höchster Stelle erhielt.[18]

In den 50er und 60er Jahren konzentrierte sich die zum Teil sehr lebhafte wissenschaftliche Debatte daher vor allem auf die Frage, ob die Identifikation des Grabes unter dem τροπαῖον mit dem des Petrus zutreffend und – damit oft verbunden – wie zuverlässig die römische Petrustradition sei. Eine nahezu unübersehbare Fülle von oft sehr kontroversen Publikationen erschien. Leider mussten dabei manche Fragen offen bleiben, nicht zuletzt auch wegen mancher Versäumnisse in der Dokumentation der Befunde während der Grabungen, nicht immer sachgerechter Aufbewahrung bestimmter Fundteile und zum Teil recht widersprüchlicher Äußerungen der mit der Publikation der Funde betrauten Wissenschaftler.[19] Mit dem Erscheinen von Engelbert Kirschbaums quasi-offizieller

16. Vorgebracht v.a. in Guarducci, *Gebeine des Apostelfürsten*.

17. Eck umschreibt die Motivlage zutreffend: „Aus dem Zusammenklang von wissenschaftlicher Bildung und Verteidigung des päpstlichen Primats entstand bei Pius XII. der Plan, die Berechtigung des Bischofs von Rom zur Führung der Gesamtkirche durch archäologische Untersuchungen zu erhärten. (…) Konnte man die Begräbnisstätte des Apostels durch die Archäologie nachweisen, dann konnte zumindest niemand mehr die Anwesenheit und das Martyrium Petri in der römischen Hauptstadt bezweifeln" ('Inschriften', p. 55).

18. Radiobotschaft Papst Pius XII. am 24.12.1950 (bei Jordan, *Apostelgrab*, p. 3). Papst Paul VI. ging sogar noch einen Schritt weiter, als er – inzwischen vorgenommene Nachuntersuchungen miteinbeziehend – am 28.06.1968 bei einer Generalaudienz verkündete: „Ja, der historische Beweis nicht nur für das Grab des Petrus, sondern darüberhinaus auch für seine verehrungswürdigen sterblichen Überreste ist erbracht. Petrus ist hier (…). Damit besitzen wir zu unserem Trost direkten Kontakt mit der Quelle der angesehensten apostolischen Tradition Roms, die uns die Gewissheit von der leibhaftigen Anwesenheit des Hauptes im Kollegium der ersten Jünger Jesu Christi in Rom gibt, und uns von der Verpflanzung der Kirche aus Jerusalem und Antiochien in die Hauptstadt des Römischen Reiches überzeugt" (L'Osser vatore Romano, Wochenausgabe in deutscher Sprache vom 07.07.19678, Nr. 27, Kap. 12 zitiert nach Jordan, *Apostelgrab*, p. 77). Die Tendenz der Inanspruchnahme archäologischer Ergebnisse durch den Papst ist überdeutlich, die wissenschaftliche Vorgeschichte der Radiobotschaft findet sich u.a. bei Guarducci, *Petrus*, pp. 126–61. Freilich wird der archäologische Befund selbst durch die päpstliche Verlautbarung nicht klarer.

19. Vgl. Thümmel, *Memorien*, pp. 15–20 zu den zahlreichen Versäumnissen und Unklarheiten der Grabung und Dokumentation.

Publikation kam die Diskussion zu einem vorläufigen Ende, ohne dass freilich auch nur annähernd ein Konsens zur heiß umstrittenen Frage der „Authentizität" des „Petrusgrabes" erreicht wurde. In den letzten Jahren ist es um die Funde stiller geworden. Einen Fortschritt markiert erst wieder die Arbeit von Lampe über die stadtrömischen Christen in den ersten beiden Jahrhunderten,[20] in der er die Untersuchung der Gräber völlig zu Recht von der verengenden Fragestellung nach der Authentizität der Petrustradition und allen damit verbundenen sekundären Fragestellungen löst und sie unter konsequent sozialgeschichtlicher Perspektive auswertet. Erst die grundlegende Untersuchung von Hans Georg Thümmel aus dem Jahre 1999 erlaubt jedoch eine kritische Neubewertung der Fundsituation und der komplizierten Publikationslage. Eine wesentliche Bereicherung der Diskussion stellen die Arbeiten von Mielsch und v. Hesberg[21] gowie Eck[22] dar, die sich mit der heidnischen Nekropole und den Inschriften auf den Mausoleen aus archäologischer und epigraphischer Sicht befassen und den architektonischen und funeralen Kontext der umstrittenen Gräber viel klarer ins Blickfeld rücken. Insofern hat sich die Perspektive dank der neueren Arbeiten wohltuend erweitert. Ich folge den neueren Ansätzen in ihrer kritischen Tendenz, blende die Frage nach der möglichen Identität der in den Gräbern bestatteten Personen zunächst aus und versuche, ein Bild der Situation im 1. Jh. herauszuarbeiten, um zu eruieren, welche Rückschlüsse sich hinsichtlich der Bestattungspraktiken früher Christen aus dem *vor die Errichtung der Gräberstraße des 2. Jh. zu datierenden* archäologischen Befund ziehen lassen.

2. Die Befunde aus der Zeit vor der Errichtung der mittelkaiserzeitlichen Gräberstraße

Beginnen wir zunächst mit den Gräbern selbst. Im einzelnen lassen sich folgende Gruppen unterscheiden:

2.1. Gräber südlich des τροπαῖον parallel zur Außenwand von Mausoleum S

α, δ, ε   Drei Einzelbestattungen jeweils in Marmorkästen. Da sie in die konstantinischen Aufschüttungen eingesenkt sind und über der ehemals natürlichen Hangkante des Vatikanhügels liegen, hängen sie stratigraphisch mit der Basilika zusammen und scheiden für unsere Frage daher als zu spät aus.

β   Da unter dem Niveau des Mosaikfußbodens von P gelegen, stammt dieses Einzelgrab noch aus vorkonstantinischer Zeit. Es war „aus Marmorplatten angelegt und mit großen Ziegeln dachartig nach oben abgeschlossen".[23]

---

20. Lampe, *Christen*, pp. 82–94.
21. Mielsch u.a., *Nekropole I*; Mielsch u.a., *Nekropole II* (Publikation der heidnischen Mausoleen A-D, E-I und Z-Psi). Da wir uns im vorliegenden Kapitel mit den Bestattungen des 1. Jh. n. befassen, muss die Diskussion der heidnischen Nekropole der 2. Hälfte des 2. Jh. unterbleiben.
22. Eck, 'Inschriften'.
23. Kirschbaum, *Gräber*, p. 83.

Der Inhalt des Grabes war bis auf eine wenige Zentimeter dicke braune Schicht zusammengesunken, in der einige Goldfäden wohl eines kostbaren Gewandes (Papstgrab?) befanden. Da das Westende von β direkt an der Roten Mauer endet und sich an der Fassade der Roten Mauer noch Reste von zum Grab gehörigen Verzierungen fanden,[24] setzt das Grab die Mauer voraus und muss später als sie entstanden sein. Grab β kann daher ebenfalls nicht zum ältesten Bestand des Bestattungsplatzes gehören.

2.2. *Gräber nördlich des* τροπαῖον *parallel zur Außenwand von* Q

μ   (Nach)konstantinische Einzelbestattung.

κ, λ   Zwei übereinander liegende Tonsärge. Die Ausrichtung längs der Roten Mauer, ihre Lage unter μ und ihre Form weisen diese Gräber dem späten 2. oder 3. Jh. zu.[25] Beide Gräber zeigen, dass also noch nach der Errichtung der Gräberstraße Einzelbestattungen außerhalb der Mausoleen vorgekommen sind.

2.3. *Ein Grab östlich des* τροπαῖον *parallel zur Außenwand von* O

ζ   „Äußerst armes" Grab aus vorkonstantinischer Zeit, bestehend „nur aus ein paar gegen die Mauer [scil. der Westwand von O] gestellten Ziegelplatten".[26]

2.4. *Gräber östlich des* τροπαῖον

η   Grab η[27] liegt über Grab θ, muss also jünger als dieses sein. Es liegt parallel zum in den Hügel gesetzten Aufgang (Clivus), d.h. rechtwinklig zum Hang und setzt offensichtlich die Planierung des Geländes voraus. Grab η nutzt die Aufschüttungen, die mit der Errichtung von Mausoleum S einher gingen, muss daher in „der kurzen Zeit zwischen der Erbauung von S und der Roten Mauer", d.h. Mitte des 2. Jh. oder kurz vorher, entstanden sein.[28] Da das Grab im Verlauf der Ausgrabungen schon früh zerstört worden ist, ist eine Rekonstruktion seines Aussehens nur noch schwer möglich:[29] „Es handelt sich um eine Grube, die unten auf dem Boden und an den Seiten mit Platten (Ziegeln) ausgelegt war und nach

---

24. Kirschbaum, *Gräber*, p. 148.
25. Kirschbaum, *Gräber*, pp. 85.148.
26. Kirschbaum, *Gräber*, p. 148; Josi u.a., *Esplorazioni*, p. 114 und Fig. 83. Vgl. den Plan bei Kirschbaum, *Gräber*, p. 84 Abb. 18a, auf Abb. 18b (*ibidem*) trägt dieses Grab versehentlich das Siglum ξ.
27. Vgl. dazu auch die neuen Überlegungen von Thümmel, *Memorien*, p. 19 (zur Grabung und Dokumentation) und pp. 28–32.
28. Thümmel, *Memorien*, p. 29.
29. Thümmel, *Memorien* schreibt: „Die Berichterstattung über dieses Grab ist verwirrend. Text, Zeichnungen und Fotos in den Esplorazioni zeigen große Differenzen. [...] Ich kann mir die Widersprüche nicht anders erklären, als dass nach weitgehender Zerstörung des Bestandes die Ausgräber den Befund anhand von Fotos rekonstruiert haben" (pp. 29 und 32).

der Bestattung mit weiteren Platten (Ziegeln) abgedeckt und dann zugeschüttet wurde".[30]

2.5. *Ältere Gräber im Umfeld des* τροπαῖον

γ Unter η und ihm daher vorausgehend liegt γ[31]. Dieses Grab besteht aus einer nur 1,26 m langen Terrakottakiste mit einer spitzwinklig darauf gesetzten Ziegelabdeckung, vermutlich eine Kinderbestattung. In der Bauart unterscheidet es sich von allen übrigen Gräbern der Umgebung: „Etwa in Brusthöhe mündete in den Sargdeckel aus dachartig gegeneinander gestellten Ziegelplatten das Ende einer Libationsröhre, durch die nach römischem Brauch Wein und ähnliches geschüttet wurde. Diese lange Ziegelröhre, und zum Teil auch das Grab selbst, ist durch einen turmartigen Aufbau von etwa 1,70 m Höhe geschützt. Dieser ist in seinem unteren Teil verhältnismäßig roh aus Tuff und Mörtel zusammengefügt. Der obere, etwa 80 cm hohe Teil ist aus Ziegeln gemauert, allerdings auch ziemlich roh. Hier ist nochmals eine Zweiteilung erkennbar. Die untere Hälfte ist heute noch an der Süd- und Westseite durch eine Ziegelplatte abgedeckt. Die andere Hälfte, die auf der Nordseite im Mauerwerk durch einen Rücksprung gekennzeichnet ist, ragt frei heraus".[32] Grab γ war über die Bleileitung mit einem Spendealtar verbunden. Im Grab vermauerte Ziegel sind sicher auf 115–123 datiert, was das frühest *mögliche* Datum der Erbauung darstellt; eine Sekundärverwendung der Ziegel in etwas späterer Zeit ist freilich nicht ausgeschlossen,[33] den *terminus ad quem* gibt die Umgestaltung des Geländes zwischen 160–165. Grab γ „steht am Anfang einer größeren Anzahl von Bestattungen in der näheren Umgebung, die freilich meist viel ärmer waren".[34]

θ Liegt nahe bei γ und setzt wohl die gleiche Beschaffenheit der Hangkante voraus wie γ; zugleich liegt θ etwa 1m tiefer als der zerstörte Teil von η, dem Hügelanstieg folgend: „Es liegt vollkommen Parallel zu γ, nur so weit nach Norden und Osten verschoben, dass seine südwestliche Ecke von der nordöstlichen des Maueraufbaues von γ ungefähr 50 cm entfernt ist".[35] Nur der westliche Teil von θ ist ausgegraben. Es handelt sich um ein ausgesprochenes Armengrab: „Eigentlich kann man nur von einem

---

30. Thümmel, *Memorien*, p. 31 gegen Kirschbaum, *Gräber*, p. 85, der noch von einer Abdeckung des Grabes mit einer Marmorplatte sprach.

31. Prandi, *Zona*, pp. 37–41; vgl. dazu jetzt auch Thümmel, *Memorien*, pp. 27–28.

32. Kirschbaum, *Gräber*, p. 86.

33. Wohl aber eine Errichtung bereits im 1. Jh. n. Chr., wie Thümmel, *Memorien*, p. 28 zu Recht unterstreicht.

34. Thümmel, *Memorien*, p. 28 mit Verweis auf Prandis Untersuchungen des Umfelds von Hof P, die neben den durch die ersten Ausgrabungen bekannten sechs vorkonstantinischen Gräbern „etwa 25 weitere ans Licht gebracht [...haben...], von denen sich jedoch für keines eine Entstehung vor dem 2. Jahrhundert nachweisen läßt" (*ibidem*, Anm. 127).

35. Kirschbaum, *Gräber*, p. 87.

Grabdeckel sprechen. Man hat den Leichnam mit dem Kopf nach Westen ohne irgendwelchen Boden- oder Seitenschutz in eine Erdgrube gelegt und darüber sechs Ziegelplatten dachförmig gegeneinander gestellt. Dabei wurden zum Teil richtige Dachziegel verwendet".[36] Auf einem der Deckziegel befindet sich ein Stempel aus den 60er bis 80er Jahren des 1. Jh. Die Ausgräber halten Grab θ daher für das möglicherweise älteste datierbare Grab des Bestattungsplatzes.[37] Freilich ist auch hier eine Zweitverwendung der Ziegel nicht ausgeschlossen,[38] sodass eine Datierung ins späte 1. Jh. nicht zwingend ist; allein der *terminus ante quem* steht fest: Grab θ muss vor der Errichtung der MR angelegt worden sein, da es tiefer als deren Fundament liegt.[39]

ι   Dieses Grab liegt im rechten Winkel zu θ auf gleicher Tiefe und überlagert dessen Nordwestspitze mit seiner Südostecke um einige Zentimeter. Wegen der gemeinsamen Nähe sind θ und ι wohl gleichzeitig und, weil sie unterhalb des Niveaus der Roten Mauer liegen, früher als diese entstanden. „Auch ι ist ein einfaches Bodengrab, das, ohne Boden- und Seitenschutz, nur oben mit Ziegelplatten zugedeckt ist. Diese sind aber diesmal nicht dachförmig gegeneinander gestellt, sondern liegen flach auf. Auf diese Weise benötigte man nur drei Ziegelplatten".[40] Freilich besteht dadurch noch kein Grund, Grab ι in das 1. Jh. zu datieren, vielmehr könnte es etwa gleichzeitig mit dem Umbau der ehemaligen Zisterne Q in ein Mausoleum angelegt worden sein (Anfang 3. Jh.).[41]

2.6. *Gräber an der westlichen Seite der Roten Mauer*

Nicht nur östlich des τροπαῖον bzw. der Roten Mauer wurden Gräber gefunden, sondern auch westlich davon. Zwei davon seien exemplarisch erwähnt:

Grab I   Grab I liegt unter Grab II und konstituiert sich aus „Elemente(n) einer älteren, zerstörten Grabanlage (…), die ohne Zweifel noch dem ersten Jahrhundert angehört. Die Tiefenlage ist ungefähr die Gleiche der nahebei liegenden Gräber ι und θ. Es handelt sich bei diesem Funde außer Knochen und Eierschalen-Resten vor allem um Fragmente von Tonlampen und Glasgefäßen. Einer der Glasreste weist eine Goldstaub-Technik auf, die als ägyptischer Import nur im 1. Jh. n. Chr. bekannt ist. Derselben Zeit entstammt eine der Tonlampen, die auf der Unterseite noch die Reste des Fabrikstempels bewahrt hat. Es handelt sich demnach um einen L.Munatius Threptus, dessen Lampen nur ungefähr bis zum Jahr 70

---

36. Kirschbaum, *Gräber*, p. 88.

37. Kirschbaum, *Gräber*, p. 88 weist die Möglichkeit der Zweitverwendung zurück, weil derart einfache Ziegel selbst für Arme erschwinglich gewesen seien und keiner der verwendeten Ziegel irgendwelche Spuren von Mörtel aufweist, vgl. Lampe, *Christen*, pp. 87–90. Freilich ist auch dies kein absolut stringentes Argument.

38. Dinkler, 'Petrus', p. 12 Anm. 17.

39. Thümmel, *Memorien*, p. 28.

40. Kirschbaum, *Gräber*, p. 88.

41. Thümmel, *Memorien*, p. 47.

nachweisbar sind".[42] Doch geben diese Funde nur den frühest *möglichen* Entstehungszeitpunkt an, eine spätere Verwendung der Gegenstände ist dadurch nicht ausgeschlossen.

Grab II   Reste eines Grabes aus der ersten Hälfte des 2. Jh. n. Chr.[43] (Prandi Grab 28).

2.7. *Ein Grab unter dem* τροπαῖον? *„Grab X"*

Die Ausgräber interpretierten eine Reihe von Indizien dahin gehend, dass sich unter dem τροπαῖον ein weiteres Grab befunden haben muss (hier als „Grab X" bezeichnet).[44] Vor allem eine in der Achse der Aedicula verschobene „Deckplatte" im Boden zwischen den Säulchen des τροπαῖον sahen sie als untrüglichen Hinweis auf die Existenz eines weiteren, unter der Platte liegenden Grabes an. Ferner behaupteten sie, dass die frühen Gräber γ, ι und θ (dann aber auch die übrigen, jüngeren Gräber) in eigentümlicher Weise auf dieses unter dem τροπαῖον befindliche Grab hin ausgerichtet sind, woraus gefolgert wurde, dass auch „Grab X" zur frühesten Belegungsphase des Bestattungsplatzes gehört. Zwei kleine Mäuerchen (m1 und m2) verliefen südlich und nördlich seitlich am Grab entlang, wohl um es vor der starken Hangerosion durch Abschwemmung zu schützen.[45] Die originale Höhe des Grabes war freilich nicht mehr feststellbar, da es – dies gaben die Ausgräber zu – nicht mehr in seinem ursprünglichen Zustand aufgefunden wurde. Zu einem bestimmten Zeitpunkt hatte man das Grab, so wurde vorgetragen, geöffnet und die Gebeine entnommen, um sie in einem Fach in der erst um die Mitte des 3. Jh. entstandenen Graffitimauer (Mauer g) zweitzubestatten. Die Umbettung könne frühestens in der Mitte des 2. Jh. vorgenommen worden sein, ihre Umstände seien jedoch nicht mehr eindeutig zu klären. Die ursprüngliche Herkunft der Knochen aus dem Erdgrab ist für die Ausgräber durch mit ihnen gefundene Erde gesichert. Anthropologische Untersuchungen hätten zudem ergeben, dass die Knochenreste zu einem männlichen Individuum von 60–70 Jahren gehörten.[46] Insofern waren sich die Ausgräber sicher, dass sie zwar nicht das Petrusgrab mit den sterblichen Überresten des Apostels selbst gefunden haben, wohl aber die Stelle, wo es sich bis zur Umbettung der Gebeine befand: unter der Deckplatte zwischen den Säulen der Aedicula. Exakt an der Stelle, an der

---

42. Kirschbaum, *Gräber*, p. 89, vgl. p. 129 Anm. 17: „Nach dem Plan Prandis (*Zona*, Abb. 18b) wurden unter der Treppe vier Grabanlagen gefunden: 27, 28, 29, 30. Von diesen müssen jedenfalls 27 und 28 schon vor der Treppe angelegt worden sein. Dazu kommt noch der Grabrest unter 28 aus der Zeit Neros" (i.e. unser „Grab I").

43. Kirschbaum, *Gräber*, p. 89.

44. Kirschbaum, *Gräber*, pp. 90–91. Nicht nur ein „Ehrenmal" oder Kenotaph: „Dort unter der Erde war etwas Konkretes, das Breite, Länge und eine klare Richtung hatte, ein Grab und nicht etwa bloß die Erinnerungsstätte des Martyriums. Diese hätte weder Breite noch Länge und noch weniger eine bestimmte Richtung aufzuweisen brauchen" (*ibidem*, p. 91), vgl. auch P. Saint-Roch, 'Das Petrusgrab', *WUB* 7/1 (1998), pp. 26–29 (hier p. 29).

45. Guarducci, *Gebeine des Apostelfürsten*, pp. 10–11.

46. Dazu ausführlich Guarducci, *Gebeine des Apostelfürsten*, pp. 17–23; anders noch Kirschbaum, *Gräber*, p. 91.

die Rote Mauer über das ehemalige Grab hinweg lief, habe man dann das τροπαῖον errichtet. Die erwähnte Deckplatte in der Mitte des Bodens des τροπαῖον habe das 30 cm tiefer liegende Knochendeposit geschützt und markiere so die Ausmaße des ehemaligen Grabes. Weiter habe die Rote Mauer auf das Knochendeposit insofern „Rücksicht" genommen, als dessen Fundamentierung an dieser Stelle in einer recht primitiven dreieckigen Aussparung gleichsam darüber hinweg geführt wurde.[47] Über die Gründe für diese ungewöhnliche Maßnahme konnte man nur spekulieren: wollte man das Grab mit der „profanen" Mauer nicht berühren,[48] oder sparte man einen inzwischen verlorenen Grabstein (*cippus*) aus[49] oder deutet die Aussparung auf ein hölzernes Baugerüst, das eine ehemals vorhandene dachförmige Ziegelabdeckung schützen sollte[50]? Wie immer man das auch beurteilen mag, bezeichnend ist dann doch, dass offensichtlich keine „materiellen Bestandteile [des ehemaligen] Grabes, wie Ziegelplatten oder ähnliches" in das neue Ensemble einbezogen wurden.[51] Das Grab existiert nicht mehr. Die Ausgräber schlossen daraus, dass es sich auch bei „Grab X" um ein ebensolches Armengrab gehandelt hat wie die in der unmittelbaren Nähe gefundenen Gräber θ, ι, I und II.[52] Nur etwas mehr als die halbe ursprüngliche Länge des Grabes sei durch die Deckplatte erschließbar. Aufgrund der Lage der benachbarten Gräber γ, θ und ι könne man jedoch annehmen, dass sich das Grab in westliche Richtung unter der Roten Mauer hinweg in den Raum hinein erstreckte habe, der von ca. 160 n.Chr. an von einem Treppenaufgang, dem sog. Clivus, beansprucht wurde.

Die Annahme eines „Grabes X" unter dem τροπαῖον wurde freilich schon von Prandi mit schwerwiegenden Argumenten bestritten.[53] Auch Thümmel kommt nach einer gründlichen Prüfung aller von den Ausgräbern angeführten Argumente

47. Es ist sehr bedauerlich, dass nur wenige brauchbare Fotos (mit Maßstab) des vermeintlichen Erdgrabes veröffentlicht wurden, die diese in der Forschung sogenannte „Nische N¹" zeigen, was zumindest zum Teil wohl durch die ungewöhnlich schwierigen Grabungsumstände zu erklären sein mag. Zur Fundlage von „Grab X" vgl. das Foto auf Tafel 49 bei Guarducci, *Gebeine des Apostelfürsten*, p. 200.

48. So etwa Kirschbaum, *Gräber*, p. 91.

49. So Prandi, *Zona*, pp. 69–73; *idem*, 'Tomba', pp. 390–97; Guarducci, *Gebeine des Apostelfürsten*, pp. 10–11, doch vgl. unten Anm. 55.

50. Guarducci, *Petrus*, p. 64. Angesichts der doch sehr einfachen Bauweise (selbst Guarducci, *ibidem*, spricht von einer „eher plumpe[n] Einbuchtung") halte ich jede Spekulation darüber, ob es sich um die Aussparung für einen inzwischen verlorenegegangenen Grabstein (so Prandi) oder um ein „Gebilde zum Schutz des alten Petrusgrabs beim Mauerbau" (so Guarducci, *ibidem*) haudelt, für äußerst unsicher.

51. Kirschbaum, *Gräber*, p. 92.

52. Kirschbaum, *Gräber*, p. 92 bezeichnet es wohl zu Recht als „überdeckte Erdmulde". Die dreieckige Fundamentüberführung könnte nach Kirschbaum auf eine dachförmige Abdeckung des Grabes schließen, doch ist dann zu fragen, warum nicht Teile der Abdeckung in der dreieckigen Höhlung der Roten Mauer noch erhalten sind. Besaß Grab X nicht einmal eine Ziegelabdeckung? Sind sie beim Bau der Roten Mauer oder des τροπαῖον verwendet worden? Angesichts der Verehrung, die man um 160 dem Grab angeblich erwies, kann man sich kaum vorstellen, dass man ehemals zur Abdeckung verwendete Ziegel einfach vernichtet hätte. Sicherheit ist hier jedenfalls nicht zu gewinnen.

53. Prandi, 'Tomba', bes. p. 412; Dinkler, 'Petrus', p. 14.

zu dem Ergebnis, dass unter der Aedicula kaum jemals ein weiteres „Grab X" existiert hat, nach dessen Ausmaßen sich die Rote Mauer mit ihrer Nische (das ursprüngliche τροπαῖον) hätte richten können.[54] Auch von der Existenz eines Grabcippus ist mangels entsprechender Hinweise nicht auszugehen.[55] Rätselhaft ist ferner, dass bei der Untersuchung des Erdgrabes Knochen von drei Individuen vermischt mit Tierknochen gefunden wurden, „zu einem Häuflein zusammengerafft" (in einem Textil- oder Holzbehälter?).[56] Auf letzteren Punkt werden wir im Verlauf der Diskussion noch zurückkommen.

Damit kristallisiert sich eine Gruppe von Gräbern heraus, die nach Maßgabe der Stratigraphie älter sein müssen als die Neuerrichtung der Gräberstraße inklusive des Grabhofes P, der Roten Mauer und des τροπαῖον. Für diese erste Begräbnisgruppe ergibt sich etwa das Jahr 160 als definitiver *terminus ante quem*. Wie weit ins 1. Jh. zurück die ältesten dieser Gräber zu datieren sind, ist unklar. Nichts *nötigt* dazu, eines der Gräber überhaupt ins 1. Jh. hinabzudatieren, in Falle von Grab θ ist eine derart frühe Entstehung aufgrund der vespasianischen Ziegel aber durchaus *möglich*, im Falle von Grab I westlich der Roten Mauer angesichts des neronischen Lampenfragments sogar durchaus *wahrscheinlich*.[57] Für keines der Gräber kann aber eine Entstehung im 1. Jh. als *erwiesen* gelten,[58] allein der *terminus ad quem* steht durch die schrittweise Errichtung der Mausoleen der Gräberstraße fest.

Damit kann man die zeitliche Abfolge der Bestattungen wie folgt angeben:

Vorkonstantinisch	β, κ, λ, ζ
Mitte des 2. Jh.	η
Vor MR	γ, θ, ι, Grab I, Grab II

Dies ist in mehrfacher Hinsicht ein bemerkenswerter Befund, den es nun auszuwerten gilt.

3. *Auswertung der Befunde*

Welche Rückschlüsse lassen sich aus den oben dargestellten Befunden ziehen?

3.1. *Das topographische Arrangement der Einzelgräber*
Zunächst rücken die vor dem Bau der mittelkaiserzeitlichen Gräberstraße angelegten einfachen Gräber in ihren ursprünglichen sachlichen Kontext. Obwohl insbesondere die älteren Befunde nicht immer leicht zu interpretieren und daher manche Details dieser Nekropole noch unbekannt sind, lässt sich die Frage nach der Größe des ursprünglichen Bestattungsplatzes doch mit einer gewissen Sicherheit

---

54. Thümmel, *Memorien*, p. 72.
55. So Thümmel, *Memorien*, p. 37 gegen Prandi, 'Tomba', pp. 390–7; *idem, Zona*, pp. 69–73. Noch Dinkler, 'Petrus', pp. 13–14 hat sich Prandis Hypothese angeschlossen.
56. Kirschbaum, *Gräber*, p. 91.
57. Vgl. Lampe, *Christen*, pp. 87–90.
58. Vgl. Gerkan in Dinkler, 'Petrus', p. 13; Thümmel, *Memorien*, p. 28.

beantworten.[59] So wurden auf dem Gebiet der heutigen Vatikanstadt an zwei nur etwa 300 m bis 500 m von der Konstantinsbasilika entfernten Stellen ähnliche Gräber entdeckt, die aus der Zeit vom Ende des 1. bis zum Beginn des 2. Jh. („Annona"-Grabung 1930) bzw. vom Anfang des 1. bis ins 2. Jh. n. Chr. (Grabungen von 1957 westlich davon) stammen.[60] Freilich müssen die Gräber unter dem Petersdom mit den eben genannten nicht unmittelbar zu ein- und demselben Gräberfeld gehören, doch ist die Nutzung der gesamten Region zwischen Tiber und Vatikanhügel als Bestattungsort seit dem Beginn des 1. Jh. n. Chr. evident.[61] Es gibt ferner genügend Hinweise darauf, dass das Areal am und zunehmend auch im ehemaligen Zirkus des Nero (also im engeren Sinne das uns interessierende Gebiet unter dem Petersdom) seit dem späten 1. Jh. von Gräbern eingenommen wurde.[62] Schließlich befand sich das gesamte Gebiet außerhalb des *pomerium* und stand für die Nutzung als Bestattungsplatz für die Bevölkerung der benachbarten Wohngebiete offen. Diese lockere Grabbelegung im Umfeld des Zirkus des Nero, nicht aber die im 2. Jh. hinzukommende Gräberstraße mit dem τροπαῖον ist der primäre archäologische und historische Kontext, in dem die Erdgräber unter St.Peter zu interpretieren sind.

3.2. *Die Machart der Gräber*

Deutlich ist: Die früheste Grabgruppe unter dem Petersdom besteht aus Einzelgräbern mit unterschiedlicher „architektonischer" Gestaltung (einfaches Erdgrab, mit Ziegelabdeckung, Tonsarg; über die Brandbestattung ist eine Aussage nicht möglich, s.u.). Alle Gräber sind zumindest in der uns interessierenden Phase Primärbestattungen. Den menschlichen Knochenresten nach zu urteilen wurden Männer, Frauen und (angesichts der Größe von Grab γ) wohl auch Kinder nebeneinander bestattet.[63] Da keine Grabinschriften gefunden wurden, sind die sozialen Bezüge der einzelnen Bestatteten nicht mehr zu eruieren, doch deutet die generell einfache Machart und die geringen Beigaben darauf hin, dass die Bestatteten eher den unteren sozialen Schichten Roms angehört haben. Lampe zählt sie

59. Kirschbaum, *Gräber*, p. 148.

60. Guarducci, *Petrus*, p. 24 mit Anm. 19; Kirschbaum, *Gräber*, pp. 20.45–6.

61. M. Guarducci, 'Documenti del primo secolo nella necropoli vaticane', *RPARA* 29 (1956–57), pp. 111–37: „(T)utta l'area compresa fra i palazzi vaticani e l'attuale Piazza Risorgimento era occupata de una vasta necropoli, venutasi a formare lungo il precorso della via Trionfale e die suoi diverticoli, e databile, per la sua massima parte, fra l'età di Augusto e quella di Traiano" (p. 111).

62. Zum Zirkus, der sowohl archäologisch als auch literarisch belegt ist, vgl. F. Magi, 'Un nuovo mausoleo presso il circo Neroniano e altre minori scoperte', *RPARA* 42 (1966), pp. 207–26; F. Castagnoli, 'Il circo di Nerone in Vaticano', *RPARA* 32 (1959–60), pp. 97–121; L. Richardson, *A New Topographical Dictionary of Ancient Rome* (Baltimore, London: The Johns Hopkins University Press, 1992), pp. 83–84. Zur generellen Beschaffenheit der Umgebung des Vatikans im 1. Jh. n. Chr. vgl. Toynbee, 'Shrine', pp. 3–23; Guarducci, *Petrus*, pp. 19–25; Thümmel, *Memorien*, pp. 26–28 und der Plan bei von Hesberg, 'Planung', p. 44.

63. Nach der Untersuchung der unter dem Fundament der Roten Mauer (Gruppe T) und aus dem Boden des Grabhofes P (Gruppe K) gefundenen Gebeine durch den Anthropologieprofessor Venerando Correnti, vgl. Guarducci, *Gebeine des Apostelfürsten*, pp. 117–35 und 136–46; *idem*, *Petrus*, p. 122.

wohl zu Recht zu den *humiliores*.[64] Begräbnisse diesen Typs sind nichts Ungewöhnliches und wurden auch an anderen Orten in hinreichend aussagekräftiger Anzahl gefunden (Isola Sacra, Ostia, Sarsina).[65]

3.1. Beobachtungen zu „Grab X" und dessen Umfeld

Von besonderer Bedeutung für die Fragestellung ist seit je her „Grab X", das hier nochmals gesondert betrachtet werden soll. Auch hier kann man aus den Befunden einige überraschende Rückschlüsse ziehen.

a) Wenn man Prandi, Dinkler und Thümmel folgt ist die Existenz eines aufgrund der Lage des τροπαῖον identifizierbaren Petrusgrabes *hinfällig*. Hinter diese Erkenntnis gibt es kein Zurück. Die Anlage der Roten Mauer mit ihrer Nische als ursprüngliche Petrusmemoria der Zeit um 160–165 hätte damit auf *kein* einzelnes Grab Bezug genommen. Dafür wird aber der Kontext der frühen Bestattungen γ, θ, und ι deutlicher. Bisher wurde in der Literatur oft vermutet, dass alle *östlich* der Roten Mauer gelegenen Gräber ein zusammenhängendes, irgendwie auf das ominöse „Grab X" Bezug nehmendes Ensemble bilden. So erwähnt Kirschbaum zwar Gräber I und II westlich der Roten Mauer, konzentriert seine Aufmerksamkeit sonst aber fast ausschließlich auf die Bestattungen in unmittelbarer Umgebung zu „Grab X" *östlich* der Roten Mauer, obwohl er selbst zugibt, dass die durch die Errichtung der Roten Mauer verursachte Trennung künstlich und später ist. Bei Lampe spielen Gräber I und II überhaupt keine Rolle. Doch sollte man die Interpretationsbasis nicht zu eng fassen. Sicher ist nämlich, dass die in der unmittelbaren Nähe der Memoria befindlichen Bestattungen nur ein kleiner Teil einer weit größeren Gräbergruppe des 1./frühen 2. Jh. n. Chr. darstellen. Eine isolierte Betrachtung allein der östlich von MR liegenden Gräber ist nicht zu rechtfertigen.

b) Es ist nicht unsere Aufgabe darüber zu spekulieren, wie sehr das von Kirschbaum u.a. entworfene Bild des „Petrusgrabes" davon abhängig ist, welche Gräber in die Überlegungen einbezogen und welche ausgeschlossen worden sind.

---

64. Lampe, *Christen*, p. 92. Freilich sind die ärmlichen Einzelbestattungen wohl nicht der ganz unteren Schicht der stadtrömischen Bevölkerung zuzuweisen, da noch individuelle Grablegen vorliegen und ein Mindestmaß an ritueller Gestaltung des Begräbnisses feststellbar ist. Im Gegensatz dazu stehen anonyme Massenbegräbnisse namenloser Toter, die archäologisch bisher nur in Ausnahmefällen zu fassen sind, dazu vgl. J. LeGall, 'La sépolture des pauvres à Rome', *BAntFr* 1980–1981, pp. 148–52; J. Zangenberg, *Haus der Ewigkeit. Archäologische und literarische Studien zur jüdischen und frühchristlichen Bestattungskultur in Palästina* (Habilitationsschrift in Kooperation zwischen der Kirchlichen Hochschule Wuppertal und der Bergischen Universität Wuppertal, Februar 2003, in Druckvorbereitung für WUNT I; Tübingen: Mohr-Siebeck, 2005), pp. 252–57; U. Volp, *Tod und Ritual in den christlichen Gemeinden der Antike* (VC.Sup, 65; Leiden und Boston: Brill, 2002), p. 75 (mit Verweis auf Lancianis Entdeckungen in den 80er Jahren des 19. Jh.)

65. Zur Grabanlage auf der Isola Sacra vgl. G. Calza, *La necropoli del Porto di Roma nell' Isola Sacra* (Rom: La Libreria dello Stato, 1940) und I. Baldassare, 'La necropoli dell'Isola Sacra (Porto)', in v. Hesberg und Zanker, *Gräberstraßen*, pp. 125–38; zu Ostia s. D. Boschung, 'Die republikanischen und frühkaiserzeitlichen Nekropolen vor den Toren Ostias', in v. Hesberg und Zanker, *Gräberstraßen*, pp. 111–24; zu Sarsina s. J. Ortalli, 'La via dei sepolcri di Sarsina. Aspetti funzionali, formali e sociali', in v. Hesberg und Zanker, *Gräberstraßen*, pp. 155–82.

In jedem Fall ist aber davor zu warnen, bei der Bestimmung des religionsgeschicht-lichen Profils des Bestattungsplatzes unter Grabhof P oder auch nur eines seiner Gräber den Blick künstlich nur auf die unmittelbar bei „Grab X" befindliche Gruppe zu verengen. Betrachtet man aber die Umgebung von „Grab X", wird besonders deutlich, wie fragmentarisch unsere Befunde tatsächlich sind. Eine ganze Reihe von frühen Gräbern dürfte nämlich noch vor der Errichtung der hadrianisch/frühantoninischen Mausoleen durch künstliche Erdbewegungen, die an manchen Stellen beträchtliche Hangerosion des Vatikanhügels und Einwirkungen durch Schwemmwasser vernichtet worden sein.[66] Dennoch reichen die Befunde für eine weiterführende, kritische Überprüfung der bisherigen Interpretation aus. Kein Zweifel besteht zunächst daran, dass keines der oben zur ersten Phase der Begräb-nisse gerechneten Gräber aus dem Rahmen einfacherer Bestattungen herausfällt. Dies ist in der Literatur bisher auch nie bestritten worden.[67] Doch ist auf drei weitere Beobachtungen hinzuweisen, die die bisherigen Theorien hinsichtlich des Petrusgrabes deutlich relativieren. Um des Experimentes willen nehmen wir trotz der berechtigten Einwände Thümmels an, dass „Grab X" tatsächlich existiert habe. Es zeigt sich schnell, dass selbst *wenn* „Grab X" existiert *hätte*, dessen Bedeutung kaum die weit reichenden Hypothesen der Ausgräber rechtfertigen würde:

c) Fragwürdig ist zunächst die Behandlung der *Orientierung* der Gräber γ, θ und ι um das angeblich durch das $\tau\rho o\pi\alpha\hat{\iota}ov$ hervorgehobene „Grab X". Bei allen dreien kommt es zu Überschneidungen untereinander (bis auf Grab η), nicht aber mit „Grab X". Die Achsen von zwei der ältesten Gräber (γ und θ) laufen parallel zum unter dem $\tau\rho o\pi\alpha\hat{\iota}ov$ befindlichen Grab (dessen eigene Achse hingegen um 11° von der der Roten Mauer abweicht!), Grab ι liegt etwa im rechten Winkel dazu. Alle *späteren* Gräber orientieren sich im Unterschied dazu eher an der Roten Mauer, wobei Gräber α, β, δ und ε im rechten Winkel zur Roten Mauer und κ, μ und λ parallel zu ihr verlaufen. Alle diese Gräber liegen auch höher als die ältesten Gräber γ, θ und ι. Nun ist aber die Frage der Ausrichtung der Gräber zueinander von der Frage nach der Gesamtorientierung der Gräber „X", γ, θ und ι methodisch zu unterscheiden. Nicht „Grab X" ist der Orientierungspunkt für Gräber γ, θ und ι, sondern „X" *und* die um es herum befindlichen Gräber sind, da es sich um Teile eines größeren Gräberfeldes handelt, *gemeinsam* auf ein anderes Objekt hin orientiert. Der Vergleich mit anderen aus Einzelbestattungen bestehenden Gräb–ergruppen zeigt, dass diese oft im rechten Winkel *oder* längs zur einer das Gräberfeld durchziehenden *Straße* orientiert sind.[68] Da Einzelgräber oft

---

66. Guarducci, 'Ausgrabungen', p. 367; *idem, Petrus*, p. 150 verweist auf ein Epigramm des Papstes Damasus (366–384), der sich rühmt, „die ‚Asche und Gebeine' (!) vieler, gerade im Bereich der Peterskirche gerettet zu haben vor der Einwirkung des unterirdischen Wassers" (Epigrammata 4).

67. Schließlich kann, um im traditionellen Modell zu bleiben, der Leichnam des hingerichteten Petrus durchaus inmitten von Armengräbern bestattet worden sein.

68. Dabei macht es keinen Unterschied, ob es sich um Körperbestattungen wie im Fall des Vatikanbereichs oder um Brandgräber handelt. Auch die Brandgruben in Mainz-Weisenau sind längs *oder* rechtwinklig auf die Gräberstraße hin orientiert (vgl. M. Witteyer, P. Fasold [eds.], *Des Lichtes beraubt. Totenehrung in der römischen Gräberstraße von Mainz-Weisenau* [Wiesbaden: Graphische Betriebe, 1995]). Das Gräberfeld Mainz-Weisenau eignet sich trotz seiner georgra-

mit Grabmonumenten auf einem Grundstück vergesellschaftet sind, kämen als weitere Möglichkeiten etwaige Begrenzungen von Grabgrundstücken oder ein benachbartes Großgrab in Frage. Ähnliches ist auch im Fall der Vatikangräber zu beobachten.

Wie der Vergleich mit Einzelinhumationen an anderen Orten zeigt, kann es immer wieder zur Bildung von Grabgruppen („*cluster*") kommen.[69] Ob es bei den in solchen Gruppen Bestatteten um Angehörige einer Familie oder Freunde bzw. Nachbarn handelt, lässt sich mangels Inschriften nicht feststellen; denkbar wären auch topographische Faktoren, die die Häufung von Gräbern an einem bestimmten Ort fördern. Klar ist jedenfalls: die Zusammenballung um das imaginäre „Grab X" ist also nichts, was notwendigerweise auf den besonderen Charakter dieses Grabes hinweisen würde, es ist kein Zug, der nicht auch anderenorts in derselben Nekropole anzutreffen gewesen wäre. Auch die Vermeidung von Überschneidungen der Gräber γ, θ und ι mit „X" ist daher nicht ungewöhnlich. Auch an anderen Orten überschneiden sich zeitgleich angelegte Gräber nicht. Überschneidungen können vorkommen, wenn die Erbauer neuerer Bestattungen nicht mehr um früher angelegten Gräber wussten. Diese Zurückhaltung hatte rechtliche und religiöse Gründe.[70] Eine Grabstelle galt als Besitz des Toten und (im Falle eines Mausoleums) seiner Familie, ihre Verletzung hätte zu rechtlichen Konsequenzen durch den Erben bzw. die Nachkommen des darin Bestatteten geführt. Wohlhabendere Familien erwarben das Grundstück, auf dem das Grabmal stand und grenzten es durch eine Hecke oder eine kleinere Mauer ab. Bei Armengräbern kam der Erwerb größerer Grundstücke freilich nicht infrage. Doch galt hier dasselbe Prinzip des Eigentums an der Grabstätte und das Grabgrundstück fiel lediglich mit dem Ausmaß des Grabes selbst zusammen. Zur Verletzung der Integrität des Grabes durch die späteren Generationen konnte es erst kommen, wenn niemand mehr die Unverletzlichkeit des Grabes einfordern konnte. Zudem war jedes Grab, sei es noch so ärmlich, ein den Totengeistern geweihter Ort, den die Sterblichen nicht nur bei der Anlage neuer Bestattungen zu achten hatten. Auf Grabinschriften wohlhabenderer Familien oder Individuen finden wir immer wieder scharfe Warnungen vor Verletzung der Totenruhe und deftige Flüche gegen die, die mit dem Gedanken an eine solche Tat zu spielen wagen. Obwohl uns Vergleichbares im Falle von Armengräbern fehlt

---

phischen Distanz für einen Vergleich mit den Gräbern unter der Peterskirche, da es im Unterschied zu anderen Mainzer Gräberfeldern starke italische Einflüsse verrät und ebenfalls während des 1. Jh. n. belegt worden ist (vgl. den Plan in Witteyer und Fasold, *Totenehrung*, pp. 20–21 und denjenigen von Sarsina *ibidem*, p. 105). Aufschlussreich ist die Zusammenballung und Ausrichtung der Körpergräber auf der südwestlichen Seite der Nekropole unter dem Parkplatz des Vatikans bei Steinby, 'Necropoli', Plan 1.

69. Vgl. die Befunde aus Mainz-Weisenau und Sarsina (s. vorige Anm.).

70. Zum juristischen Tatbestand des *sepulchrum violatum* vgl. Dig 47,12; zum römischen Grabrecht vgl. M. Kaser, 'Zum römischen Grabrecht', *ZSRG.R* 95 (1978), pp. 15–92 (bes. pp. 33–34); Toynbee und Ward Perkins, *Excavations*, pp. 12–13; J.M.C. Toynbee, *Death and Burial in the Roman World* (Baltimore und London: Johns Hopkins University Press, 1971), pp. 73–79; Eck, 'Inschriften', p. 58; Volp, *Tod*, pp. 86–89. Die Unverletzlichkeit des Grabes war auch bei anderen Völkern anerkannt, vgl. die auffallend ähnlich formulierten Inschriften aus dem nabatäischen Hegra bei J.F. Healey, *Nabatean Tomb Inscriptions of Mada'in Salih* (JSSt.Sup, 1; Oxford: Oxford University Press, 1993), p. 46 u.ö..

(da sie zumeist keine Grabsteine hatten), galten auch sie als Gräber und standen zumindest theoretisch unter religiösem und rechtlichem Schutz. Die „Heiligkeit", die die Erbauer der Gräber bewogen hat, ist also nicht zwangsläufig die eines bestimmten Bestatteten wie etwa des Petrus, sondern entspricht dem rechtlich-religiösen Tabubereich, das jedem auch noch so armen Grab zukommt. Die Tatsache, dass sich die Gräber γ, θ und ι nicht mit „X" überschneiden, belegt nur, dass „X" bei der Anlage von γ, θ und ι noch oberirdisch sichtbar war und man dessen Störung vermeiden wollte.

d) Im Zusammenhang der Diskussion des „Petrusgrabes" wird zweitens immer wieder auf die Tatsache hingewiesen, dass im Umkreis von „Grab X" *keinerlei Brandbestattungen* angetroffen wurden. So hat zuletzt Lampe betont, dass der „Platz ‚P' nirgendwo eine Spur von Feuerbestattung" aufweist, sondern nur Erdbestattungen, während „wir auf vergleichbaren Grabfeldern der 1. Hälfte des 2. Jh. stets ein *Nebeneinander* von beiden Bestattungsformen vorfinden". Er schließt daraus: „‚P' ist eine Ausnahme!".[71]

Das Gegenteil ist der Fall! Deutlich ist nur, dass Gräber „X" (falls es existiert hat!), γ, θ und ι keine Brandbestattungen darstellen. Doch schreibt Guarducci, dass man „(i)n der Nähe" von Grab θ „verschieden(e), teils verbrannt(e) Grabrest(e)" fand.[72] Sie scheinen durch den Fund einer Lampe des 1. Jh. (Stempel des L. Munatius Threptus) klar in dieselbe Zeitspanne wie die Erdbestattungen zu datieren.[73] Die einfachste und angesichts der Nutzung des Areals als Friedhof nächstliegende Interpretation der „teils verbrannten Grabrest(e)" ist m.E., dass es sich dabei entweder um die Relikte von öffentlichen Scheiterhaufen (*rogae*) und/oder ärmlichen Brandbestattungen handelt. Dass davon nur schwer fassbare Spuren vorhanden sind, sollte nicht verwundern. Aus zahlreichen Grabungen wissen wir, dass bei Armenbestattungen die Aschenreste nach der Verbrennung der Leiche oft nur in eine Holzkiste geschüttet oder in ein Tuch eingeschlagen wurden, um schließlich in einer einfachen Erdgrube beigesetzt zu werden.[74] Mitunter errichtete man den Scheiterhaufen auch gleich über der Grube, die man nach dem Niederbrennen zudeckte und als Grab nutzte (sog. *busta*).[75] Diese ärmlichen Aschenbeisetzungen

71. Lampe, *Christen*, p. 90 (Kursive von Lampe); vgl. schon Kerschbaum, *Gräber*, p. 83.

72. Guarducci, 'Ausgrabungen', p. 368. Dieser bedauerlich knappe Hinweis verdient stärkere Beachtung als ihm in der Forschung bisher zuteil wurde.

73. Abbildung der Lampe bei Guarducci, 'Ausgrabungen', p. 368 Abb. 3.

74. Witteyer und Fasold, *Totenehrung* liefern interessantes Anschauungsmaterial zur Kremation; vgl. auch T. Bechert, 'Zur Terminologie provinzialrömischer Brandgräber', *ArchKorr* 10 (1980), pp. 253–8; C.Vismara (ed.), *Incinerations et inhumations dans l'occident romain aux trois premiers siècles des notre ère. Actes du Colloque International de Toulouse-Montréjeau* (Toulouse: Ministère de la culture et de la communication, Direction du patrimoine, Sous-direction de l'archêologie. Association pour la promotion du patrimonie archéologique et historique en Midi-Pyrénées, 1992).

75. F. Naumann-Steckner in *idem*, (ed.), *Tod am Rhein. Begräbnisse im frühen Köln* (Köln: Römisch-Germanisches Museum, 1997), p. 26 schreibt über Bestattungen in Köln: „Knochen und Asche der Ärmsten wurden wohl lediglich in Tücher oder Stoffsäckchen gesammelt, sie sind bei Ausgrabungen nur als dunkle Erdverfärbung zu erkennen". Genau dies scheint mir bei den Brandspuren der Fall zu sein. Insofern ist der häufige Hinweis auf das Gräberfeld der Isola Sacra

können durchaus, selbst wenn das Grab durch einen Ziegel o.ä. abgedeckt worden sein sollte, durch die beträchtliche Erosion am Vatikanhügel noch leichter verschwemmt worden sein als die ohnehin schon stark gestörten Ganzkörperbestattungen.[76] Insofern ist auch in dieser Hinsicht die Behauptung besonderer Auffälligkeit der Bestattungen unter dem Petersdom hinfällig.

Doch wie schlagkräftig ist das Argument fehlender Brandbestattungen überhaupt? Vorausgesetzt ist dabei stets, dass die Brandbestattung von Christen aus religiösen Gründen nicht praktiziert wurde.[77] Nimmt man dieses Axiom einmal als zutreffend an, dann kann daraus nur folgen, dass *allein* die möglicherweise vorhandenen Brandbestattungen *nicht* christlichen Ursprungs sein können. Keinesfalls jedoch ist dadurch umgekehrt schon gesichert, dass die Erdgräber des Bestattungsplatzes im Umkreis von „Grab X" zwangsläufig christlich sein *müssen*. Über den religiösen Kontext der Erdbestattungen erfahren wir durch dieses Argument nichts; sie können paganen Ursprungs sein und dokumentieren, dass die in der frühen Kaiserzeit allgemein geübte Praxis der Brandbestattung die ältere Sitte der Erdbestattung auch im späten 1./frühen 2. Jh. noch nicht völlig verdrängt hatte.[78] Sie können aber auch von Angehörigen anderer, ebenfalls die Brandbestattung ablehnender Gruppen stammen. In Kleinasien z.B. war Erdbestattung nie durch die Kremation verdrängt worden, und auch Juden lehnten die Verbrennung strikt ab.

bei Ostia zur Erklärung des Befundes auf dem Vatikan (vgl. etwa Lampe, *Christen*, p. 90) zu relativieren. Die Isola Sacra ist nur dahingehend repräsentativ, dass Brand- und Ganzkörperbestattungen nebeneinander angelegt wurden, *nicht* dafür, dass Reste von Brandbestattungen stets in Amphoren beigesetzt wurden. Also sollte man den Befund auf der Isola Sacra nicht mit dem des Vatikans *kontrastieren* (wie dies oft geschieht), im Gegenteil: Der Befund der Isola Sacra deckt sich prinzipiell mit dem des Vatikans. Nicht auszuschließen ist, dass auch auf dem Vatikan Aschenbeisetzungen in Amphoren vorgenommen wurden, diese aber durch Erosion und spätere Planierung zerstört sind. Angesichts dessen ist es ein bedauerliches Versäumnis, dass außer dem erwähnten Lampenfragment keinerlei Keramik angemessen besprochen, geschweige denn publiziert wurde. Daher kommen wir hier über Hypothesen nicht hinaus.

76. Auch spricht das oben Anm. 66 zitierte Epigramm des Damasus dafür, dass auf dem Vatikan Brand- und Erdbestattungen zur selben Zeit existierten.

77. Volp, *Tod*, p. 107 weist zu Recht darauf hin, dass bisher lediglich keine christlichen Brandbestattungen *nachgewiesen* wurden, ihre Existenz aber aufgrund der großen Ähnlichkeit christlicher und paganer Erdbestattungen in der Frühzeit aber nicht von vorn herein ausgeschlossen werden kann. Ich verweise in diesem Zusammenhang auf Minucius Felix, Oct 34.10 der wohl um 200 die Erdbestattung allein mit dem Hinweis auf die *vetus et melior consuetudo* propagiert. Minucius Felix schreibt zu einer Zeit, als die Feuerbestattung im Römischen Reich bereits allgemein zurückging. Die später nachweisbare christliche Aversion gegen Brandbestattungen könnte somit einen Zustand perpetuieren, der ursprünglich keine spezifisch christlichen Wurzeln besaß (zu diesem komplexen Thema vgl. den klassischen Artikel A.D. Nock, ‚'Cremation and Burial in the Roman Empire', *HTR* 25 [1932], pp. 321–59 und jüngst Volp, *Tod*, pp. 186–95).

78. Lampe, *Christen*, p. 90: „Erdbestattung kam (…) erst seit Hadrian wieder in Mode"; Nock, 'Cremation'; Eck, 'Inschriften', pp. 66–67 zur Vatikannekropole: „In der Nekropole fassen wir (…) den Umbruch, der sich in den Formen der Totenbestattung seit der 1. Hälfte des 2. Jh.s langsam vollzog und sich zu Beginn des 3. Jh. vollständig durchgesetzt hatte. Was die Gründe dafür waren, ist umstritten und läßt sich wohl auch nicht eindeutig klären. Die Vatikannekropole liefert jedenfalls keinen Hinweis darauf, dass dies mit einem durch das Christentum herbeigeführten religiösen Wandel zu verbinden wäre".

e) Schließlich ist auf einen weiteren Befund hinzuweisen. Dem Charakter der Bestattungen unter der Gräberstraße der hadrianisch/frühantoninischen Zeit kommen wir einen Schritt näher, wenn wir eine Fundgruppe in den Blick nehmen, die bisher noch in keiner Publikation die erforderliche Beachtung gefunden hat. Bei der anthropologischen Untersuchung der menschlichen Knochen stellte man nämlich fest, dass bei den einzelnen untersuchten Knochengruppen stets Reste von *Tieren* beigemischt waren.[79] Aufgrund der nach heutigem Verständnis ungenügenden Bergung und Dokumentation dieser zentralen Fundgattung[80] ist eine Interpretation natürlich mit einer beträchtlichen Unsicherheit befrachtet, zumal der Zusammenhang von Fundort und Knochenfund in aller Regel nicht mehr rekonstruierbar ist. Leider richtete sich das Interesse der Forschung aus sachfremden Gründen (Erörterung der Petrusfrage) im Wesentlichen nur auf die menschlichen Knochenreste, doch besitzen wir immerhin eine sorgfältige typologische Bestimmung der Knochen durch Cardini, die die folgenden Überlegungen rechtfertigen.[81] Aufschlussreich sind zunächst die durch die Knochen repräsentierten Species von Tieren (Hühner, Schafe/Ziegen, Schweine, Rind). Dabei zeigt die Art der erhaltenen Knochen, dass die einzelnen Species nie durch ganze Exemplare, sondern stets nur durch bestimmte Teile davon repräsentiert sind.[82] Vor allem die große Anzahl von Rippen und Röhrenknochen ist bemerkenswert, wenn auch nicht allzu aussagekräftig, da diese postdepositionale Prozesse in der Regel besser überstehen als andere Skelettteile. Von entscheidender Bedeutung ist erst, dass eine ganze Anzahl dieser Knochen deutliche Schnitt- und Hackspuren bzw. Bohrungen aufweisen.[83]

Für diesen auffälligen Befund muss es eine Erklärung geben. Guarducci interpretiert die Knochen als Reste weidender Tiere in den ehemaligen Gärten des Nero (d.h. auf den späteren Grabgrundstücken), weist die Tierknochen also der Zeit vor der Errichtung des Gräberfeldes zu und sieht keinen unmittelbaren Zusammenhang mit den Begräbnissen.[84] Dies kann man aufgrund der spärlichen Informationen

---

79. Guarducci, *Petrus*, p. 125 berichtet von folgendem Wortwechsel: „‚Haben nicht auch Sie', so fragte ich Professor Correnti, ‚einen Tierknochen festgestellt?' – ‚Selbstverständlich! Sogar mehrere. Auch in den Gruppen T und K waren Tierknochen'."

80. Zu den abenteuerlichen Umständen der Entdeckung und der Wiederauffindung der menschlichen und tierischen Knochen vgl. Guarducci, *Petrus*, pp. 103–15 und oben Anm. 1. Betont sei, dass Tierknochen nicht nur bei Grabungen der 40er Jahre, sondern zuweilen auch heute noch mit der nötige Aufmerksamkeit finden, vgl. J. Lev-Tov, ‚ "Upon What Meet Doth This Our Caesar Feed…?". A Dietary Perspective on Hellenistic and Roman Palestine', in S. Alkier, J. Zangenberg (eds.), *Zeichen aus Text und Stein. Studien auf dem Weg zu einer Archäologie des Neuen Testaments* (*TANZ*, 42; Tübingen: Francke, 2003), pp. 420–446.

81. Guarducci, *Gebeine des Apostelfürsten*, pp. 173–79; vgl. auch die Abbildungen von Tierknochen auf Tafeln 2-7 *ibidem*, pp. 91–96.

82. Die einzige Ausnahme bildet das vollständige Skelett einer Maus, das in dem konstantinischen Repositorium (Gruppe VMG) gefunden wurde. Die Maus könnte, wie Guarducci unter Berufung auf Luigi Cardini zu Recht meint, durchaus in späterer Zeit dorthin gelangt und verendet sein (Guarducci, *Petrus*, pp. 132–3; *idem*, *Gebeine des Apostelfürsten*, pp. 178–79.

83. Guarducci, *Gebeine des Apostelfürsten*, p. 94 (Tafel 4).

84. Guarducci, *Gebeine des Apostelfürsten*, pp. 48–49: „Es ist keine andere Erklärung möglich, als dass sie [scil. die Knochen] schon in der Erde waren, bevor die bescheidenen Gräber geschaufelt wurden" (p. 48); vgl. *idem*, *Petrus*, pp. 127–28 und 133. Leider verrät Guarducci nicht,

über die Fundzusammenhänge und des Charakters des Vatikanhügels im 1. Jh. zwar nicht grundsätzlich ausschließen,[85] es ist aber angesichts der Arten von Knochen und der Bearbeitungsspuren sicherlich nicht die einzig mögliche Erklärung, zumal die Tierknochen offensichtlich stets in unmittelbarer Nähe der menschlichen Knochen der jeweiligen Bestattungen gefunden worden sind. Auch das Weiden von Tieren auf Gräberfeldern ist sicher dennbar, jedoch verträgt sich die Annahme, die Reste verendeter Tiere wären auf dem Gräberfeld einfach liegengelassen worden, nicht mit der Würde eines Bestattungsplatzes. Auch mag nicht grundsätzlich auszuschließen sein, dass die Knochen Reste von Abfall darstellen, der entweder vor oder während der Verwendung des Areals als Begräbnisplatz abgeladen worden sein soll, doch scheint nicht einsichtig, weshalb man Küchenabfall auf ein Gräberfeld oder – vor dessen Einrichtung- in der Umgebung des noch in Betrieb befindlichen Zirkusses deponiert haben soll.

Also liegt ein *ursächlicher* Zusammenhang ihres Vorkommens mit den Bestattungen selbst durchaus nahe, und es verwundert, dass Guarducci und andere dieser Frage nicht nachgegangen sind. In der Tat gibt es viele Gelegenheiten, in denen Tiere bei Begräbnissen eine Rolle spielten. Zum einen könnten die Tierknochen als Reste von Mählern (*silicerna*, so etwa bei den Rinderknochen: Schnittspuren, zudem Bohrungen zum Aufhängen eines Fleischstücks im Hause oder zum Räuchern) zu interpretieren sein, zum anderen Reste ritueller Schlachtungen (so besonders im Falle der Schweineknochen)[86] darstellen oder als Speisebeigaben ins Grab gelangt sein (besonders beliebt dafür waren Hühner.[87] Essen und Totengedenken waren ja seit Urzeiten eng miteinander verbunden.[88] Dazu würden auch die

welche Faktoren sie im Einzelnen zu diesem Schluss geführt haben, ihre Bemerkung über eine Umfrage unter „befreundete[n] Archäologen in den für die Ausgrabungen zuständigen Aufsichtsbehörden, besonders [...] solche[n], die mit den Ausgrabungen von Rom und Ostia zu tun hatten" (*ibidem* p. 127), bleiben kryptisch. Wegweisend scheint eine Überlegung Cardinis gewesen zu sein, der den Fund eines Rinderknochens im Marmorsarkophag des 16. Jh. auch darauf zurückführte, dass eine ehemals in der Erde bestattete Leiche in den Sarkophag umgebettet wurde (Guarducci, *Petrus*, p. 133). Die Ausführungen zum Thema Tierknochen übersteigen bei Guarducci jedoch jeweils kaum mehr als eine knappe Seite, was wohl die geringe Bedeutung verdeutlicht, die sie dieser Fundgattung zugemessen hat.

85. Guarducci, *Petrus*, pp. 19–25 erwähnt weite Freiflächen, die als Weideplatz genutzt wurden: „Zusammenfassend läßt sich sagen, dass der Vatikan zur Zeit Neros, abgesehen von der Gegend des Tiberufers, eine öde ländliche Zone war, in der Bauern und Hirten arbeiteten, und zahlreiche Tote in ihren reichen oder armen Gräbern ruhten" (pp. 24–25).

86. Vgl. Cicero, *De Legibus* II 22,57: *nec tamen eorum ante sepulchrum est quam iusta facta et porcus caesus est* und Toynbee, *Death*, p. 50; vgl. dazu J. Zias, 'Whose Bones? Were They Really Jewish Defenders? Did Yadin Deliberately Obfuscate?', *BARev* 24/6 (1998), pp. 40–45 und 64–66 und *idem*, 'Human Skeletal Remains from the Southern Cave of Masada and the Question of Ethnicity', in L.H. Schiffman, E. Tov, J.C. VanderKam (eds.), *The Dead Sea Scrolls Fifty Years After their Discovery. Proceedings of the Jerusalem Congress July 20–25, 1997* (Jerusalem: Israel Exploration Society, 2000), pp. 732–38 über Schweineknochen unter den Resten der angeblichen Verteidiger von Masada.

87. Geflügelknochen finden sich oft als Beigabe in Gräbern; vgl. Plutarch, *Crassus* 19.

88. Zum Thema vgl. H.Lindsay, 'Eating with the Dead. The Roman Funerary Banquet', in I. Nielsen and H.S. Nielsen (eds.), *Meals in a Social Context. Aspects of the Communal Meal in the*

vereinzelt gefundenen Eierschalen passen, die ebenso als Speisebeigaben und wohl auch aufgrund ihres Symbolgehaltes (neues Leben schlüpft aus totem Ei) im Totenkult eine Rolle gespielt haben.[89] Erwägenswert ist ferner, ob nicht auch zumindest manche der Lampen- und Glasfragmente (so in Grab I) Reste von Beigaben oder bestimmter Aktivitäten des Totenkults (Parfümieren des Leichnams bei der Beisetzung/Verbrennung, Beigaben, Bestandteil des Totenmahls) darstellen. Auch die Libationsröhre von Grab γ, durch die flüssige Gaben direkt in das Grab gegossen werden konnten, ordnet sich problemlos in diesen Zusammenhang ein.[90] Obwohl im einzelnen nicht mehr genau zu entscheiden ist, welche Tierknochen und Objektfragmente welchem Kontext des Totenkults zuzuweisen sind, scheint durchaus plausibel, sie als Bestandteil ritueller Totenmähler der Hinterbliebenen bzw. als Beigaben zur Speisung der Toten zu interpretieren. Trotz der recht einfachen Machart der Gräber unter St. Peter lässt sich interessanterweise doch ein komplexes Spektrum an Funden und Befunden beobachten, das auf eine verhältnismäßig differenzierte Totenpflege schliessen lassen.

4. *Fazit: Zur „Christlichkeit" der Bestattungen unter der Peterskirche*

Nach all diesen Beobachtungen stellt sich die Frage nach der „Christlichkeit" der, mancher oder zumindest einer Bestattung unter der Peterskirche erneut und mit umso größerem Nachdruck. Nach all dem, was wir bisher festgestellt haben, steht außer Zweifel: *Beweisbar* ist der christliche Charakter *keiner* der Bestattungen, da sie sich weder in ihrer Form noch Ausrichtung oder hinsichthich der Begleitfunde (Lampenfragmente, Tierknochen, Glasscherben) von dem unterscheiden, was wir über stadtrömische Armenbestattungen des späten 1./frühen 2. Jh. n. Chr. wissen.[91] Auch die höchst unwahrscheinliche Identifikation der in Mauer g gefundenen Knochen als „Gebeine Petri" bietet keine Hilfe bei der Frage nach dem religionsgeschichtlichen Profil auch nur einer einzigen frühkaiserzeitlichen Bestattung im Umfeld von „Grabhof P".[92] Will man aber auch nur eines dieser Erdgräber als

---

Hellenistic and Roman World (ASMA 1; Aarhus: Aarhus University Press, 1998), pp. 67–80; Toynbee, *Death*, pp. 50–52; Volp, *Tod*, pp. 77–86.

89. Zu Eiern als Bestandteil des Totenmahls vgl. Lindsay, 'Eating', p. 73 mit Anm. 47 (zitiert Juvenal 5.85; Lucian, *Catapl* 7; Tacitus, *Ann.* 6.5).

90. Zu Libationsröhren vgl. Volp, *Tod*, p. 62 und v.a. p. 77.

91. Wenn Lampe, *Christen*, p. 90 schreibt: „Gegen die Christlichkeit von γ können weder die durchgehende Libationsröhre noch der altarähnliche Aufbau sprechen. Da wir kein zeitgenössisches Vergleichsmaterial kennen, das ‚vorschriebe', wie ein christliches Grab dieser frühen Zeit auszusehen hätte, ist mit petitiones principii – im Stile von 'das kann gar nicht sein' – nichts zu machen", ist ihm aus theoretisch begründeter Vorsicht vor Überinterpretationen zwar grundsätzlich zuzustimmen, doch hilft das Argument nicht weiter. Es geht hier nicht darum, Aussagen darüber zu machen, was „gar nicht sein" *kann*, sondern danach zu fragen, was *positiv dafür* spricht, etwas bestätigt zu finden (die Christlichkeit des Grabes γ etwa), was in der Literatur behauptet wird. Letztlich geht es darum, eine Aussage zu unterlassen, deren Basis nicht erwiesen ist, um sich vor unbegründeten Schlussfolgerungen zu bewahren.

92. Thümmel, *Memorien*, pp. 68–72 hat die Argumente erneut zusammengestellt, vgl. auch Dinkler, 'Petrus', pp. 15–17 und 33. Jegliche Diskussion der Knochen hat davon auszugehen, dass

christlich ansprechen, muss man weitere Argumente vorbringen, die ein über das Übliche hinausgehendes religionsgeschichtliches Profil plausibel machen.

Als ausschlaggebendes Argument für die Anwesenheit christlicher Gräber, allen voran des Petrusgrabes, im Umfeld des τροπαῖον galt seit jeher die Annahme einer Lokaltradition, die um den authentischen Ort des Petrusgrabes wusste und auf die die Errichtung des τροπαῖον zurückgeht. An dieser Annahme sind nun deutliche Zweifel angebracht. Vor allem der zentrale Punkt des Arguments wankt: Da die Existenz von „Grab X" in Frage steht, kann sich die Lokaltradition nicht auf ein bestimmtes Grab beziehen, das die Position des τροπαῖον bestimmt hätte. Thümmel fragt daher zu Recht, ob die Errichtung des von Gaius erwähnten τροπαῖον zwingend voraussetzt, dass man um die *exakte* Lage des Petrusgrabes wusste und dieses mit dem Bauwerk markieren wollte.[93] Nach Wegfall von „Grab X" kann es sich bei dem τροπαῖον bestenfalls um eine allgemeine Memoria handeln, die keinen Bezug zu einem bestimmten Grab aufweist. Der archäologische Befund vermag nicht zu erklären, warum das τροπαῖον an dieser Stelle errichtet wurde. Er kann auch nicht zur Bestätigung der so oft bemühten „Lokaltradition" dienen und die Historizität eines Petrusgrabes verbürgen. Dazu folgende Überlegungen: Vorauszusetzen ist, dass die Rote Mauer mit der als τροπαῖον interpretierten Nische nur *einen* Teil einer ganzen Gräberstraße darstellt, die ab etwa 135 sukzessive entstand. Nun ist durchaus möglich, dass die Erbauer der Roten Mauer mit der Nische um 160–165 von der Existenz älterer Gräber wussten, da bei den hangseitigen Planierungsarbeiten zur Anlage der mittelkaiserzeitlichen Gräberstraße sicherlich zahlreiche ältere Bestattungen angeschnitten und wohl auch abgeräumt wurden. Offensichtlich bestanden jedoch zwischen den in den älteren Gräbern Bestatteten und den Eigentümern der einzelnen Parzellen der neuen, im Entstehen befindlichen Gräberstraße des 2. Jh. keinerlei verwandtschaftliche oder rechtliche Beziehungen. Möglicherweise wurde das Gelände außerhalb des Zirkus mit seinen verstreuten „Armengräbern" überhaupt erst mit der Anlage der Gräberstraße des 2. Jh. in klare rechtliche Eigentumstitel überführt, die so möglicherweise vorher noch gar nicht existierten. Da man sich anscheinend generell nicht die Mühe machte, ältere Gräber in die neuen Anlagen einzubeziehen, ist es erstaunlich, dass dies gerade im Fall der Roten Mauer und des Grabhofes P der Fall gewesen sein soll. Abgesehen davon ist nicht sicher, ob Petrus, der ja als Verbrecher im Zirkus hingerichtet wurde, überhaupt in einem identifizierbaren Individualgrab beigesetzt werden konnte. Man sollte sich vor der romantischen Annahme hüten, dass Petrus dasselbe Schicksal beschieden war wie Jesus von Nazaret, für den ein Vertrauter für ein „anständiges" Begräbnis sorgen konnte.[94]

die Reste *mehrerer* Individuen in dem Fach in Mauer g bestattet wurden. Für die Annahme, dass ausgerechnet das männliche Skelett aus dem unter den τροπαῖον postulierten Grab stammen sollen, gibt es keinen Beweis. So dürfte wohl Thümmels Vermutung dem Befund angemessen sein, wonach man in dem Fach in Mauer g „Gebeine deponierte, die bei den konstantinischen Bauarbeiten zutage gekommen waren" (*ibidem*, p. 70), ohne dass den konstantinischen Bauleuten deren Identität bekannt gewesen wäre. Auch die in Mauer g geritzten Graffiti stellen keine „Echtheitserklärung" dieser Gebeine dar.

93. Thümmel, *Memorien*, p. 72.

94. Üblicherweise wurden im Zirkus hingerichtete Delinquenten (*noxii*) in Massengräbern

Ferner ist zu fragen, ob die frühen Christen Roms, falls sie denn um das Petrusgrab gewusst hätten, die Errichtung der Roten Mauer mit der Nische überhaupt nach einem einzelnen älteren Grab hätten ausrichten *können*. Wenn die Rote Mauer und Grabhof P in erster Linie im Kontext der mittelkaiserzeitlichen Neuregulierung des gesamten Geländes nördlich des Nerozirkus zu sehen sind, dann hieße dies, dass sowohl die Besitzer des Hof P benachbarten Grabgrundstücks O, als auch die des ursprünglichen Wasserbeckens und späteren Mausoleums Q mit dem Clivus und die Eigentümer des Grabhauses S auf den Wunsch der Christengemeinde Rücksicht zu nehmen bereit waren, gerade dort ihr τροπαῖον errichten zu dürfen, wo diese das „Petrusgrab" lokalisierten. Welche Belege haben wir dafür? Ferner müsste man voraussetzen, dass die christliche Gemeinde im rechten Zeitpunkt mit ihrem Kaufwunsch zum Zuge kommen konnte, um Eigentümer des Grabhofes P oder zumindest der Roten Mauer zu werden, als der Ausbau des westlichen Teils der Gräberstraße im Gange war. Freilich ist auch dies nicht unmöglich; zu fragen ist aber wieder, welche Belege wir für diese Annahme wirklich haben. Selbst wenn es also eine derartige Lokaltradition über die Lage des Grabes Petri gegeben hätte, so müsste erst einmal geklärt werden, ob die notwendigen rechtlichen und praktischen Voraussetzung gegeben waren, dass jene tatsächlich auch architektonisch wirksam werden konnte.

Angesichts dieser Schwierigkeiten bleiben zwei Möglichkeiten, den Zusammenhang zwischen τροπαῖον und den ältesten Gräbern zu erklären.

Einerseits kann man mit Thümmel davon ausgehen, dass die Erbauer der Petrusmemoria keine genaue Kenntnis von der Lage des „echten" Apostelgrabes (mehr) hatten, sich aber wohl entweder auf Nachrichten stützen konnten, dass es einst in der Nähe des Zirkus gelegen habe[95] oder sich ohne jeglichen Bezug zum tatsächlichen Grab lediglich einen Platz zum Gedenken sicherten, der möglichst nah an der überlieferten Hinrichtungsstätte lag.[96] Will man keinen simplen Abbruch einer ursprünglich existenten Erinnerung annehmen (was angesichts der kurzen Zeit zwischen dem vermutlichen Tod des Petrus im Zuge der neronischen Verfolgungen im Juli 64 (Tacitus, *Ann.* XV 44.2.4–5)[97] und der Errichtung des τροπαῖον doch

---

verscharrt oder einfach in den Tiber oder einen anderen Fluss geworfen, vgl. die Befunde aus dem 4. Jh. außerhalb des Trierer Amphitheaters bei H.-P. Kuhnen, 'An der Trierer Arena. Ausgrabungen im Grabungsschutzgebiet „Amphitheater – Petrisberg" ', *FABT* 29 (1997), pp. 17–31 (hier pp. 26–28). Nur erfolgreichere Gladiatoren (zu denen Petrus sicher nicht gehörte) hatten die Chance, ein individuelles Grab mit Grabstein zu erhalten, vgl. das Inschriftfragment eines *myrmillo* aus der Umgebung des Nerozirkus bei M. Guarducci, 'Nuove iscrizioni nella zona del circo di Nerone in Vaticano', *RPARA* 32 (1959–60), pp. 123–60 (hier pp. 124–25); zur Bestattung von Opfern des Arenageschehens vgl. M. Junkelmann, 'Familia Gladiatoria. Die Helden des Amphitheaters', in E. Köhne, C. Ewigleben (eds.), *Caesaren und Gladiatoren. Die Macht der Unterhaltung im antiken Rom*. (Mainz: Philipp von Zabern, 2000), pp. 39–80 (hier p. 79). Zum Grab Jesu vgl. Zangenberg, *Haus der Ewigkeit*, pp. 484–515.

95. Zur Motivation der Errichtung der Petrusmemoria vgl. bes. Thümmel, *Memorien*, pp. 96–102.

96. Gegen Lampe, *Christen*, p. 91 Anm. 272, der vermutet, dass „das verehrte Grab bereits im 1. Jh. ein 'Petrusgrab'" war.

97. Zu den quellenkundlichen und chronologischen Problemen vgl. Dinkler, 'Petrus', pp. 6–7; Thümmel, *Memorien*, pp. 10–14.

recht unwahrscheinlich ist), dann kann man sich des Eindrucks nicht erwehren, dass das Grab des Petrus zunächst keine besondere Aufmerksamkeit auf sich zog. Erst im Laufe späterer Generationen, vielleicht gar erst zur Zeit des Gaius, scheint man der potentiellen Gegend von Hinrichtung und Grab Petri größere Bedeutung beigemessen zu haben. Folge davon war der Bau des τροπαῖον, das freilich *nicht* den Ort des wirklichen Petrusgrabes oder der Hinrichtung markiert, sondern nur in möglichst großer Nähe zur Stätte seines Todes an den Apostel *erinnert*.[98] Es gibt keine Hinweise dafür, dass die Nische lediglich als architektonische Unterstützung des mit ihr korrespondierenden „eigentlichen" τροπαῖον (etwa einem Grabcippus) konzipiert war.[99] Ursprünglich war die Nische selbst das τροπαῖον. Verwendet Gaius deshalb den allgemeineren Begriff τροπαῖον (Sieges-, Erinnerungszeichen)[100] und nicht das Wort τάφος (Grab), das sein montanistischer Gegenspieler gebraucht, um die Gräber der Philippustöchter in Hierapolis hervorzuheben? Träfe dies zu, dann läge die Steigerung darin, dass Rom die *Sieges*zeichen der *Apostel* und *Märtyrer* Petrus und Paulus zu bieten hat und nicht lediglich die Gräber von vier Töchtern eines urchristlichen Propheten.[101]

Man nutzte den Neubau der Gräberstraße, um ein recht unscheinbares Erinnerungsmal in Form einer einfachen Nische an einem Platz anzubringen („Hof P"), der offensichtlich inmitten der Mausoleen „übrig war" und sich gut für kleinere Versammlungen eignete. Die Nische hatte sicher keine dekorative Funktion (dazu ist sie zu primitiv), sondern könnte als Orientierungspunkt für diejenigen gedient haben, die sich im Hof P versammelten. Form und Orientierung von Hof P scheinen allein durch die Raumaufteilung der Gräberstraße (Nachbarschaft von Mausolea O und S und dem damals noch als Zisterne genutzten Bereich Q) diktiert gewesen zu sein, eine besondere „symbolische" Bedeutung der Lage im Westen des Hofes scheint mir nicht gegeben. In Anbetracht der Nische und ihrer vermutlichen Funktion sollte man P nicht als „*Grab*hof" bezeichnen. Viel eher haben wir es hier mit dem wohl ältesten datierbaren christlichen Versammlungsraum in Rom zu tun. Die fehlende Kontinuität der Memoria zu den älteren Einzelgräbern ist nicht primär dadurch gegeben, dass die Gräber allesamt ins 2. Jh. zu datieren wären,[102] sondern liegt allein in deren paganem Charakter. Die Erbauer des Hofes P interessierten sich schlicht nicht für sie.

Falls aber einige der frühkaiserzeitlichen Gräber doch von Christen angelegt worden sind (was trotz fehlender positiver Indizien letztlich nicht ausgeschlossen

---

98. Ich gehe insofern noch einen Schritt weiter als Dinkler, 'Petrus', p. 33, der zwar die Interpretation „Grab" zu Recht ablehnt, aber von „Martyriums-Ort" spricht. Zutreffend wäre „Ort der Erinnerung an den Sieg des Petrus im Martyrium".

99. Vgl. oben Anm. 49 und 55.

100. Dinkler, 'Petrus', p. 32 verweist zu Recht darauf, dass die einschränkende Deutung von τροπαῖον als „Grab" erst durch den Kontext des Gaius-Zitats in Eusebs Kirchengeschichte gegeben ist.

101. Dinkler, 'Petrus', p. 8.

102. Dinkler, 'Petrus', p. 14 und 33 misst der Datierung der Gräber ins 2. Jh. zu großes Gewicht bei. Der Befund ist zu komplex und undeutlich, als dass man pauschal ein Datum im 2. Jh. postulieren könnte.

werden kann), dann könnten wir sie als Beleg dafür ansehen, dass christliche Gräber nicht nur dieselbe Form wie zeitgenössische schichtspezifische pagane Bestattungen aufweisen und mit diesen zusammen auf ein- und demselben Friedhof angelegt sein können, sondern dass sich in dieser frühen Zeit noch bemerkenswerte Parallelen hinsichtlich des *Grab- und Totenkultes* beobachten lassen. Dann wären Totenmähler und Speisebeigaben auch in christlichem Kontext vorgekommen und christliche Gräber wären ohne erkennbare Abgrenzung inmitten von heidnischen Bestattungen angelegt worden. All dies wäre nicht ungewöhnlich: „Das Nebeneinander von heidnischen und christlichen Gräbern auf engem Raum begegnet immer wieder".[103] Insofern wären dann die Gräber unter dem Petersdom ein Beleg dafür, dass sich frühestchristliche Bestattungen hinsichtlich der Form und Begleitrituale weitgehend an dem orientieren, was in der jeweiligen Umwelt praktiziert wurde.[104]

ABSTRACT

Ever since the excavations under St Peter's Cathedral started in the 1940s and culminated in the official announcement of Pope Pius XII in 1953 that the true remains of St Peter had been found, many scholars have remained sceptical about the significance of the discoveries. Even the strongest proponents of the authenticity of the discovery cannot deny that little if anything about the earliest graves shows any clear Christian character. The first and second century CE graves very much resemble contemporaneous simple interments of common people from the neighbouring quarters of Rome. Many archaeological details, however, have been found that help to reconstruct burial practices and cultic activities. It is not before around 160 CE that we see some kind of interest of Roman Christians in the site by the construction of a simple monument that consisted of a niche and a courtyard (the *Tropaion Gaii*). The monument was probably used for gatherings, but not as marker of an individual grave, since memory of the Peter's original burial place was lost by the time the *Tropaion* was erected. The existence of the *Tropaion* did not result in the development of a Christian burial site, but was integrated into a middle-class non-Christian burial street. Only in the age of Constantine the site was firmly and finally taken over by Christians, thereby obliterating all earlier traces of burial activity apart from the immediate space around the *Tropaion*. In conversation with Peter Lampe's and Hans Georg Thümmel's recent studies, the article assesses the various phases of archaeological evidence and reflects upon their respective cultural and historical context.

103. Lampe, *Christen*, p. 18–19; Kirschbaum, *Gräber*, pp. 20–39.
104. Diese These entfalte ich näher in Zangenberg, *Haus der Ewigkeit*.

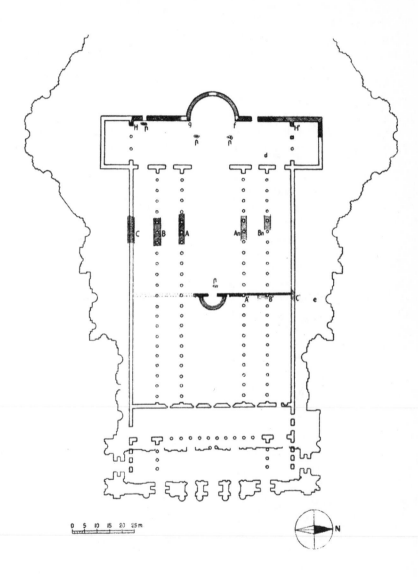

1. *St. Peter. Grundriss der konstantinischen Basilika*

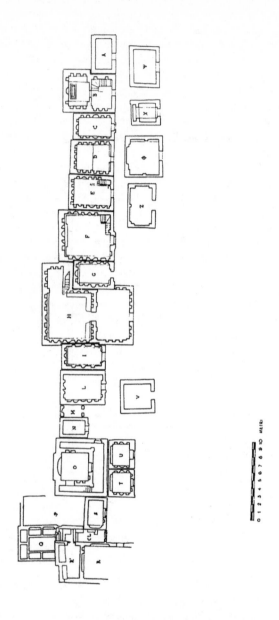

2. *Die mittelkaiserzeitliche Nekropole unter St. Peter*

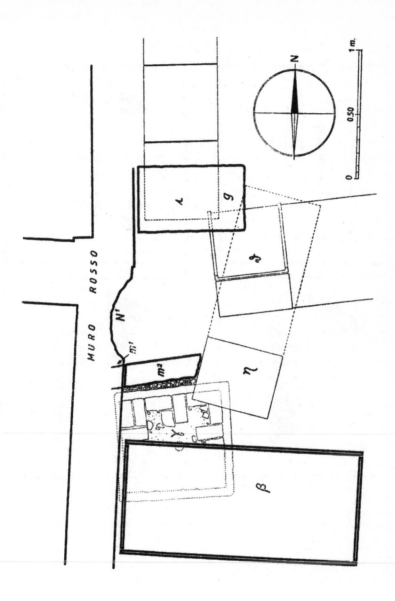

3. *St. Peter, Nische N¹ mit den umliegenden Gräbern*

4. *Rekonstruktion der Petrusmemorie in ihrer Entwicklung nach Thümmel*

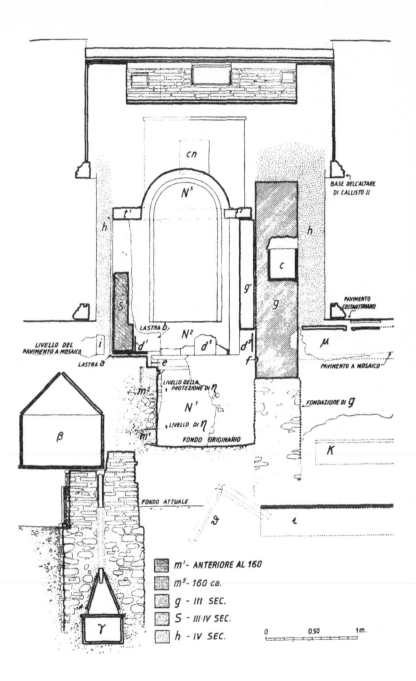

5. *St. Peter, Aufriss der Petrusmemorie*

Abbildungen

1. St. Peter. Grundriss der konstantinischen Basilika (aus: Thümmel, *Memorien*, Abb. 46 auf Tafel XLVI unter Verwendung von Apollonii Ghetti u.a., *Esplorazioni*, Fig. 103).

2. Die mittelkaiserzeitliche Nekropole unter St. Peter (aus: Prandi, *Zona*, Fig. 3).

3. St. Peter, Nische N^1 mit den umliegenden Gräbern (aus: Thümmel, *Memorien*, Abb. 7 auf Tafel VII).

4. Rekonstruktion der Petrusmemorie in ihrer Entwicklung nach Thümmel:
    a) Die Rote Mauer mit der Nische nach der Errichtung um 160–165. Der obere Abschluss der Nische ist hypothetisch.
    b) Die Memorie vor dem Bau von Mauer g. Die hinter der Nische gelegene Zisterne Q ist in eine Grablege verwandelt, deren Mauerwerk bis an die Nische heranreicht. Das Laufniveau ist gestiegen.
    c) Die Memorie mit Mauer g.
    d) Die vorkonstantinische Memorie. Auf einem wiederum erhöhten Niveau ist die Ädikula errichtet und eine Marmorverkleidung angebracht worden. Der Boden vor der Nische wurde tiefergelegt, die Umgebung erhielt einen Mosaikboden. Ergänzt sind Kapitelle und Architrav, der obere Abschluss der Nische ist weiterhin hypothetisch. (aus: Thümmel, *Memorien*, Abb. 45 auf Tafel XLV).

5. St. Peter, Aufriss der Petrusmemorie (aus: Thümmel, *Memorien*, Abb. 22 auf Tafel XXII unter Verwendung von Apollonii Ghetti u.a., *Esplorazioni*, Fig. 91).

Das Christentum in Rom im Spiegel des ersten Clemensbriefes

Martin Meiser

Versucht man, dem nicht wirklich gesichert zu datierenden[1] ersten Clemensbrief konkrete kirchen- und theologiegeschichtlich verwertbare Aussagen über das Christentum zu Rom bzw. eine seiner Formationen zu entnehmen, sieht man sich in mehrfacher Weise methodischen Bedenken gegenüber.

a) Der erste Clemensbrief ist ein situatives Dokument, dem die Abzweckung „auf die Stirn geschrieben"[2] steht, die Korinther zur ὁμόνοια und εἰρήνη zurückzurufen[3] und den Opponierenden die freiwillige Selbstunterwerfung oder die Auswanderung zu empfehlen; er ist kein geschichtlicher Rückblick auf die Entwicklung der römischen Gemeinde[4] und auch keine Gemeindeordnung, die die

---

1.   Üblicherweise wird der erste Clemensbrief in das letzte Jahrzehnt des ersten Jahrhunderts datiert (dazu forschungsgeschichtlich T.J. Herron, 'The Most Probable Date of the First Epistle of Clement to the Corinthians', *StPatr* 21 (1989), pp. 106–21, hier pp. 106–07.). Zieht O.M. Bakke, *„ Concord and Peace". A Rhetorical Analysis of the First Letter of Clement with an Emphasis on the Rhetoric of Unity and Sedition* (WUNT, 2.143; Tübingen: Mohr-Siebeck, 2001), p. 11 auch das erste Jahrzehnt des zweiten nachchristlichen Jahrhunderts in Betracht, so sind jüngst T.J. Herron und K. Erlemann für eine Frühdatierung eingetreten (Th.J. Herron, 'Date', passim; K. Erlemann, 'Die Datierung des ersten Klemensbriefes – Anfrage an eine Communis Opinio', *NTS* 44 (1998), pp. 591–607). Zwar scheint Herrons Argument naheliegend, dass der Verweis auf die immer-währenden Opfer in 1 Clem. 40–1 sinnlos wäre, wenn sie momentan nicht fortdauerten (p. 109) – T. Schmitt, *Paroikie und Oikoumene. Sozial- und mentalitätsgeschichtliche Untersuchungen zum 1. Clemensbrief* (BZNW, 110; Berlin, New York: W. de Gruyter, 2002), p. 120, wertet um des willen 1 Clem. als Beleg für die Wiederaufnahme des Opferkultes in Jerusalem vor dem Bar-Kochba-Aufstand (zu dieser Frage vgl. M. Tilly, *Jerusalem – Nabel der Welt* [Stuttgart: W. Kohlhammer], 2002, p. 26), doch ist die Ältestenverfassung längst als Selbstverständlichkeit akzeptiert; die Apostel sind in Kap. 43-4 schon als Größe der Vergangenheit gezeichnet (vgl. W. Wrede, *Untersuchungen zum ersten Klemensbrief* [Göttingen: Vandenhoeck & Ruprecht, 1891], p. 102).

2.   Wrede, Untersuchungen, p. 1; vgl. A.W. Ziegler, *Neue Studien zum ersten Klemensbrief* (München: Manz, 1958), p. 34; D. Powell, Art. 'Clemens von Rom', *TRE* 8 (1981), pp. 113–20.

3.   1 Clem. ist nach textpragmatischen Gesichtspunkten am ehesten als νουθεσία zu charakterisieren (O.B. Knoch, 'Im Namen des Petrus und Paulus. Der Brief des Clemens Romanus und die Eigenart des römischen Christentums', *ANRW* II 27,1 [1993], pp. 3–54, hier p. 12; M. Günther, *Einleitung in die Apostolischen Väter* [ARGU, 4; Frankfurt (Main) u.a.: Peter Lang, 1997], p. 51). Die Parallelität von νουθετεῖν (1 Clem. 7.1) und ἔντευξις (1 Clem. 63.2) legt es nahe, in keinem der beiden Ausdrücke eine Gattungsdefinition *klassischer* formgeschichtlicher Prägung zu erblicken.

4.   Nicht durchgesetzt hat sich O. Cullmanns These, die Verfolgung der beiden Apostelfürsten Petrus und Paulus sei durch Auseinandersetzungen innerhalb der römischen christlichen Gemeinde

stadtrömischen kirchlichen Verhältnisse um ihrer selbst willen widerspiegelt,[5] und keine Selbstvorstellung, die von sich aus die Bewältigung der multikulturellen Situation der Hauptstadt Rom thematisiert.

b) Manches muss den Korinthern nicht gesagt werden, weil sie um ihre eigene Situation wissen[6] – wir können im Nachhinein kaum feststellen, ob der erste Clemensbrief den Konflikt schärfer darstellt, als er in Wirklichkeit war,[7] und ob die Wahl der Terminologie staatspolitischer Rhetorik statt der des Vereinswesens[8] eine solche Verschärfung nur unbewusst bewirkt oder doch bewusst intendiert. Manches

begünstigt worden (O. Cullmann, 'Les causes de la mort de Pierre et de Paul d'apres le témoignage de Clément Romain', *RHPhR* 10 (1930), pp. 294–300; zur Kritik daran vgl. O.B. Knoch, 'Im Namen des Petrus', p. 40 mit Anm. 173; G. Schneider, *Clemens von Rom: Epistola ad Corinthios / Brief an die Korinther, übers. u. eingel.* (FC, 15; Freiburg u.a.: Herder, 1994), p. 64 u.a. Skeptisch ist auch H. Löhr, 'Zur Paulus-Notiz in 1 Clem. 5,5–7', in F.W. Horn (ed.), *Das Ende des Paulus. Historische, theologische und literaturgeschichtliche Aspekte* (BZNW, 106; Berlin, New York: W. de Gruyter, 2001), pp. 197–213, hier p. 211).

5.   H.-G. Leder, 'Das Unrecht der Presbyterabsetzung in Korinth. Zur Interpretation von 1. Cl. 44,1-6', *ThV* 10 (1979), pp. 107–27, hier pp. 109.117, hat 1 Clem. 44.1–2 auf die Übereinstimmung der Kirchenverfassung der römischen Gemeinde mit dem kirchenordnenden Handeln der Apostel in 1 Clem. 42 gedeutet. Doch hat sich diese Interpretation nicht durchgesetzt; zur Kritik vgl. A. Lindemann, *Die Clemensbriefe* (HNT, 17; Tübingen: Mohr-Siebeck, 1992), p. 130; H.E. Lona, *Der erste Clemensbrief übersetzt und erklärt* (KAV, 2; Göttingen: Vandenhoeck & Ruprecht, 1998), pp. 455–46.

6.   Dem heutigen Leser „erscheinen…die korinthischen Verhältnisse nur in der Beleuchtung, in welcher er (scil. Der erste Clemensbrief) sie sieht und sehen lässt" (Wrede, *Untersuchungen*, p. 8).

7.   So Chr. Eggenberger, *Die Quellen der politischen Ethik des 1. Klemensbriefes* (Zürich: Zwingli-Verlag, 1951), p. 35 unter Berufung auf A. v. Harnack, *Einführung in die alte Kirchenge-schichte. Das Schreiben der römischen Kirche an die korinthische aus der Zeit Domitians (1. Clemensbrief) übersetzt und den Studierenden erklärt* (Leipzig: Hinrichs, 1929), p. 104; vgl. R. Knopf, *Die Lehre der zwölf Apostel. Die zwei Clemensbriefe* (HNT, 17; Tübingen: Mohr-Siebeck, 1920), 48: „αἰχμαλωσία ist übertreibend und bildlich, wie auch πόλεμος". Eggen-bergers weitergehende These, der auf die Anfangszeit Hadrians zu datierende Brief sei nur fiktiv nach Korinth, eigentlich aber an die römische Staatsmacht adressiert und solle eigentlich „als getarnte Apologie … bei Hofe einen für das Christentum günstigen Eindruck erwecken" (p. 191), machen wir uns in dieser Zuspitzung nicht zu eigen.

8.   Zu den Begriffen *consentire* und *seditio* vgl. die Satzung des Begräbnisvereins von *Lanuvium* (136 n. Chr.; *ILS* II/2, 7212 pag. I 16 / pag. II 25, aber nicht in unmittelbarer Gegenüberstellung). Eine generelle christliche Zurückhaltung dieser Terminologie gegenüber begründet B. Kötting, Art. 'Genossenschaften D. Christlich', *RAC* 10 (1978), pp. 142–52, hier p. 147, mit dem Anspruch „der vollständigen Einbeziehung aller Lebensvorgänge" der Christen durch die christliche Gemeinde. – Der Begriff πόλεμος wird offensichtlich nur in 1 Clem. 3.2; 46.5 auf innergemeindliche Zwistigkeiten angewandt, höchstens vielleicht noch in Jak 4.1, sofern das in Jak 4 angesprochene Fehlverhalten der Christen auf ihr Verhalten in der Gemeinde (H. Frankemölle, *Der Brief des Jakobus* [ÖTK, 17/2, GTB 18, Gütersloh: Gütersloher Verlagshaus und Würzburg: Echter Verlag, 1994], p. 580; F. Schnider, *Der Jakobusbrief übersetzt und erklärt* [RNT, Regensburg: Pustet, 1987], pp. 97–98) und nicht in ihrem persönlichen Umfeld referiert (so m.E. zu Recht M. Dibelius, *Der Brief des Jakobus erklärt* [KEK, 15, 11. Aufl., hg. u. erg. v. H. Greeven; Göttingen: Vandenhoeck & Ruprecht 1964], p. 259; W. Popkes, *Der Brief des Jakobus* [ThHK. NT, 14; Leipzig: Evangelische Verlagsanstalt, 2001], p. 262). *TestGad* 5.1 ist eine nur undeutliche Parallele; unsicher ist *4Q183* frg. 1 col. ii.

über die römischen Verhältnisse und Geschehnisse, z.B. die συμφοραὶ καὶ περιπτώσεις von 1 Clem. 1.1, mag ihnen bekannt sein oder durch die in 1 Clem. 65.1 genannten römischen Gemeindegesandten mündlich mitgeteilt werden. Für andere Fälle unspezifischer Redeweise mag eine Interpretation zu erwägen sein, dergemäß die angeredeten Korinther[9] sich strikt darauf konzentrieren sollen, die ihnen seitens der Absender zugedachte Rolle in diesem Kommunikationsgeschehen auszufüllen,[10] d.h. die Zurechtweisung dieses Briefes zu akzeptieren[11] – dazu mussten sie über die römischen Verhältnisse nicht mehr wissen, als der Brief zu erkennen gibt. Der Verweis auf „den selben Kampfplatz" 1 Clem. 7.1[12] hätte ähnlich wie das „wir" von 1 Clem. 56.2; 63.1 die Funktion, die römischen Ausführungen von dem Verdacht jeglicher Willkür speziell den Korinthern gegenüber zu befreien, gäbe aber keine Auskunft über Konflikte innerhalb der römischen Gemeinde[13] oder über gegenwärtige Verfolgungen.[14]

c) Der erste Clemensbrief hält die Selbstpräsentation als Schreiben *der Gemeinde* zu Rom konsequent durch; das Ausmaß an Schriftkenntnis und rhetorischer

---

9.   Ein expliziter Kommunikationsvorgang mit den abgesetzten Presbytern ist nicht unmittelbar greifbar; ob der erste Clemensbrief durch ihre Beschwerde veranlasst war (so H.-J. Vogt, Rez. A. Lindemann, *Die Clemensbriefe, JAC* 38 [1995], pp. 167–70, hier p. 169), muss fraglich bleiben. Dass die Presbyter im Fall der Unterwerfung der Aufständischen Verzeihung gewähren sollen, mag impliziert sein, wird aber nicht gesagt, um dem Brief nicht seine Stoßkraft zu nehmen.

10.   Vgl. die Wendung τὸν τῆς ὑπακοῆς τόπον ἀναπληρῶσαι in 1 Clem. 63.1.

11.   Kaum verhüllt wird in 1 Clem. 58.2; 59.1 das eschatologische Geschick zumindest der Rädelsführer der στάσις von ihrem Gehorsam gegenüber den Ausführungen des ersten Clemensbriefes abhängig gemacht, die nach eigenem Selbstverständnis von Gott gesagt sind (59.1) und dem Wollen des göttlichen πνεῦμα entsprechen (vgl. 1 Clem. 63.2 und dazu Lindemann, *Die Clemensbriefe*, p. 178). Vgl. auch C. Caragounis, 'From Obscurity to Prominence: The Development of the Roman Church between Romans and 1 Clement', in K.P. Donfried und P. Richardson (eds.), *Judaism and Christianity in First-Century Rome* (Grand Rapids, Cambridge: Eerdmans, 1998), pp. 245–79, hier p. 276: „Its (scil. des ersten Clemensbriefes) συμβουλή sounds more like an ultimatum"; vgl. auch p. 278. – Das Adjektiv ἄθραυστον in der Bitte, dass die Christenheit unversehrt bewahrt bleibe (1 Clem. 59.2), könnte, beachtet man die biblischen Bezüge der Wortgruppe θραύω, ebenfalls auf das *göttliche* Endgericht verweisen: Ein vom Herrn kommendes θραύειν steht in Num 17.11–5 zu befürchten (auf Num 17 wird in 1 Clem. 43 Bezug genommen), vgl. auch 2 Chr 20.37; Ps. 106.23, 30.

12.   Für den hier vorauszusetzenden übertragenen Gebrauch von σκάμμα vgl. Epiktet, *Diss.* IV 8, 26.

13.   So aber die vorsichtigen Mutmaßungen bei L.L. Welborn, 'On the Date of First Clement', *BR* 29 (1984), pp. 35–54, hier pp. 46–48 und die Behauptungen bei B.E. Bowe, *A Church in Crisis: Ecclesiology and Paraenesis in Clement of Rome* (HDR, 23; Minneapolis: Fortress Press, 1988), p. 157; Bakke, „*Concord and Peace*", pp. 100–103, dessen Verweis auf die συμφοραὶ καὶ περιπτώσεις 1 Clem. 1.1 m.E. nicht überzeugt: Hätten Maßnahmen zur Behebung einer στάσις innerhalb der römischen Gemeinde durch freiwillige Unterordnung der Aufrührer Erfolg gehabt, wäre das auch in der Mahnung gegenüber den Korinthern ein brauchbares *exemplum* gewesen; wären die συμφοραὶ καὶ περιπτώσεις nicht im Sinne des Verfassers des ersten Clemensbriefes behoben worden, hätte er besser daran getan, sie völlig zu verschweigen.

14.   So aber T. Schmitt, *Paroikie*, p. 123; doch wäre die folgende Mahnung zur Buße damit nicht wirklich motiviert. Ταῦτα in 7.1 greift nicht die Verfolgungen als solche auf, sondern die Beispielreihe zu ζῆλος und ἔρις (1 Clem. 6.4).

Stilisierung dürfte jedoch gerade angesichts ihrer sozialen Spannbreite[15] nicht jedem einzelnen ihrer Mitglieder erschwinglich gewesen sein.

1. *Historische und sozialgeschichtliche Daten*

Nach dem bisher Ausgeführten ergeben sich äußere Kontrolldaten weder für die Situation der römischen Gemeinde noch für den Verfasser des ersten Clemensbriefes. So muss es historisch ungewiss bleiben, ob die Wendung αἰφνίδιοι καὶ ἐπαλλήλοι | συμφοραί καὶ περιπτώσεις in 1 Clem. 1.1 auf eine kürzlich zu Ende gegangene lokale Verfolgung zurückblickt.[16] Die erst sekundär[17] mit dem Schreiben verbundene Person des Klemens ist nicht weiter eingrenzbar;[18] das Christentum des ersten Clemensbriefes ist möglicherweise nur eine der Manifestationen römischen Christentums zu seiner Zeit.[19]

15. Caragounis, 'Prominence', 272, mit Verweis auf 1 Clem. 38.2; 59.4; 55.2. Auch wenn einige dieser Belege topisch sein sollten (vgl. Lindemann, *Die Clemensbriefe*, p. 155, zu 1 Clem. 55.2), dürfte Caragounis' Gesamtergebnis zutreffen.

16. So M. Dibelius, 'Rom. und die Christen im ersten Jahrhundert', in *idem, Botschaft und Geschichte. Gesammelte Aufsätze, Bd. II*, hrsg. v. G. Bornkamm (Tübingen: Mohr-Siebeck, 1956), pp. 177–228, hier p. 192; zuletzt wieder J. Molthagen, 'Die Lage der Christen im römischen Reich. Zum Problem einer domitianischen Verfolgung', *Hist.* 44 (1995), pp. 422–58; A. Brent, *The Imperial Cult and the Development of Church Order. Concepts and Images of Authority in Paganism and Early Christianity before the Age of Cyprian* (VC.Sup Wel, 45; Leiden: E.J. Brill 1999), pp. 143–44, der mit einer lokal begrenzten Aktion Domitians rechnet. Doch συμφορά und περίπτωσις „sind keine für Christenverfolgungen üblichen Termini" (Lindemann, *Die Clemensbriefe*, p. 26). Zur Problematik der These einer Christenverfolgung in Rom unter Domitian vgl. J. Ulrich, '*Euseb, Hist. Eccl.* III 14–20 und die Frage nach der Christenverfolgung unter Domitian', *ZNW* 87 (1996), pp. 269–89. T. Schmitt, *Paroikie*, p. 124, hält eine generelle Zuspitzung der Gefährdungssituation für die Christen in spätflavischer Zeit für wahrscheinlich.

17. Vgl. noch Irenäus, *Adversus haereses* III 3.3: „Als es zur Zeit dieses Klemens zu einem nicht geringfügigen Aufstand bei den Brüdern in Korinth kam, sandte *die römische Gemeinde...*" (Hervorhebung M.M.).

18. Gelegentlich wird behauptet, Clemens sei Heidenchrist und evtl. Freigelassener des römischen Konsuls Titus Flavius Clemens gewesen, der zusammen mit seiner Frau wegen Atheismus und Hinneigung zu jüdischen Sitten verurteilt worden sei (D.F.W. Wong, 'Natural and Divine Order in 1 Clem', *VC* 31 [1977], pp. 81–87; mit Verweis auf den archäologischen Befund unter der stadtrömischen Basilika San Clemente J.S. Jeffers, 'The Influence of the Roman Family and Social Structures on Early Christianity in Rome', *SBL.SP* 27 [1988], pp. 370–84, hier p. 371; als Erwägung auch bei Bakke, „*Concord and Peace*", p. 7). Aus dem Text geht das nicht hervor. Außerdem wäre auf den Freigelassenen das *gentilicium*, d.h. der Name „Flavius" übertragen worden, nicht das *cognomen* Clemens. Dass Vf. einstens als Sekretär in der kaiserlichen Kanzlei tätig war (als Vermutung Bakke, „*Concord and Peace*", p. 326) ist ebenfalls nicht nachzuweisen: Die Textbasis für eine solche Behauptung ist zu schmal. Zu Recht warnt P. Lampe, *Die stadtrömischen Christen in den ersten beiden Jahrhunderten. Untersuchungen zur Sozialgeschichte*² (WUNT, 2.18; Tübingen: Mohr-Siebeck, 1989), p. 172: „Die Person des Autors lässt sich sozialgeschichtlich nicht näher eingrenzen; anderslautende Hypothesen greifen fehl".

19. Vgl. N. Brox, *Der Hirt des Hermas übersetzt und erklärt* (KAV, 7; Göttingen: Vandenhoeck & Ruprecht, 1991), p. 23; Jeffers, 'Influence', p. 370. – C. Caragounis, 'Prominence', p. 271, rechnet mit der Existenz einzelner Hausgemeinden für die Zeit des ersten Clemensbriefes ebensowenig wie für die Zeit des Römerbriefes (pp. 260–62), m.E. nicht zwingend zu Recht.

Textintern ein wenig günstiger sind die Voraussetzungen für die sozial-geschichtliche Einordnung des Verfassers und der von ihm repräsentierten (Teile der) Gemeinde. Sie versteht sich, wie das Proömium ausweist, als fremde Größe in der Welt,[20] und doch sind in der Betonung der ὁμόνοια und der εἰρήνη pagane, staatspolitischer Rhetorik entstammende Wertmaßstäbe speziell der politischen Oberschicht leitend.[21] So könnte der erste Clemensbrief ähnlich wie einige neutes-tamentliche Spätschriften zeigen, dass das Christentum allmählich auch in höhere Gesellschaftsschichten,[22] möglicherweise schon in die Schicht der Gefolgsleute der politischen Eliten eindringt.[23]

Die genannte Wertorientierung bestimmt das Gottesbild genauso wie das allge-meinchristliche und das speziell ekklesiale Ethos: Das Prinzip der ὑποταγή prägt das Verhältnis der Schöpfung zu ihrem Schöpfer (1 Clem. 20.1) und Wohltäter (1 Clem. 20.11; 23.1) ebenso wie das Verhältnis zwischen politischen Eliten und Nichteliten (1 Clem. 61.1)[24] und, zusammen mit dem Prinzip der

20. So mit Nachdruck betont von T. Schmitt, *Paroikie*, p. 5 u.ö., p. 137 mit dem Verweis auf die Doppelung des Verbums παροικεῖν in 1 Clem. 1.1 – E. Peterson, 'Das Praescriptum des 1. Clemensbriefes', in *idem, Frühkirche, Judentum und Gnosis. Studien und Untersuchungen* (Rom, Freiburg, Wien: Herder 1959), pp. 129–36, hier 129–30, leitet παροικεῖν von Sir prol. 34 ab und versteht ἐκκλησία παροικοῦσα nicht als Ausdruck der Fremdlingschaft der Kirche in der Welt, sondern Bezeichnung der heidenchristlichen Kirche außerhalb des Mutterlandes Israel; der erste Clemensbrief sei im Grunde an die ganze Ökumene außerhalb Israels gerichtet. Dem widersprechen die Parallelen zu παροικεῖν in 1 Pt 1.17; EpPolyk prooem; Dg 5.5 sowie die konkrete Bezugnahme auf die Verhältnisse in Korinth.

21. Umstritten ist, ob die Betonung auf den zu Beginn des 2. Jh. n. Chr. „in griechischen Städten (besonders des Ostens) auffallend" thematisierten Begriff der Eintracht zurückverweist (so K. Thraede, Art. 'Homonoia [Eintracht]', *RAC* 16 [1994], pp. 176–289, hier p. 244) oder ob „die römische, vor dem Hintergrund der Erfahrungen der Bürgerkrieges des ersten vorchristlichen Jahrhunderts entstandene Idee der Kaiserherrschaft als einer Ordnung des Friedens" (T. Schmitt, *Paroikie*, 92 Anm 122) den Brief wie den Verstehenshorizont der Korinther als einer römischen Kolonie prägt. Zur Frage nach einer Bezugnahme des Briefes auf die pax Romana vgl. auch K. Wengst, *Pax Romana. Anspruch und Wirklichkeit. Erfahrungen und Wahrnehmungen des Friedens bei Jesus und im Urchristentum* (München: Kaiser, 1986), p. 136 sowie ohne negative Wertung Jeffers, 'Influence', p. 373.

22. Wengst, *Pax Romana*, p. 136, hat Vf. als gutsituierten Römer bezeichnet. Dies Gesamturteil scheint mir plausibel, weniger dessen Begründung mit 1 Clem. 38.2; 34.1: Dass der Reiche dem Armen geben soll, ist allgemein urchristlicher Topos, und die Beziehung des Christen zu Gott ist, wenn man als Bildspender das Verhältnis zwischen Arbeitgeber und Arbeitnehmer verwendet, kaum anders als in 1 Clem. 34.1 zu beschreiben und sachlich durch die Gleichnisse der Jesus-tradition abgedeckt.

23. So Caragounis, 'Prominence', p. 273.

24. Schmitt, *Paroikie*, pp. 40–60 hat bestritten, dass sich 1 Clem. 60.4–61.2 auf die staatlichen Regenten bezieht und stattdessen die Deutung auf die kirchlichen „Amtsträger" vorgeschlagen. M.E. widersprechen dieser Interpretation die Wendung ἐπὶ τῆς γῆς (1 Clem. 60.4), die Bezeich-nung der genannten Tätigkeit als βασιλεία (1 Clem. 61.1) und die im Falle seiner Deutung zur Tautologie herabsinkende Wendung μηδὲν ἐναντιουμένους τῷ θελήματί σου (1 Clem. 61.1). Ferner hat Schmitt m.E. den frühjüdischen traditionsgeschichtlichen Hintergrund dieser Theologie (Dan. 4; EpArist) nicht beachtet. Dass die *divi fili* in 1 Clem. 61.2 als υἱοὶ τῶν ἀνθρώπων bezeichnet werden, ist tatsächlich eine auch in anderer christlicher Literatur bekannte Einschränkung des kaiserlichen Selbstverständnisses (zu T. Schmitt, *Paroikie*, p. 45).

τιμή, die Beziehungen zwischen Eliten[25] und Nichteliten innerhalb der christlichen Gemeinde (1 Clem. 1.3);[26] dem Vorbild einiger Angehöriger politischer Eliten sollen die Aufrührer gerade durch die Bereitschaft zum Verzicht auf die Realisierung ihrer Pläne und zur Auswanderung entsprechen.[27] Das christliche Ethos, etwa hinsichtlich der Entfaltungsmöglichkeiten der Frau,[28] entspricht konservativen, an Vorstellungen altrömischen Rechtes orientierten Idealen.[29] Ob die für das klassische Rom kennzeichnende Viereinigkeit von „Autorität, Ordnung, Gesetz und Gehorsam"[30] den Verfasser des ersten Clemensbriefes wenigstens unbewusst bestimmt hat, muss freilich offen bleiben. Was explizit fehlt, ist eine Begründung des römischen Eingreifens unter Bezug auf die Welthauptstadt Rom oder auf die Geschichte der christlichen stadtrömischen Gemeinde. Eine gelegentliche Anlehnung an Ideale der geistigen Eliten in der paganen Umwelt wird sichtbar in der Beschreibung der Gotteserkenntnis als „Schau Gottes mit dem Verstand" (1 Clem. 19.3) und in einzelnen Zügen des Gottesbildes,[31] in der Charakterisierung der Aufrührer u.a. als ἄφφρονες

25. Das faktische Verhalten der bisher amtierenden Presbyter wird als Verhalten im Sinne urchristlicher, für Funktionsträger geltender Ideale beschrieben: Die Motive der ταπεινοφροσύνη (vgl. Apg 20.19, zum sachlichen Anliegen auch 1 Pt 5.3) und der ἡσυχία (vgl. 1 Tim. 2.2) implizieren, dass die Presbyter keinen Anlass zum Aufruhr gegeben haben, das Motiv der μαρτυρία durch die Gemeinde verweist auf ihre allgemeine Anerkennung (vgl. Apg 6.3 von den Diakonen sowie die Forderung 1 Tim. 3.7, den ἐπίσκοπος betreffend). Auch diese Charakterisierung der korinthischen Presbyter soll, unabhängig von ihrem Realitätsgehalt, das Verhalten der Aufrührer in ein negatives Licht rücken.

26. Begegnet die ὑποταγή schon in neutestamentlichen Texten im innergemeindlichen Kontext (1 Kor. 16.16 gilt sie bestimmten Personen, in 1 Pt 5.5a den Presbytern, wird dort freilich durch die Forderung der ταπεινοφροσύνη im gegenseitigen Umgang ergänzt), so wird die Wortgruppe τιμᾶν, in Neuen Testament das Verhältnis zur staatlichen Obrigkeit bezeichnend (Röm. 13.7; 1 Pt 2.17; dort im Unterschied zur Gottesfurcht), erst nachneutestamentlich auf kirchliche ἡγούμενοι übertragen (vgl. zu 1 Clem. 1.3 auch 1 Clem. 21.6; Ignatius, *Smyrn* 9.1; zum Begriff ἡγούμενοι vgl. aber schon Heb. 13.7,17,24).

27. Die Aufrührer sind keine βασιλεῖς καὶ ἡγούμενοι (1 Clem. 55.1)!

28. Für Frauen gelten, unbeschadet der Anerkennung von Martyrien und von tapferen Taten (1 Clem. 55.3–5; zu den Parallelen in der zeitgenössischen Rhetorik vgl. Ziegler, *Studien*, p. 79) und der Anerkennung der προφητεία bei Rahab (1 Clem. 12.8) als Ideale Unterordnung und Gattenliebe (1 Clem. 1.3), Keuschheit, Sanftmut, Schweigsamkeit und unprätentiöse Nächstenliebe (1 Clem. 21.7) sowie die Selbstdemütigung (1 Clem. 55.6). Als Presbyter kommen für den ersten Clemensbrief nur Männer in den Blick (1 Clem. 44.2–3). Andererseits wird nicht tadelnd erwähnt, dass Frauen im besonderen an der Erhebung gegen die korinthischen Presbyter beteiligt gewesen sein sollen. – Immerhin stellt das Prädikat „die selige Judith" (1 Clem. 55.4) diese Frau „auf die gleiche Ebene der Vollendeten wie Mose (43.1) und Paulus (47.1)" (Lona, *Der erste Clemensbrief*, p. 565).

29. Vgl. K. Thraede, Art. 'Frau', *RAC* 8 (1972), pp. 197–269, hier pp. 239–40 – Ob in 1 Clem. 38.2 die Beziehung zwischen arm und reich nach der römischen Patron-Klient-Beziehung geschildert wird (so Jeffers, 'Influence', p. 382), ist umstritten (zur Kritik vgl. Lona, *Der erste Clemensbrief*, p. 418).

30. V. Harnack, *Einführung*, p. 98.

31. Gott ist frei vom Zorn gegenüber seiner Schöpfung (1 Clem. 19.3), und er ist bedürfnislos (1 Clem. 52.1).

(1 Clem. 3.3)[32] oder in der Wertschätzung der σωφροσύνη als christlicher Tugend (1 Clem. 62.2); wichtiger aber ist die Anlehnung an Ideale der Frommen Israels in der Betonung der Demut,[33] vor allem aber der Umstand, dass die Beispiele alttestamentlicher und christlicher Vorbilder einen Wissensschatz bereitstellen, der es der christlichen Gemeinde hinfort erlaubt, ihre Ideale unabhängig von heidnischen *exempla* zu illustrieren. So gehört der erste Clemensbrief zu den Texten, die wie Heb. 11 wohl nicht der Intention nach, aber faktisch zur Formulierung eines neuen binnenchristlichen Bildungskanons beitragen, der auf der Grundlage beanspruchter geistiger und ethischer Suffizienz[34] die Abgrenzung von der nichtchristlichen Umwelt ermöglicht und so seinen Beitrag zur Ausbildung einer christlichen Gruppenidentität leistet.

Das Griechisch des Briefes ist i.w. korrekt;[35] nicht selten ist rhetorische Stilisierung erkennbar.[36] Ob der erste Clemensbrief eine wirkliche Vertrautheit mit der zeitgenössischen rhetorischen Tradition voraussetzt,[37] muss allerdings offen bleiben; vielleicht reichte ihm das als Kenntnis aus, was in der Grammatikerschule an einschlägigem, klassischem Bildungsgut vermittelt wurde.[38] Gewisse jüdische bzw. christliche[39] Bildungsgüter müssen verfügbar gewesen sein, z.B. Schriftrollen einiger alttestamentlicher Texte und Textcorpora,[40] aber auch Texte bzw. (über entsprechende Sozialkontakte vermittelte?) Traditionen, die als Vorlage für Partien

32. Vgl. auch die indirekte Charakteristik in 1 Clem. 21.5 (u.a. als ἄφρονες und ἀνόητοι), in 1 Clem. 39.1 sowie in 1 Clem. 45.7 (die Feinde Daniels, Ananias, Azarias und Misaels [nach Dan. 3.88] sind nach 1 Clem. 45.7 στυγητοὶ καὶ πάσης κακίας πληρεῖς).

33. Zur Forderung der Demut vgl. u. a. Ps. 119.75; Prov 11.2; 1 QS 2.24 sowie vor allem Jes 53.8 LXX. Dort wird das ganze Geschick des Gottesknechtes als ταπείνωσις gesehen; deshalb kann Jes 53 LXX ethisch verwendet werden.

34. Vgl. in 1 Clem. 62,1 die Wendung περὶ ... τῶν ὠφελιμωτάτων εἰς ἐνάρετον βίον sowie 1 Clem. 7.2. Zur ethischen Suffizienz des Christentums vgl. 1 Clem. 19.1 (zu dem hier angesprochenen Motiv der Besserung im einzelnen vgl. Justin, *1. Apol* 14.1).

35. Wrede, *Untersuchungen*, p. 109 Anm. 1.

36. Vgl. P. Vielhauer, *Geschichte der urchristlichen Literatur. Einleitung in das Neue Testament, die Apokryphen und die Apostolischen Väter* (Berlin: W. de Gruyter, 1975), p. 533.

37. So Bakke, *„Concord and Peace"*, p. 61, mit Verweis auf seine Fähigkeit, zu einem dafür geeigneten Thema deliberative Rhetorik in Dienst zu nehmen und auch die Beispiele entsprechend zu wählen. Nach Lampe, *Die stadtrömischen Christen*, p. 181, hat Clemens die Argumentationsart der Paradigmenreihen „wiederum nur via jüdisch-christliche Tradition, letztlich via Tradition der hellenistischen Synagoge kennengelernt".

38. Lampe, *Die stadtrömischen Christen*, pp. 180–82.

39. Literarische Beziehungen bestehen sicher zum 1. Korintherbrief, wahrscheinlich zum Römerbrief, möglicherweise zum Hebräerbrief; die Anklänge an den ersten Petrusbrief oder den Jakobusbrief sind eher mit dem Aufkommen einer allgemein-christlichen Binnensprache zu erklären. Eine *literarische* Abhängigkeit von den synoptischen Evangelien ist für 1 Clem. 13.2; 46.8 unwahrscheinlich; der Begriff εὐαγγέλιον in 1 Clem. 47.2 (auf den ersten Korintherbrief bezogen) ist wie das Verbum in 1 Clem. 42.1 literaturgeschichtlich gesehen unspezifisch gebraucht.

40. Man kann aufgrund der relativen Nähe vieler AT-Passagen zum LXX-Text den Zugang zu Schriftrollen der Thora und der hinteren Nebiim vermuten, vielleicht auch zu Teilen der Ketubim, wo alles außer Canticum und Kohelet zum Zitat herangezogen wird. Einzelne, an Sir und SapSal anklingende Wendungen lassen nicht zwingend auf den Zugang zu entsprechenden Schriftrollen schließen.

wie 1 Clem. 20 in Frage kommen.[41] Der religionsgeschichtliche Befund für diese Passagen ergibt allerdings keine Entscheidung darüber, ob der Verfasser einen „profan antiken Ausbildungsgang" durchlaufen hat. An rein paganem Bildungsgut verbleibt nicht viel, was zu einer Revision dieses Urteils führen müsste.[42]

2. *Das religionsgeschichtliche Profil des ersten Clemensbriefes*

Kann als die religionsgeschichtliche Hauptfrage zum ersten Clemensbrief die Frage nach dem Verhältnis zwischen alttestamentlich-frühjüdischen,[43] christlichen und paganen Motiven und Traditionen gelten, so hat die allgemeine erneute Hinwendung zu Geschichte und Literatur des frühen Judentums auch für den ersten Clemensbrief eine neue Verhältnisbestimmung veranlasst.

Ältere Forschung war zu 1 Clem. 5–6 (Märtyrer als Athleten), 1 Clem. 6.2 (Danaiden und Dirken), 1 Clem. 37.2 (Ordnung des Heeres),[44] 1 Clem. 37.4 (Satz von der Mischung), 1 Clem. 54.2 (Auswanderungsrat)[45] und 1 Clem. 55.1 (pagane Beispiele freiwilliger Selbstaufopferung) von allgemein paganer Beeinflussung, vor allem zu 1 Clem. 20 und zur Frage nach der Relevanz des ὁμόνοια-Prinzips für den Makrokosmos der Schöpfung bis zum Mikrokosmos der christlichen Gemeinde von speziell stoischem Einfluss ausgegangen.

Demgegenüber hat sich die Forschungslage vor allem für 1 Clem. 20 völlig verschoben. Der Nachweis *jüdisch*-hellenistischer Parallelen zu Texten wie 1

---

41.   Nach Lampe, *Die stadtrömischen Christen*, pp. 174–78, beweist der erste Clemensbrief keine stoische Spezialbildung, sondern eine Vertrautheit mit Elementen allgemein-antiken Denkens, das im hellenistischen Judentum, vor allem bei Philo breit rezipiert wurde (s.u.). Deshalb kann auf einen „profan antiken Ausbildungsgang stadtrömischer Christen" (*ibidem*, p. 178, kursiv durch P.L.) nicht zurückgeschlossen werden. Bereits für Wrede, *Untersuchungen*, p. 101 Anm. 1, zeugen die wenigen heidnischen Beispiele davon, „dass Klemens über eine gewisse, allerdings doch wohl bescheidene weltliche Bildung verfügte".

42.   Für die Formulierung des Auswanderungsrates fallen Parallelen aus Cicero, *Pro Milone* 93 (vgl. v. Harnack, *Einführung*, p. 82) und Seneca, *Medea* 449 (vgl. Ziegler, *Studien*, p. 91) auf; ferner zitiert Ziegler, *Studien*, p. 101, Beispiele für den Rat bzw. Befehl zur Flucht oder Auswanderung durch ein Orakel.

43.   Biblische Zitate sind zumeist der Septuaginta entnommen (Vgl. dazu D.A. Hagner, *The Use of the Old and New Testaments in Clement of Rome* [NT.Sup, 34; Leiden: E.J. Brill, 1973], dort pp. 37–79 auch zu der notwendigen Differenzierungen. Nach Powell, Art. 'Clemens von Rom', p. 113, besteht keine durchgehende Nähe zu einer der Hauptrezensionen der LXX, diese ist also auch nicht in einer „akzeptierten Standardform" benutzt. – Hebräische oder aramäische Sprachkenntnisse sind nicht erkennbar (Hagner, *Use*, p. 80); biblische Beispielreihen setzen gelegentlich Zusätze der Septuaginta (vgl. Lona, *Der erste Clemensbrief*, p. 566 Anm. 4 zu 1 Clem. 55.6) bzw. die *hellenistisch*-jüdische Rezeption einer biblischen Person (zu Jona als Bußprediger der Menschheit [1 Clem. 7.6] vgl. Josephus, *Ant.* 1.74) voraus. Die Heilige Schrift wird in aller Regel wörtlich ausgelegt (als Ausnahme ist nur 1 Clem. 12.7 zu benennen); die alttestamentlichen Weisungen werden bruchlos als für die christliche Gemeinde gültig in Anspruch genommen, wenn auch an zentraler Stelle (1 Clem. 40–41) nur dem allgemeinen Sinn nach.

44.   So noch zuletzt Knoch, 'Im Namen des Petrus und Paulus', p. 42.

45.   Nach Knoch, 'Im Namen des Petrus und Paulus', p. 42, sieht sich der Verfasser des ersten Clemensbriefes als hellenistischen Kosmopoliten.

Clem. 20 und selbst 1 Clem. 25[46] muss hier nicht wiederholt werden;[47] es lässt sich nicht belegen, dass stoische Literatur im ersten Clemensbrief unmittelbar rezipiert worden sein muss. Der Zusammenhang zwischen Naturerkenntnis und Ethik ist in griechischer Philosophie wie in jüdischer Literatur formuliert,[48] und in 1 Clem. 20 liegt der Hauptakzent nicht auf der Selbstevidenz der Naturordnung, sondern auf dem Machtwort Gottes, dessen Willensoffenbarung sie ist.[49]

Die genannte Verschiebung betrifft aber auch Partien außerhalb von 1 Clem. 20: Die Topik „Märtyrer als Athleten" begegnet in 4 Makk. 17; in 1 Clem. 37.2 wird nicht auf das römische Heer, sondern auf ein Heer nach biblischen Vorstellungen (Dtn 1.15)[50] verwiesen. Dazu fügt sich, dass der Verfasser des ersten Clemensbriefes ohne nähere Kommentierung die Gottesbezeichnungen „König der Äonen" (1 Clem. 61.2)[51] und „Herr der Geister" (1 Clem. 64.1) rezipieren und innerhalb biblischer Terminologie selbst sprachschöpferisch tätig[52] werden kann, wie auch wesentliche christliche Erziehungsideale sich biblischer Tradition verdanken.[53]

Für das hier erörterte Thema der Bewältigung der multikulturellen Situation ist jedoch unter rezeptionsästhetischer Perspektive zu bedenken, dass den Lesern des ersten Clemensbriefes die oben genannten frühjüdischen Parallelen zu Texten wie 1 Clem. 20; 25 nicht notwendig bekannt sein mussten, damit sie den Brief

46. Der Phönix wird im übrigen nicht aufgrund seiner Herkunft aus dem Heidentum und auch nicht wegen des Mirakulösen des Vorganges, „sondern als Naturerscheinung" (v. Harnack, *Einführung*, p. 62), vergleichbar dem Wechsel von Tag und Nacht etc., zum Argument für die Auferstehung der Toten. Das Argument ist auf Unwiderleglichkeit aus.

47. Vgl. insgesamt dazu Lampe, *Die stadtrömischen Christen*, 178–88; Lona, *Der erste Clemensbrief*, pp. 267–74, hier p. 273 (zu 1 Clem. 20). Brent, *Imperial Cult*, pp. 145–46, lässt die frühjüdischen Parallelen sowie die Diskussion um 1 Clem. 20 völlig außer acht, auch seine Ausführungen zum Zusammenhang zwischen stoischer Kosmologie, Divination und der Rechtfertigung des Kaiserkultes sind zu undifferenziert, wie er auch das Vorhandensein einer gerade von Stoikern getragenen Opposition gegen die Herrschaft Domitians nicht berücksichtigt. – Zur Nähe von 1 Clem. 1.1 zu frühjüdischer Briefliteratur vgl. Peterson, 'Praescriptum', p. 129; zur Nähe von 1 Clem. 1–7 zu frühjüdischer Märtyrertradition vgl. K. Beyschlag, *Clemens Romanus und der Frühkatholizismus. Untersuchungen zu I Clemens 1–7* (BHTh, 35; Tübingen: Mohr-Siebeck, 1966), passim. – Forschungsgeschichtlich ist an W. Bousset, *Kyrios Christos. Geschichte des Christusglaubens von den Anfängen des Christentums bis Irenäus* (FRLANT, 21; Göttingen: Vandenhoeck & Ruprecht, 2. Aufl. 1921), p. 291, zu erinnern, der den ersten Clemensbrief als „entschränktes … Diaspora-Judentum" bezeichnet hatte.

48. Für die griechische Philosophie vgl. hier nur die stoische Telosformel ὁμολογουμένως τῇ φύσει ζῆν (*SVF* I 179), für jüdische Literatur vgl. Hi 28.27–8; *äthHen* 2.1–5.5; *TestNaph* 3,2; *AssMos* 12.9–10.

49. W. C. van Unnik, 'Is 1 Clem. 20 purely Stoic? ', *VC* 4 (1950), pp. 181–89, hier p. 184; ihm folgend A. Stuiber, Art. 'Clemens Romanus I', *RAC* 3 (1957), pp. 188–97, hier p. 196.

50. Zur Wirkungsgeschichte von Dtn 1.15 vgl. auch 1 Makk. 3.55; 1 QS 2.21–2; 1QSa 1.14,29.

51. Vgl. auch die Schlusswendung 1 Clem. 65.2.

52. Vgl. die Aufforderung „Beugt die Knie des Herzens" in 1 Clem. 57.1 und dazu die Redeweise von der Beschneidung des Herzens Jer. 4.4; Dtn 10.16; Ez 44.7; 1QS 5.5,26; vgl. Röm. 2.28; 4.11–12.

53. Vgl. die Ideale der ταπεινοφροσύνη und des φόβος τοῦ κυρίου in 1 Clem. 21.8. – Die Wortgruppe ταπεινός ist in der paganen Gräzität m.W. nie positiv konnotiert.

richtig verstehen konnten. Auch für andere Termini wie σώφρων εὐσέβεια (1 Clem. 1.2), καθῆκον (1 Clem. 1.3; 3.4), τὸ καλῶς ἔχον (1 Clem. 14.2), ἀθανασία (1 Clem. 35.2), θνητός (1 Clem. 39.2), θρησκεία (1 Clem. 62.1)[54] ist bei heidenchristlichen Lesern natürlicherweise ein Verständnis auf hellenistischem Hintergrund eher zu erwarten. Ferner bleibt, auch forschungsgeschichtlich, die Feststellung der Herkunft der Begriffe ὁμόνοια und εἰρήνη aus paganer[55] staatspolitischer Rhetorik. Ähnliches gilt für die Terminologie der Bewertung des korinthischen Aufstandes, die für den geistes- und religionsgeschichtlichen Hintergrund des ersten Clemensbriefes ebenfalls mehr als bisher fruchtbar gemacht werden sollte. Stärker als in den Bibelzitaten ist die eigentlich politische pagane Terminologie bei den Eigenformulierungen des Vf. vertreten;[56] biblische Maßstäbe vor allem *ad vocem* ἀλλότριον,[57] spät- und nachneutestamentlicher Wortschatz[58]

54. Für das Ideal der ἀγάπη mag, zumal angesichts der Rezeption von 1 Kor. 13 in 1 Clem. 49–50, paulinischer Sprachgebrauch verantwortlich sein. Gleichwohl ist an das von O. Wischmeyer, 'Vorkommen und Bedeutung von Agape in der außerchristlichen Antike', *ZNW* 69 (1978), pp. 212–38, hier p. 224 mit Anm 57, zitierte Beispiel einer paganen Ethisierung des ἀγάπη-Begriffes (es handelt sich um ein Grabepigramm aus Tiberias aus dem 3. Jh. n. Chr.) zu erinnern.

55. Zum pagan-antiken Hintergrund der Begriffe ὁμόνοια und εἰρήνη und ihrer Verbindung vgl. W.C. van Unnik, 'Tiefer Friede (1 Clem. 2,2)', *VC* 24 (1970), 261–79; G. Brunner, *Die theologische Mitte des Ersten Klemensbriefes. Ein Beitrag zur Hermeneutik frühchristlicher Texte* (FThSt, 11; Frankfurt [Main]: Knecht 1972), pp. 134–41, mit Verweis auf die römische Münzprägung zur Zeit Trajans (p. 138 Anm. 149); Thraede, Art. 'Homonoia', pp. 244–45; Bakke, *„Concord and Peace"*, pp. 72–79; zum pagan-antiken Hintergrund des Vorwurfs der Hybris (1 Clem. 59.3) vgl. H.O. Maier, '1 Clement and the Rhetoric of ὕβρις', *StPatr* 31 (1997), pp. 136–42. Von diesen Aufstellungen her ist die Wortstatistik bei Lona, *Der erste Clemensbrief*, pp. 31–35, nicht in jeder Hinsicht überzeugend. – Eine Wiederannäherung an paganes Denken beobachtet M. Walter, *Gemeinde als Leib Christi. Untersuchungen zum Corpus Paulinum und zu den „Apostolischen Vätern"* (NTOA, 49; Freiburg [Schweiz]: Universitäts-Verlag; Göttingen: Vandenhoeck & Ruprecht, 2001), p. 256, bei dem Gebrauch der Leib-Metaphorik im Rahmen des „hierarchische(n) Duktus".

56. Bakke, *„Concord and Peace"*, 159. Dass der Vf. des ersten Clemensbriefes die Termini στάσις und ὁμόνοια verwendet, obwohl diese im ersten Korintherbrief fehlen, begründet Bakke, *„Concord and Peace"*, p. 90 Anm. 431 mit der besseren Kenntnis der rhetorischen Tradition durch den Vf. von 1 Clem.

57. Zu ἀλλότρια vgl. immerhin den Verweis auf das ungehörige Feueropfer, das Nadab und Abihu, die Söhne Aarons, darbrachten (Lev. 10.1; 16.1 LXX: Num 3.4; 26.61) sowie den Verweis auf das ungehörige Feueropfer der 250 Mann von Num 16.17,35 im Zusammenhang mit dem Aufstand der Rotte Korah. Das Handeln Jerobeams wird in 3 Reg 11.27, das Handeln des Gottlosen wird in Ps. 9.23 (10.2); SapSal 5.8; Prov 3.34 LXX mit ὑπερηφανία (vgl. noch Hi 38.15), in Ps. 37 (36).35 mit ἐπαίρομαι (vgl. die Warnungen in Prov 3.5; 19.18; Sir 6.2) belegt (vgl 1 Clem. 16.1). Die Ereignisse von Num 16 werden in *4Q423*, frgm. 4,2 offensichtlich als allgemeines Beispiel für Gottes Gerichtshandeln rezipiert, in *4Q491* frgm. 1-3.1 illustrieren sie möglicherweise Gottes Gerichtshandeln im Krieg, dienen aber m.E. nicht als Beispiele für Fehlverhalten innerhalb des Gottesvolkes.

58. Zur innerchristlichen στάσις vgl. Apg 15.2, zur ὀργή als Fehlverhalten von Christen vgl. Kol 3.8; Eph 4.31; zur ἀλαζονεία vgl. Jak 4.16; Hermas, *Mand* VI 2.5; zur Wortgruppe τυφόομαι vgl. 1 Tim. 3.16; 6.4; 2 Tim. 3.4; zur ὑπερηφανία vgl. Jak 4.6; 1 Pt 5.5; Did 5.1; Hermas, *Mand* VI 2.5. In Jak 3.16 begegnet das in LXX nur spärlich belegte φαῦλος. Der Begriff ξένος von unpassenden Lehren Heb. 13.9; Hermas, *Sim* 8.6.

sowie gelegentliche Parallelen bei Josephus[59] verändern dieses Bild nicht wesentlich.[60] Ähnlich ist die Auferstehungshoffnung nur im biblischen Zitat Hi 19.26 = 1 Clem. 26.3 als Hoffnung auf die Auferstehung des Fleisches benannt, nicht in der Eigenformulierung 1 Clem. 24.1.

Gerade in Hinsicht auf die leitende Frage, wie Christen im ersten Jahrhundert die multikulturelle Situation ihrer Umwelt bewältigt haben, bleibt die Aufgabe bestehen, das Miteinander biblischer wie paganer Termini im ersten Clemensbrief zu erklären. Unbeschadet des griechisch-philosophischen Einflusses auf antikjüdisches Denken blieb in beiden Lagern das Wissen um die je eigene kulturelle Prägung präsent,[61] und unbeschadet ihrer weitgehenden Integration in das Sozialgefüge des Imperium Romanum konnten sich Christen immer auch als Fremde verstehen.[62] Ist im ersten Clemensbrief für die Hereinnahme nichtbiblischer Traditionen eine gewisse „Weltoffenheit, ja Weltlichkeit"[63] oder wenigstens „Unbefangenheit"[64] verantwortlich? Ist der allumfassende Grundsatz der Ordnung „nach Belieben"[65] mit profanen oder mit biblischen Beispielen gestützt? Oder muss es bei allgemeinen Feststellungen des Zusammenfindens hellenistischer Bildung und christlicher Tradition[66] oder der „eigenartigen Synthese"[67] sein Bewenden haben?

Festzuhalten ist, dass dieser Text über das genannte Miteinander nicht explizit hermeneutisch reflektiert und der Rückschluss von einer expliziten Argumentation auf die genannte hermeneutische Intentionalität im Blick auf generelle Tendenzen der terminologischen Umbildung christlicher Sprachwelt weniger gesichert ist als es den Anschein hat. Die Indienstnahme hellenistisch verständlicher Abstracta wie εὐσέβεια und θρησκεία und der Bezug auf die pagane Heilshoffnung der Unsterblichkeit (1 Clem. 24.1) helfen den Christen, ihr Selbstverständnis als *religio* auch in den Kategorien pagan-antiker Religiosität zu verstehen und nach außen verständlich zu machen. In Fragen der Ethik gilt wie schon zu Phil. 4.8, der Anspruch an die Christen, dass sie bei feststehender Wahrheit der christlichen

---

59. Überprüft wurde die Wiedergabe von Num 16–7 in Josephus, *Ant.* 4.12–76. Prägend sind die Begriffe στάσις und στασιάζειν für den Aufruhr; als terminologische Parallelen zu 1 Clem. sind neben der Wendung ὁμόνοια καὶ εἰρήνη (in Moses Bitte für Israel, *Ant.* 4.50) die Motivation mit φθόνος (*Ant.* 4.14), die Bewertung ὑβρίζειν (*Ant.* 4.16) und die Bezeichnung von Datam und Abiram als ὑπερηφανήσαντες (*Ant.* 4,38) zu benennen.

60. Teilweise mögen aber auch literatursoziologische Gründe ausschlaggebend sein: Die biblische Tradition bietet erzählende Texte zum Thema (Num 16 wird denn auch in 1 Clem. 51.3, Num 16 in 1 Clem. 43.1–6 rezipiert), aber wenig abstrahierende und subsumierende Begrifflichkeit; ὁμόνοια ist an einer einzigen Stelle (4 Makk. 3.21) im vergleichbaren Sinn verwendet.

61. Vgl. *EpArist* 139–42 einerseits, Tacitus, *Hist.* 5.5 andererseits. – Dass die Christen „*die* hellenischen Götter ablehnten", dafür vgl. Lukian, *Peregrinus Proteus* 13 (Hervorhebung M. M.).

62. W. Wischmeyer, *Inschriftliche Quellen zur Sozialgeschichte der Alten Kirche* (TKTG, 14; Gütersloh: Mohn, 1984), pp. 8–9.

63. Beyschlag, *Clemens*, p. 340.

64. Lindemann, *Die Clemensbriefe*, p. 20.

65. H. v. Campenhausen, *Kirchliches Amt und geistliche Vollmacht in den ersten drei Jahrhunderten* (BHTh, 14; Tübingen: Mohr-Siebeck, 2. Auflage, 1963), p. 101.

66. J.A. Fischer, *Die apostolischen Väter, eingeleitet, herausgegeben, übertragen und erläutert*[7] (SUC, 1; München: Kösel, 1976), p. 8.

67. Knoch, 'Im Namen des Petrus und Paulus', p. 53.

Verkündigung hinter dem, was sie bei der nichtchristlichen Umwelt als höchsten, biblisch akzeptablen Wert beobachten, nicht zurückbleiben sollen – die partielle relative Nähe jüdischer und christlicher Ethik zu philosophischer Ethik in der einzelnen Forderung (weniger in deren Begründungen!) hat die Übernahme paganer Terminologie erleichtert.

Doch ist genauer nach den Bedingungen der Aufnahme paganer Vorstellungen im ersten Clemensbrief zu fragen, in dem wenigstens versuchsweise dessen „Nähe zur „Glaubens- und Vorstellungswelt Israels"[68] fruchtbar gemacht werden soll: Wenigstens unbewusst hat möglicherweise frühjüdisches Denken nachgewirkt, demgemäß die Aufnahme paganer Vorstellung bei feststehender Wahrheit der Religion Israels[69] u.a. dazu dienen kann, den Anspruch des Gottes Israels an seine Verehrer in größtmöglicher Schärfe herauszustellen.[70] So erscheinen auch im ersten Clemensbrief einige der heidnischen Beispiele als geeignet, den Anspruch des Christentums gegenüber seinen Anhängern prägnant zu formulieren. Die Beispiele aus 1 Clem. 25 und 1 Clem. 55 werden in einem Schluss *a minore ad maius* verwendet: Wenn Gott selbst durch einen Vogel die Totenauferstehung bezeugt, um wie viel mehr sollte man seinem Wort glauben (1 Clem. 26.1),[71] und wenn schon heidnische Könige zur Selbstaufopferung bereit sind, um wie viel mehr sollten es die Christen sein (1 Clem. 55.1).[72] Die Bezeichnung des Menschen als θνητός (1 Clem. 39.2)[73] führt seine Unterschiedenheit von Gott vor Augen, welchem allein es zukommt, die Art und Weise seiner Verehrung in einer für die Menschen verbindlichen Weise festzulegen (1 Clem. 40). Der Vergleich der

68. Fischer, *Die apostolischen Väter*, p. 8.

69. Der Terminus schließt nicht aus, sondern ein, dass biblische Traditionen dabei nach aktuellen Bedürfnissen rezipiert oder auch übergangen werden. So dürfte es im ersten Clemensbrief kein Zufall sein, dass auf das Beispiel Jerobeams verzichtet wird: Auf Rehabeam als den möglichen τύπος der Ältesten in Korinth fällt in der Vorgeschichte der Reichsteilung kein günstiges Licht. Ähnlich begründet Lona, *Der erste Clemensbrief*, p. 565, die vom Buch Judit abweichende Darstellung in 1 Clem. 55.4–5 mit der Intention des Verfassers, die Autorität der korinthischen Ältesten nicht implizit zu untergraben.

70. Vgl. etwa die unter dem Einfluss stoischer Affektenlehre verkürzende und zugleich verschärfende Rezeption von Ex 20,17 LXX (μὴ ἐπιθυμήσεις) in frühjüdischer Literatur. – Andere Möglichkeiten sind der Verweis auf die Überlegenheit der jüdischen über die griechische Kultur (vgl. die Vereinnahmung Abrahams und Moses im Sinne der πρῶτος-εὑρέτης-Thematik durch Ps.-Hekataios II, bei Josephus, *Ant.* 1,154–5; vgl. ferner die Gesprächssituation in der Gastmahlsszene des sog. Aristeasbriefes [*EpArist* 187–294]: Der ptolemäische König fragt, die jüdischen Weisen antworten) oder die Abgrenzung gegenüber der nichtisraelitischen Umwelt (vgl. 1 Reg 7.3; 15.23 LXX diff MT): Wenn nach *äthHen* 8.1 Azalel die Menschen die Herstellung von Kriegswaffen und Augenschminke lehrt, ist diese Zusammenordnung m.E. am ehesten als Verweis auf die äußere militärische und die innere moralische Gefährdung Israels durch die nichtjüdische Umwelt zu verstehen.

71. 1 Clem. 26 wendet sich wie 2 Pt 3.4 gegen Zweifel, die aus der Parusieverzögerung erwachsen.

72. 1 Clem. 55.1 ist mit 1 Clem. 26.1 hinsichtlich des steigernd anreihenden καί vergleichbar. Im übrigen kommen pagane Beispiele zumeist nicht allein zu stehen, sondern als Ergänzung biblischer oder christlicher Beispiele (1 Clem. 6.3; 54.2) oder als durch biblische Beispiele weitergeführt (1 Clem. 55.1).

73. Vgl. hierzu wie für ἀθανασία schon 1 Kor. 15,53.

Misshandlungen an Christinnen mit dem Schicksal von Dirken und Danaiden soll wohl die Grausamkeit der Misshandlungen dartun[74] und beleuchtet insofern einerseits die vorfindliche *Erfahrung* der Fremdheit der Christen, illustriert andererseits die Tapferkeit der Märtyrerinnen, die wiederum den Beweis für die Richtigkeit des Christentums liefert, und zwar in dem Verständnis des Verfassers. Der Auswanderungsrat 1 Clem. 54.2 aktualisiert Moses Bereitschaft zur Selbstaufopferung (1 Clem. 53.4); das Zitat aus Ps. 24.1 besagt, dass dem *bußfertigen* Sünder (nicht nur dem zu Unrecht Verfolgten und der Buße nicht bedürfenden griechischen Weisen) Gottes Fürsorge nicht entzogen bleiben wird. Auch der Einbezug der Unsterblichkeitshoffnung ist paränetisch motiviert: Die Unverbrüchlichkeit der Verheißung Gottes soll betont und damit wieder die religiöse Bindung des Christen bestärkt werden. Die Rezeption der hellenistischen, schon im Frühjudentum bekannten Terminologie der ἀθανασία ist durch 1 Kor. 15.53 gedeckt. Anders als dort bleibt im ersten Clemensbrief die Frage nach der Art und Weise des neuen Lebens offen, doch ist nicht explizit von der Unsterblichkeit der Seele die Rede;[75] zu dieser Redeweise führt auch nicht der Umstand, dass in 1 Clem. 35.2 die διάνοια als der anthropologische Ort gilt, an dem wir der uns verliehenen Heilsgüter inne werden.[76] So ist in 1 Clem. 24.1 und vergleichbaren Fällen wohl am ehesten eine unbewusst eingegrenzte Unbekümmertheit zu konstatieren.

Vergleicht man den ersten Clemensbrief mit dem ebenfalls in Rom geschriebenen, wohl um 140 n. Chr. entstandenen „Hirt des Hermas", so sind Kontinuitäten der Gemeindestruktur,[77] Ähnlichkeiten religionsgeschichtlicher Prägung und gravierende sozialgeschichtliche Unterschiede zu beobachten: Auch der „Hirt des Hermas" ist in seiner Vorstellungswelt größtenteils frühjüdisch beeinflusst,[78] wenngleich pagane Elemente nicht fehlen,[79] und im Wortschatz,[80]

---

74. Nach H.C. Brennecke, 'Danaiden und Dirken', *ZKG* 88 (1977), pp. 302–08, erfolgen die mythologischen Anspielungen nicht *ad vocem* der Strafen im Hades, sondern berühren einen Seitenzweig des Danaidenmythos. „Wie die Danaostöchter stehen die Märtyrerinnen auf der Rennbahn und kämpfen wie die Athleten bis zum Tode" (p. 307).

75. So kann selbst die Interpretation von 1 Clem. 24.1 bezeugen, dass das frühjüdische Prinzip der Freiheit der materialen, nicht auf die Ethik bezogenen Aussage weiterhin wirksam ist. Für die Abwendung von diesem Prinzip dürfte die Auseinandersetzung mit Marcion und dann mit der Gnosis verantwortlich sein, die eine radikale, aber auch teilweise großkirchlich akzeptierte Ethik mit einer aus der Sicht der Großkirche nicht mehr akzeptablen Weltdeutung verbanden, die gegen das Grundgebot des biblischen Monotheismus verstieß.

76. Diese Hochschätzung der διάνοια begegnet auch in manchen neutestamentlichen Spätschriften, vgl. Hebr 10.16; 1 Joh 5.20; Lk. 10.27.

77. Nach wie vor stehen mehrere Presbyter an der Spitze der Gemeinde (*Vis* II 4.3; auch in *Vis* III 5.1 ist im Bezug auf die ἐπίσκοποι, διδάσκαλοι und διάκονοι die pluralische Redeweise festgehalten).

78. Als ein Beispiel unter vielen vgl. die Vorstellung der Schaffung aller Dinge um der Kirche willen (*Vis* I 1.6); die Kirche ist präexistent, und um ihretwillen ist alles geschaffen (*Vis* II 4.1), wie im frühen Judentum u.a. die Thora, die Buße und der Messias.

79. Vgl. Hermas, *Vis* I 1.1–2; *Sim* IX 10.6–11.8. Das geistige Niveau der Traditionen und ihrer Verarbeitung sticht durchaus von 1 Clem. 6 und vor allem 1 Clem. 55.1 ab. Auf paganen Einfluss gehen auch die Personifikationen der Tugenden und der Laster in *Sim* IX 15,2–3 zurück.

80. Einige Beispiele mögen genügen: Sünder können bezeichnet werden als „Söhne des

aber nicht in der Grammatik[81] durch das biblische Griechisch geprägt; doch belegen die begrenzten literarischen Fähigkeiten des Verfassers[82] sowie seine soziale Selbsteinordnung, dass er und der durch ihn repräsentierte Teil der Gemeinde sozialökonomisch auf einem niedereren Niveau anzusiedeln ist.[83]

3. Wie kommen Nichtchristen in den Blick?

Für diese Frage ist an den eingangs genannten methodischen Vorbehalt zu erinnern, dass der erste Clemensbrief als situationsbezogenes Dokument keine Veranlassung hat, von sich aus diese Fragestellung zu thematisieren.

Ob die Nichtchristen die christlichen Gemeinden noch als jüdische Sondergruppe oder als eigenständige Gruppe neben dem Judentum wahrgenommen haben, wird nicht gesagt.[84]

Über das gegenwärtige nicht an Jesus glaubende Israel finden sich keine Aussagen. Die Christen sind wohl von den nicht an Jesus glaubenden Juden getrennt, wie neben der Wendung θρησκεία ἡμῶν (1 Clem. 62.1) der Umstand nahelegt, dass Existenz und Dignität zeitgleicher jüdischer Ämter nicht thematisiert werden. Fragen der rituellen Thora treten situationsbedingt nicht als Gegenstand der Kontroverse zwischen Christen und Juden in den Blick.[85]

Unrechts" (*Vis* III 6.1); παραβολή ist nicht nur „Gleichnis", sondern „Weisheitswort" (משל), deswegen kann auch sim. 7 als παραβολή bezeichnet werden, obwohl es kein Gleichnis in unserem Verständnis ist. Dass sich der Geist als Kirche zeigt, diese wiederum als Frau symbolisiert wird, verweist wohl nicht auf weibliche Stadtgottheiten, sondern auf die hebr. feminine רוח.

81. Konsens der Forschung zum „Hirt des Hermas" ist, dass der Verfasser als Muttersprache keineswegs eine semitische Sprache hatte, sondern das Griechische, wenngleich nicht auf hohem Niveau. Ein Vergleich z.B. mit der Wiedergabe der Samuelbücher in LXX zeigt die Unterschiede: In Hermas sich weitaus häufiger das Partizip auch jenseits der *conjugatio periphrastica* (z.B. *Vis* I 1.2), der *genitivus absolutus* (z.B. *Vis* II 2.1), die Partikel δέ (z.B. *Vis* I 1.2), das Paar μέν - δέ (z.B. *Vis*. III 2.6–7).

82. Zu den nur begrenzten schriftstellerischen Fähigkeiten des Hermas vgl. Lampe, *Die stadtrömischen Christen*, pp. 195–97. – Dass mit der Ausnahme von *Vis* II 3.4 keine Zitate begegnen, kann auf den Unterschied im Bildungsgrad ebenso hindeuten wie auf das Selbstverständnis einer Offenbarungsschrift (vgl. M. Leutzsch, *Die Wahrnehmung sozialer Wirklichkeit im „Hirten des Hermas"* [FRLANT, 150; Göttingen: Vandenhoeck & Ruprecht, 1989], p. 71 Anm. 49).

83. Vgl. Jeffers, 'Influence', p. 370.

84. Noch für die Interpretation von Tacitus, *Ann.* 15,44, ist umstritten, ob Tacitus die Christen als Gruppe neben dem Judentum (H. Wolff, 'Die Juden im antiken Rom', in K. Rother (ed.), *Minderheiten im Mittelmeerraum* [Passauer Mittelmeerstudien, 2; Passau: Passavia-Universitäts-Verlag, 1989], pp. 35–62, hier p. 51) oder als jüdische Sekte ansieht (H. Botermann, *Das Judenedikt des Kaisers Claudius. Römischer Staat und Christiani im 1. Jahrhundert* [Hermes Einzelschriften, 71; Stuttgart: Steiner 1996], p. 182).

85. Insofern ist von dem impliziten Autor nicht ohne weiteres auf den realen Autor zurückzuschließen (Lona, *Der erste Clemensbrief*, p. 48). So lässt der erste Clemensbrief nicht auf ungetrübte Beziehungen zwischen Juden und Christen schließen, sondern gibt für die Rekonstruktion dieser Beziehungen für die römische(n) Gemeinde(n) schlichtweg nichts her.

Die Nichtchristen[86] kommen in realen Beziehungen zu Christen vornehmlich als Feinde, im innerpaganen Verhalten auch als Vorbild in den Blick,[87] ferner – um hier schon den weiteren Ausführungen summierend vorzugreifen – in der Hoffnung des Verfassers als Bekenner des Christengottes (1 Clem. 59.4).

Dass Nichtchristen in 1 Clem. 1.1 in der Wendung „euer allen Menschen liebenswerter Name" als mögliche Bewunderer benannt werden, ist ebenso biblischer Topos[88] wie die Feststellung, dass die innergemeindlichen Vorgänge in Korinth die Nichtchristen zu einem negativen Urteil über das Christentum veranlassen.[89] Diese Topik schließt tatsächliches Erleben von Bewunderung bzw. entsprechend begründeter Kritik nicht aus, gibt aber keinen Blick frei auf die realen Beziehungen[90] zwischen Christen und Nichtchristen.[91]

Als reale Widerfahrnisse durch Nichtchristen werden ungerechtfertigter Hass (1 Clem. 60.3) und Verfolgung (1 Clem. 5.1–6.4)[92] angesprochen. Nicht spezifiziert wird, von wem die Verfolgungen im einzelnen ausgehen und wie sie begründet werden; unter den verschiedenen Formen von Pression (gesellschaftliche Diskriminierung, ökonomische Pression, Exilierung, Martyrium) wird nur das Martyrium explizit erwähnt. Aussagen über reales Verhalten von Nichtchristen sind ferner die in 1 Clem. 55.1 genannten, den korinthischen Rädelsführern zur Nachahmung anempfohlenen Beispiele.

4. Wie bewältigt die Gemeinde die Erfahrung der multikulturellen Situation?

Zur Beantwortung der Frage empfiehlt sich angesichts der Zurückhaltung der Aussagen des ersten Clemensbriefes der Schritt vom Detail zum Allgemeinen.

86. Λαός bezeichnet das Gottesvolk, ἔθνη die Heiden, analog zum Sprachgebrauch der LXX.

87. J.C. Salzmann, 'Vorbildliche Heiden: Überlegungen zum 1. Clemensbrief 55,1', in R. Feldmeier *et al.* (eds.), *Die Heiden. Christen, Juden und das Problem des Fremden. Mit einer Einleitung von M. Hengel* (WUNT, 70; Tübingen: Mohr-Siebeck, 1994), pp. 317–24, hier p. 320–21, konstatiert, die theologische Spannung zwischen beiden Momenten sei hier noch nicht verarbeitet, sondern erst mit der These der Apologeten, das, was positiv sei am Heidentum, sei eigentlich christlich.

88. Vgl. Dtn 4.6; Mt. 5.16 sowie in späterer Zeit 2 Clem. 13.1–4.

89. Vgl. Jes 52.5 LXX.

90. Wiederum ist der „Hirt des Hermas" zu vergleichen: Er konstatiert Fehlverhalten von Christen, das u.a. auch in deren Außenkontakten begründet liegt (*Sim* VIII 9,1). Der erste Clemensbrief hat aufgrund seiner Situationsbezogenheit keinen Anlass, das zu thematisieren.

91. Nach P. Mikat, 'Die Bedeutung der Begriffe Stasis und Aponoia für das Verständnis des 1. Clemensbriefes', in *idem*, *Religionsrechtliche Schriften II* (Berlin: Duncker & Humblot, 1974), pp. 719–51, will der erste Clemensbrief die στάσις in Korinth unterbinden, um ein Eingreifen der römischen Staatsmacht wegen Erregung öffentlicher Unruhe zu verhindern (skeptisch dazu Lona, *Der erste Clemensbrief*, p. 512 u. a.). Es ist nicht zwingend zu erweisen, aber auch nicht völlig ausgeschlossen, dass 47.7 tatsächlich mit einem Eingreifen römischer Staatsorgane rechnet; Topik schließt Bezug zur historischen Realität nicht aus (so auch Bakke, *„Concord and Peace"*, p. 250). – Die Verweise auf die „Gefahr" in 1 Clem. 14.2; 41.4; 59.1 sind allgemein gehalten. Ist das Vorsichtsmaßnahme oder rhetorische Strategie der Verunsicherung?

92. In 1 Clem. 45.6–7 ist jedoch nicht auf die Verfolgung von Christen durch Nichtchristen abgehoben; dort sind nur exempla für die These genannt, Verfolgungen gebe es nur durch die Ungerechten (gegen Schmitt, *Paroikie*, p. 25).

Die christenfeindlichen Verhaltensweisen der Nichtchristen führt der Verfasser im Gebet auf die anti*göttlichen* Pläne der Nichtchristen zurück (1 Clem. 59.3), während die Christen unbeschadet ihres Fehlverhaltens im einzelnen als auf der Seite Gottes stehend gelten.[93] Die ursprünglich Israel geltende Theologie der Erwählung und des Eigentums und das Selbstverständnis Israels[94] wird bruchlos auf die christliche Gemeinde übertragen, frühjüdische theologische Erkenntnis nimmt 1 Clem. 59.3 auf, wo die Existenz der Fremdvölker und zugleich ihre Unterschiedenheit von der Heilsgemeinde im Schöpfungswillen Gottes verankert werden.[95] Ebenfalls frühjüdischem Denken entspricht es, wenn nach 1 Clem. 61.1 den „Herrschenden und Regierenden auf Erden" (1 Clem. 60.4) ihre Herrschaft als durch Gott gegeben gilt. Von einem Strafgericht Gottes über die Nichtchristen ist nicht die Rede, vielmehr wird die Gotteserkenntnis aller Völker erbeten (1 Clem. 59.4).[96] Eine solche Bitte geschieht nicht ohne Aussicht auf partielle Erhörung, haben doch die Christen selbst ihre „Berufung aus der Finsternis zum Licht, von der Unkenntnis zur Kenntnis der Herrlichkeit seines Namens" (1 Clem. 59.2) erfahren.[97] Die Bewältigung der Erfahrung der multikulturellen Situation erfolgt in der christlichen Gemeinde zu Rom nicht prinzipiell anders als in anderen christlichen Gemeinden, nämlich so, dass das Christentum für seine Mitglieder eine neue Identität bereitstellt und sich für Nichtmitglieder offenhält, soweit diese dazu bereit sind, sich restlos auf diese neue Identität einzulassen.[98] Diese neue Identität verspricht ihnen die transformierende Erfüllung von Heilshoffnungen[99] ebenso, wie sie einen Lebenswandel fordert, der für die bisherige Bandbreite ethischer Positionen im pagan-antiken Kontext keinen Raum mehr bietet, sondern auf Ideale verpflichtet, die den Idealen etwa eines Musonius Rufus nahestehen.

93. Vgl. die schon angesprochenen Selbstprädikationen „Schafe seiner Weide" (1 Clem. 59.3) und „wir, dein Volk" (1 Clem. 59.4).

94. Vgl. die nunmehr christliche Selbstprädikation „Schafe seiner Weide" (1 Clem. 59.3) und die Wendungen ἡμεῖς λαός σου in 1 Clem. 59.4 bzw. λαὸς περιούσιος in 1 Clem. 64.1. Zur zeitnahen christlichen Rezeption alttestamentlicher Erwählungstheologie vgl. auch Tit. 2.11–4.

95. Vgl. das Zitat von Dtn 32.8–9 in 1 Clem. 29.2. Die paränetische Rezeption der alttestamentlichen Erwählungstheologie ist nur eine der im ersten Clemensbrief wahrgenommenen Möglichkeiten.

96. Der Topos ist biblisch; zu 1 Clem. 59.4 vgl. 2 Reg 19.19b; Sir 36.17; 2 Makk. 1.27. – Das wird im ersten Clemensbrief aber nicht explizit mit einem missionarischen Handeln der Gemeinde in Verbindung gebracht, wenngleich in der Wendung „euer…allen Menschen liebenswerter Name" in 1 Clem. 1.1 wenigstens topisch die faktische Außenwirkung christlichen Normalverhaltens mitbedacht ist.

97. Das altkirchliche *sola gratia*, das Bekenntnis, nicht aus eigener Kraft den rettenden Weg gefunden zu haben (vgl. Eph 2.8; EpPolyk 2.3; 2 Clem. 1.4–8), hat ebenfalls Parallelen in Mysterienreligionen (Apuleius, *Metamorphosen* 11.22.5). Zum Wechsel von der Finsternis zum Licht vgl. Apg 26.18; 1 Pt 2.9; 2 Clem. 1.6; als indirekte Traditionsgrundlage vgl. die Wendung „Licht der Heiden" in Jes 49.6, die in frühjüdischer Literatur als Selbstaussage Israels stehen kann.

98. Hierin zeigt der erste Clemensbrief eine gewisse Nähe zur kontaktorientierten frühjüdischen Literatur (vgl. aber auch Apuleius, *Metamorphosen* 11.6.4), ebenso darin, dass dieser positive Kontakt zu den Heiden keine Assimilation an heidnische Kultur bedeutet. Für die frühjüdische Literatur vgl. *JosAs* 21.1: „nicht ziemt es einem israelitischen Manne …".

99. Im Falle der Hoffnung auf Unsterblichkeit liegt die Transformation in dem Einbezug des Gerichtshorizontes 1 Clem. 28.1.

Warum sieht sich die christliche Gemeinde zu Rom trotz aller Nähe zu konservativen Idealen, wie sie auch von Teilen der Gesellschaft vertreten werden, als Fremde? Einerseits ist diese Fremdheit in der Heterokulturalität der Umwelt begründet, die von ihrem Standpunkt aus die Christen als Fremde empfindet und sie ihre Fremdheit öfters auch leidvoll spüren lässt. Diese äußere Fremdheit wird hinsichtlich ihrer leidvollen Dimensionen im ersten Clemensbrief vornehmlich im Gebet bewältigt.[100] Andererseits wird das Bewusstsein der Fremde greifbar in dem Motiv des παροικεῖν, aber auch in den Motiven der Erwählung, Berufung und Heiligung (1 Clem. 1.1; 29.1–3; 64.1); diese Fremdheit wird in Aufnahme alttestamentlicher Theologie der Erwählung Israels als Erfahrung der gottgewollten Fremdheit verstanden.[101] Zusätzlich wird dieses Selbstverständnis des Christentums als einer Existenz in der Fremde durch konversionale Sprache gefördert, näherhin durch das Bewusstsein, den rettenden Weg nicht durch einen weltimmanenten Rückschluss der reflexiven Vernunft, sondern kraft göttlicher Offenbarung erkannt zu haben. So gibt der erste Clemensbrief trotz der in der Einleitung benannten methodischen Vorbehalte durchaus „von dem, was central und peripherisch im Christentum des Vf. war, uns einen sehr guten Begriff".[102]

5. Zusammenfassung

Zwar zielt die Fragestellung dieses Beitrages nicht unmittelbar auf den Abfassungszweck des ersten Clemensbriefes, der dessen Gestaltung bis ins einzelne hinein bestimmt, und doch lassen sich mit der gebotenen Vorsicht folgende Aussagen treffen: Werte der paganen politischen Oberschicht werden in der Betonung der ὁμόνοια und der εἰρήνη reflektiert, Werte der pagane geistigen Elite in einzelnen Zügen des Gottesbildes. Vielzahl und Qualität biblischer Beispiele lassen auf ein beachtliches Maß an Kenntnis der Heiligen Schrift (= des Alten Testamentes in Gestalt der Septuaginta) schließen. Religionsgeschichtlich ist mit der neueren Forschung die Verwurzelung in der Geistigkeit des hellenistischen Judentums zu betonen, gleichzeitig die Offenheit für die Hereinnahme paganer Werte und Motive und ihre Gewichtung gegenüber biblischen Vorgaben zu beschreiben und mit dem Prinzip der relativen Freiheit der nichtethischen materialen Aussage zu begründen: Leitend für das christliche Lebensideal sind Werte wie Nächstenliebe, Demut und Gottesfurcht; die herangezogenen paganen Beispiele erscheinen als geeignet, der Intention des ersten Clemensbriefes besonderen Nachdruck zu verleihen; pagane Heilshoffnungen können unter Adaption an biblische Normalvorstellungen integriert werden.

Nichtchristen kommen vorwiegend als Subjekte antichristlicher Aktionen in den Blick (von den möglichen Formen ist nur die zum Martyrium führende Pression

---

100. Dieser Bewältigung dienen der Verweis auf den geschichtsmächtigen Gott in 1 Clem. 59.3; 60.3 und die Bitte um die Gotteserkenntnis seitens aller Völker in 1 Clem. 59.4.

101. Dass eine neugewonnene *religio* auch Trost in der Fremde bedeuten kann, dafür vgl. Apuleius, Metamorphosen, 11.28.6: „... *quae res* (scil. die Bindung an Isis und Osiris) *summum peregrinationi meae tribuebat solacium*".

102. Wrede, *Untersuchungen*, p. 87 (bei W. gesperrt gedruckt).

erwähnt, ohne dass andere Verhaltensweisen außer Acht bleiben dürften), dazu als vorbildlich im Handeln. Die Schilderung ihrer Bewunderung wie ihres Lästerns aufgrund christlichen Wohlverhaltens bzw. Fehlverhaltens entspringt biblischer Topik und lässt daher im einzelnen keine Rückschlüsse auf konkretes Erleben zu, wenngleich generell gesehen beides im Erfahrungshorizont der Christinnen und Christen gelegen haben dürfte. Die multikulturelle Situation wird auf der Grundlage des bereits charakterisierten christlichen Lebensideals in überbietender Adaption auch paganer ethischer Höchstwerte in ganzheitlicher Prägung der Existenz bewältigt.

ABSTRACT

This study deals with the social-historical situation of the Roman Christians represented by 1 Clem. Comparing 1 Clem. with the 'Shepherd of Hermas' we can see that Clement's group is to be located at a higher social and economical level: behaviour within the Christian community is judged according to values of the socio-political elites, and – in view of the numerous Biblical quotations and allusions – there is good reason to assume that these Christians had their own Bible texts. Yet, we do not know whether the author participated in higher pagan education. Christian morale is expressed and acted out in terms of Biblical values like charity, humility, fear of God, and is primarily illustrated by Biblical models; only few pagan examples, integrated only additively, underline the high level of Christian ethical expectations over against the own group. How should the Christians respond to the challenge of the multicultural situation at Rome? According to 1 Clem. Christians are called to surpass non-Christians in fulfilling the highly esteemed ancient virtues in their whole life. Non-Christians are described without differentiation of their political or religious identities. They are perceived as adversaries in daily life, function as models of conduct in the author's literary world, and will become Christians in the author's hope. 1 Clem. lacks any information about the relationship between Jews and Christians in Rome.

VALENTINIAN TEACHERS IN ROME

Ismo Dunderberg

Valentinian Christianity was one of the most significant early Christian groups that emerged in the second century CE. One sign of its importance is a massive attack leveled against it c. 180 CE by Irenaeus, Bishop of Lyons. From his five-volume *Against Heresies*, it can be inferred that it was very difficult to tell a Valentinian from an ordinary member of early Christian congregations. The difference *should* have been clear enough, Irenaeus believes, for the Valentinians even walked differently, 'with strutting gait and a supercilious countenance, possessing all the pompous air of a cock.'[1] Irenaeus' description reflects his insistent claim that Valentinians were an elitistic group thinking highly of themselves. They regarded themselves as 'spiritual' ones who were saved simply because of their nature, while other Christians were 'psychic' ones, who had to believe and do good works to in order to acquire salvation. Since Valentinians believed that their spiritual essence will be saved no matter what, they were, according to Irenaeus, prone to everything that was forbidden: they seduced and defiled women, ate meat offered to idols, participated pagan festivals, and attended gladiator fights.[2] There were also some better ones among them, Irenaeus admits, but they were irritatingly supercilious.[3]

Yet even Irenaeus' polemical account shows that Valentinians considered themselves Christians. 'They say the same things and hold the same doctrine', and disliked being called heretics.[4] They confess 'with the tongue one God the Father, and that all things derive their existence from him', and they also confess 'our Lord Jesus Christ.'[5] Valentinians were, apparently, not so deviant from Irenaeus' orthodox standards as he would have hoped. What made the difference, according to him, was that Valentinians *thought* differently. They were also reluctant to disclose to outsiders their real ideas, teaching divine mysteries only to the chosen few in secrecy.[6] Curiously enough, though, Irenaeus also maintains that his account of the Valentinians is based upon his conversations with them and reading their books.[7] Valentinians appear, thus, a less exclusive group and more open to discussing their views also with outsiders than Irenaeus is willing to admit.

1. Irenaeus, *Adv. Haer.* 3.15.2 (*ANF*).
2. Irenaeus, *Adv. Haer.* 1.6.2–3; cf. also ibid. 1.13.6.
3. Irenaeus, *Adv. Haer.* 3.15.2.
4. Irenaeus, *Adv. Haer.* 3.15.2.
5. Irenaeus. *Adv. Haer.* 4.33.3.
6. Irenaeus, *Adv. Haer.* 1.15.2.
7. Irenaeus, *Adv. Haer.* 1, preface.

Valentinian teachers were dispersed in different areas of the Roman empire. They were no doubt active and found supporters in Rome as well. In this article, I will focus on those Valentinian teachers who have been located in Rome more or less securely. I concur in this article with the scholars who have suggested that Valentinianism is best understood in the setting of a school.[8] Based on this view, I will try to sketch a picture of the general outlook of the Valentinian *paideia*. Finally, I will point out that there is one Valentinian group to which the school setting does not apply. This group is the followers of Marcus who seem to have formed a church organization of their own in Rome.

1. *Problems with Evidence*

Irenaeus' account has usually served as a point of departure for general descriptions of Valentinians. Yet when it comes to the question of what we know about Valentinians in Rome, his account proves difficult to use. Since Irenaeus was a man of great mobility, it is impossible to tell where his personal contacts with Valentinians took place. Did he meet Valentinians in Rome during his temporary stays there? Did he already argue with them in Asia Minor, where he came from? Or does he have in mind Valentinian groups in, or close to, remote Lyons, where he wrote his anti-Valentinian treatise? Hints at each of these possibilities have been preserved. Irenaeus occasionally refers to his personal knowledge of Valentinian groups in Asia Minor.[9] He also mentions those 'in our own regions around the Rhone.'[10] Remnants of his correspondence related to Florinus, the Valentinian presbyter of Victor, Bishop of Rome (189–199 CE), shows that Irenaeus also knew some Valentinians in Rome.[11] It is possible, therefore, that Irenaeus' account is

---

8.   G. Lüdemann, 'The History of Earliest Christianity in Rome', *The Journal of Higher Criticism* 2 (1995), pp. 112–41 (129) (German original: 'Zur Geschichte des ältesten Christentums in Rom', *ZNW* 70 (1979), pp. 86–114); B. Layton, *The Gnostic Scriptures: A New Translation with Annotations and Introductions* (New York: Doubleday, 1987), p. 267; C. Markschies, 'Valentinian Gnosticism: Towards the Anatomy of a School', in A. McGuire, J.D. Turner (eds.), *The Nag Hammadi Library after Fifty Years: Proceedings of the Society of Biblical Literature Commemoration* (NHMS, 44; Leiden: E.J. Brill, 1997), pp. 401–38 (436–38). Notably, in the latter study, Markschies revises his earlier opinion that there was no διαδοχή that the followers of Valentinus could have used to trace their teaching back to him; cf. C. Markschies, *Valentinus Gnosticus? Untersuchungen zur valentinianischen Gnosis mit einem Kommentar zu den Fragmenten Valentin* (WUNT, 65; Tübingen: Mohr-Siebeck, 1992), p. 394. Now he affirms that 'the "school of Valentinus" is constituted by a teacher-student relation; it knows a διαδοχή or *successio* of teachers' ('Valentinian Gnosticism', p. 437). For the view that Valentinin in general should be understood as an independent church, see E. Thomassen, 'Ortodoksi og heterodoksi i det andre århundrets Roma', in S. Rubenson (ed.), *Patristica Nordica 4* (Religio, 44; Lund: Teologiska institutionen, 1995), pp. 39–55 (54–55).

9.   Irenaeus calls upon personal knowledge in relating that Marcus the Magician seduced Christian women in Asia Minor (*Adv. Haer.* 1.13.5).

10.   Irenaeus, *Adv. Haer.* 1.13.7 (trans. Unger-Dillon).

11.   Irenaeus affirms that, as a child, he already saw Florinus in Asia Minor (Irenaeus to Florinus: Eusebius, *Hist. Eccl.* 5.20.4). Irenaeus also urged Victor to acquaint himself with Florinus' books and get rid of them (Irenaeus, frg. syr. 28 [Harvey II, p. 457; nr. 51 in the translation of

partly based upon his knowledge about the situation in Rome, but there is no way of telling which parts of his presentation exactly refer to this specific situation.

Similar problems pertain to Justin, from whom stems the earliest condemnation of Valentinians.[12] Justin is often closely associated with Rome, but 'it remains unclear how long Justin stayed in Rome altogether, how long the contact with the Roman community was.'[13] Hippolytus of Rome is more relevant at certain points, for he reports protests of some Valentinian groups against Irenaeus' account,[14] and it can be assumed that these protests were most likely raised in Rome.

It does not make our inquiry any easier that Valentinian teachers were as mobile as Irenaeus and Justin. Evidence for the views of those teachers who can be located in Rome more or less securely stems largely from the patristic authors of Alexandria. This raises the question of whether we can be sure that the views attributed to Valentinian teachers in these sources were really taught by them in *Rome*. It is, of course, possible that their teachings recorded in Alexandrian sources were developed only after they had left Rome. It is also possible that they held these views earlier but no longer in Rome, or that they did not find the specific illustrations of their views attested to by Alexandrian fathers suitable in Rome. Any portrayal of Valentinian teachers in Rome is therefore based upon mixing two separate kinds of data, one locating them in Rome and another bearing witness to their views. This approach cannot be abandonded completely, but in what follows I have tried to be as careful as possible in distinguishing clearly between the two different sets of data.

2. *Valentinus: Cosmic Sympathy and Dualism*

Valentinus came to Rome most probably from Egypt in the late 130s and stayed there at least for 15–20 years.[15] Tertullian and Epiphanius agree with each other in claiming that Valentinus left Rome at some point, but provide us with completely different stories as to why this happened. Tertullian tells us that Valentinus left Rome and became a heretic, since he had been embittered by not being

---

Irenaeus' fragments in *ANF* I, pp. 568–78]). Cf. P. Lampe, *Die stadtrömischen Christen in den ersten beiden Jahrhunderten: Untersuchungen zur Sozialgeschichte* (WUNT, 2/18; Tübingen: Mohr-Siebeck, 2nd edn, 1989), pp. 327–28.

12. Justin, *Dial.* 35.

13. G. Schöllgen, 'Probleme der frühchristlichen Sozialgeschichte: Einwände gegen Peter Lampe's Buch über "Die stadtrömischen Christen in den ersten beiden Jahrhunderten"', *JAC* 32 (1989), pp. 23–40 (29–30).

14. See below p. 170.

15. Irenaeus, *Adv. Haer.* 3.4.5, dates Valentinus' stay in Rome by mentioning three bishops, Hyginus (136–140), Pius (140–155), and Anicetus (155–166). Tertullian, *Praes. Her.* 30.1–2, says that Valentinus (and Marcion) lived during the time of the emperor Antoninus Pius (138–161). This fits well with Irenaeus, but confusion arises from Tertullian's mentioning of Bishop Eleutherus (174–189) in this connection. For a critical review of the data related to Valentinus' life, see C. Markschies, *Valentinus Gnosticus? Untersuchungen zur valentinianischen Gnosis mit einem Kommentar zu den Fragmenten Valentin* (WUNT, 65; Tübingen: Mohr-Siebeck, 1992), pp. 294–336.

elected the bishop of Rome, though he had considerable support for this office.[16] Epiphanius, on the other hand, claims that Valentinus traveled to Cyprus and went mad there; hence the beginning of his heresy.[17] Since the historical value of both stories remains questionable,[18] we cannot be sure whether Valentinus ever left Rome. The strongly Alexandrian provenance of the fragments of his lost writings may suggest, however, that he returned to Egypt at some point.[19]

Already in patristic sources, Valentinus is considered the founder of a school (διδασκαλεῖον).[20] In recent years, however, there has been a considerable debate as to Valentinus' relationship to 'the school of Valentinus'. This debate was launched by Christopher Markschies who argued that Valentinus was neither a gnostic nor really a Valentinian.[21] Markschies must be given credit for pointing out that features which could be considered gnostic or distinctly Valentinian are strikingly absent in the fragments of Valentinus. Sophia's fall and restitution, the ignorant creator-God, three classes of humankind, the bridal chamber are not mentioned in them. Markschies's study, however, has not found full acceptance by other scholars, and they have carried on the discussion about Valentinus' affinity with gnostic ideas.[22]

It is not my primary concern here to assess Valentinus' relationship to gnosticism.[23] I find more intriguing a tension between his emphasis on cosmic sympathy and his dualistic view about Adam's creation. The former idea comes to expression in Valentinus' poem entitled *Harvest*, which runs as follows:[24]

16. Tertullian, *Val.* 4.1–2.

17. Epiphanius, *Panarion* 31.7.2.

18. Cf. Lüdemann, 'The History of Earliest Christianity in Rome', p. 119; Lampe, *Die stadtrömischen Christen*, p. 329 n. 87; Markschies, *Valentinus Gnosticus?*, p. 308.

19. Out of ten or eleven fragments of Valentinus, six stem from Clement's *Stromateis* (2.36.2–4; 2.114.3–6; 3.59.3; 4.89.1–3; 4.89.6–90.1; 6.52.3–53.1). The ratio becomes even more significant, if fragments 9 and 10 in Pseudo-Anthimus and Photius are not genuine, as has been argued convincingly by Markschies (*Valentinus Gnosticus?*, pp. 260–75). In that case, in addition to the six fragments of Valentinus in Clement, we are left with only two or three genuine ones in Hippolytus' *Refutatio* (6.42.2; 6.37.7; possibly 10.13.4).

20. Irenaeus, *Adv. Haer.* 1.11.1; cf. also *Adv. Haer.* 1.30.15 (*Valentini schola*). διδασκαλεῖον denotes often a philosophical school; cf. A.M. McGuire, *Valentinus and the Gnostike Hairesis: An Investigation of Valentinus' Position in the History of Gnosticism* (PhD dissertation, Yale University, 1983), pp. 20–21. For other examples of school terminology attached to Valentinians' in patristic sources and the *Testimony of Truth* (56.1–5), see Markschies, 'Valentinian Gnosticism', pp. 411–19.

21. Markschies, *Valentinus Gnosticus?*, pp. 392–407.

22. Cf., e.g., J. Holzhausen, 'Gnosis und Martyrium: Zu Valentins viertem Fragment', *ZNW* 85 (1994), pp. 116–31; G. Quispel, 'Valentinus and the Gnostikoi', *VC* 50 (1996), pp. 1–4; *idem*, 'The Original Doctrine of Valentinus the Gnostic', *VC* 50 (1996), pp. 327–52; P. Schüngel, 'Gnostische kontra neutestamentliche Soteriologie: Zu Valentins viertem Fragment', *VC* 50 (1996), pp. 257–65.

23. This would require a closer discussion as to how 'gnosticism' itself should be defined, for it has been a very elusive category even in scholarly usage, as has been effectively demonstrated by M.A. Williams, *Rethinking 'Gnosticism': An Argument for Dismantling a Dubious Category* (Princeton, NJ: Princeton University Press, 1996), *passim*.

24. Hippolytus, *Refutation* 6.37.7.

> I see that all is hung up by the spirit,
> I understand that all is carried by the spirit,
> Flesh, hanging from soul,
> Soul, depending on air,
> Air, hanging from aether,
> Fruits that are borne from the depth,
> A babe that is brought forth from the womb.

Valentinus' poem lends expression to a basically Stoic world view in which 'the permeation of πνεῦμα held all cosmic parts in tension...and created as it were a cosmic "bond"...'.[25] Nonetheless, it does not have to be assumed that Valentinus was taught by Stoic teachers of philosophy. The idea of cosmic sympathy was common coin in antiquity, and also other Stoic cosmological views were embraced by many non-Stoic authors in the Roman era.[26] I find it significant that Stoic ideas were adapted in Hermetic traditions in a manner that brings these ideas closer to Valentinus' poem. For example, no close Stoic parallel can be found to Valentinus' contention that 'all is carried by the spirit', but a similar statement occurs in a Hermetic description of the primeval distinction between heavy and light cosmic elements.[27] The parallel suggests that Valentinus and Hermetic authors drew upon similar (Egyptian?) traditions based upon Stoic cosmology. In addition, it may be inferred from this parallel that Valentinus' poem was not only a praise of cosmic sympathy in the spirit of Stoicism, but could be part of, or presuppose, a speculation on the origins of the universe.

A strikingly different edge to Valentinus' teaching is lent by his interpretation of Adam's creation.[28] Valentinus provides us with a description of antagonism between Adam and the creator angels. Adam is here characterized by 'a seed of the essence from above' deposited in him without the angels' knowledge. The superior seed becomes visible, as Adam speaks words which surpass what the angels had created. This shows that in him exists 'the pre-existent human being.' The creator angels are afraid of this essence and attempt to destroy Adam (or conceal him).[29] Valentinus' description of the malevolent creator angels not only presupposes a dualistic understanding of creation but also resembles closely an account of Adam's creation found in the *Apocryphon of John*. This may suggest that Valentinus was familiar with distinctly Sethian gnostic traditions attested in the latter text.[30]

The obvious question is, how Valentinus' dualistic view fits together with his more positive view about cosmic sympathy. It seems that his teaching is one of

---

25. M. Lapidge, 'Stoic Cosmology and Roman Literature, First to Third Centuries AD', *ANRW* 2.36.3, pp. 1379–429 (1384).

26. Lapidge, 'Stoic Cosmology', pp. 1411–12, 1418–21.

27. *CH* 3.2: 'While all was unlimited and unformed, light elements were set apart to the heights and the heavy were grounded in the moist sand, the whole of them delimited by fire and raised aloft, to be carried by the spirit' (trans. Copenhaver).

28. Clement, *Strom.* 4.89.6–4.90.1.

29. The Greek verb ἀποφανίζειν Valentinus uses here can have both meanings.

30. Cf. I. Dunderberg, 'Valentinian Views about Adam's Creation: Valentinus and the *Gospel of Philip*' (forthcoming).

those cases where negative views related to cosmogony do *not* lead to a strictly dualistic view of the present world.[31] The radical dualism inherent in gnostic cosmogonies can be toned down in several ways. Some Valentinians contended that, as spiritual beings, they 'were loved more than the others by the demiurge.'[32] It does not seem very likely that these Valentinians considered the world an utterly hostile place to live. In a similar manner, although it is affirmed in the Valentinian *Gospel of Truth* that the material world emerged from error and confusion,[33] it has been correctly pointed out that the world view of this text is 'Stoic and pantheistic: that is, a universe in which all is enclosed by god, and ultimately all *is* god.'[34]

Valentinus' joining together of dualistic cosmogony with a positive world view was, thus, not exceptional in Valentinianism. There is no way of telling whether he saw any dichotomy between the two views, and if he did, how he coped with this difficulty. It may have been that, in his teaching, both ideas simply went hand in hand, as they do in the *Gospel of Truth*. Another possibility is that the two fragments presuppose different levels of instruction. I find it noteworthy that a similar tension between cosmic sympathy and more dualistic views about the world occurs in Hermetic writings. Garth Fowden has argued, convincingly in my opinion, that cosmic sympathy is affirmed in the Hermetic tractates meant for initial instruction, while clearly dualistic views appear in those addressed to the more advanced.[35] Based upon this analogy, it may be that the implied recipients of Valentinus' poem *Harvest* and those of his teaching about Adam were at different levels of development and, thus, in need of different instruction.

3. *Ptolemy and Heracleon vs. Marcion*

While we have strong evidence for locating Valentinus in Rome, evidence related to Ptolemy and Heracleon remains more dubious. Hippolytus mentions them in connection with what he designates the 'Italian' version of Valentinian Christology.[36] This provides us with some justification for locating Ptolemy and Heracleon in Rome, for it seems natural to assume that the version Hippolytus calls 'Italian' was the prevalent one among the Valentinians in Rome which he knew best.[37] Caution is warranted in this case, however, for Hippolytus does not claim that the 'Italian' Christology was restricted to Rome, nor that the alternative, 'eastern' Valentinian Christology had no supporters there.[38]

---

31. Cf. Williams, *Rethinking 'Gnosticism'*, pp. 98–108.

32. Irenaeus, *Adv. Haer.* 1.7.3.

33. *Gos. Truth* 17.

34. Layton, *The Gnostic Scriptures*, p. 222.

35. Cf. G. Fowden, *The Egyptian Hermes: A Historical Approach to the Late Pagan Mind* (Princeton, NJ: Princeton University Press, 1986), pp. 103–04.

36. Representatives of this Christology thought that Jesus had a psychic body to begin with and received the spirit only with baptism (Hippolytus, *Ref.* 6.35.5–6).

37. Cf. Lampe, *Die stadtrömischen Christen*, p. 255.

38. Representatives of eastern Valentinian Christology claimed that the Savior had a spiritual body to begin with (Hippolytus, *Ref.* 6.35.7). The designation 'eastern teaching' appears also in the

Additional evidence for Ptolemy could perhaps be obtained from Justin. In his *2 Apology*, Justin mentions a Christian teacher called Ptolemy who suffered martyrdom in Rome under the prefect Urbicus (144–160 CE). This must also have taken place before the completion of Justin's *2 Apology* (ca. 152). The teacher mentioned by Justin may be identical with the Valentinian Ptolemy,[39] though this is not entirely certain.[40] It has also been suggested that Ptolemy's *Letter to Flora* could have been originally an 'appeal to the Christian church of Rome',[41] but this is a less likely option.[42] As for Heracleon, a recent study by Ansgar Wucherpfennig suggests that he stayed in Rome only temporarily and then returned to Egypt where he had come from originally.[43] This accounts for the Alexandrian provenance of the data related to Heracleon's literary production, above all his commentary on John known to us from Origen.

The fact that both Ptolemy and Heracleon reacted to Marcion's teachings in their writings points to Rome as well. Wucherpfennig traces several reactions to Marcionite opinions in the surviving fragments of Heracleon.[44] Discussion with Marcion's programme is even more clearly indicated in Ptolemy's *Letter to Flora*.[45] This text also provides us with clear evidence for the idea of progressive instruction, which was suggested above as a possibility in the case of Valentinus. The *Letter to Flora* presents itself as initial instruction, for it ends up with a promise of further teaching, if the addressee proves 'worthy of the apostolic tradition.'[46] In addition, Ptolemy's writing bears witness to the literary skill of Valentinian teachers. Since the letter is clearly written following the rules of an ideal public speech taught in rhetorical schools,[47] Ptolemy must have had education in rhetoric. It can be assumed, moreover, that it was especially the educated who could appreciate his skillful composition in accordance with rhetorical conventions. We cannot be sure whether Flora was only a fictional addressee or a real historical figure. In the latter case, she could have been Ptolemy's benefactor.[48] Since patronage was often a prerequisite for the

---

title of Excerpts of Theodotus, but it remains unclear, from whom this title stems; cf. Markschies, 'Valentinian Gnosticism', pp. 433–35.

39. In recent studies, the identification is supported in, e.g., Lüdemann, 'The History of Earliest Christianity in Rome', pp. 127–29; Lampe, *Die stadtrömischen Christen*, pp. 202–03; M. Müller, *Gnostikerne og Bibelen: Ptolemaeus og hans brev till Flora* (Text & Tolkning, 9; s. l. [Danmark]: Akademisk Forlag, 1991), p. 11.

40. One of the problems with the identification is that Justin condemns Valentinians in his Dialogue with Trypho (see above p. 159 n. 12). The latter work was, however, written after *2 Apology*, so it is possible that Justin changed his opinion about Valentinians between the two writings.

41. R. M. Grant, 'Notes on Gnosis', *VC* 2 (1957), pp. 145–51 (147).

42. Cf. Lüdemann, 'The History of Earliest Christianity in Rome', p. 133 n. 63.

43. A. Wucherpfennig, *Heracleon Philologus. Gnostische Johannesexegese im zweiten Jahrhundert* (WUNT, 142; Tübingen: Mohr-Siebeck, 2001), pp. 360–71.

44. Cf. Wucherpfennig, *Heracleon Philologus*, pp. 156–58, 178, 231, 367.

45. Epiphanius, *Panarion*, 33.3.1–33.7.10.

46. Epiphanius, *Panarion*, 33.7.9.

47. For the composition of public speech, see C. Walde, 'Rhetorik (I–V)', *Der Neue Pauly* 10.958–78 (971).

48. It has been suggested that Flora could be the anonymous noble woman Justin mentioned in

production of texts in antiquity,[49] it is even possible that she had ordered this treatise from Ptolemy.[50]

Ptolemy's *Letter to Flora* is a concise but skillfully organized treatise about the law in the Hebrew Bible. Ptolemy's purpose is to convince his addressee that the God of the Hebrew Bible who gave the law is neither the supreme God nor the devil, but a figure midway between them. This god is the creator-God, the demiurge, who is neither good nor bad but only righteous. To prove his point, Ptolemy first distinguishes in this law between divine legislation and two types of human additions, those of Moses and those stemming from the elders of the people. Then he argues that even the divine law can be divided into three groups which are the perfect law, laws interwoven with injustice, and ritual laws. The perfect law is the decalogue which is valid also for Christians. As to ritual laws, Ptolemy recommends that they should be interpreted not literally but allegorically.

It is in the second group consisting of the laws interwoven with injustice that Ptolemy finds evidence for his point that the Old Testament God is righteous but not good. These laws are based upon retaliation ('an eye for an eye, a tooth for a tooth'). Though their good intention is to prevent greater evil, they fail to do so. If murder is punished with death, as the law orders, this not only contradicts the commandment in the perfect law 'You shall not kill', but also duplicates the evil, for two murders are commited instead of one. The God who gave this law was 'fooled by necessity'. He had the best intentions, but his legislation remains inconsequent and increases evil. Thus, this God cannot be the perfect God, Ptolemy argues.

The scholarly consensus is that Ptolemy wrote his treatise *against* Marcion,[51] but I believe that this assessment must be reconsidered. It has been suggested that Ptolemy had the Marcionites in mind, as he mentions at the outset of his study those who think that the biblical law stems from the devil.[52] Identification of the

his account of Ptolemy's martyrdom. This identification cannot be affirmed with certainty, but it cannot be ruled out either. It is an interesting coincidence that Ptolemy deals with divorce in his *Letter to Flora* (arguing that it is against the divine law of the Savior but can be beneficial in certain cases, 33.4.6–33.4.10), while the Christian noble woman in Justin's account who reluctantly decides to divorce her adulterous husband (*2 Apology* 2.2–10). For recent discussions about the identification of Flora with the anonymous noble woman in Justin, see Lüdemann, 'The History of Earliest Christianity in Rome', p. 133 n. 62; Lampe, *Die stadtrömischen Christen*, pp. 202–03; Müller, *Gnostikerne og Bibelen*, pp. 11–12.

49. Cf. Wucherpfennig, *Heracleon Philologus*, p. 33.

50. The best evidence for early Christian writings made to order is Origen's commentary on the Gospel of John which was ordered and generously funded by his wealthy patron Ambrose (Eusebius, *Hist. Eccl.* 6.23.1). For Ambrose's role as the patron of Origen, see Wucherpfennig, *Heracleon Philologus*, pp. 15–21.

51. E.g., R. M. Grant, *Heresy and Criticism: In Search for Authenticity in Early Christian Literature* (Louisville, KY: Westminster/John Knox Press, 1993), p. 51; Lüdemann, 'The History of Earliest Christianity in Rome', pp. 133–34; Markschies, 'Valentinian Gnosticism', p. 429; Müller, *Gnostikerne og Bibelen*, 13; G. Quispel, 'Introduction', in *idem, Ptolémée: Lettre a Flora: Texte, Traduction et Introduction* (SC 23a; Paris: Cerf, 1949), pp. 12–13.

52. Quispel, 'Introduction', pp. 9–11. Yet Quispel also points out that this was not Marcion's own view.

God in the Hebrew Bible with the devil was, however, an extremist position even among Marcionites, and it was certainly not Marcion's own view.[53] Marcion himself considered, like Ptolemy, the Jewish God to be neither good nor evil but righteous in the weaker sense of the term. In fact, the distinction between 'good' and 'righteous' itself seems characteristic of Marcion; it was not widely accepted among other early Christian authors.[54] This suggests, in my view, that Ptolemy adopts a distinctly Marcionite teaching about the demiurge in his *Letter to Flora*. Ptolemy appears, thus, a moderate Marcionite rather than an anti-Marcionite polemicist; moderate in the sense that he did not accept the radical consequences of Marcion's program. Ptolemy clearly did not abandon the Old Testament entirely as Marcion did, but emphasized the continuing value of certain parts of it for Christians. In addition, Ptolemy's quotations from Matthew and John, as well as the fact that he does not use the Gospel of Luke at all, show that he did not follow the Marcionite canon.

It is often thought that, with his *Letter to Flora*, Ptolemy attempted to entangle orthodox Christians in his toils and planned to reveal to them his distinctly gnostic teachings only later.[55] Yet it is not so much the catholic position with which Ptolemy flirts in this writing but the Marcionite one. This suggests that the implied audience of the *Letter to Flora* was already engaged in discussions about Marcion's views.[56] It seems unlikely that this audience consisted of those already converted to these views, for Ptolemy is still able to use the gospels of Matthew and John as his proof texts. Accordingly, the implied audience of his treatise must have accepted their authoritative status as well. Ptolemy shows agreement with Marcion's demiurgical view, but otherwise his letter seems like an attempt to swing the pendulum back from Marcion's radical suggestions to a more catholic direction.[57]

4. *Valentinian Paideia and School Setting*

We cannot tell with certainty what Ptolemy planned to teach to Flora at the more advanced level – if she proved worthy of it, as he wished. Attempts to disclose

---

53. Cf. Quispel, 'Introduction', pp. 9–11; Lüdemann, 'The History of Earliest Christianity in Rome', p. 134.

54. E.g. Irenaeus, *Adv. Haer.* 1.27.1 (for Cerdo); Origen, *Princ.* 2.7.1; Clemens, *Strom.* 2.8.39 (referring to the Marcionite understanding of the law). For these passages and refutation of this distinction by other early Christian authors, see A. von Harnack, *Marcion: Das Evangelium vom fremden Gott: Eine Monographie zur Geschichte der Grundlegung der katholischen Kirche* (Leipzig: J.C. Hinrich, 2nd edn, 1924; reprint: Darmstadt: Wissenschaftliche Buchgesellschaft, 1985), pp. 262*–63*, 271*.

55. Cf. Grant, *Heresy and Criticism*, p. 49; Müller, *Gnostikerne og Bibelen*, p. 13.

56. For a different view, see Scholten, 'Quellen zur Sozialgeschichte', p. 259: it is sufficient for 'Valentinian Flora…to understand Ptolemy's letter that she is able to read and has some knowledge of the scripture.'

57. Cf. W.A. Löhr, 'Die Auslegung des Gesetzes bei Markion, den Gnostikern und den Manichäern', in G. Schöllgen, C. Scholten (eds.), *Stimuli. Exegese und ihre Hermeneutik in Antike und Christentum* (Festschrift E. Dassmann; JAC.E, 23; Münster: Aschendorffsche Verlagsbuchhandlung, 1996), pp. 77–95 (84, 94).

Ptolemy's 'hidden agenda' simply by recourse to Irenaeus' account in *Against Heresies* 1.1–8 seem to me unwarranted.[58] In the introduction of this section, Irenaeus mentions Ptolemy's disciples but not Ptolemy himself,[59] whereas a short remark 'Thus in truth Ptolemaeus (*et Ptolomaeus quidem ita*)' at the end of this passage is absent in the Greek version of text and may be secondary.[60]

In any case, Ptolemy's *Letter to Flora* shows that he was engaged in progressive instruction. This brings us to the exoteric and esoteric teachings of the Valentinians. The distinction between the two types of instruction became visible in Irenaeus' portrayal of Valentinians as double-dealers, saying one thing and meaning another, and in his complaint that they betrayed their real thoughts only to limited audiences in secrecy. I have already pointed out that there is a tension between this complaint and the fact that Irenaeus talked with his opponents and in so doing learned about their 'real' views. Therefore, it seems justified to try to paint a picture of Valentinianism that takes into account the possibility of progressive instruction but is not so completely coloured by Irenaeus' polemic attitude towards this idea.

Nonetheless, only a very tentative sketch of Valentinian *paideia* can be drawn. The evidence employed in this connection is no longer confined to the Valentinians in Rome, but must be gathered from various sources. The emerging picture of "the school of Valentinus" will be, thus, of a very general nature. We may assume, however, that the situation in Rome was perhaps not totally different from this general picture.

One important starting point to our inquiry is that already Irenaeus conceived of Valentinians as a 'school'.[61] Accordingly, this group must have born some resemblance to philosophical schools in antiquity. These schools tolerated variably deviant opinions.[62] The school of Valentinus seems to have belonged to those open to diverse interpretations. Not only were they ready to converse with Irenaeus, but also their own teachings point to strikingly different backgrounds. While Valentinus seems to have been familiar with Sethian gnostic traditions, Ptolemy's view about the demiurge stood very close to Marcion's position, though he did not go as far as Marcion. The setting of a school offered a context in which such interpretations stemming from different traditions could be discussed and elaborated.

The school setting is also compatible with the idea of instruction at different levels. As it seems, some parts of Hermetic *paideia* were confined to the spiritually advanced. In rabbinic Judaism, passages in scripture 'which were difficult or easily misunderstood were to be taught only to a few pupils at a time and not to the

---

58. E.g., Grant, *Heresy and Criticism*, pp. 51–52, takes Irenaeus' account at face value in describing Ptolemy's scriptural exegesis. He also speaks of Ptolemy's 'hidden agenda' in this connection (ibid. p. 47).

59. Irenaeus, *Adv. Haer.* 1, preface.

60. Irenaeus, *Adv. Haer.* 1.8.5.; cf. Lüdemann, 'The History of Earliest Christianity in Rome', p. 126.

61. See above, p. 160.

62. Cf. R.A. Culpepper, *The Johannine School: An Evaluation of the Johannine-School Hypothesis Based on an Investigation of the Nature of Ancient Schools* (SBL.DS, 26; Missoula, MT: Scholars Press 1975), pp. 252–53.

public.'[63] Discussion of difficult passages in the Torah was, thus, restricted to the specialists. One sign of this kind of esotericism of the learned are rabbinic discussions as to which passages in the Hebrew Bible should be left untranslated in synagogue meetings.[64] It has even been suggested that rabbis took a strictly orthodox and monotheistic line in the synagogue, but endulged in more speculative discussions among themselves. Vivid rabbinic speculations as to Adam's original form have been explained as emerging from the latter context. [65] Speculation seems here a scholarly enterprise confined to, and characteristic of, an inner circle of the learned. It is not necessary to assume that rabbis thought that views they expressed within the school setting challenged their public teaching. The ability to deal with speculative issues and to offer new innovations seems simply to be part of being learned.

The idea of esoteric instruction can also be seen in Origen, who, for instance, 'approves a Jewish custom of keeping the Song of the Songs … out of the hands of the spiritually immature.'[66] It is possible that Valentinian teachers thought in a similar manner, and this may have triggered the patristic accusation that they keep their real teachings to themselves. The example of Irenaeus shows, however, that admittance to Valentinian school discussions was not restricted to those initiated in specific cult practices such as the bridal chamber and redemption. In addition, I believe that we can rule out the possibility that Irenaeus infiltrated a Valentinian group in order to gain information of their real views, though this strategy is attested for curious Romans, who 'sent spies to discover what the rabbis were teaching.'[67] This leaves us with the other possibility that Irenaeus' Valentinian discussion partners considered him learned enough to be included in advanced discussions, though they knew that his theological stance was squarely opposed to theirs.

63. S.J.D. Cohen, 'The Rabbi in Second-Century Jewish Society', *CHJ* III, pp. 922–90 (955).

64. Cf. G.A. Wewers, *Geheimnis und Geheimhaltung im rabbinischen Judentum* (RVV, 35; Berlin: W. de Gruyter, 1975), pp. 33–44, 204.

65. J. Jervell, *Imago Dei. Gen. 1,26f. im Spätjudentum, in der Gnosis und in den paulinischen Briefen* (FRLANT, 58; Göttingen: Vandenhoeck & Ruprecht, 1960), pp. 72–74, 119. On public instruction in the early synagogue, see L. I. Levine, *The Ancient Synagogue: The First Thousand Years* (New Haven: Yale University Press, 1999), pp. 144–47. Levine also reminds us, however, that rabbinic involvement in the ancient synagogue, however, should not be exaggerated; its degree 'is far more complex and varied than any sweeping and facile generalization of yes and no' (ibid. 441). C. Hezser, *The Social Structure of the Rabbinic Movement in Roman Palestine* (TSAJ, 66; Tübingen: Mohr-Siebeck, 1997), p. 100, argues even that, in tannaitic traditions, 'there are no references to rabbis teaching the community in public.' Yet Hezser's study offers abundant evidence to the contrary: rabbis could offer public instruction if they deemed the audience worthy of it (ibid. pp. 101–02) – and sometimes even if the audience was not at all interested; *Songs R.* 1.15 relates that, as a rabbi was teaching, 'the congregation fell asleep' (ibid. p. 104). Nevertheless, rabbinic influence on the ancient synagogue should not be exaggerated.

66. J.W. Trigg, *Origen* (The Early Church Fathers; London: Routledge, 1998), p. 47 (with reference to Origen, *Comm. Cant.* 1.4–7); cf. also Cohen, 'The Rabbi in Second-Century Jewish Society', p. 956. Esoteric instruction was probably offered also in the school of Philo; cf. Culpepper, *The Johannine School*, pp. 211–12.

67. Cohen, 'The Rabbi in Second-Century Jewish Society', p. 955 n. 150, with reference to *Sifre Dtn* 344.

There is no evidence that Valentinians made vows to keep silent about their teachers' instruction, as did the students of Ammonius.[68] Yet Irenaeus contends that Valentinian teachers preferred 'living speech' to 'written documents'.[69] From this may be inferred that their advanced instruction was mainly delivered orally. This would also be consistent with what we know about other early Christian teachers and Jewish rabbis.[70]

According to Irenaeus' account of the Valentinian system of thought, the advanced Valentinian discussion was heavily concentrated on speculation related to the origins of the visible world. Discussion about these issues provides us, I suggest, with a case of 'esotericism of the learned' similar to that implied by rabbinic school discussions. It may be that Valentinian teachers, like rabbis, conceived of themselves as experts able to discuss speculative issues, but thought that public meetings of Christians were not the right places for such discussions.

5. *The School of Valentinus and Christian Communities in Rome*

No evidence is available as to the organization of the school of Valentinus either in Rome or in general. We do not know whether they had specific properties where people gathered to receive instruction and discussions among the more advanced took place, or whether this all happened more informally.[71] In any case, we must assume that Valentinian teachers enjoyed some popularity and their success continued even after the first signs of criticism against their views. Justin's condemnation of Valentinians seems to have been ineffective, and it must be assumed that Bishop Victor still had his Valentinian presbyter in Rome for some time after the completion of Irenaeus' *Against Heresies*.

The house churches in Rome were in general surprisingly tolerant as to diversity of Christian interpretations.[72] This general atmosphere made it possible for Valentinian teachers to continue their teaching despite the first signs of opposition to it in

68.   On the esotericism of Ammonius and his students, see R. Valantasis, *Spiritual Guides of the Third Century. A Semiotic Study of the Guide-Disciple Relationship in Christianity, Neoplatonism, Hermetism, and Gnosticism* (HDR, 27; Minneapolis, MN: Fortress, 1991), p. 46.

69.   Irenaeus, *Adv. Haer.* 3.2.1.

70.   As is well known, Papias also preferred oral traditions to the written ones (Eusebius, *Hist. Eccl.* 3.39); for his way of using this distinction, see R. Uro, 'Thomas and Oral Gospel Tradition', in *idem* (ed.), *Thomas at the Crossroads* (Edinburgh: T. & T. Clark, 1998), pp. 8–32 (20–21). For rabbis, see Cohen, 'The Rabbi in Second-Century Jewish Society', p. 955: 'Rabbinic law...was always studied orally.' As an analogy, Cohen (ibid. p. 956) mentions Clement of Alexandria, who was apologetic for laying bare his thoughts in writing (cf. Strom. 1.1.1–16).

71.   For different categories of philosophers who may offer an analogy for early Christian teachers, see Markschies, 'Valentinian Gnosticism', p. 404. Markschies mentions visiting lectures, domestic philosophers, parlor (or popular) philosophers, and professional philosophers. Yet I am not entirely convinced by Markschies's suggestion that Valentinus and Ptolemy 'attempted to measure up to the qualitative level...of professional philosophers' whereas 'the mythologoumena' of other Valentinians hint at 'at the level of parlor philosophy' (*ibidem*, pp. 437–38). It seems to me that we simply do not have enough evidence to warrant the strong value judgment inherent in this division between Valentinian teachers.

72.   Lampe, *Die stadtrömischen Christen*, pp. 323–30.

the writings of Justin and Irenaeus. Tolerance towards deviant teachings was connected to the loose structure of house churches in Rome that made possible a great variety of Christian interpretations in the first and second centuries.[73] The organization of communities was based upon the 'extended family structures of the Greco-Roman households.'[74] Wealthy Christian patrons who opened their houses for communal meetings were responsible for different aspects of leadership in these communities, including maintenance for the teachers.[75]

In house churches, therefore, the recruitment of teachers must have been largely dependent on patrons' personal tastes. This situation was most likely very favourable to educated early Christian teachers like those of the school of Valentinus. Since wealth and education usually went hand in hand in antiquity, it can be assumed that many patrons belonged to the educated class sensitive to the merits of the Valentinian teachers in literacy and artistic expression.[76] Valentinus himself was skilled in poetry, Ptolemy in rhetoric, and Heracleon in rules of textual interpretation. This must have contributed to their success as teachers in Rome.

6. *Marcosians in Rome*

Thus far, I have argued, concurring with many other scholars, that Valentinians are best understood in the setting of a school. I assume that this explanation also applies to the Valentinians in Rome. The representatives of this school did not drift apart from the ordinary (whatever that may mean in the context of second-century Rome) Christian church. On the contrary, the Valentinian Florinus was able to become a member of church hierarchy still at the end of the second century CE.[77]

This general picture would remain, however, one-sided without a discussion of Marcosians in Rome. This group was obviously more distinct from ordinary Christian communities than other Valentinians. Already Irenaeus characterizes Marcosians in terms of their own ritual practices and meetings.[78] In addition, clear boundaries between them and other Christian communities had begun to be established in Asia Minor, when Irenaeus still was there, for those returning from Marcosian groups to 'the church of God'[79] were subjected to public confessions prior to their admittance to the Christian community of Irenaeus.[80]

---

73. Cf. Lampe, *Die stadtrömischen Christen*, pp. 320–23; Lüdemann, 'The History of Earliest Christianity in Rome', p. 127.

74. William L. Lane, 'Social Perspectives on Roman Christianity during the Formative Years from Nero to Nerva: Romans, Hebrews, 1 Clement', in K.P. Donfried and P. Richardson (eds.), *Judaism and Christianity in First-Century Rome* (Grand Rapids, Michigan/Cambridge, UK: Eerdmans, 1998), pp. 196–244, on p. 213; cf. Lampe, *Die stadtrömischen Christen*, pp. 315–16.

75. Lane, 'Social Perspectives', 211–12.

76. Valentinus' reputation for eloquence was still known to Tertullian (*Val.* 4.1–2). He no doubt mentions this feature not as compliment to Valentinus but thinking of the contrast often drawn in antiquity between the truth and the deceptive beauty of rhetorical skill (thus, e.g., Philo, *Vit. Cont.* 31).

77. Cf. E. Pagels, *The Gnostic Gospels* (New York: Vintage Books, 1989 [1979]), pp. 44–45.

78. Irenaeus, *Adv. Haer.* 1.13.1–7, 1.21.1–5.

79. Irenaeus, *Adv. Haer.* 1.13.5.

80. Irenaeus, *Adv. Haer.* 1.13.8.

Marcus himself is located in Rome in the *Universal History* (*Kitab al-'Unvan*) written in Arabic in 10th century CE by the church historian Agapius.[81] Though this text is late, it is based upon earlier sources which may be reliable.[82] It is, in any case, certain that there were Marcosians in Rome, for their protests against Irenaeus' account of Marcus and his followers are reported by Hippolytus of Rome.[83] Hippolytus' account also suggests that Marcosians formed a distinct church organization with their own bishop (ἐπίσκοπος). He was responsible for whispering the secret instruction into the ears of the dying ones in a deathbed ritual called 'redemption' peculiar to Marcosians.[84] The fact that the bishop is not mentioned in an earlier description of this ritual by Irenaeus[85] indicates that Marcosian groups developed into a more organized church movement at the turn of the third century, after Irenaeus but prior to Hippolytus.[86]

I am also inclined to believe that there is a link between the famous epitaph dedicated to Flavia Sophe (*IGUR* 15884) and Marcosians. This inscription found in the Via Latina in Rome is one of two inscriptions associated with Valentinians in scholarly literature.[87] The two-sided inscription runs as follows:

(A)
After having yearned for the paternal light, sister and wife, my Sophē,
anointed in baths of Christ with imperishable, holy oil,
you hastened to gaze at the divine features of the eternal beings (aeons),
the great angel of the great council, the true Son,
entering [into] the bridal chamber and ascending to […]
[…] paternal […]

81. Agapius (Mahboub) de Menbidj, *Kitab al-'Unvan: Histoire Universelle* (ed. A. Vasiliev; vol. 2: *PO* 7 [1911], pp. 459–591 [511]).

82. Cf. N. Förster, *Marcus Magus. Kult, Lehre und Gemeindeleben einer valentinianischen Gnostikergruppe. Sammlung der Quellen und Kommentar* (WUNT, 114; Tübingen: Mohr-Siebeck, 1999), pp. 44–53.

83. Hippolytus, *Ref.* 6.42.1; cf. Förster, *Marcus Magus*, pp. 28–29.

84. Hippolytus, *Ref.* 6.41.4–5.

85. Irenaeus, *Adv. Haer.* 1.21.5.

86. Cf. Förster, *Marcus Magus*, p. 155.

87. For this evidence, see M. Guarducci, 'Valentiniani a Roma: Ricerche epigrafiche ed archeologiche', *MDAI.R* 80 (1973), pp. 169–89 (and the tables 46–52); eadem, 'Ancora sui Valentiniani a Roma', *MDAI.R* 81 (1974), pp. 341–43; Lampe, *Die stadtrömischen Christen*, pp. 257–64. The other inscription has quite extensive lacunae which make its interpretation very difficult. In Lampe's translation based upon his restoration the inscription runs as follows: 'Cobrothers (?) of the bridal chambers celebrate with torches the baths (?) for me,/ They hunger for banquets in our rooms (?),/ Lauding the Father and praising the Son,/ O, may there be flowing (?) of the only spring (?) and of the truth in that very place.' P. Lampe, 'An Early Christian Inscription in the Musei Capitolini', in D. Hellholm, H. Moxnes, T. Karlsen Seim (eds.), *Mighty Minorities: Minorities in Early Christianity – Positions and Strategies* (Festschrift J. Jervell; Oslo: Scandinavian University Press, 1995), pp. 79–92 (80–81). This study is Lampe's response to C. Scholten, 'Gibt es Quellen zur Sozialgeschichte der Valentinianer Roms?' *ZNW* 79 (1988), pp. 244–61, who contends that the Valentinian origin of this inscription 'is highly unlikely and can virtually be excluded' (ibidem, p. 253) and suggests that we are dealing with a secular wedding inscription.

(B)
This deceased had no ordinary end of life,
she died, and she lives and sees the truly imperishable light.
She lives for the living ones, she is dead to those who are really dead.
Earth, why do you wonder at the race of the dead one? Are you seized with fear?

Earlier scholarship has shown sufficient basis for this inscription being of Valentinian origin.[88] For example, the description of Sophe's salvation in terms of seeing the aeons fits well with Valentinian speculation about these beings attested in patristic sources.[89] The Valentinian usage of 'the angel of the great council' from Is 9.6 LXX as a Christological title is attested in *Excerpts of Theodotus* 43.2.[90] The bridal chamber imagery occurs frequently in Valentinian sources.[91] Though it is not confined to Valentinian sources in early Christian literature,[92] it rarely appears elsewhere in writings that show interest in aeons, while other 'gnostic' writings occupied with aeons do not usually employ the bridal chamber imagery. Hence, I find the combination of 'aeons' and 'bridal chamber' in the Flavia Sophe inscription characteristically Valentinian.

As to the possible linkage of this inscription with Marcosians, Irenaeus specifically mentions that some Marcosians performed a bridal chamber ritual which was understood as effecting a spiritual marriage drawn after the image of heavenly syzygies.[93] I also find the second line of the inscription noteworthy: Sophe has been 'anointed in the baths of Christ with imperishable, holy oil.' Anointing

88. For the opposite view, see Scholten, 'Quellen zur Sozialgeschichte', p. 255: the Valentinian provenance of this inscription is 'only a remote possibility'.

89. E.g. Irenaeus, *Adv. Haer.* 1.1.1. Scholten, 'Quellen zur Sozialgeschichte', p. 255, maintains, with reference to *LPGL*, that 'also non-Gnostic Christian authors speak quite naturally (*selbstverständlich*) of aeons as overcosmic entities.' So natural is not the evidence offered in *LPGL* s.v. (p. 56) for aeons as personified divine entities: it stems almost completely from descriptions of positions that can be considered 'gnostic'; the only clear exception in this group is Tatian (Irenaeus, *Adv. Haer.* 1.28.1).

90. For non-Valentinian early Christian authors referring to Isa. 9.6, see C.A. Gieschen, *Angelomorphic Christology: Antecedents & Early Evidence* (*AGAJ*, 42; Leiden: E.J. Brill, 1998), pp. 176, 189 (Justin), 195 (Origen), 197 (Novatian). (*Exc. Theod.* 43.2 goes unnoticed in Gieschen's study.)

91. The word πάστος used in the inscription does not appear in patristic references to the Valentinian 'bridal chamber', but it occurs frequently in the *Gospel of Philip*, pp. 69–71 (§§ 73, 76, 79, 82). The most common term for the Valentinian 'bridal chamber' is νύμφων (Irenaeus, *Adv. Haer.* 1.7.1; 1.21.3; 1.13.3, 6; Clement, *Exc. Theod.* 64; 65.1; *Gos. Phil.*, pp. 65, 67, 69, 72, 74, 76, 82, 86 [§§ 61, 67, 68, 76, 87, 88, 95,102, 122, 127]). That πάστος and νύμφων could be understood as synonyms is shown by *Gospel of Philip*, p. 69 (§ 76). In addition, γάμος (Clement, *Exc. Theod.* 63.2; 65.1; Origen, *Comm. Joh.* 10.19; cf. *Gos. Phil.*, p. 64 [§ 60]) and κοιτών (*Gos. Phil.*, p. 84–5 [§§124/5–126]) are used. These terms, however, are not always synonyms in Valentinian texts; in *Gos. Phil.*, p. 72 (§§ 87–88), the children of νύμφων and those of γάμος are presented as two separate groups.

92. In non-Valentinian early Christian writings, 'bridal chamber' is mentioned, e.g., in Matt 9.15; 25.1–13; *Gos. Thom.* 75, 104; *Dial. Sav.* 138; *Exeg. Soul* 134; for further references, see Scholten, 'Quellen zur Sozialgeschichte', p. 255 n. 50.

93. Irenaeus, *Adv. Haer.* 1.21.3: 'Some of them prepare a bridal chamber and complete the mystic teaching with invocations on those who are being initiated (trans. Unger-Dillon).'

with oil was also part of the Marcosian ritual of redemption according to Irenaeus. He says that this ritual was performed by pouring oil, or a mixture of oil and water, upon a person's head. Marcosians conceived of this ritual as the second 'baptism' (βάπτισμα) or 'bath' (λουτρόν);[94] the latter word would account for 'baths' as a description of anointing in the inscription. In addition, the plural 'baths' coincides with 'baths and redemptions' (λούσματα καὶ ἀπολυτρώσεις) which Hippolytus mentions in his account of the Marcosian ritual practices.[95] Hippolytus differs at this point from Irenaeus, who only speaks of one redemption performed in different manners by Marcosians.[96] Hence, Hippolytus' version may go back to his specific knowledge of Marcosians and their ritual practices in Rome.

What would, then, the inscription tell us about Valentinians in Rome? Although caution is always advisable in interpreting ancient epitaphs, I believe that certain inferences can be drawn. First, a marble epitaph of this quality could not have been unexpensive. Admittedly, people in antiquity might spend to the commemoration of the deceased more than their economic situation would have allowed.[97] Even so, a poor family could scarcely have afforded such a lengthy, carefully composed and skillfully engraved epitaph. Accordingly, Sophe's spouse must have been a man of some fortune. This is consistent with the patristic complaint that Marcus recruited adherents among the wealthy.[98] Second, the composition of the epitaph in hexameter shows the husband's respect of literary skill.[99] Hence, the inscription adds strength to the general picture drawn above of the adherents to Valentinian groups in Rome.

94. Irenaeus, *Adv. Haer.* 1.21.2; Hippolytus, *Ref.* 6.41.1–2. (Marcovich adds in both cases <πρῶτον> to Hippolytus' text when referring to baptism. This would make the point even clearer, but I do not believe that the addition is necessary.) As to Hippolytus' account at this point, Förster, *Marcus Magus*, 154, claims that 'the description of the apolytrosis as a baptismal bath (λουτρόν) ...does not fit in with the form and course of this ritual among Marcosians in Hippolytus' description'. Thus, he argues that 'the second baptism' in Hippolytus' account refer to 'other Valentinian groups and not to Marcosians.' It is true that, as Förster points out, Hippolytus does not mention anointing in his description of how the apolytrosis was performed, but speaks only of laying of hands on the recipient. Nevertheless, it is possible that Hippolytus took anointing for granted, because it was already described already by Irenaeus as part of the apolytrosis. This is implied, in my view, in Hippolytus' expression 'baths and redemptions' (*Ref.* 6.42.1; for this expression, see below).

95. Hippolytus, *Ref.* 6.42.1.

96. Irenaeus, *Adv. Haer.* 1.13.6; cf. Förster, *Marcus Magus*, p. 29.

97. Cf. A. Samellas, *Death in the Eastern Mediterranean (50–600 AD): The Christianization of the East: An Interpretation* (STAC, 12; Tübingen: Mohr-Siebeck, 2002), p. 230.

98. Irenaeus, *Adv. Haer.* 1.13.3, claims that Marcus sought followers among rich women. Their high status is shown by their purple clothes Irenaeus mentions in this connection. In the Roman empire, purple was 'the colour of prestige' (R. Saller, 'Status and Patronage', *CAH* 11, pp. 817–54 [821]); and purple clothes were carried by those of 'high social classes, above all in the emperor's house' (Förster, *Marcus Magus*, p. 96).

99. I think this much can be concluded, even if the sublime style in the epitaph was only meant for status display. It can be, of course, that the husband composed the epitaph himself, but it is equally possible that he ordered it from someone able to do this for him.

Third, the inscription betrays a special group identity. There is emphasis on the 'race' of the deceased; it is affirmed that she 'had no ordinary end of life'; and she is portrayed superior to the earth which may be seized with fear, as it encounters her. The inscription, hence, reflects a similar attitude towards the hereafter as the Marcosian deathbed instruction. In the latter, the initiated affirms the superiority of his or her origin in comparison to that of the gatekeepers and, in so doing, shames them because of their humble origin.[100] Fourth, though the epitaph is often said to bear witness to the privileged status of women in gnostic groups,[101] it says in fact relatively little about that issue. The inscription bears witness to the admission of women into a group of initiates, but it does not reveal whether they assumed a more active role in performing rituals. The active role of women may be assumed, however, if the inscription is of Marcosian origin.[102]

The Flavia Sophe inscription reminds us that Valentinianism in Rome was not confined to school discussions of the learned. There were real people who put their trust in Valentinian instruction and expressed their eschatological hopes in terms of it.

7. Conclusion

In light of this study, I believe that it is advisable to separate between two different strands of Valentinianism, one that resembled ancient philosophical schools and another that developed into a distinct church organization. The former was most likely the dominant context of Valentinian groups in antiquity. The evidence for the 'Valentinian' church is restricted in early sources to the followers of Marcus, who also in many other ways differed from 'mainstream' Valentinianism.

I have suggested above that Valentinian teachers in Rome (and elsewhere) were engaged in progressive instruction. This possibility involves a distinction between an 'exoteric' or initial instruction and an 'esoteric' or advanced instruction. It may seem natural to assume that the latter was based upon what was learned at the initial level.[103] This, however, cannot be taken for granted. Hermetic treatises bear witness that the advanced teaching could be in contradiction to what had been taught earlier. One Hermetic treatise opens with Asclepius' saying to his addressee Ammon that 'you will find that it contradicts even some of my own discourses.'[104] Another Hermetic text shows that 'a more mystical interpretation' was withheld

---

100. Scholten, 'Quellen zur Sozialgeschichte', p. 255, remains one-sided, as he speaks only of 'the fear of soul because of the gatekeepers' in this connection. As result of their meeting with the dead one who knows the right answers, the gatekeepers 'are very much upset and condemn their root and the origin of their Mother' (Irenaeus, *Adv. Haer.* 1.21.5; trans. Unger-Dillon).

101. E.g. K. Rudolph, *Die Gnosis: Wesen und Geschichte einer spätantiken Religion* (Göttingen: Vandenhoeck & Ruprecht, 3rd edn, 1990), p. 229; G. Filoramo, *A History of Gnosticism* (Oxford: Basil Blackwell, 1991), p. 176.

102. At least prophesying was, as Irenaeus tells in dismay, equally allocated to men and women by drawing lots in each meeting of Marcosians; cf. Irenaeus, *Adv. Haer.* 1.13.4.

103. Cf. Markschies, *Valentinus Gnosticus*, p. 394.

104. *CH* 16.1.

from newcomers and granted only to the advanced;[105] similar tendencies are attested also in Rabbinic writings.[106] In Hermetic texts, 'doctrinal variations …reflect an intention that different *successive* levels (or "steps") of spiritual enlightment should provide access to different *successive* levels of truth about Man, the world and God…'.[107]

It is difficult to say whether Valentinian *paideia* was occupied with successive levels of spiritual enlightment in a manner similar to that attested in Hermetic tractates. We have evidence for progressive education in Ptolemy's *Letter to Flora*, but we cannot be sure what the subsequent step brought with it. It could have been advanced spiritual instruction, as in Hermetic tractates, but it may also have consisted of advanced 'theological' education that prepared the recipient for a better understanding of learned discussions both within the school of Valentinus and between Valentinian and other early Christian teachers.

---

105. *CH* 14.1.

106. Cf. Wewers, *Geheimnis und Geheimhaltung*, pp. 104–05, referring to *y. 'Aboda sara* 41d (and its parallels). According to this midrash to Prov 27.26, 'the words of Torah' should be hidden, when students are 'small'. 'The secrets of Torah' can be revealed to them only when they have grown up and become as strong as goats.

107. Fowden, *The Egyptian Hermes*, p. 103.

Jürgen Wehnert

Das Thema dieses Beitrags ist aus einem langjährigen Forschungsprojekt an der Theologischen Fakultät der Universität Göttingen erwachsen. Sein Gegenstand ist die Übersetzung und Kommentierung der pseudoklementinischen Homilien. Dieses Projekt hat großzügige Förderung seitens der Deutschen Forschungs Gemeinschaft (DFG) sowie der Fritz Thyssen Stiftung gefunden und wird unter der fachlichen Ägide von Prof. Eduard Lohse in hoffentlich naher Zukunft abgeschlossen werden können.

1. *Zum Forschungsgegenstand*

Hinter dem etwas merkwürdigen Titel „Pseudoklementinen" (nachfolgend: PsKl) verbirgt sich der in zwei verschiedenen Versionen überlieferte erste christliche Roman. Seine Bedeutung liegt weniger in seinem eher bescheidenen Unterhaltungswert als vielmehr in den darin verarbeiteten Traditionsstoffen, die früher kurzerhand unter dem Etikett „judenchristlich" eingeordnet wurden. Wegen dieser Traditionen wurden die PsKl seit Mitte des 19. Jahrhunderts zu einem wichtigen Gegenstand der neutestamentlichen und kirchengeschichtlichen Forschung. So fußt z.B. Ferdinand Christian Baurs berühmte These von der Entstehung des Katholizismus aus Paulinismus und Petrinismus unmittelbar auf der Beschäftigung mit den PsKl, die Baur als Quelle für ein petrinisches Christentum heranzog.[1] Zahlreiche Monographien und Aufsätze (u.a. von Adolf Hilgenfeld, Gerhard Uhlhorn, Wilhelm Bousset, Hans Waitz, Hans-Joachim Schoeps und Georg Strecker) haben Baurs Untersuchungen fortgeführt und beträchtlich vertieft.

Leider sind die PsKl als wichtige Quelle für die Geschichte und Theologie des frühen Christentums in der zweiten Hälfte des 20. Jahrhunderts an die Peripherie des Forschungsinteresses geraten[2] – trotz der sorgfältigen Edition beider Fassungen

---

1. Vgl. bes. die Schriften F.C. Baur, 'Die Christuspartei in der korinthischen Gemeinde, der Gegensatz des petrinischen und paulinischen Christenthums in der ältesten Kirche, der Apostel Petrus in Rom', *TZTh* 1831, pp. 61–206 (Reprint in: ders., *Historisch-kritische Untersuchungen zum Neuen Testament* [hg. v. K. Scholder; Ausgewählte Werke in Einzelausgaben I; Stuttgart-Bad Cannstatt: Frommann, 1963, pp. 1–146]) und: ders., *Paulus, der Apostel Jesu Christi. Sein Leben und Wirken, seine Briefe und seine Lehre. Ein Beitrag zu einer kritischen Geschichte des Urchristenthums* (Stuttgart: Becker & Müller, 1845).

2. Siehe den Forschungsüberblick von F. Stanley Jones, 'The Pseudo-Clementines: A History of Research', *The Second Century* 2 (1982), pp. 1–33 und 63–96.

in den „Griechischen Christlichen Schriftstellern" durch Bernhard Rehm[3] und mancher neuen Einzeluntersuchung.[4] Mitverantwortlich für das Stagnieren der Forschung ist sicher, dass in wichtigen Einleitungsfragen, speziell über das Verhältnis der beiden vorhandenen Romanfassungen, und deren Entstehungsgeschichte, bisher kein Konsens erzielt werden konnte. Ich möchte deshalb im ersten Teil meines Beitrags einen Abriss der Entstehungsgeschichte der PsKl geben, so wie sie sich mir darstellt. Im zweiten Teil will ich dann ein bemerkenswertes Stück aus der ältesten Literarschicht, ein antipaulinisches Streitgespräch, näher vorstellen.

2. Zur Entstehungsgeschichte des pseudoklementinischen Romans[5]

Bei den beiden Romanversionen handelt es sich einerseits um die sog. Rekognitionen („Wiedererkennungen", im folgenden: R), andererseits um die Homilien („Predigten", im folgenden: H). Beide Rezensionen wurden in griechischer Sprache verfasst. Die Rekognitionen sind allerdings in der Originalsprache verloren gegangen und heute nur in lateinischer und zum Teil in syrischer Übersetzung zugänglich. Das erschwert die Untersuchung dieser Literatur erheblich, weil der synoptische Vergleich der beiden Rezensionen dabei eine wichtige Rolle spielt. Eine synoptische Textausgabe ist deshalb für das „Corpus Christianorum, Series Apocryphorum" geplant; sie wird durch eine Arbeitsgruppe innerhalb der „Association pour l'étude de la littérature apocryphe chrétienne", Lausanne-Genf-Paris, unter der Leitung von Jean-Daniel Kaestli vorbereitet.

Homilien und Rekognitionen sind zwei Bearbeitungen desselben Romanstoffs, der seinerseits eine lange literarische Vorgeschichte hat. Worum es in den disparaten Teilen dieses Werkes geht, wird hoffentlich deutlich, wenn ich seine mutmaßliche Entstehungsgeschichte kurz skizziere:

a) Älteste und theologiegeschichtlich wohl bedeutsamste Schicht der PsKl ist eine Novelle, die den Kampf zwischen dem Apostel Petrus und seinem Widersacher, dem Zauberer Simon Magus, schildert – ein Konflikt, dessen literarische Wurzeln bis Apg 8,9–24 zurückreichen. Die Auseinandersetzung der beiden Kontrahenten findet in drei Teilen statt: Der erste ist eine Disputation im judäischen Cäsarea, die mit der Flucht des Magiers endet. Der zweite Teil beschreibt eine Verfolgungsjagd von Cäsarea bis in die syrische Hauptstadt Antiochien. (Petrus heftet sich an die Fersen seines Gegenspielers, der die Bewohner verschiedener phönizischer Küstenstädte gegen den Apostel aufhetzt; doch nützt ihm das nichts, denn Petrus zieht die Bevölkerung durch ausführliche Missionspredigten auf seine Seite, gründet in jeder

---

3.   Homilien im Jahre 1953, [2]1969, [3]1992; Rekognitionen im Jahre 1965, [2]1994.

4.   Siehe zuletzt die Monographien F. Stanley Jones, *An Ancient Jewish Christian Source on the History of Christianity: Pseudo-Clementine Recognitions 1.27–71* (SBL Texts and Translations 37 = Christian Apocrypha Series, 2; Atlanta: Scholars Press, 1995); M. Vielberg: *Klemens in den pseudoklementinischen Rekognitionen. Studien zur literarischen Form des spätantiken Romans* (TU, 145; Berlin: Akademie Verlag, 2000).

5.   Vgl. ausführlicher J. Wehnert, 'Abriß der Entstehungsgeschichte des pseudoklementinischen Romans', *Apocrypha* 3 (1992), pp. 211–35.

Stadt eine christliche Gemeinde und setzt Bischöfe ein.) Den dritten Teil bildet eine weitere Disputation, in der Petrus den Magier erneut überwindet.

Die Datierung dieser Novelle ergibt sich daraus, dass sie die sog. Petrusakten voraussetzt. Jene apokryphe Apostelgeschichte stammt aus der zweiten Hälfte des 2. Jahrhunderts; sie schließt mit der endgültigen Niederlage des Simon Magus und mit dem Tod des Apostels Petrus in Rom. Im ausgehenden 2. Jahrhundert dürfte die vorpseudoklementinische Petrus/Simon-Novelle entstanden sein, um die Lücken im Erzählbericht der Petrusakten zu schliessen, die sich auf Ereignisse in Jerusalem und Rom beschränken. Diese Novelle lässt sich literarkritisch relativ leicht aus den übrigen PsKl herauslösen, weil sie in auktorialer Erzählperspektive, also in 3. Person, verfasst wurde; der spätere Protagonist Klemens spielt darin noch keine Rolle.

b) Mitte des 3. Jahrhunderts wurde die Petrus/Simon-Novelle zu einem auto-biographisch stilisierten Ich-Roman umgearbeitet. *Terminus post quem* ist die Benutzung der Schrift „Buch der Gesetze der Völker" des Syrers Bardesanes (gest. 222 n. Chr.). Ich-Erzähler des Romans ist der adlige Jüngling und spätere Bischof Klemens von Rom – also eine historische Person aus dem Ende des 1. Jahrhunderts. Der Klemensroman hat zwei Teile. Die erste Hälfte ist ein Entwicklungsroman: Der von den Sinnfragen des Lebens umgetriebene Klemens hört in Rom eine Predigt des Barnabas, reist daraufhin nach Judäa, schließt sich dort dem Schüler-kreis um Petrus an, wird von diesem zum Christentum bekehrt und getauft. Die zweite Hälfte ist ein Familien- bzw. Anagnorismen- (= Wiedererkennungs-) Roman: In der Mitte des Werkes erfährt der Leser überraschenderweise, dass Klemens in seiner Jugend durch Schicksalsschläge von seinen Zwillingsbrüdern, seiner Mutter und seinem Vater getrennt wurde, die seitdem verschollen sind. Dank Petrus' Hilfe wird Klemens während der Reise von Cäsarea nach Antiochien nach und nach wieder glücklich mit allen Familienmitgliedern vereint. Wegen ihres fiktiven Ich-Erzählers hat die zum Doppelroman erweiterte Petrus/Simon-Novelle den Namen „Pseudoklementinen" erhalten. Da der Ausgangspunkt dieses Werks Rom ist und, wie in der nächster Bearbeitungsstufe ansatzweise ausgeführt, auf die Rückkehr des Protagonisten und seiner Familie nach Rom zielt, mag der Roman in der Hauptstadt des Imperiums entstanden sein. Der ingeniöse Verfasser griff hier die populäre pagane Literaturform auf, um das gebildete Lesepublikum mit christlichen Anschauungen zu konfrontieren.

c) Das so entstandene Romanwerk wurde auf einer dritten Stufe, vielleicht vom selben Autor, nochmals erweitert: Durch zwei einleitende Briefe an den Herren-bruder Jakobus (Epistula Petri mit Contestatio; Epistula Clementis [Bericht vom Tod des Petrus in Rom und von der Einsetzung des Klemens zum dortigen Bischof]) sowie durch gelegentlich eingestreute Anreden in 2. Person ist es zu einer überdimensionalen brieflichen Mitteilung des Klemens an das Oberhaupt der Jerusalemer Christen umgestaltet worden. Jakobus gilt auf dieser Stufe der Bear-beitung als christlicher Oberbischof („Bischof der Bischöfe", Epistula Clementis 1.1), der die ordnungsgemäße Verkündigung aller Apostel überwacht. Zu diesem Zweck müssen ihm regelmäßig Mitschriften der Petruspredigten übersandt werden, was Klemens als Sekretär des Petrus erledigt.

d) Dieser zum Brief mutierte pseudoklementinische Roman war Grundlage für die beiden überlieferten Fassungen des Werkes, H und R. Homilien und Rekognitionen stammen aus dem Ende des 3., spätestens aus dem Anfang des 4. Jahrhunderts. Die Redaktoren, die dafür verantwortlich sind, haben den Stoff nochmals unabhängig voneinander bearbeitet. Dabei haben die 20 Bücher von H die Vorlage oft besser bewahrt als die zehn Bücher von R. In R wurde vieles gestrichen oder entschärft, was in großkirchlichen Kreisen Häresieverdacht hätte erregen können.

Das von R unterdrückte Material ist jedoch von höchstem Interesse, weil es Traditionen enthält, die auf ein nicht-katholisch geprägtes hellenistisches Christentum mit starken jüdischen Wurzeln zurückgehen. Sein besonderes Gewicht erhält dieses Material dadurch, dass es vorwiegend in die älteste Schicht der PsKl eingebettet ist, also in die anfangs skizzierte Petrus/Simon-Novelle. Das theologische Grundprofil dieser Novelle lässt sich in vier Punkten zusammenfassen: 1. Der jüdische Monotheismus wird stark betont (der Gott Israels ist der einzige Gott). Dem korrespondiert 2. eine sehr reduzierte Christologie (von Kreuz und Auferstehung Jesu ist nirgends die Rede; seine Würde gewinnt Jesus als Inkarnation des von Gott gesandten „wahren Propheten", der die Menschen lehrt, was ihnen zum Heil dient). 3. Es findet sich eine rigoristische Ethik, die auch einen Teil der jüdischen Reinheitsbestimmungen einschließt, die durch die Taufe nicht obsolet geworden sind. Dem entspricht 4. ein kaum verhüllter Antipaulinismus, der auf die Verwerfung der gesetzesfreien Verkündigung des Völkerapostels hinausläuft. Den zweiten und vierten Punkt illustriert eindrucksvoll der Abschnitt H 17.13–20, dem ich mich nun zuwenden möchte.

3. Ein Streitgespräch über Vision und Wirklichkeit (H 17.13–20)

H 17.13–20 enthält einen Disput zwischen Simon Magus und Petrus über die Frage, ob eine Vision zuverlässigere Erkenntnis verschafft als Mitteilungen in einem persönlichen Gespräch. Seit der Untersuchung Ferdinand Christian Baurs von 1831[6] ist durchweg unbestritten, dass diese Debatte eine Polemik gegen den Apostel Paulus darstellt – er ist es, der sich in diesem Abschnitt hinter der Maske des Simon Magus verbirgt. Die Gründe für diese Annahme sind zwingend:

a) Nur in H 17.13–20 beansprucht Simon Magus, ein Schüler Jesu zu sein, der durch eine Jesuserscheinung zum Lehrer befähigt worden ist. Dieser Sachverhalt ist Voraussetzung sowohl der Gesprächssituation in 17.13.1–2 als auch der abschließenden Aufforderung des Petrus, Simon möge als Schüler der zwölf Apostel ein echter Jesusjünger werden (17.19.7). In den übrigen PsKl spielt Simon Magus hingegen die Rolle des *advocatus diaboli*, der die jüdisch-christliche Lehre des Petrus bekämpft und aufgrund seiner magischen Fähigkeiten eigene göttliche Würde beansprucht. Der schroffe Rollenwechsel Simons in 17.13–20 wird durch den Kunstgriff abgemildert, dass der Magier in den Rahmenstücken (H 17.4–5; H 18) als Verfechter der markionitischen Zwei-Götter-Lehre auftritt, die von

---

6. Baur, 'Christuspartei', pp. 126ff.

Petrus erfolgreich widerlegt wird. Der theologisch unverdächtige antimarkionitische Kontext kaschiert den antipaulinischen Disput, doch hat das eine mit dem anderen ursprünglich nichts zu tun.[7]

b) Während die paulinischen Briefe in den PsKl durchweg ignoriert werden, ist der Abschnitt H 17.13–20 gespickt mit Anspielungen darauf sowie auf die Paulus-traditionen der Apg.[8] Im Zentrum des Interesses stehen die visionäre Christuserfahrung des Paulus, durch die er sich zum Völkerapostel berufen sah, sowie sein Zusammenstoß mit Petrus in Antiochien. Die Visionsterminologie des Neuen Testaments ist breit reflektiert.[9] Die ὀπτασίαι und ἀποκάλυψεις, die empfangen zu haben sich Paulus in 2 Kor. 12.1 rühmt, bilden den Ausgangspunkt der Diskussion (17.13; vgl. die Parallelen R 2.61.4–6; 65.5–7, wo die Entrückung in die oberste Himmelsregion ausführlich referiert wird). Theologumena wie die Gottessohnschaft Jesu (17.16.4.6; 17.4) und die Totenauferstehung der Gerechten, bei der sie eine nicht-sarkische, engelgleiche Natur erhalten (17.16.5), reflektieren paulinisches Denken und finden sich in den PsKl sonst nie. Am Ende des Disputs steht, unter Zitation von Gal. 2.11, der Vorwurf, Simon (= Paulus) stehe Petrus, dem wahren Apostel Jesu, feindlich gegenüber und habe ihn „verurteilt" genannt (vgl. 17.19.4 und 6: ἐναντίος ἀνθέστηκάς μοι [sc. Petrus], κατεγνώσμενος με λέγει, mit Gal. 2.11: κατὰ πρόσωπον αὐτῷ ἀντέστην, ὅτι κατεγνωσμένος ἦν.

---

7.   Teile der älteren Forschung haben im Anschluß an Baur in 17.13–20 eine primär gegen Markion gerichtete Tendenz erkennen wollen (Paulus als „Apostel Markions": A. Hilgenfeld, *Die clementinischen Recognitionen und Homilien, nach ihrem Ursprung und Inhalt dargestellt* [Jena: Schreiber, 1848], pp. 265–66. 269; vgl. J. Lehmann, *Die Clementinischen Schriften mit besonderer Rücksicht auf ihr literarisches Verhältniss* [Gotha: Perthes, 1869], pp. 382–83), doch wird das dem traditionsgeschichtlichen Befund nicht gerecht.

8.   Vgl. die Zusammenstellungen bei H. Waitz, *Die Pseudoklementinen. Homilien und Recognitionen. Eine quellenkritische Untersuchung* (TU, 25.4; Leipzig: Hinrich, 1904), pp. 138–39 und H.J. Schoeps, *Theologie und Geschichte des Judenchristentums* (Tübingen: Mohr-Siebeck, 1949; Reprint: Gesammelte Schriften, 2; Hildesheim usw.: Olms, 1998), pp. 424–26.

9.   Die Fülle der terminologischen Berührungen kann hier nur summarisch angedeutet werden: ὀπτασία („Erscheinung"; vgl. 2 Kor. 12.1) ist neben ὅραμα (s.u.) Leitbegriff der Diskussion in 17.13–20. Er erscheint in 17.13.1–20.1 15mal (in H sonst nur noch zweimal in Vers 17.5,6b, der die spätere Diskussion vorbereitet). ὅραμα („Vision"; vgl. Apg 9.12; 16.9–10; 18.9) begegnet in 17.13.1–19.1 ebenfalls 15mal (in H sonst nur 14.7.3; 18.21.3). Aktivisches ὁρᾶν erscheint 17.7.3–18.6 16mal im Präsens, 17.7.4–16.6 zehnmal im Aorist (vgl. Apg 9.12,27; 16.10; 22.14,18; 26.13,16) und 17.15.2–3; 17,2 dreimal im Perfekt (vgl. 1 Kor. 9.1). Im Passiv findet sich das Verb 17.16.3–4 zweimal im Aorist 1 und 17.13.2; 16.6 bis 19.1–4 siebenmal im Aorist 2 (vgl. 1 Kor. 15.8; Apg 9.17; 16.9; 26.16). Das Vorkommen von ἀποκάλυψις („Offenbarung"; vgl. 2 Kor. 12.1,7; Gal. 1.12; 2.2) beschränkt sich auf fünf Belege in 17.18.1–19.6, im selben Abschnitt auch viermal das Verb ἀποκαλύπτειν (vgl. Gal. 1.16). Angesichts der aus einer Auslegung von Mt. 16.13–8 erschlossenen besonderen Semantik des Begriffs (im Sinne einer unvermittelten inneren Erleuchtung), die auch die nachfolgende antimarkionitische Debatte in H 18 bestimmt (dort ἀποκάλυψις fünfmal in 18.6.3–10.5, ἀποκαλύπτειν 29mal in 18.4.2–21.3), ist jedoch sehr fraglich, ob die Passage 17.17.5b–18.3 sowie die darauf Bezug nehmenden Sätze in 17.18.4; 19.1.4 und 6 ursprüngliche Bestandteile des antipaulinischen Disputs sind (s.u. Anm. 14). Ferner begegnen die Termini ἐνύπνιον („Traumbild", zwölfmal in 17.14,3–19,1, sonst nur in H 18.21,3) und ὄνειρος („Traum", achtmal in 17.15.2–18.2, 14 weitere Belege in H), die in der ntl. Paulustradition nicht vorkommen. Sie zielen darauf ab, den paulinischen Visionsbegriff im Sinne einer Traumerscheinung auszulegen.

c) Der Abschnitt 17.13–20 steht in Zusammenhang mit einer Reihe weiterer antipaulinischern Passagen in H und R (vor allem R 1.70–1; Epistula Petri 2; H 2.17; 11.35).[10] Sie scheinen sie einem gemeinsamen Traditionsstrom anzugehören, dem Paulus als „feindlicher Mensch" (Epistula Petri 2,3; R 1.70.1; 71.3; 73.4) gilt, weil er eine der jüdischen Religion zuwiderlaufende ungesetzliche Lehre verbreite.

4. Zum Alter des Traditionsstücks H 17.13–20

Das nur von H überlieferte, am Anfang wohl leicht abgekürzte Traditionsstück,[11] das sich auch durch sprachliche Besonderheiten abhebt,[12] ist bis zum Beweis des Gegenteils der Petrus/Simon-Novelle zuzuordnen, in die es eingebettet ist.[13] Die thematische Disparatheit des Streitgesprächs läßt darauf schließen, dass es nicht vom Novellisten geschaffen wurde. Er hat es vorgefunden und in seinen Text integriert, indem er den Namen Paulus durch Simon Magus ersetzte.[14] Ebenfalls auf das Konto des Novellisten dürfte die Einführung eines rationalen Offenbarungsbegriffs in 17.17.5b–18.3 zu setzen sein, der die Debatte sprengt[15] und sie mit

10.   Vgl. G. Strecker, *Das Judenchristentum in den Pseudoklementinen* (2. Auflage; TU, 70; Berlin: Akademie-Verlag, 1981), pp. 187–96; G. Lüdemann, *Paulus, der Heidenapostel II: Antipaulinismus im frühen Christentum* (FRLANT, 130; Göttingen: Vandenhoeck & Ruprecht, 1983), pp. 228–57; weitere mögliche Belege bei R.A. Lipsius, *Die Quellen der römischen Petrussage* (Kiel: Schwers, 1872), pp. 42–44.

11.   Der traditionelle Charakter ergibt sich aus der mangelhaften Verknüpfung des Disputs mit dem Kontext: Simons Behauptung, Petrus habe „gestern" die Vision als Medium der Vermittlung von Jesu Lehre in Frage gestellt (17.5.6b; vgl. 13.1), findet in der Darstellung von H keinen Anhalt; tatsächlich vertritt Petrus diese Auffassung ausschließlich in 17.13–19. Die Parallele in R 2.61–66 deutet darauf hin, dass der Disput ursprünglich durch einen deutlichen Hinweis auf die visionären Erfahrungen des Paulus auf der Grundlage von 2 Kor. 12,1ff. eröffnet wurde. (Bei den R-Parallelen 2.61–69; 3.29–30 und 44 handelt es sich um eine verharmlosende Bearbeitung des in H vorliegenden Materials, durch die „all taint of its original virus has been neutralized", so C. Bigg, 'The Clementine Homilies', *Studia Biblica et Ecclesiastica* 2 [1890], p. 177).

12.   Siehe dazu B. Rehm, 'Zur Entstehung der pseudoclementinischen Schriften', *ZNW* 37 (1938), pp. 77–184 (150–51).

13.   Die Frage nach dem Ursprung des Disputs wird in der Literatur kontrovers beantwortet: Rehm, 'Entstehung', pp. 152–54, hält 17.13–20 für eine ebionitische Interpolation in H (vgl. J. Rius-Camps, 'Las Pseudoclementinas. Bases filológicas para una nueva interpretación', *Revista Catalana de Teologia* 1 [1976], pp. 79–158 [157]), doch scheitert diese Annahme an den Parallelen in R 2 und 3 (Anm. 11). Schoeps, *Theologie und Geschichte*, pp. 54.384.418–434, A. Salles, 'La diatribe antipaulinienne dans le "Le roman pseudo-clémentin" et l'origine des "Kérygmes de Pierre"', *RB* 64 (1957), pp. 518–25 und Strecker, *Judenchristentum*, pp. 191–94, möchten den Abschnitt einer Quelle von PsKl zuweisen, nämlich den sog. „Kerygmata Petrou" (Strecker) bzw. sogar einer Quelle dieser Kerygmen (Schoeps: das Stück sei Teil „Ebionitischer Apostelakten", der ältesten Schicht der PsKl). Obwohl diese Quellenpostulate unbegründet sind (J. Wehnert, 'Literarkritik und Sprachanalyse. Kritische Anmerkungen zum gegenwärtigen Stand der Pseudoklementinenforschung', *ZNW* 74 [1983], pp. 268–301 bes. pp. 286–91), betonen diese Autoren zu Recht das hohe Alter des Stückes.

14.   Der Sinn dieser literarischen Tarnung ist evident: „der Schriftsteller kann sich immer dahinter zurückziehen, dass er von Simon und nicht von Paulus geredet hat" (E. Schwartz, 'Unzeitgemäße Beobachtungen zu den Clementinen', *ZNW* 31 [1932], pp. 151–99 [184]).

15.   Der Offenbarungsbegriff in 17.17.5b–18.3 sowie in den damit zusammenhängenden Formulierungen von 18.4; 19.1.4,6 (s. Anm. 8) steht in Spannung zu 18.5–19.7, wonach Wissen

der antimarkionitischen Diskussion in H 18 verklammern soll, sowie die Schlus–snotiz 17.20.1–2, die die Simons Paulusrolle als nur vorgetäuscht wieder aufhebt. Der nach Abzug dieser Eingriffe verbleibende Text (ein Produkt des frühen 2. Jahrhunderts?) spiegelt die Auseinandersetzungen eines judenchristlich-petrinischen Christentums mit der grundsätzlich anders strukturierten Theologie des Völkerapostels Paulus wider.

Höchst optimistisch hat die ältere Forschung in der Frage geurteilt, ob die im Disput verarbeiteten Argumente bis in die Zeit des historischen Paulus und Petrus zurückreichen. Hier ist jedoch deutliche Zurückhaltung geboten. Bei genauerem Hinsehen zeigt sich, dass der Disput keine Einheit darstellt, sondern aus zwei Teilen wohl unterschiedlichen Alters besteht: a) Den Anfang bildet eine breite Debatte über die Frage, ob Erfahrungen in einer Vision oder Unterweisungen durch einen Lehrer höheren Erkenntniswert besitzen (13.1–19.1). b) Am Schluß steht eine vehemente Attacke des Petrus gegen seinen Widersacher. Petrus bezieht sich darin auf den antiochenischen Konflikt und stellt die apostolische Würde des Paulus grundsätzlich in Frage (19.2–7).

Betrachten wir beide Teile etwas genauer. Die einleitende Debatte will die Frage, ob Paulus durch eine Christusvision zum Völkermissionar legitimiert worden sein kann, auf einer theoretischen Ebene beantworten. Die Argumentation verläuft wie folgt: Paulus alias Simon Magus behauptet, dass eine Vision bzw. Audition – anders als menschliche Rede – göttlichen Ursprungs ist und jeder menschlichen Rede überlegen (17.5,6; 13.2) und dass gerechte Menschen (Anspielung auf die paulinische Rechtfertigungslehre?) gottgesandte Visionen empfangen (17.15.4). Petrus weist diese Behauptung mit drei Argumenten zurück: 1. Der göttliche Ursprung einer Vision ist zweifelhaft. Es kann sich auch um „Teufelswerk"[16] handeln, nämlich um die Erscheinung eines Dämons, der sich als ein anderer ausgibt (17.14.4–5.; 16.6). 2. Kein Mensch kann in einer Vision den Vater oder den Sohn sehen, da ihre immense göttliche Lichtfülle den Menschen töten würde (17.16.2–4). 3. Eine Kette atl. Zitate beweist, dass Visionen nicht gerechten, sondern nur ungerechten Menschen widerfahren und Ausdruck des Zorns Gottes sind (17.18.4–6). Daraus ergibt sich als Fazit: Selbst wenn Paulus, wider alle Wahrscheinlichkeit, eine Christusvision gehabt haben sollte, ist ihm Jesus darin als Feind und im Zorn erschienen.

Hier ist nicht der Raum, um die einzelnen Argumente genauer zu würdigen. Es genügt die Feststellung, dass keins mit dem historischen Petrus in Zusammenhang stehen kann. Da Petrus seine führende Stellung im frühen Christentum seinerseits durch eine Christuserscheinung erlangt hat (1 Kor. 15.5; Lk. 24.34), kann er den göttlichen Ursprung einer solchen Vision kaum in Frage gestellt haben – egal, wem sie widerfahren ist. Der theoretische Disput in 17.13.1–19.1 kann also keinesfalls die Autorität des historischen Petrus beanspruchen[17] und wird als schriftgelehrtes Produkt des 2. Jahrhunderts einzustufen sein.

---

allein durch persönliche Belehrung Jesu bzw. des wahren Propheten vermittelt wird. Der Passus durchbricht zudem die Kette der atl. Beweise in 17.1–4; 18.5–6.

16. Schoeps, *Theologie und Geschichte*, p. 449.

17. Der Verfasser der vorpseudoklementinischen Novelle hat dieses historische Problem

Anders verhält es sich mit dem folgenden Teil 17.19.2–7, dessen besondere Bedeutung ein Zitat rechtfertigt.

> 19.2. (Petrus:) Ob aber jemand aufgrund einer Erscheinung zur Lehre befähigt werden kann? Und wenn du sagst: Es ist möglich, warum blieb der Lehrer ein ganzes Jahr bei wachen (Schülern) und redete mit ihnen? 19.3. Selbst dass er dir erschienen ist – wie sollen wir dir das glauben? Wie kann er dir denn überhaupt erschienen sein, wenn du denkst, was im Widerspruch zu seiner Lehre steht? 19.4. Wenn du aber von ihm eine Stunde lang mit einer Erscheinung bedacht und belehrt worden bist und sein Apostel wurdest, verkündige seine Aussprüche, lege seine (Worte) aus, liebe seine Apostel, kämpfe nicht mit mir, seinem Schüler! Denn mir, dem festen Fels, dem Grundstein der Kirche (Mt. 16.18), stehst du feindlich gegenüber (vgl. Gal. 2.11). 19.5. Wenn du nicht (mein) Widersacher wärst, würdest du mich nicht in Verruf bringen und die Verkündigung von mir nicht verleumden, damit man mir nicht glaubt, wenn ich sage, was ich vom Herrn mit eigenen Ohren gehört habe, so als sei ich verurteilt worden, während du in gutem Ruf stehst. 19.6. Wenn du mich verurteilt nennst (vgl. Gal. 2.11), klagst du Gott an, der mir den Christus offenbarte, und setzt den herab, der mich wegen dieser Offenbarung seligpries (Mt. 16.17). 19.7. Wenn du jedoch wirklich am (Werk) der Wahrheit mitarbeiten willst, lerne zuerst von uns, was wir von ihm gelernt haben, und wenn du ein Jünger der Wahrheit geworden bist, werde unser Mitarbeiter!

Die glasklare Argumentation dieser Verse lässt sich in aller Kürze zusammenfassen: Paulus' Verkündigung unterscheidet sich von der des Petrus. Folglich kann er keine Erscheinung Jesu gehabt haben, denn sonst würde er dasselbe lehren wie der Jesusschüler Petrus und ihm nicht feindlich entgegentreten. Daraus ergibt sich die Pointe: Wenn Paulus ein Mitarbeiter an der Wahrheit werden will, muß er erst bei den wirklichen Jüngern Jesu in die Schule gehen.

Es erscheint mir nicht abwegig, dass diese biographisch geprägte Argumentation, die ausdrücklich auf den antiochenischen Zwischenfall anspielt, ein Nachhall der historischen Konflikte zwischen beiden Aposteln ist. Hier wird – anders als im einleitenden Disput – nicht der Offenbarungscharakter von Christusvisionen in Frage gestellt, sondern lediglich der Anspruch des Paulus, als Empfänger einer solchen Vision legitimer Völkerapostel geworden zu sein (vgl. Gal. 1.11–2 und 15–6). Dies entspricht dem historischen Befund, dass die Apostelwürde des Paulus von judenchristlicher Seite bestritten wurde (vgl. bes. 1 Kor. 9.1ff.; 2 Kor. 11.5; 12.11). Es daher durchaus glaubhaft, dass in der parteilichen und polemischen Attacke 17.19.2–7 Argumente verarbeitet sind, die seinerzeit gegen Paulus ins Feld geführt wurden. Paulus hat seine judaisierenden Gegner – Petrus und Jakobus ebenso wie die von ihm so genannten „Falschbrüder" (Gal. 2.4) und „Superapostel" (2 Kor. 11.5,13; 12.11) – nicht geschont. Der pseudoklementinische Disput macht deutlich, dass er seine Gegner zu Antworten provozierte, die seine Autorität grundsätzlich in Frage stellten. Die hier dokumentierten Vorwürfe können illustrieren, warum

---

erkannt und es dadurch zu lösen versucht, dass er auf der Grundlage von Mt. 16.13–19 einen nicht-visionären Offenbarungsbegriff entwickelt (s.o. Anm. 14), der Petrus' Doppelrolle als Visionskritiker und Offenbarungsempfänger begreiflich machen soll.

Paulus an sich selbst als „Fehlgeburt" gelitten hat (1 Kor. 15.8): Er wusste, dass er sich durch seine Lebensgeschichte von den anderen Offenbarungsempfängern unterschied, ohne deshalb je an der Gewissheit seiner Christusoffenbarung irre zu werden.

Fazit: Die Entstehungsgeschichte von H 17.13–20 dürfte so zu rekonstruieren sein, dass sich an den alten, polemischen Traditionskern in 19.2–7 sekundär ein Disput über die Vision als Modus göttlicher Offenbarung angelagert hat, der auf die vollständige Verwerfung von Visionen als Medium göttlicher Selbstmitteilung hinausläuft und damit den Antipaulinismus der Frühzeit auf die Spitze treibt.

Gewiß wäre es interessant zu erfahren, was paulinische Christen des 2. Jahrhunderts, die die impliziten Adressaten des Disputs sind, auf die (pseudo-)petrinischen Argumente erwidert, in welcher Form sie auf einer Unterscheidung zwischen vorösterlicher Jesus- und österlicher Christuserfahrung beharrt hätten (vgl. 2 Kor. 5.16). Doch darüber schweigt die Überlieferung. Der Dissens zwischen den Parteien wurde nicht im Dialog beigelegt, sondern durch die Geschichte erledigt, in der die Jesusverehrung judenchristlicher Provenienz untergegangen ist.

ABSTRACT

The Purpose of the Paper

The Pseudo-Clementines (PsCl) represent the first Christian novel. It survived in two recensions: a) the so-called Recognitions (in 10 books; today completely extant only in the Latin translation of Rufin of Aquileia [about 406 CE]) and b) the so-called Homilies (in 20 books). Both versions are the final result of a long history of literary development. Until now, no generally accepted theory of this process has been found. In the first part of this paper, therefore, I outline my own theory of the genesis of the Pseudo-Clementine literature. The second part deals with a passage of the Homilies, book 17, which contains a controversy between the apostles Paul and Peter – obviously an old tradition with anti-Pauline tendency.

I. *The History of Pseudo-Clementine Literature*

My analysis of the material led me to the conclusion that four literary layers need to be distinguished in PsCl:

a) The oldest layer is a pre-Pseudo-Clementine novella from the end of the second century. It focuses on Peter and his disciples on one side and the magician Simon (cf. Acts 8.9–24) and his adherents on the other. Two discussions between Peter and Simon Magus in Caesarea Strationis and Antiochia/Syria provide the narrative framework. Simon's defeat in Caesarea marks the beginning of his persecution along the shores of the Eastern Mediterranean which ends in Antiochia with another defeat of the magician. The prime literary characteristic of this layer is its perspective: The author narrates in the third person (omniscient narrator).

b) In the mid-third century (after 222 CE), this novella has been transformed to a novel, which pretends to be the autobiography of Clement, the later bishop of

Rome. The author of this layer narrates in the first person (autoptic narrator; therefore: Pseudo-Clementines). The novel, perhaps of Roman origin, consists of two parts: In the first part the pagan Clement becomes acquainted with the Christian preacher Barnabas in Rome, travels to Judaea, becomes a pupil of Peter and is finally baptized by him. The second part is sort of a family-novel (Anagnoriseis = Recognitions). The reader learns that Clement has lost all his relatives – his mother, his twin brothers and his father. With the help of Peter, he finds them again on the way from Caesarea to Antiochia – in the end all are reunited as a Christian family.

c) This novel has later been transformed (perhaps by the same author) into an oversized letter to Jacob, bishop of Jerusalem (who ranks as 'bishop of bishops'). To this purpose, the author added one letter by Peter and one by Clement directed to Jacob, as well as some remarks in the text that address Jacob directly in the second person.

d) This edition of the novel provided the literary basis for the Homilies and Recognitions, which originate around the end of the third or the beginning of the fourth century. In general, the Homilies have preserved the PsCl better than the Recognitions – the latter dropped much material that might have aroused suspicion of heresy.

II. *A Controversy between Peter and Paul on the Value of Visions (Homilies 17.13–20)*

Part of the material lacking in the Recognitions is a dialogue between Paul (in the guise of Simon Magus) and Peter on the relevance of visions: Do they furnish insight in the will of God as Paul maintains who founded his apostleship on a revelation of Christ (Gal. 1 etc.)? This dialogue is part of the old pre-Pseudo-Clementine novella and seems to be one of its sources, because here Simon is arguing – quite differently from the rest of the PsCl – as an alter ego of Paul. In the literature since Ferdinand Christian Baur, it is generally assumed that this dialogue with its anti-Pauline tendency reflects the historical conflict between the two apostles and has its roots in the first century. An analysis of the text shows, however, that this impression is – at least – partly wrong. Homilies 17.13–20 is no homogeneous entity, but consists of two parts:

a) 17.13,1–19,1 is an anti-Pauline discussion on the value of visions, but its 'Petrine' arguments cannot be traced back to the historical Peter. The arguments are: 1. A vision is not necessarily of divine origin, it might as well have been triggered by a demon. 2. No man can see the Father or the Son in a vision, because their divine light would kill him. 3. Citations from the Old Testament prove that visions are only sent to unjust people as signs of God's wrath. As Peter himself gained his leading position in the early church by a vision of the risen Christ (1 Cor. 15.5; Lk. 24.34), none of these arguments can be his own. Conclusion: This dialogue is a later work, perhaps from the early second century, intended to undermine the influence of Pauline Christianity by an attack on its very roots.

b) 17.13,1–19,1 seems to be the oldest part of the tradition used in Homilies 17.

Its argumentation runs differently: Simon's (= Paul's) doctrine differs from that of Peter and he even attacks Peter (cf. Gal. 2.11–4). Consequently, Paul cannot have received a vision of Christ – otherwise he would teach as Peter, the true disciple of Jesus, does. These biographically founded reproaches, which do not doubt the existence and dignity of divine visions, might indeed reflect the historical conflict between Peter and Paul. Thus, they might furnish us with some of the arguments which were put forward against Paul in contemporary Jewish-Christian circles.

INDEX

INDEX OF REFERENCES

BIBLE

INDEX OF AUTHORS